MORALS BY AGREEMENT

MORALS BY AGREEMENT

DAVID GAUTHIER

Professor of Philosophy
University of Pittsburgh

CLARENDON PRESS · OXFORD

This book has been printed digitally and produced in a standard specification in order to ensure its continuing availability

OXFORD
UNIVERSITY PRESS

Great Clarendon Street, Oxford OX2 6DP

Oxford University Press is a department of the University of Oxford.
It furthers the University's objective of excellence in research, scholarship, and education by publishing worldwide in

Oxford New York

Auckland Cape Town Dar es Salaam Hong Kong Karachi
Kuala Lumpur Madrid Melbourne Mexico City Nairobi
New Delhi Shanghai Taipei Toronto

With offices in

Argentina Austria Brazil Chile Czech Republic France Greece
Guatemala Hungary Italy Japan South Korea Poland Portugal
Singapore Switzerland Thailand Turkey Ukraine Vietnam

Oxford is a registered trade mark of Oxford University Press in the UK and in certain other countries

Published in the United States
by Oxford University Press Inc., New York

Reprinted 2006

ISBN 0-19-824992-6

PREFACE

THE present enquiry began on a November afternoon in Los Angeles when, fumbling for words in which to express the peculiar relationship between morality and advantage, I was shown the Prisoner's Dilemma. (The unfamiliar reader will be shown it in section 3.2 of Chapter III.) Almost nineteen years later, I reflect on the course of a voyage that is not, and cannot be, completed, but that finds a temporary harbour in this book.

The Prisoner's Dilemma posed a problem, rather than solving one. The problem concerns practical rationality, understood in maximizing terms, and it is resolved, or so I now think, in Chapter VI.

It proved to be the second of three core problems that required resolution before my enquiry could issue in this book. The first was to formulate the principle of rational co-operation, which I believe is central to morality. In my account, this principle is related to a rational agreement or bargain, and I was able to develop a game-theoretic treatment of bargaining, which has evolved into Chapter V. The second was to demonstrate the rationality of complying with this principle, which turns out to be the problem of rational behaviour in a Prisoner's Dilemma. And the third was to determine the appropriate initial position from which co-operation proceeds, which requires showing the rationality of accepting a Lockean proviso on initial acquisition. (The unfamiliar reader will meet the proviso in section 3.1 of Chapter VII.) This third problem proved the most recalcitrant; from the initial idea of a contractarian moral theory, which captured my imagination in 1966, some thirteen years elapsed before the role of the proviso became clear.

During those years I published several papers, developing what I now consider proto-versions of parts of the present theory. A reader familiar with those papers will find in them both arguments and attitudes that are contradicted or modified in the present account. I should like to think that this represents progress in my enquiry.

Perhaps changes in attitude deserve a further remark. I have had, and continue to have, somewhat mixed feelings about morals by agreement. Indeed, at one time I thought of setting out much of the present book as a study of a set of conceptual interconnections with no claim that the whole constitutes the correct moral theory. But now I am willing to make that claim. Incorporation of the Lockean proviso, and of the idea of the liberal individual (in the final chapter), have alleviated some of my earlier worries. But perhaps most important, the conception of practical rationality that I accept at the root of my argument seems to me the only one capable of withstanding critical examination, and the moral theory that I then develop seems to me, in outline if not in every detail, the only one compatible with that conception of rationality. Yet, as Richard Rorty or Alasdair MacIntyre might remind me, perhaps I lack the vocabulary for talking perspicuously about morality.

The first draft of most of the book was written in Aix-en-Provence in 1979–80; I am grateful for financial support during that year from the University of Toronto and from the Social Sciences and Humanities Research Council of Canada. The second draft of Chapters II–IX was written in Toronto in the spring of 1982; the final chapters refused to fall into place until the summer of 1983. The present draft was written in Pittsburgh from January to May 1984; I am grateful to the University of Pittsburgh for releasing me from teaching duties during that term, and to Ruth Durst for her typing.

Were I to attempt to thank by name all those individuals who have contributed to an enquiry as extended as this one, my list would inevitably be marred by omission. Many, many colleagues and students, at the Universities of Toronto and Pittsburgh, at other universities where I have visited or read papers, and at professional meetings, have helped me to rethink my ideas and to reformulate my thoughts. To all, my gratitude. To Clark Glymour, who pointed out that I could avoid the horrendous 's/he' and 'him/her' of earlier drafts by resorting to an appropriately programmed randomizing device, I am sure that I can add the gratitude of readers to my own. And to Howard Sobel, who among those who have provided philosophical aid occupies the first place, for it was Howard who showed me the Prisoner's Dilemma and introduced me to the basic ideas of the theory of games, mere gratitude would not be enough.

And so I come to an end, aware that it is also a beginning, for I shall surely find myself embarked again on the quest to understand how morality and rationality are related.

DAVID GAUTHIER

Pittsburgh
24 May 1984

CONTENTS

NOTE TO READER

ONE should begin at the beginning and end at the end. But *en route*, some sections and sub-sections may well be omitted on a first reading, in order more easily to grasp the main line of argument. And some few sections are intended only for those with specialized interest in the theories of games and rational choice.

After gaining the overview offered in Chapter I, the reader who wishes to move more rapidly to the main theses of the moral theory may omit sections 2 and 3 in Chapter II, in which preference is discussed in some detail, section 2 in Chapter III (of interest to specialists only, I suspect), and the concluding section 4 in Chapter IV, on utilitarian and Marxian reactions to the market. Although there are later references back to some of these sections, omitting them on a first reading should not impede understanding.

Chapters V, VI, and VII are the argumentative centre of the book. But even here some omissions are possible. The reader may wish to pass from section 1 in Chapter V to 2.3, omitting discussion of rejected alternatives *to* bargaining, and to leave aside the specialized discussion in 3.4, on a rejected alternative *in* bargaining. In Chapter VI the discussion of Hobbes in 1.2 and 1.3, and the concluding mention of reciprocal altruism in 3.3, may initially be omitted. In Chapter VII only the brief treatment of the threat point in 2.2 may safely be ignored.

The positive argument of Chapter VIII is found in sections 1 and 4; the critical discussions of Harsanyi and Rawls in the intermediate sections 2 and 3 may be postponed. Chapter IX sketches applications of the theory and could be omitted entirely in grasping the main line of argument, but section 1 may provide a useful overview of the various applications, and 5.1, which offers criteria for ordering ways of life, is particularly important. In Chapter X the reader may wish to pass from 2.1 to 2.5, omitting the detailed discussion of economic man. Chapter XI should, I think, be read without omissions.

Slightly more than two-thirds of the whole remains for a first reading.

I

OVERVIEW OF A THEORY

1 What theory of morals can ever serve any useful purpose, unless it can show that all the duties it recommends are also the true interest of each individual?[1] David Hume, who asked this question, seems mistaken; such a theory would be too useful. Were duty no more than interest, morals would be superfluous. Why appeal to right or wrong, to good or evil, to obligation or to duty, if instead we may appeal to desire or aversion, to benefit or cost, to interest or to advantage? An appeal to morals takes its point from the failure of these latter considerations as sufficient guides to what we ought to do. The unphilosophical poet Ogden Nash grasped the assumptions underlying our moral language more clearly than the philosopher Hume when he wrote:

> 'O Duty!
> Why hast thou not the visage of a sweetie or a cutie?'[2]

We may lament duty's stern visage but we may not deny it. For it is only as we believe that some appeals do, alas, override interest or advantage that morality becomes our concern.

But if the language of morals is not that of interest, it is surely that of reason. What theory of morals, we might better ask, can ever serve any useful purpose, unless it can show that all the duties it recommends are also truly endorsed in each individual's reason? If moral appeals are entitled to some practical effect, some influence on our behaviour, it is not because they whisper invitingly to our desires, but because they convince our intellect. Suppose we should find, as Hume himself believes, that reason is impotent in the sphere of action apart from its role in deciding matters of fact.[3] Or suppose we should find that reason is no more than the handmaiden of

[1] See David Hume, *An Enquiry concerning the Principles of Morals*, sect. ix, pt. ii, in L. A. Selby-Bigge (ed.), *Enquiries concerning Human Understanding and concerning the Principles of Morals*, 3rd edn. (Oxford, 1975), p. 280.

[2] Ogden Nash, 'Kind of an Ode to Duty', *I Wouldn't Have Missed It: Selected Poems of Ogden Nash* (Boston, 1975), p. 141.

[3] See David Hume, *A Treatise of Human Nature*, bk. ii, pt. iii, sect. iii, ed. L. A. Selby-Bigge (Oxford, 1888), pp. 413–18.

interest, so that in overriding advantage a moral appeal must also contradict reason. In either case we should conclude that the moral enterprise, as traditionally conceived, is impossible.

To say that our moral language assumes a connection with reason is not to argue for the rationality of our moral views, or of any alternative to them. Moral language may rest on a false assumption.[4] If moral duties are rationally grounded, then the emotivists, who suppose that moral appeals are no more than persuasive, and the egoists, who suppose that rational appeals are limited by self-interest, are mistaken.[5] But are moral duties rationally grounded? This we shall seek to prove, showing that reason has a practical role related to but transcending individual interest, so that principles of action that prescribe duties overriding advantage may be rationally justified. We shall defend the traditional conception of morality as a rational constraint on the pursuit of individual interest.

Yet Hume's mistake in insisting that moral duties must be the true interest of each individual conceals a fundamental insight. Practical reason is linked to interest, or, as we shall come to say, to individual utility, and rational constraints on the pursuit of interest have themselves a foundation in the interest they constrain. Duty overrides advantage, but the acceptance of duty is truly advantageous. We shall find this seeming paradox embedded in the very structure of interaction. As we come to understand this structure, we shall recognize the need for restraining each person's pursuit of her own utility, and we shall examine its implications for both our principles of action and our conception of practical rationality. Our enquiry will lead us to the rational basis for a morality, not of absolute standards, but of agreed constraints.

2.1 We shall develop a theory of morals. Our concern is to provide a justificatory framework for moral behaviour and principles, not an explanatory framework. Thus we shall develop a normative theory. A complete philosophy of morals would need to explain, and perhaps to defend, the idea of a normative theory. We shall not do this. But we shall exemplify normative theory by sketching the theory of rational choice. Indeed, we shall do more. We shall develop a theory of morals as part of the theory of rational

[4] Thus one might propose an error theory of moral language; for the idea of an error theory, see J. L. Mackie, *Ethics: Inventing Right and Wrong* (Harmondsworth, Middx:, 1977), ch. 1, esp. pp. 35, 48–9.

[5] The idea that moral appeals are persuasive is developed by C. L. Stevenson; see *Ethics and Language* (New Haven, 1944), esp. chs. vi, ix.

choice. We shall argue that the rational principles for making choices, or decisions among possible actions, include some that constrain the actor pursuing his own interest in an impartial way. These we identify as moral principles.

The study of choice begins from the stipulation of clear conceptions of value and rationality in a form applicable to choice situations.[6] The theory then analyses the structure of these situations so that, for each type of structure distinguished, the conception of rationality may be elaborated into a set of determinate conditions on the choice among possible actions. These conditions are then expressed as precise principles of rational behaviour, serving both for prescription and for critical assessment. Derivatively, the principles also have an explanatory role in so far as persons actually act rationally.

The simplest, most familiar, and historically primary part of this study constitutes the core of classical and neo-classical economic theory, which examines rational behaviour in those situations in which the actor knows with certainty the outcome of each of his possible actions. The economist does of course offer to explain behaviour, and much of the interest of her theory depends on its having explanatory applications, but her explanations use a model of ideal interaction which includes the rationality of the actors among its assumptions. Thus economic explanation is set within a normative context. And the role of economics in formulating and evaluating policy alternatives should leave us in no doubt about the deeply prescriptive and critical character of the science.

The economist formulates a simple, maximizing conception of practical rationality, which we shall examine in Chapter II. But the assumption that the outcome of each possible choice can be known with certainty seriously limits the scope of economic analysis and the applicability of its account of reason. Bayesian decision theory relaxes this assumption, examining situations with choices involving risk or uncertainty. The decision theorist is led to extend the economist's account of reason, while preserving its fundamental identification of rationality with maximization.

Both economics and decision theory are limited in their analysis of

[6] Our sketch of rational choice owes much to J. C. Harsanyi; see 'Advances in Understanding Rational Behavior', in *Essays on Ethics, Social Behavior, and Scientific Explanation* (Dordrecht, 1976), pp. 89–98, and 'Morality and the theory of rational behaviour', in A. Sen and B. Williams (eds.), *Utilitarianism and beyond* (Cambridge, 1982), pp. 42–4.

interaction, since both consider outcomes only in relation to the choices of a single actor, treating the choices of others as aspects of that actor's circumstances. The theory of games overcomes this limitation, analysing outcomes in relation to sets of choices, one for each of the persons involved in bringing about the outcome. It considers the choices of an actor who decides on the basis of expectations about the choices of others, themselves deciding on the basis of expectations about his choice. Since situations involving a single actor may be treated as limiting cases of interaction, game theory aims at an account of rational behaviour in its full generality. Unsurprisingly, achievements are related inversely to aims; as a study of rational behaviour under certainty economic theory is essentially complete, whereas game theory is still being developed. The theory of rational choice is an ongoing enterprise, extending a basic understanding of value and rationality to the formulation of principles of rational behaviour in an ever wider range of situations.

2.2 Rational choice provides an exemplar of normative theory. One might suppose that moral theory and choice theory are related only in possessing similar structures. But as we have said, we shall develop moral theory as part of choice theory. Those acquainted with recent work in moral philosophy may find this a familiar enterprise; John Rawls has insisted that the theory of justice is 'perhaps the most significant part, of the theory of rational choice', and John Harsanyi explicitly treats ethics as part of the theory of rational behaviour.[7] But these claims are stronger than their results warrant. Neither Rawls nor Harsanyi develops the deep connection between morals and rational choice that we shall defend. A brief comparison will bring our enterprise into sharper focus.

Our claim is that in certain situations involving interaction with others, an individual chooses rationally only in so far as he constrains his pursuit of his own interest or advantage to conform to principles expressing the impartiality characteristic of morality. To choose rationally, one must choose morally. This is a strong claim. Morality, we shall argue, can be generated as a rational constraint from the non-moral premisses of rational choice. Neither Rawls nor Harsanyi makes such a claim. Neither Rawls nor Harsanyi treats moral principles as a subset of rational principles for choice.

Rawls argues that the principles of justice are the objects of a

[7] J. Rawls, *A Theory of Justice* (Cambridge, Mass., 1971), p. 16; J. Harsanyi, 'Morality and the theory of rational behaviour', p. 42.

rational choice—the choice that any person would make, were he called upon to select the basic principles of his society from behind a 'veil of ignorance' concealing any knowledge of his own identity.[8] The principles so chosen are not directly related to the making of individual choices.[9] Derivatively, acceptance of them must have implications for individual behaviour, but Rawls never claims that these include rational constraints on individual choices. They may be, in Rawls's terminology, reasonable constraints, but what is reasonable is itself a morally substantive matter beyond the bounds of rational choice.[10]

Rawls's idea, that principles of justice are the objects of a rational choice, is indeed one that we shall incorporate into our own theory, although we shall represent the choice as a bargain, or agreement, among persons who need not be unaware of their identities. But this parallel between our theory and Rawls's must not obscure the basic difference; we claim to generate morality as a set of rational principles for choice. We are committed to showing why an individual, reasoning from non-moral premisses, would accept the constraints of morality on his choices.

Harsanyi's theory may seem to differ from Rawls's only in its account of the principles that a person would choose from behind a veil of ignorance; Rawls supposes that persons would choose the well-known two principles of justice, whereas Harsanyi supposes that persons would choose principles of average rule-utilitarianism.[11] But Harsanyi's argument is in some respects closer to our own; he is concerned with principles for moral choice, and with the rational way of arriving at such principles. However, Harsanyi's principles are strictly hypothetical; they govern rational choice from an impartial standpoint or given impartial preferences, and so they are principles only for someone who wants to choose morally or impartially.[12] But Harsanyi does not claim, as we do, that there are situations in which an individual must choose morally in order to choose rationally. For Harsanyi there is a rational way of choosing

[8] See Rawls, p. 12.

[9] See ibid., p. 11; 'the principles . . . are to assign basic rights and duties and to determine the division of social benefits.' Principles for individuals are distinguished from the principles of justice; see p. 108.

[10] See Rawls's distinction of 'the Reasonable' and 'the Rational', in 'Kantian Constructivism in Moral Theory', *Journal of Philosophy* 77 (1980), pp. 528–30.

[11] See Rawls, *A Theory of Justice*, pp. 14–15, and Harsanyi, 'Morality and the theory of rational behaviour', pp. 44–6, 56–60.

[12] See Harsanyi, 'Morality and the theory of rational behaviour', p. 62.

morally but no rational requirement to choose morally. And so again there is a basic difference between our theory and his.

Putting now to one side the views of Rawls and Harsanyi—views to which we shall often return in later chapters—we may summarize the import of the differences we have sketched. Our theory must generate, strictly as rational principles for choice, and so without introducing prior moral assumptions, constraints on the pursuit of individual interest or advantage that, being impartial, satisfy the traditional understanding of morality. We do not assume that there must be such impartial and rational constraints. We do not even assume that there must be rational constraints, whether impartial or not. We claim to demonstrate that there are rational constraints, and that these constraints are impartial. We then identify morality with these demonstrated constraints, but whether their content corresponds to that of conventional moral principles is a further question, which we shall not examine in detail. No doubt there will be differences, perhaps significant, between the impartial and rational constraints supported by our argument, and the morality learned from parents and peers, priests and teachers. But our concern is to validate the conception of morality as a set of rational, impartial constraints on the pursuit of individual interest, not to defend any particular moral code. And our concern, once again, is to do this without incorporating into the premisses of our argument any of the moral conceptions that emerge in our conclusions.

2.3 To seek to establish the rationality of moral constraints is not in itself a novel enterprise, and its antecedents are more venerable than the endeavour to develop moral theory as part of the theory of rational choice. But those who have engaged in it have typically appealed to a conception of practical rationality, deriving from Kant, quite different from ours.[13] In effect, their understanding of reason already includes the moral dimension of impartiality that we seek to generate.

Let us suppose it agreed that there is a connection between reason and interest—or advantage, benefit, preference, satisfaction, or individual utility, since the differences among these, important in other contexts, do not affect the present discussion. Let it further be agreed that in so far as the interests of others are not affected, a

[13] This conception of practical rationality appears with particular clarity in T. Nagel, *The Possibility of Altruism* (Oxford, 1970), esp. ch. x. It can also be found in the moral theory of R. M. Hare; see *Moral Thinking* (Oxford, 1981), esp. chs. 5 and 6.

person acts rationally if and only if she seeks her greatest interest or benefit. This might be denied by some, but we wish here to isolate the essential difference between the opposed conceptions of practical rationality. And this appears when we consider rational action in which the interests of others are involved. Proponents of the *maximizing* conception of rationality, which we endorse, insist that essentially nothing is changed; the rational person still seeks the greatest satisfaction of her own interests. On the other hand, proponents of what we shall call the *universalistic* conception of rationality insist that what makes it rational to satisfy an interest does not depend on whose interest it is. Thus the rational person seeks to satisfy all interests. Whether she is a utilitarian, aiming at the greatest happiness of the greatest number, or whether she takes into independent consideration the fair distribution of benefit among persons, is of no importance to the present discussion.

To avoid possible misunderstanding, note that neither conception of rationality requires that practical reasons be self-interested. On the maximizing conception it is not interests in the self, that take oneself as object, but interests of the self, held by oneself as subject, that provide the basis for rational choice and action. On the universalistic conception it is not interests in anyone, that take any person as object, but interests of anyone, held by some person as subject, that provide the basis for rational choice and action. If I have a direct interest in your welfare, then on either conception I have reason to promote your welfare. But your interest in your welfare affords me such reason only given the universalistic conception.

Morality, we have insisted, is traditionally understood to involve an impartial constraint on the pursuit of individual interest. The justification of such a constraint poses no problem to the proponents of universalistic rationality. The rational requirement that all interests be satisfied to the fullest extent possible directly constrains each person in the pursuit of her own interests. The precise formulation of the constraint will of course depend on the way in which interests are to be satisfied, but the basic rationale is sufficiently clear.

The main task of our moral theory—the generation of moral constraints as rational—is thus easily accomplished by proponents of the universalistic conception of practical reason. For them the relation between reason and morals is clear. Their task is to defend their conception of rationality, since the maximizing and universalistic conceptions do not rest on equal footings. The maximizing conception possesses the virtue, among conceptions, of weakness. Any consideration affording one a reason for acting on the maximizing conception, also affords one such a reason on the universalistic conception. But the converse does not hold. On the universalistic conception all persons have in effect the same basis for rational choice—the interests of all—and this assumption, of the impersonality or impartiality of reason, demands defence.

Furthermore, and perhaps of greater importance, the maximizing conception of rationality is almost universally accepted and employed in the social sciences.[14] As we have noted, it lies at the core of economic theory, and is generalized in decision and game theory. Its lesser prominence in political, sociological, and psychological theory reflects more the lesser concern with rationality among many practitioners of those disciplines, than adherence to an alternative conception. Social scientists may no doubt be mistaken, but we take the onus of proof to fall on those who would defend universalistic rationality.

In developing moral theory within rational choice we thus embrace the weaker and more widely accepted of the two conceptions of rationality that we have distinguished. Of course, we must not suppose that the moral principles we generate will be identical with those that would be derived on the universalistic conception. Its proponents may insist that their account of the connection between reason and morals is correct, even if they come to agree that a form of morality may be grounded in maximizing rationality. But we may suggest, without here defending our suggestion, that few persons would embrace the universalistic conception of practical reason did they not think it necessary to the defence of any form of rational morality. Hence the most effective rebuttal of their position may be, not to seek to undermine their elaborate and ingenious arguments, but to construct an alternative account of a rational morality grounded in the weaker assumptions of the theory of rational choice.

3.1 Morals by agreement begin from an initial presumption against morality, as a constraint on each person's pursuit of his own

[14] See Harsanyi, 'Advances in Understanding Rational Behavior', p. 89; also J. Elster, *Ulysses and the Sirens: Studies in rationality and irrationality* (Cambridge, 1979); 'The "rational-choice" approach to human behaviour is without much doubt the best available model . . .', p. 112.

interest. A person is conceived as an independent centre of activity, endeavouring to direct his capacities and resources to the fulfilment of his interests. He considers what he can do, but initially draws no distinction between what he may and may not do. How then does he come to acknowledge the distinction? How does a person come to recognize a moral dimension to choice, if morality is not initially present?

Morals by agreement offer a contractarian rationale for distinguishing what one may and may not do. Moral principles are introduced as the objects of fully voluntary *ex ante* agreement among rational persons. Such agreement is hypothetical, in supposing a pre-moral context for the adoption of moral rules and practices. But the parties to agreement are real, determinate individuals, distinguished by their capacities, situations, and concerns. In so far as they would agree to constraints on their choices, restraining their pursuit of their own interests, they acknowledge a distinction between what they may and may not do. As rational persons understanding the structure of their interaction, they recognize a place for mutual constraint, and so for a moral dimension in their affairs.

That there is a contractarian rationale for morality must of course be shown. That is the task of our theory. Here our immediate concern is to relate the idea of such a rationale to the introduction of fundamental moral distinctions. This is not a magical process. Morality does not emerge as the rabbit from the empty hat. Rather, as we shall argue, it emerges quite simply from the application of the maximizing conception of rationality to certain structures of interaction. Agreed mutual constraint is the rational response to these structures. Reason overrides the presumption against morality.

The genuinely problematic element in a contractarian theory is not the introduction of the idea of morality, but the step from hypothetical agreement to actual moral constraint. Suppose that each person recognizes himself as one of the parties to agreement. The principles forming the object of agreement are those that he would have accepted *ex ante* in bargaining with his fellows, had he found himself among them in a context initially devoid of moral constraint. Why need he accept, *ex post* in his actual situation, these principles as constraining his choices? A theory of morals by agreement must answer this question.

Historically, moral contractarianism seems to have originated among the Greek Sophists. Glaucon sketched a contractarian account of the origin of justice in Plato's *Republic* but significantly, he offered this view for Socrates to refute, not to defend.[15] Our theory of morals falls in an unpopular tradition, as the identity of its greatest advocate, Thomas Hobbes, will confirm. Hobbes transformed the laws of nature, which lay at the core of Stoic and medieval Christian moral thought, into precepts of reason that require each person, acting in his own interest, to give up some portion of the liberty with which he seeks his own survival and well-being, provided others do likewise.[16] But this agreement gives rise to actual constraint only through the efficacy of the political sovereign; from the standpoint of moral theory, the crucial step requires the intervention of a *deus ex machina*. Nevertheless, in Hobbes we find the true ancestor of the theory of morality that we shall present. Only recently has his position begun to acquire a significant following. G. R. Grice has developed an explicitly contractarian theory, and Kurt Baier has acknowledged the Hobbesian roots of his central thesis, that 'The very *raison d'être* of a morality is to yield reasons which overrule the reasons of self-interest in those cases when everyone's following self-interest would be harmful to everyone.'[17]

To the conceptual underpinning that may be found in Hobbes, Grice, and Baier, we seek to add the rigour of rational choice. Of course the resulting moral theory need not be one that they would endorse. But the appeal to rational choice enables us to state, with new clarity and precision, why rational persons would agree *ex ante* to constraining principles, what general characteristics these principles must have as objects of rational agreement, and why rational persons would comply *ex post* with the agreed constraints.

3.2 A useful vantage point for appreciating the rationale of constraint results from juxtaposing two ideas formulated by John Rawls. A contractarian views society as 'a cooperative venture for mutual advantage' among persons 'conceived as not taking an interest in one another's interests'.[18] The contractarian does not

[15] See Plato, *Republic*, 358b–359b.

[16] Thomas Hobbes, *Leviathan* (London, 1651), ch. 14, pp. 64–5.

[17] See G. R. Grice, *The Grounds of Moral Judgement* (Cambridge, 1967), and K. Baier, *The Moral Point of View: A Rational Basis of Ethics* (Ithaca, NY, 1958); the quotation is from p. 309.

[18] Rawls, *A Theory of Justice*, pp. 4, 13.

claim that all actual societies are co-operative ventures; he need not claim that all afford the expectation of mutual advantage. Rather, he supposes that it is in general possible for a society, analysed as a set of institutions, practices, and relationships, to afford each person greater benefit than she could expect in a non-social 'state of nature', and that only such a society could command the willing allegiance of every rational individual. The contractarian need not claim that actual persons take no interest in their fellows; indeed, we suppose that some degree of sociability is characteristic of human beings. But the contractarian sees sociability as enriching human life; for him, it becomes a source of exploitation if it induces persons to acquiesce in institutions and practices that but for their fellow-feelings would be costly to them. Feminist thought has surely made this, perhaps the core form of human exploitation, clear to us. Thus the contractarian insists that a society could not command the willing allegiance of a rational person if, without appealing to her feelings for others, it afforded her no expectation of net benefit.

If social institutions and practices can benefit all, then some set of social arrangements should be acceptable to all as a co-operative venture. Each person's concern to fulfil her own interests should ensure her willingness to join her fellows in a venture assuring her an expectation of increased fulfilment. She may of course reject some proposed venture as insufficiently advantageous to her when she considers both the distribution of benefits that it affords, and the availability of alternatives. Affording mutual advantage is a necessary condition for the acceptability of a set of social arrangements as a co-operative venture, not a sufficient condition. But we suppose that some set affording mutual advantage will also be mutually acceptable; a contractarian theory must set out conditions for sufficiency.

The rationale for agreement on society as a co-operative venture may seem unproblematic. The step from hypothetical agreement *ex ante* on a set of social arrangements to *ex post* adherence to those arrangements may seem straightforward. If one would willingly have joined the venture, why would one not now continue with it? Why is there need for constraint?

The institutions and practices of society play a co-ordinative role. Let us say, without attempting a precise definition, that a practice is co-ordinative if each person prefers to conform to it provided (most) others do, but prefers not to conform to it provided (most) others do not.[19] And let us say that a practice is beneficially co-ordinative if each person prefers that others conform to it rather than conform to no practice, and does not (strongly) prefer that others conform to some alternative practice. Hume's example, of two persons rowing a boat that neither can row alone, is a very simple example of a beneficially co-ordinative practice.[20] Each prefers to row if the other rows, and not to row if the other does not. And each prefers the other to row than to act in some alternative way.

It is worth noting that a co-ordinative practice need not be beneficial. Among peaceable persons, who regard weapons only as instruments of defence, each may prefer to be armed provided (most) others are, and not armed provided (most) others are not. Being armed is a co-ordinative practice but not a beneficial one; each prefers others not to be armed.

The co-ordinative advantages of society are not to be underestimated. But not all beneficial social practices are co-ordinative. Let us say that a practice is beneficial if each person prefers that (almost) everyone conform to it rather than that (most) persons conform to no practice, and does not (strongly) prefer that (almost) everyone conform to some alternative practice. Yet it may be the case that each person prefers not to conform to the practice if (most) others do. In a community in which tax funds are spent reasonably wisely, each person may prefer that almost everyone pay taxes rather than not, and yet may prefer not to pay taxes herself whatever others do. For the payments each person makes contribute negligibly to the benefits she receives. In such a community persons will pay taxes voluntarily only if each accepts some constraint on her pursuit of individual interest; otherwise, each will pay taxes only if coerced, whether by public opinion or by public authority.

The rationale for agreement on society as a co-operative venture may still seem unproblematic. But the step from hypothetical agreement *ex ante* on a set of social arrangements to *ex post* adherence may no longer seem straightforward. We see why one might willingly join the venture, yet not willingly continue with it. Each joins in the hope of benefiting from the adherence of others, but fails to adhere in the hope of benefiting from her own defection.

In the next two chapters we shall offer an account of value,

[19] The discussion here is related to my characterization of a convention in 'David Hume, Contractarian', *Philosophical Review* 88 (1979), pp. 5–8.

[20] See Hume, *Treatise*, iii. ii. ii, p. 490.

rationality, and interaction, that will give us a precise formulation of the issue just identified. Prior to reflection, we might suppose that were each person to choose her best course of action, the outcome would be mutually as advantageous as possible. As we fill in our tax forms we may be reminded, *inter alia*, that individual benefit and mutual advantage frequently prove at odds. Our theory develops the implications of this reminder, beginning by locating the conflict between individual benefit and mutual advantage within the framework of rational choice.

3.3 Although a successful contractarian theory defeats the presumption against morality arising from its conception of rational, independent individuals, yet it should take the presumption seriously. The first conception central to our theory is therefore that of a morally free zone, a context within which the constraints of morality would have no place.[21] The free zone proves to be that habitat familiar to economists, the perfectly competitive market. Such a market is of course an idealization; how far it can be realized in human society is an empirical question beyond the scope of our enquiry. Our argument is that in a perfectly competitive market, mutual advantage is assured by the unconstrained activity of each individual in pursuit of her own greatest satisfaction, so that there is no place, rationally, for constraint. Furthermore, since in the market each person enjoys the same freedom in her choices and actions that she would have in isolation from her fellows, and since the market outcome reflects the exercise of each person's freedom, there is no basis for finding any partiality in the market's operations. Thus there is also no place, morally, for constraint. The market exemplifies an ideal of interaction among persons who, taking no interest in each other's interests, need only follow the dictates of their own individual interests to participate effectively in a venture for mutual advantage. We do not speak of a *co-operative* venture, reserving that label for enterprises that lack the natural harmony of each with all assured by the structure of market interaction.

The perfectly competitive market is thus a foil against which morality appears more clearly. Were the world such a market, morals would be unnecessary. But this is not to denigrate the value of morality, which makes possible an artificial harmony where

[21] This is the theme of ch. IV, below. See also my earlier discussion in 'No Need for Morality: The Case of the Competitive Market', *Philosophic Exchange* 3, no. 3 (1982), pp. 41–54.

natural harmony is not to be had. Market and morals share the non-coercive reconciliation of individual interest with mutual benefit.

Where mutual benefit requires individual constraint, this reconciliation is achieved through rational agreement. As we have noted, a necessary condition of such agreement is that its outcome be mutually advantageous; our task is to provide a sufficient condition. This problem is addressed in a part of the theory of games, the theory of rational bargaining, and divides into two issues.[22] The first is the bargaining problem proper, which in its general form is to select a specific outcome, given a range of mutually advantageous possibilities, and an initial bargaining position. The second is then to determine the initial bargaining position. Treatment of these issues has yet to reach consensus, so that we shall develop our own theory of bargaining.

Solving the bargaining problem yields a principle that governs both the process and the content of rational agreement. We shall address this in Chapter V, where we introduce a measure of each person's stake in a bargain—the difference between the least he might accept in place of no agreement, and the most he might receive in place of being excluded by others from agreement. And we shall argue that the equal rationality of the bargainers leads to the requirement that the greatest concession, measured as a proportion of the conceder's stake, be as small as possible. We formulate this as the principle of minimax relative concession. And this is equivalent to the requirement that the least relative benefit, measured again as a proportion of one's stake, be as great as possible. So we formulate an equivalent principle of maximin relative benefit, which we claim captures the ideas of fairness and impartiality in a bargaining situation, and so serves as the basis of justice. Minimax relative concession, or maximin relative benefit, is thus the second conception central to our theory.

If society is to be a co-operative venture for mutual advantage, then its institutions and practices must satisfy, or nearly satisfy, this principle. For if our theory of bargaining is correct, then minimax relative concession governs the *ex ante* agreement that underlies a fair and rational co-operative venture. But in so far as the social arrangements constrain our actual *ex post* choices, the question of compliance demands attention. Let it be ever so rational to agree to

[22] For references to the literature on rational bargaining, see notes 12–14 to ch. V, below.

practices that ensure maximin relative benefit; yet is it not also rational to ignore these practices should it serve one's interest to do so? Is it rational to internalize moral principles in one's choices, or only to acquiesce in them in so far as one's interests are held in check by external, coercive constraints? The weakness of traditional contractarian theory has been its inability to show the rationality of compliance.

Here we introduce the third conception central to our theory, constrained maximization. We distinguish the person who is disposed straightforwardly to maximize her satisfaction, or fulfil her interest, in the particular choices she makes, from the person who is disposed to comply with mutually advantageous moral constraints, provided he expects similar compliance from others. The latter is a constrained maximizer. And constrained maximizers, interacting one with another, enjoy opportunities for co-operation which others lack. Of course, constrained maximizers sometimes lose by being disposed to compliance, for they may act co-operatively in the mistaken expectation of reciprocity from others who instead benefit at their expense. Nevertheless, we shall show that under plausible conditions, the net advantage that constrained maximizers reap from co-operation exceeds the exploitative benefits that others may expect. From this we conclude that it is rational to be disposed to constrain maximizing behaviour by internalizing moral principles to govern one's choices. The contractarian is able to show that it is irrational to admit appeals to interest against compliance with those duties founded on mutual advantage.[23]

But compliance is rationally grounded only within the framework of a fully co-operative venture, in which each participant willingly interacts with her fellows. And this leads us back to the second issue addressed in bargaining theory—the initial bargaining position. If persons are willingly to comply with the agreement that determines what each takes from the bargaining table, then they must find initially acceptable what each brings to the table. And if what some bring to the table includes the fruits of prior interaction forced on their fellows, then this initial acceptability will be lacking. If you seize the products of my labour and then say 'Let's make a deal', I may be compelled to accept, but I will not voluntarily comply.

[23] This conclusion rests on a reinterpretation of the maximizing conception of rationality, which we develop in ch. VI, below; see especially the opening paragraph of 3. 1.

We are therefore led to constrain the initial bargaining position, through a proviso that prohibits bettering one's position through interaction worsening the position of another.[24] No person should be worse off in the initial bargaining position than she would be in a non-social context of no interaction. The proviso thus constrains the base from which each person's stake in agreement, and so her relative concession and benefit, are measured. We shall show that it induces a structure of personal and property rights, which are basic to rationally and morally acceptable social arrangements.

The proviso is the fourth of the core conceptions of our theory. Although a part of morals by agreement, it is not the product of rational agreement. Rather, it is a condition that must be accepted by each person for such agreement to be possible. Among beings, however rational, who may not hope to engage one another in a co-operative venture for mutual advantage, the proviso would have no force. Our theory denies any place to rational constraint, and so to morality, outside the context of mutual benefit. A contractarian account of morals has no place for duties that are strictly redistributive in their effects, transferring but not increasing benefits, or duties that do not assume reciprocity from other persons. Such duties would be neither rationally based, nor supported by considerations of impartiality.

To the four core conceptions whose role we have sketched, we add a fifth—the Archimedean point, from which an individual can move the moral world.[25] To confer this moral power, the Archimedean point must be one of assured impartiality—the position sought by John Rawls behind the 'veil of ignorance'. We shall conclude the exposition of our moral theory in Chapter VIII by relating the choice of a person occupying the Archimedean point to the other core ideas. We shall show that Archimedean choice is properly conceived, not as a limiting case of individual decision under uncertainty, but rather as a limiting case of bargaining. And we shall then show how each of our core ideas—the proviso against bettering oneself through worsening others, the morally free zone afforded by the perfectly competitive market, the principle of minimax relative concession, and the disposition to constrained maximization—may be related, directly or indirectly, to Archimedean choice. In embrac-

[24] For the idea of the proviso, see note 1 to ch. VII, below.

[25] For the idea of an Archimedean point, see Rawls, *A Theory of Justice*, pp. 260–5.

ing these other conceptions central to our theory, the Archimedean point reveals the coherence of morals by agreement.

4 A contractarian theory of morals, developed as part of the theory of rational choice, has evident strengths. It enables us to demonstrate the rationality of impartial constraints on the pursuit of individual interest to persons who may take no interest in others' interests. Morality is thus given a sure grounding in a weak and widely accepted conception of practical rationality. No alternative account of morality accomplishes this. Those who claim that moral principles are objects of rational choice in special circumstances fail to establish the rationality of actual compliance with these principles. Those who claim to establish the rationality of such compliance appeal to a strong and controversial conception of reason that seems to incorporate prior moral suppositions. No alternative account generates morals, as a rational constraint on choice and action, from a non-moral, or morally neutral, base.

But the strengths of a contractarian theory may seem to be accompanied by grave weaknesses. We have already noted that for a contractarian, morality requires a context of mutual benefit. John Locke held that 'an Hobbist ... will not easily admit a great many plain duties of morality'.[26] And this may seem equally to apply to the Hobbist's modern-day successor. Our theory does not assume any fundamental concern with impartiality, but only a concern derivative from the benefits of agreement, and those benefits are determined by the effects that each person can have on the interests of her fellows. Only beings whose physical and mental capacities are either roughly equal or mutually complementary can expect to find co-operation beneficial to all. Humans benefit from their interaction with horses, but they do not co-operate with horses and may not benefit them. Among unequals, one party may benefit most by coercing the other, and on our theory would have no reason to refrain. We may condemn all coercive relationships, but only within the context of mutual benefit can our condemnation appeal to a rationally grounded morality.

Moral relationships among the participants in a co-operative venture for mutual advantage have a firm basis in the rationality of the participants. And it has been plausible to represent the society that has emerged in western Europe and America in recent centuries

[26] Locke MS, quoted in J. Dunn, *The Political Thought of John Locke* (Cambridge, 1969), pp. 218–19.

as such a venture. For Western society has discovered how to harness the efforts of the individual, working for his own good, in the cause of ever-increasing mutual benefit.[27] Not only an explosion in the quantity of material goods and in the numbers of persons, but, more important, an unprecedented rise in the average life span, and a previously unimaginable broadening of the range of occupations and activities effectively accessible to most individuals on the basis of their desires and talents, have resulted from this discovery.[28] With personal gain linked to social advance, the individual has been progressively freed from the coercive bonds, mediated through custom and education, law and religion, that have characterized earlier societies. But in unleashing the individual, perhaps too much credit has been given to the efficacy of market-like institutions, and too little attention paid to the need for co-operative interaction requiring limited but real constraint.[29] Morals by agreement then express the real concern each of us has in maintaining the conditions in which society can be a co-operative venture.

But if Locke's criticism of the scope of contractarian morality has been bypassed by circumstances that have enabled persons to regard one another as contributing partners to a joint enterprise, changed circumstances may bring it once more to the fore. From a technology that made it possible for an ever-increasing proportion of persons to increase the average level of well-being, our society is passing to a technology, best exemplified by developments in medicine, that make possible an ever-increasing transfer of benefits to persons who decrease that average.[30] Such persons are not party to the moral relationships grounded by a contractarian theory.

[27] We offer no explanation of this discovery. There seems no reason to suppose that it resulted from deliberate search.

[28] For the increase in average life span, see N. Eberstadt, 'The Health Crisis in the U.S.S.R.', *New York Review of Books* 28, no. 2 (1981), p. 23. For the broadening in the range of accessible occupations, note that 'As late as 1815 three-quarters of its [Europe's] population were employed on the land ...', *The Times Concise Atlas of World History*, ed. G. Barraclough (London, 1982), p. 82.

[29] Thus the idea of economic man as an unlimited appropriator comes to dominate social thought. The effects of this conception are one of the themes of my 'The Social Contract as Ideology', *Philosophy and Public Affairs* 6 (1977), pp. 130–64.

[30] The problem here is not care of the aged, who have paid for their benefits by earlier productive activity. Life-extending therapies do, however, have an ominous redistributive potential. The primary problem is care for the handicapped. Speaking euphemistically of enabling them to live productive lives, when the services required exceed any possible products, conceals an issue which, understandably, no one wants to face. Without focusing primarily on these issues, I endeavour to begin a

Beyond concern about the scope of moral relationships is the question of their place in an ideal human life. Glaucon asked Socrates to refute a contractarian account of justice, because he believed that such an account must treat justice as instrumentally valuable for persons who are mutually dependent, but intrinsically disvaluable, so that it 'seems to belong to the form of drudgery'.[31] Co-operation is a second-best form of interaction, requiring concessions and constraints that each person would prefer to avoid. Indeed, each has the secret hope that she can be successfully unjust, and easily falls prey to that most dangerous vanity that persuades her that she is truly superior to her fellows, and so can safely ignore their interests in pursuing her own. As Glaucon said, he who 'is truly a man' would reject moral constraints.[32]

A contractarian theory does not contradict this view, since it leaves altogether open the content of human desires, but equally it does not require it. May we not rather suppose that human beings depend for their fulfilment on a network of social relationships whose very structure constantly tempts them to misuse it? The constraints of morality then serve to regulate valued social relationships that fail to be self-regulating. They constrain us in the interests of a shared ideal of sociability.

Co-operation may then seem a second-best form of interaction, not because it runs counter to our desires, but because each person would prefer a natural harmony in which she could fulfil herself without constraint. But a natural harmony could exist only if our preferences and capabilities dovetailed in ways that would preclude their free development. Natural harmony would require a higher level of artifice, a shaping of our natures in ways that, at least until genetic engineering is perfected, are not possible, and were they possible, would surely not be desirable. If human individuality is to bloom, then we must expect some degree of conflict among the aims and interests of persons rather than natural harmony. Market and morals tame this conflict, reconciling individuality with mutual benefit.

contractarian treatment of certain health care issues in 'Unequal Need: A Problem of Equity in Access to Health Care', *Securing Access to Health Care: The Ethical Implications of Differences in the Availability of Health Services*, 3 vols., President's Commission for the Study of Ethical Problems in Medicine and Biomedical and Behavioral Research (Washington, 1983), vol. 2, pp. 179–205.

[31] *Republic*, 358a, trans. A. Bloom (New York, 1968), p. 36.

[32] ibid., 359b, p. 37.

We shall consider, in the last chapters of our enquiry, what can be said for this interpretation of the place of moral relationships in human life. To do so we shall remark on speculative matters that lead beyond and beneath the theory of rational choice. And we may find ourselves with an alternative reading of what we present as a theory of morals.[33] We seek to forge a link between the rationality of individual maximization and the morality of impartial constraint. Suppose that we have indeed found such a link. How shall we interpret this finding? Are our conceptions of rationality and morality, and so of the contractarian link between them, as we should like them to be, fixed points in the development of the conceptual framework that enables us to formulate permanent practical truths? Or are we contributing to the history of ideas of a particular society, in which peculiar circumstances have fostered an ideology of individuality and interaction that coheres with morals by agreement? Are we telling a story about ideas that will seem as strange to our descendants, as the Form of the Good and the Unmoved Mover do to us?

[33] The thoughts in this paragraph have been influenced by R. Rorty; see esp. 'Method and Morality', in Norma Haan, R. N. Bellah, P. Rabinow, and W. M. Sullivan (eds.), *Social Science as Moral Inquiry* (New York, 1983), pp. 155–76.

II

CHOICE: REASON AND VALUE

1 'There is nothing either good or bad, but thinking makes it so.'[1] But if things considered in themselves are neither good nor bad, if there is no realm of value existing independently of animate beings and their activities, then thought is not the activity that summons value into being. Hume reminds us, 'Reason is, and ought only to be the slave of the passions', and while Hume's dictum has been widely disputed, we shall defend it.[2] Desire, not thought, and volition, not cognition, are the springs of good and evil.

We might wish to bypass the great questions of value that have exercised Western philosophers from the time of Socrates and the Sophists. But answers to these questions are implicit in the theory of rational choice. Although the presentation of a full theory of value lies beyond the scope of our present enquiry, yet we shall find that in discussing the basic concepts of choice theory—preference, utility, maximization—we are led not only to outline a technical apparatus, but also to reflect on reason and value. In this chapter we shall consider both the apparatus and the assumptions needed to explain morality as arising from rational agreement.

But rational agreement itself, and its role in interaction, must wait to be introduced. Our present focus is on *parametric* choice, in which the actor takes his behaviour to be the sole variable in a fixed environment. In parametric choice the actor regards himself as the sole centre of action. Interaction involves *strategic* choice, in which the actor takes his behaviour to be but one variable among others, so that his choice must be responsive to his expectations of others' choices, while their choices are similarly responsive to their expectations.[3] Rational choice is well defined for parametric environments; we shall argue that morality enters in defining it for certain strategic environments. But this is to anticipate. How shall we understand parametric choice?

[1] Shakespeare, *Hamlet*, II. ii. 255–7.

[2] Hume, *Treatise*, ii. iii. iii, p. 415.

[3] For the distinction between parametric and strategic rationality, see J. Elster, *Ulysses and the Sirens: Studies in rationality and irrationality* (Cambridge, 1979), pp. 18–19, 117–23.

In Chapter I we spoke of the interest or interests of each person, relating rationality to the satisfaction of individual interest, and morality to an impartial constraint on the pursuit of that interest. But interest is a conception that hovers uneasily between an individual's own perspective and that of an outsider. The theory of rational choice takes as primary a conception even more clearly subjective and behavioural than interest, the relation of *individual preference*. Preference relates states of affairs; one speaks of preferring an apple to a pear, but more strictly one prefers the eating of an apple to the eating of a pear in some given environment or set of environments. The theory of rational choice is of course primarily concerned with preferences between states of affairs conceived as alternative possibilities realizable in action. These states of affairs are therefore not direct objects of choice, but rather are possible outcomes of the actions among which one chooses. The theory does not analyse particular relations of preference, which are treated as ultimate data, but sets of these relations, each set representing the preferences of one individual over the pairs of realizable outcomes in a choice situation.

Practical rationality in the most general sense is identified with maximization. Problems of rational choice are thus of a well-known mathematical type; one seeks to maximize some quantity subject to some constraint. The quantity to be maximized must be associated with preference; we have spoken loosely of advantage, or benefit, or satisfaction, but the theory of rational choice defines a precise measure of preference, *utility*, and identifies rationality with the maximization of utility. Utility is thus ascribed to states of affairs considered as objects of preference relations. The constraint under which utility is to be maximized is set by the possibilities of action. The rational actor maximizes her utility in choosing from a finite set of actions, which take as possible outcomes the members of a finite set of states of affairs.

An objector might agree to identify practical rationality with maximization, but insist that a measure of individual preference is not the appropriate quantity to maximize. It is rational to maximize *value*; the theory of rational choice implicitly identifies value with utility, but the objector challenges this identification. A radical challenger would insist that value is not a measure, but a norm or standard for preference. Value does not depend on preference, but rather rational preference depends on value. We shall explain our rejection of this position in clarifying our conception of value. A more moderate challenger would agree that value is a measure, but insist that it does not measure brute preferences, which may be misinformed, inexperienced, or ill-considered. We shall accept this view in so far as it concerns the manner in which preferences are held. Thus we shall develop a set of conditions for *considered preference*, which must be satisfied if utility, as a measure of preference, is to be identified with value, and the maximization of utility with rationality.

We must also sketch the formal conditions for defining utility. We have said that it is a measure of preference; more precisely it is a measure of outcomes representing relations of preference. Given a set of these relations, constituting the preferences of one individual in a choice situation, then a utility is to be assigned to each possible outcome in such a way that one may infer the person's preference between any two outcomes from the utilities. For any two possible outcomes the one with greater utility must be preferred. But not all sets of preference relations permit the definition of such a measure. Suppose for example that Bruce prefers eating an apple to eating a pear, eating a pear to eating a peach, and eating a peach to eating an apple. Then the required measure of Bruce's preferences must assign a greater value to eating an apple than to eating a pear, to eating a pear than to eating a peach, and to eating a peach than to eating an apple. But this is impossible. Bruce's preferences violate the conditions on sets of preference relations which are necessary for the definition of a measure. Preferences failing to satisfy these conditions are incoherent; we must sketch the conditions of *coherent preference*.

To avoid misunderstanding, we should note that although we may infer preferences from utilities, we do not explain preferences by utilities. Utility is simply a measure; its role is similar to that of temperature. If the temperature in Aix-en-Provence is higher than the temperature in Toronto, we may infer that it is warmer in Aix than in Toronto. But we do not explain Aix's greater warmth in terms of its higher temperature. It is not warmer because its temperature is higher, but rather its temperature is higher because it is warmer. Measures do not in themselves serve explanatory roles.

Utility is assigned directly to possible outcomes, but choice concerns actions. If the outcome of each possible action may be known with certainty, then choice among actions is equivalent to choice among their outcomes. The maximizing problem to be solved in choosing rationally is then very simple; one selects that action yielding the outcome with greatest utility. (If there are several such actions, then one chooses indifferently among them.) A purely *ordinal* measure of the outcomes suffices; rational choice under certainty requires only that the outcomes be ranked. Since most of classical economics examines choice under certainty, ordinal utility meets the economist's needs.[4]

But in most real-life situations, even if the environment may be treated as fixed, its characteristics are not fully known. And so the outcomes of some choices are risky or uncertain. (In the theory of rational choice, risk is associated with objective probability, uncertainty with subjective.)[5] Choice among actions must then be based not solely on the utilities of their possible outcomes, but also on the probabilities of those outcomes. The maximizing problem is more complex and can in general be solved only given an *interval* measure of preference. From the utilities of the members of a set of possible outcomes we must be able to infer not only the preference ordering, but also the relative strengths of the preferences. If Bruce prefers eating an apple to eating a pear to eating a peach, then from his utilities we must be able to infer whether his preference for eating an apple over a pear is stronger than his preference for eating a pear over a peach.

The formal conditions on sets of preferences that are required to define utility thus fall into two groups—those sufficient for a merely ordinal measure, and those additionally required for an interval measure. After we have sketched these two groups of conditions we shall be able to extend our account of the solution of the maximization problem from the simple case of choice under certainty to choice under risk and uncertainty. Strategic choice, involving interaction, raises further issues deferred to Chapter III.

If the conditions for coherent preferences are met, we may introduce a measure of the objects of preference. If the conditions for considered preference are also met, we may identify this measure with value, and its maximization with rationality. We may therefore speak of the conditions for coherent and considered preference as

[4] See J. C. Harsanyi, 'Advances in Understanding Rational Behavior', in *Essays on Ethics, Social Behavior, and Scientific Explanation* (Dordrecht, 1976), p. 94.

[5] See Harasanyi, *Rational Behavior and Bargaining Equilibrium in Games and Social Situations* (Cambridge, 1977), p. 9.

conditions of rational preference. But we must not be misled in so speaking, for none of the conditions addresses the content of particular preferences. Not the particular preferences, but the manner in which they are held, and their interrelations, are the concern of reason. Once more we find ourselves in agreement with Hume, in this case when he says that it is 'not contrary to reason to prefer the destruction of the whole world to the scratching of my finger'.[6] It may be contrary to reason to hold such a preference in an ill-considered manner, or to conjoin it with certain other preferences. But considered in itself we cannot assess its rationality. Of course we should not deny that such a preference may be symptomatic of severe emotional disturbance to the point of insanity. But its pathological character must be established by considering how it is acquired and maintained. Only confusion results from the all too common supposition that a malfunction of the affections must imply a failure of reason.

The conditions of rational preference do not require that the preferences of different persons be cast in a common mould. Each person's preferences determine her values quite independently of the values of others. Thus a state of affairs is characterized not by a single value, but by a set of values, one for each person into whose preferences it does or may enter. Value does not afford a single uniform measure of preference but a measure relative to each valuer. And although values are ascribed to states of affairs, the ascription is attitudinal, not observational, subjective, not objective. As a measure of preference value is and must be contingent on preferences for its very existence. Thus the theory of rational choice treats value as a subjective and relative measure, not as an objective and absolute standard.[7] These contrasts are controversial and demand commentary.

The theory of rational choice also treats practical reason as strictly instrumental. This is not quite implicit in the identification of rationality with maximization, for as we have noted, one might suppose that the quantity to be maximized was not a measure of but a standard for preference, a standard objectively inherent in states of affairs whose apprehension involves an exercise of reason. On such a

[6] Hume, *Treatise*, ii. iii. iii, p. 416.

[7] There are significant differences in the uses of 'subjective' and 'objective', 'relative' and 'absolute'. We shall seek to make our use of these terms clear in sect 4. 1–2 *infra*.

view reason would not be merely instrumental, but would also be concerned with the ends of action. But in identifying rationality with the maximization of a measure of preference, the theory of rational choice disclaims all concern with the ends of action. Ends may be inferred from individual preferences; if the relationships among these preferences, and the manner in which they are held, satisfy the conditions of rational choice, then the theory accepts whatever ends they imply.

An instrumental conception of rationality is thus linked to the identification of value with utility. Were value a standard, then reason might have a role in determining this standard which would go beyond mere maximization. Were there neither standard nor measure, then reason would have no practical role whatsoever; there would be nothing to maximize. The theory of rational choice sets its course between the dogmatism of assuming a standard for preference and the scepticism of denying a measure of preference. Since our aim is to have rational choice take moral theory in tow, we shall want to be sure that this course avoids shipwreck.

We have raised three topics to occupy the remainder of this chapter. In the next section we shall discuss considered preference. Then we shall sketch coherent preference. And in the final section we shall defend the conception of value as a subjective, relative measure.

2.1 To this point we have spoken as if preference may be distinguished from choice, not only conceptually but also operationally. We have supposed that a person's preferences over all pairs of possible outcomes are available as basic data, that a measure of these outcomes may then be defined from which her preferences may be inferred, and that a rule for maximizing this measure may then be introduced as a basis for choosing. Since preference and choice are treated as distinct, the rationality of choices may be assessed by determining whether they maximize preference fulfilment. But as the reader familiar with economics knows, this is not how the economist relates preference and choice, and consequently not how he understands utility and maximization.[8] For the economist choice alone is accessible to observation. Rationality is assumed wherever possible, so that a person is treated as behaving rationally if her choices may

[8] See R. D. Luce and H. Raiffa, *Games and Decisions* (New York, 1957), pp. 50–1, and D. M. Winch, *Analytical Welfare Economics* (Harmondsworth, Middx., 1971), p. 25.

be given a maximizing interpretation. Value is then identified with whatever she maximizes. Preferences are not given as data but are inferred; a person's preferences may be identified with the members of any set of relationships between possible outcomes such that their measure is maximized in her choices. On the economist's view preference is revealed in choice and has no independent operational significance.

Whether or not this approach is adequate for economics, it does not suffice for moral theory. The economist supposes that a person behaves irrationally, or fails to maximize value, if and only if her behaviour cannot be given a maximizing interpretation. Although reason and value play a limited normative role in prescribing and criticizing choice, that role is expressed in the single injunction, 'Maximize!' To say that one should maximize utility as a measure of preference adds nothing, since utility is simply identified with whatever one's behaviour may be interpreted as maximizing.[9]

If reason and value are to play normative roles in the framework for understanding human action afforded by the theory of rational choice, then it must be possible to give the injunction to maximize further content. If a person may behave in a maximizing way and yet not fully rationally, then maximization, although necessary, cannot be sufficient for rationality. But revealed preference is too impoverished a conception to provide this further content. If our only access to a person's preferences is through her choices, then whatever she maximizes must be the measure of those preferences. To move from the economist's account to a view of rational choice adequate to understand rational behaviour, we must begin by reconsidering the conception of preference.

Yet we must not suppose that the economist's focus on revealed preference is simply mistaken. Certainly choices reveal preferences; a conception of preference that treated the linkage between preference and choice as merely accidental would be even more evidently inadequate than one that makes preference parasitic on choice. What we must reject in the economist's account is the insistence that choice affords the sole access to preference. We must distinguish a behavioural dimension of preference revealed in choice, and an attitudinal dimension expressed in speech. Choosing an apple from a dish of apples and pears, one reveals a preference for eating an apple

[9] 'We assume that individuals attempt to maximize utility, and define utility as that which the individual attempts to maximize.' Winch, p. 25.

rather than a pear. Saying that one likes apples better than pears, one expresses a preference for eating an apple rather than a pear. Of course in some situations choice is verbal; one reveals one's preference by expressing it. But in other contexts the two dimensions of preference are quite distinct and may be in conflict. Karen expresses a preference for reading philosophical works rather than watching situation comedies on television, but she spends her free time in front of her television set while her philosophical library gathers dust.

We are now in a position to add some content, although as yet by no means sufficient, to the injunction to maximize. Utility is a measure of preference, but not of either revealed or attitudinal preference taken in isolation from the other. It is a measure of both dimensions in so far as they agree. If the two are in conflict, then even if it is possible to define a measure for each, neither may be identified with utility. If a person's revealed and expressed preferences diverge, then her values are confused and she lacks an adequate basis for rational choice. A necessary condition of supposing that a person is maximizing value, and so acting rationally, is that it be possible to interpret her choices as maximizing the measure of her expressed preferences.

Lack of a measure common to behaviour and attitudes is a sign of irrationality. But we may not without further ado ascribe this irrationality to a person's choices because they fail to conform to her attitudes, or to her attitudes because they fail to express her choices. In specific circumstances one of these ascriptions may seem clearly justified. But in general we may conclude only that the divergence between choice and attitude indicates irrationality without locating it more precisely. For it would be overcome were either the person's choices to come to conform to what she expresses, or her attitudes to come to conform to what she chooses.

In many situations a person chooses without any verbal expression of preference. In other situations a person expresses a preference without being in a position to make a choice. Of course we do not suppose that in these situations the person fails to be rational, simply because it is not possible to measure both dimensions of her preference. Rather we suppose that wherever possible, an individual would verbally confirm her choice, or behaviourally confirm her attitude. We assume the coincidence of revealed and expressed preference unless we have clear evidence of divergence. We assume a single measure of preference unless we are confronted with opposed measures. We accept the economist's assumption that rationality is to be ascribed to a person's behaviour in the absence of contrary evidence; we reject the extreme limitations on the evidence he allows.

2.2 Choice may fail in several ways. Queen Gertrude chose the poisoned cup. A young lady says 'Yes' (whether to a proposal or to a proposition) and later, although perhaps only momentarily later, realizes her mistake. A tourist newly arrived in France orders a bottle of Nuits-Saint-Georges to accompany his *sole meunière*. We may say that Gertrude's choice was uninformed, that the young lady's was unconsidered, that the tourist's was inexperienced.

Gertrude's choice, although fatally mistaken, was not irrational. She had no reason to believe that the cup contained poison. She wanted drink and chose what she took to be drink. Had she had reason to suspect the cup, then, given that her aim was not suicide, her choice would have been irrational. But we need not attribute this to her preferences; her beliefs would have been at fault. Her choice would have reflected failure to assess correctly evidence concerning her circumstances.

It might be supposed that a person's values should be identified with the measure of her informed preferences. But this we reject. Instead we relate a person's preferences to her state of belief or information. Gertrude chose poison, but she did not believe what she chose to be poison, and her choice did not reveal a preference for poison. Characterizing her preferences in relation to her beliefs, we have no reason to fault them, or to refuse to identify their measure with her values.

In some cases we may be able to infer what a person would have preferred, had she been correctly or fully informed about her circumstances. Gertrude would have preferred a cup of wine. But in other cases we may be quite unable to determine what persons would have preferred, since they will have formed no preferences in relation to the actual facts. We may relate the Aztecs' preference for human sacrifice to their belief in the hunger of the gods for human blood, but how would their preferences have been altered had they held no such belief? We do not know and have no way of knowing. The preferences of the Aztecs were formed in the context of their beliefs; beyond that context they had, or need have had, no preferences. To suppose that each person must have a set of 'real' or 'true' preferences related to her actual circumstances, although often concealed by false or incomplete beliefs, seems psychologically implausible.

A full discussion of the role of belief in relation to choice and preference would take us too far from our present concern. We accept the general explanatory schema: choice maximizes preference fulfilment given belief. We reject the trivialization of this schema that results from denying independent evidential access to each of its terms—to choice, preference, and belief. Choice may go astray because of mistaken belief; choice may be irrational because of irrational belief formation. The identification of value with the measure of preference, and the rationality of preference-based choice, are not affected by these failings of belief.

From Gertrude we turn to the inexperienced tourist. We may hope that before his departure from France he will realize that he does not prefer red wine with fish. His initial choice reflects his unfamiliarity with French cuisine; he has no firm or clear preference. Perhaps his choice is irrational; he would have done better to consult the waiter or to peruse the food-and-drink section of his guidebook; but waiters intimidate and guidebooks overwhelm. It may be that his choice reflects his preferences and beliefs as best he could ascertain them in the circumstances. But we should not want to take his initially revealed preference for red wine with fish as a basis for determining his values, since he lacks the experience to form a considered preference.

The young lady's acceptance of the proposal (or proposition) is equally not a basis for determining her values. She may not lack the experience to form a considered preference. But she fails to reflect before accepting. When she does come to reflect she realizes that her firm preference is expressed by 'No'. Does she change her initial preference, or does she correct it? Neither alternative is acceptable; the first would imply that her successive preferences stand on an equal footing; the second would imply that initially she misstates her preference. A better account is that without due consideration, she forms a tentative preference revealed in her acceptance, which she then revises. Any choice reveals (behavioural) preference, but not all preferences are equal in status, so that the rejection of a tentative preference is not to be equated with the alteration of a firm or considered preference. Of course not every rejection of a tentative preference need involve the formation of a firm one. The young lady's 'No' might have been followed by yet another 'Yes'. But we may suppose that in this case further reflection only confirms her second preference. And so we treat it as affording a basis for determining the young lady's values.

In the absence of full reflection on one's preferences choice tends to go astray. Again, this need not show it to be irrational. Circumstances may not allow adequate reflection; the gunman who says 'Your money or your life' is unlikely to accede to my request for time to think it over. Or even if time permits, the investment of effort in reflection may be unproductive; faced with fourteen brands of laundry detergent on the supermarket shelves, I simply reach for the nearest box. But if I am deciding where to spend my vacation, I shall act irrationally if I am not satisfied that further reflection would leave my preference unaltered.

If one chooses without adequate experience of the possible outcomes, one may later wish that one could undo one's choice. If one chooses without sufficient reflection on the outcomes, one may wish later to alter one's choice, should this be feasible. In neither case would one suppose one's original choice to have been successful, or to have maximized the measure of one's considered preferences. If one supposes that nevertheless one chose rationally, one must consider that one's choice was based on the best estimate that one could make in the situation of one's considered preferences—those that would pass the tests of reflection and experience.

But considered preferences, although stable, need not be unchanging. Mark, aged fifteen, prefers listening to disco to listening to Bach; twenty years later Mark prefers listening to Bach. His preference for disco indicates, we may judge, a lack of musical sensitivity and discrimination. As he acquires this sensitivity his preference changes, and he comes to think his later preference superior to his earlier one. He comes to think it better to prefer listening to Bach. But does this not imply that when earlier he prefers listening to disco, his preference is ill-considered?

Mark's lack of musical sensitivity at fifteen may invalidate any musical judgements he makes, but not his musical preferences. That he will come to prefer to listen to Bach does not give him a real preference for Bach in conflict with a merely apparent preference for disco. His current preference for disco is neither unreflective nor inexperienced; listening to disco does not make him wish to undo his choice, and should he find himself compelled to listen to Bach, he is not led to wish that he had done so voluntarily. In later life he wishes that when younger he had listened more to Bach. But nothing in his earlier preferences would have made such a choice rational. Although one may regret past choices because of their failure to maximize the fulfilment of one's considered preferences, one may also come to regret them because the fully considered preferences whose fulfilment they maximized do not correspond to one's present preferences.

An objector may point out that our argument ignores Mark's judgement that it is better to prefer to listen to Bach. He regrets his past choices, not merely because his preferences have changed, but because he has come to consider his past preferences inferior. And choices based on inferior preferences are faulty. But in the sense in which this last claim is true, it is not applicable to Mark's past choices. To suppose one preference superior to another is simply to prefer the one to the other. If one is in a position to choose among one's preferences, then one rationally chooses those preferences one considers superior. To choose inferior preferences would be to contradict expressed preference by revealed preference. But Mark does not do this. At fifteen he does not consider a preference for listening to disco inferior, and in any event he is not concerned to choose among possible musical preferences.

One chooses rationally in endeavouring to maximize the fulfilment of those preferences that one holds in a considered way in the choice situation. That these may include preferences that one will come to prefer not to have had, is a troubling feature of human life, but not of rational choice. Equally as troubling for life is that one may have preferences that at the same time one would prefer not to have. Some persons prefer to smoke—and their preference may be fully considered and all too experienced—and yet they prefer to prefer not to smoke. It may be that smoking, although obviously fulfilling the preference to smoke, diminishes the likelihood that they will come to prefer not to smoke. These persons face a hard choice, but not one that raises problems for our account of rational choice. The strength of their preferences, and the effect that choice is likely to have on their fulfilment, determine what it is rational for them to do. But surely new objections must occur to the reader. Are we not bypassing questions of interests and of prudence? To these and related issues we must therefore turn.

2.3 Preferences are considered if and only if there is no conflict between their behavioural and attitudinal dimensions and they are stable under experience and reflection. Value is the measure of considered preference, and rational choice involves the endeavour to maximize value. This view may be challenged by any one of several related positions. One may prefer smoking another cigarette to doing without, but it may be held irrational to choose to smoke since smoking is injurious to health and it is in one's *interest* to be healthy, whatever one may prefer. One may prefer pursuing one's lost love to seeking consolation elsewhere, but it may be held irrational to continue in a hopeless quest which only adds to one's misery rather than to gain greater *happiness* or *satisfaction* by directing one's efforts to some more attainable goal. One may prefer spending all one's earnings to gratify present desires rather than saving for one's old age, but it may be held irrational to maximize the measure of one's present preferences rather than *prudently* endeavouring to maximize the measure of one's considered preferences over the course of one's future life.[10]

We cannot discuss exhaustively the alternatives that might be advanced to our position, but shall simply sketch our principal reasons for rejecting the three views just mentioned. In each case the seeming plausibility of the alternative depends on contrasting it with the economic view that choice is rational in maximizing revealed preference. Once attitudinal preference, or even more reflective preference is introduced into the basis of rational choice, the plausibility of the alternative vanishes.

A person who acknowledges an interest in not smoking exhibits irrationality if she simply continues to smoke, without either endeavouring to stop or expressing some stronger considered preference for continuing. But we need not explain this irrationality by contrasting interest with preference as a basis for choice. To acknowledge an interest in not smoking is to express a preference, other things being equal, for those states of affairs furthering the interest over those not furthering it. If this acknowledgement is ignored in choice behaviour, then there is a divergence between expressed and revealed preference.

[10] Our concern is with ideal types, rather than with particular positions in the literature. A useful discussion based on interest, which rejects an objective conception of value but collapses interest into satisfaction, is found in L. W. Sumner, *Abortion and Moral Theory* (Princeton, 1981), pp. 162–86. Note that our own reference to interest in ch. I was intended as a stand-in for preference and utility, and not for the specific notion discussed here. An influential discussion of prudence is found in T. Nagel, *The Possibility of Altruism* (Oxford, 1970), pp. 27–76.

But what of the person who does not acknowledge an interest in not smoking? The defender of the view that rational choice is interest-based will insist that this person nevertheless has an interest in not smoking, and chooses irrationally in ignoring it. But here there is no overt conflict between behavioural and attitudinal dimensions of preference. Are we then not committed to the view that the smoker's behaviour is rational?

Not necessarily. Her revealed preference for smoking may fail to be contradicted by an acknowledged contrary interest because of her failure to reflect sufficiently. This failure may be inadvertent, or it may be deliberate, since the person may know that were she to reflect, she would have to acknowledge an interest in not smoking. If we may suppose that her revealed preference would not survive reflection unopposed, then we may agree that her choice is not fully rational.

But it will now be asked, what of the person who on the fullest and most careful reflection and the most extensive experience does not acknowledge an interest in not smoking? What of the person who consistently refuses to take her health into any practical account whether in word or deed? An acknowledged interest is an expressed preference, but on our view a rejected interest has no standing in determining either a person's values or the rationality of her choices.

Here then we disagree with the defender of the rationality of interest-based choice. To take an unacknowledged and indeed rejected 'interest', rather than a clear, considered preference, as the ground of choice is in effect to treat the content of preference as subject to rational assessment. And this requires an objective conception of value. If we treat the proposal to ground choice in interest as a subjectivist alternative to our view, then it fails. For if it be agreed that values are subjective, then there is no ground for appeal beyond what a person acknowledges, given that she has reflected sufficiently and is fully experienced. Of course her beliefs may be irrationally held, but this will not impugn her values, although it may show them to be inapplicable or irrelevant in her true circumstances.

There are few persons who do not acknowledge health as an interest, and even fewer who would not acknowledge it given adequate experience and reflection. For all but those few it would indeed be irrational to behave as if health were of no account. Those who believe that smoking is inimical to health must, if they are rational, choose not to smoke, unless their interest in health is outweighed by some stronger and equally considered preference. We need not take interest as the basis of rational choice to reach this conclusion, and we find no plausibility to any stronger conclusion.

A person may of course come to acknowledge as in her interest what previously she rejected, and may then regret having ignored it. This acknowledgement may reflect a change in belief, or in preference, or it may arise through the person's experience of ignoring the interest. In this last case the person's past choices have not been successful. Through inexperience she failed to ascertain correctly her considered preferences. Whether this failure indicates irrationality must of course depend on the particular circumstances.

The second position we must consider briefly is that rational choice is based on satisfaction or happiness, a measure of the quality of experience, or enjoyment or hedonic tone. No particular term suffices to express this proposed basis for choice, perhaps because it is unclear precisely what is to be measured. But what is essential is that there be a measure, distinct from utility and so independent of preference, applied to situations in virtue of the way in which they are experienced. The defender of happiness supposes that this measure is to be maximized in rational choice.

An immediate difficulty with this view is that there is in fact no measure of our experience whose credentials we may assess. But let us assume such a measure, and let what is measured be called *enjoyment*, which we shall treat in this discussion as a semi-technical term. Satisfaction or happiness is then defined as the measure of enjoyment, just as utility is the measure of preference, or temperature the measure of heat.

We suppose that people become acquainted with enjoyment and its measure, so that in forming their preferences they may take into account the expected satisfaction afforded by the possible outcomes of their choices. There are now two possibilities. The one is that their fully considered preferences do not focus exclusively on enjoyment, so that utility and satisfaction do not always correspond. Now this would surely be the best possible case against equating rationality with the maximization of satisfaction. If enjoyment is not acknowledged on full reflection to be the appropriate object of preference, then no argument can ever show that the maximization of its measure is the primary requirement of practical reason.

On the other hand it may be that fully considered preferences are exclusively concerned with enjoyment, so that the measure of expected enjoyment always corresponds to the measure of preference. Were this so, we should have made a profound psychological discovery about preference. We should have found it to have a single object—enjoyment. We should have found that it is possible to discover a person's real preference between any two states of affairs without appealing to either her choices or expressions of preference, without even requiring that she be acquainted with or even aware of the states of affairs, provided that we could determine how much enjoyment she would experience in each. And we should be able to explain a person's preferences in terms of enjoyment and its measure, so that we should be able to say that she preferred one outcome to another because the first afforded her greater satisfaction.

Were all this so, we should agree that satisfaction afforded the basis for rational choice. But this would not be opposed to our present position, for satisfaction would provide the basis for rational choice as the measure of the object of preference, enjoyment. But of course we have no reason to believe that preference has a unique, measurable object such as we have supposed enjoyment to be. It seems clear that preferences cannot be correlated with any single dimension or characteristic of the states of affairs that they relate. Indeed, it seems clear that preferences do not depend solely on the qualities of experience, as the defender of satisfaction or happiness maintains.[11] We may dismiss this alternative from further discussion.

The third position opposed to our preference-based account of rational choice identifies practical rationality with prudence. It is not rational, the defender of prudence claims, simply to maximize the fulfilment of one's present preferences, however considered they may be, if one does not take into account the preferences one will or may come to have. Of course one cannot have full knowledge of one's future, but one may form reasonable expectations, allowing for different alternatives with varying probabilities. The prudent person takes thought for the morrow and so, our objector claims, chooses rationally.

An example will illustrate how prudence-based and preference-

[11] Sumner states, 'If something enhances my welfare, it must, directly or indirectly, immediately or in the long run, either produce states of mind I find agreeable or prevent states of mind I find disagreeable', p. 184. So if value is the measure of individual welfare, or of happiness or satisfaction, a hedonistic conception of value is established by conceptual fiat.

based accounts of rational choice differ. Winter will come, and when it comes Susan will prefer her home to be well insulated. Is it not rational for her to insulate now, when prices are lower and workers and materials readily available? This would be the prudent course of action, but it is summer, and Susan is reclining by her pool without any care for winter. She believes that she will care, but right now she does not. The defender of the rationality of prudence insists that her present unconcern is irrational. But on our account, only a consideration entering into one's present preferences can provide rational support for choice. If Susan's unconcern is fully considered, then she has no reason to insulate now.

Here we face the proverbial contrast between the grasshopper and the ant; are we not defending the rationality of the heedless grasshopper? Indeed we are, in so far as the grasshopper is reflectively heedless, but we are not thereby impugning the rationality of the prudent ant. To maximize on the basis of one's present preferences need not be to ignore one's future preferences; one may take an interest in one's future well-being now, preferring a satisfying life to more immediate gratification. But also, one may not. Our view is that prudence is rational for those who have a considered preference for being prudent, but not for those who on full reflection do not.

Our disagreement with the defender of prudence does not turn on whether future preferences are to be taken into account, but on how they are to be considered. We both agree that the unreflectively heedless person, who takes no thought about the morrow, chooses irrationally. One's considered preferences for possible outcomes of one's choices must take into account the expected effects of those outcomes on oneself. But one may choose to ignore those effects in what one does; one may choose to take no thought for the morrow. And this reflective heedlessness is not irrational on our view. The defender of prudence insists that rational choice must be directed to the maximal fulfilment of all our preferences, present and future, in so far as we are able to determine what they are. On our view rational choice must be directed to the maximal fulfilment of our present considered preferences, where consideration extends to all future effects in so far as we may now foresee them.

There is a close link between the defender of interest-based choice and the defender of prudence. Both view the future in a temporally neutral way, denying any priority to the present moment in rational deliberation about what to do. Our position rejects this temporal neutrality except in so far as it is part of an individual's present stance. Or in other words, we suppose that the extent of an individual's practical identification with her future selves is determined by her present preferences, and these preferences, as all others, are not subject to rational assessment in terms of their contents. To be sure, the markedly imprudent, devotees of instant gratification, may find that when they taste the bitter fruit of their choices, they regret their past folly. But their irrationality is a contingent matter, determined by their considered preferences, and not a matter determined conceptually by the alleged atemporality of reason. Practical reason takes its standpoint in the present.[12]

Against the view that mere behavioural preference suffices as a basis for rational choice, and as a determinant of value, the defenders of interest, of enjoyment, and of prudence, may press plausible objections. But the view that rational choice rests on considered preference, exhibiting no divergence between behaviour and attitude, and manifesting adequate experience and reflection, assimilates the merits of these alternative positions. Considered preference is, however, but part of our story. Maximization itself imposes conditions on preference. But these conditions, required for the definition of an interval measure, are quite independent of the way in which preferences are held. Unconsidered preferences may meet, and considered preferences may fail, the conditions for maximization. To simplify our discussion we shall henceforth talk only of preference, leaving it understood that unless we should specifically state otherwise, our concern is with considered preference and with the maximization of utility taken as the measure of considered preference.

3.1 The formal conditions required in order to define an interval measure of preference are extensively discussed in the literature of rational choice.[13] We have nothing to contribute to the mathematical treatment. Our aim in this section is merely to offer a relatively non-technical account of coherent preference. As we noted previously our discussion falls into two parts: first we sketch the

[12] 'The correct perspective on one's life is *from now*', B. Williams, 'Persons, character and morality', in *Moral Luck* (Cambridge, 1981), p. 13. See, in addition to Williams's paper, D. Parfit, 'Later Selves and Moral Principles', in A. Montefiore (ed.), *Philosophy and Personal Relations* (London, 1973), pp. 137–69. See also the discussion of the position that 'the notion of rational man should be extended so as to include temporal considerations', in Elster, pp. 65–77.

[13] See Luce and Raiffa, ch. 2, and Harsanyi, *Rational Behavior*, ch. 3.

conditions sufficient for a merely ordinal measure of preference; then we introduce the further conditions necessary for an interval measure.

An ordinal measure may be defined over the members of a set on the basis of any relationship weakly ordering those members. The relationship places the members from first to last, best to worst, most to least, with ties permitted. Height weakly orders human beings from tallest to shortest. Lifetime major league batting average weakly orders baseball players from highest (Ty Cobb) to lowest (?). An ordinal measure of preference may be defined over the possible outcomes in any choice situation if and only if preference weakly orders those outcomes, from most preferred to least preferred (with ties—equal preference or indifference—permitted).

The first condition required if a relationship is to weakly order the members of a set is that any two members be comparable on the basis of the relationship. Thus for any two possible outcomes in a choice situation, the chooser must either prefer one to the other or be indifferent between them. This is the condition of *completeness*; it rules out preferentially non-comparable outcomes.

As a condition on behavioural preference completeness is trivial. If a person must choose between two possible outcomes, then his choice will reveal a preference between them. But of course, he may be unwilling or unable to express or acknowledge a preference. As a condition on considered preference completeness is not trivial. Its failure does not preclude choice, but only rational choice. If someone finds two possible outcomes preferentially non-comparable, then he is unable to choose rationally between them. This is a direct consequence of the view that rational choice rests on preference.

But it should be noted that the need for a condition of completeness arises because rational choice is based on a relationship among the objects of choice. Whatever that relationship is, it must satisfy such a condition. If we were to substitute interest, or enjoyment, for preference, as the basis for rational choice, then we should have to be able to compare any two possible outcomes in terms of interest fulfilment or in terms of enjoyment, in order to choose rationally between them.

Much of our discussion in this section is concerned, not so much with preference itself, as with the requirements of any account identifying rationality with the maximization of the measure of some relationship among the possible outcomes of actions. But of course we must ask if these requirements may plausibly be imposed on preference; if not, we should seek some other relationship as the basis of rational choice—or we should give up the identification of rationality with maximization. We suppose that it is plausible to require that preference satisfy completeness, that it is plausible to claim that a person who is unable to compare two states of affairs preferentially is indeed unable to choose rationally between them.

The second condition required if a relationship is to weakly order the members of a set is that the relationship be transitive. Let us illustrate the *transitivity* condition as it applies to preference by a simple example. Suppose that among the possible outcomes of Bruce's choice are eating an apple, eating a pear, and eating a peach. If Bruce prefers eating an apple to eating a pear and eating a pear to eating a peach, then if transitivity holds he prefers eating an apple to eating a peach. If Bruce is indifferent between eating an apple and eating a pear, and eating a pear and eating a peach, then if transitivity holds he is indifferent between eating an apple and eating a peach. Furthermore, if Bruce prefers eating an apple to eating a pear and is indifferent between eating a pear and eating a peach, or is indifferent between eating an apple and eating a pear and prefers eating a pear to eating a peach, then if transitivity holds he prefers eating an apple to eating a peach.

Even more than completeness, transitivity represents a standard for preference rather than a characterization of actual behaviour and attitudes. In some contexts the standard is no doubt attained. If the possible outcomes are all sums of money then we may expect perfect transitivity of preference, a larger sum always being preferred to a smaller one and equal sums being treated as indifferent. But if there is no one quantitative dimension along which the outcomes may be ranged and which is the sole object of concern in choice among them, then transitivity may be expected to fail in the actual world. This is most evident in the case of indifference. One is indifferent between a first apple and a second, between the second and a third . . . between the nineteenth and a twentieth, yet one is in no doubt about one's preference for the first to the twentieth. Each small difference between successive apples falls beneath one's threshold of discrimination, but summed the differences are clearly noticeable. Sufficiently similar objects or states of affairs are regarded as alike, but sufficient similarity is not a transitive relationship.

Gross failure to satisfy transitivity leads to a cycle of preference, as exemplified by our reference to Bruce in the first section of this chapter, who prefers eating an apple to a pear, a pear to a peach, and a peach to an apple. If manifest in behaviour, such cycles would divest choice of all rationality. Suppose that Bruce has an apple. Before he eats it we offer him a peach; he prefers the peach and so trades. Before he eats the peach we offer him a pear; he prefers the pear and so trades. But before he eats the pear we offer him his original apple; he prefers the apple and so trades. After three trades, in each of which Bruce betters his situation in terms of his preferences, he finds himself at his starting-point.

Indeed, Bruce's situation is even worse than this example suggests. If he prefers a peach to an apple, then presumably he is willing to offer more than the apple in return for the peach. Suppose he is willing to offer 1c. And suppose he is willing to offer the peach and 1c for the pear, and the pear and 1c for the apple. Then after three trades, in each of which Bruce betters his situation in terms of his preferences, Bruce finds himself with his original apple but 3c poorer. Clearly an astute trader can take advantage of Bruce's intransitive preferences to beggar him by an unending round of such trades. And clearly Bruce, who becomes ever less well off as a result of trades, each of which betters his position in terms of his preferences, is engaged in an irrational sequence of choices.

Acyclicity, or the avoidance of full preference cycles, must be required of any relationship if it is to ground rational choice. Full transitivity is a stronger requirement, demanded by the identification of practical rationality with maximization. But its plausibility does not rest on that identification alone. Were no more than acyclicity required, Bruce might be indifferent between eating an apple and eating a peach, even though he preferred eating an apple to a pear and a pear to a peach. In ruling out such preference combinations, transitivity surely expresses our pre-theoretic ideal of rationality in choice.

Completeness and transitivity are together sufficient to ensure that the preference relationship weakly orders any set of possible outcomes. Each such set then includes an outcome preferred to all others, or several outcomes, mutually indifferent, but each preferred to all others. These are the most preferred outcomes; utility, the measure of preference, is maximized by the selection of a most preferred outcome.

But as we have noted, the direct objects of choice are actions, not outcomes. Under conditions of certainty, in which each action is correlated with a definite outcome, this poses no problem for maximization. But under conditions of risk or uncertainty, in which each action is correlated only with a set of possible outcomes, each with its (objective or subjective) probability, it may not be possible straightforwardly to choose a most preferred outcome. Suppose Bruce prefers eating an apple to a pear to a peach, and that his preferences are transitive. There are two bowls of fruit, one with two apples, five pears and one peach, the other with four apples, one pear and three peaches. Bruce may choose a bowl, from which he will then receive one fruit selected at random. Which bowl should he choose? His preference ordering does not yield an answer, since it does not reveal the strength of his preference for apples to pears, in comparison with his preference for pears to peaches. If he very much prefers pears to peaches, but only slightly favours apples to pears, then the first bowl will be the better choice. But if he strongly prefers apples to pears, and only slightly favours pears to peaches, then the second bowl will be better. To determine the respective strengths of Bruce's preferences, an interval measure is needed.

3.2 Under risk or uncertainty, each action open to a person's choice is associated with a set of outcomes. Each outcome in the set is assigned a probability; under risk, as we have noted, these probabilities are objectively based, whereas under uncertainty the probabilities are determined by the individual's subjective estimates. For present purposes the distinction between objective and subjective probability may be ignored, as long as we require that the subjective probabilities be assigned so that they sum to unity. It is taken as certain that if the action is chosen, one of the outcomes in its associated set will result, and only one.

We may think of each action as a lottery, with its associated outcomes as its prizes. But we should enter a warning about this terminology, which is standard in the literature of rational choice. Each actor's preferences for any choice treated as a lottery, must depend solely on his preferences for the outcomes or prizes and on their probabilities. The lottery itself is transparent to preference; each person is indifferent to the 'gamble' which the lottery involves.

In real-life lotteries the participants are concerned, not only with the prizes and their probabilities, but with the pleasures (or displeasures) of taking a chance. But in the lotteries associated with risk and uncertainty, taking a chance is not one of the factors affecting preference.

Utility, the measure of preference, is determined by a real-valued function, that is, a function assigning real numbers to outcomes in such a way that, if outcome X is assigned a greater number than outcome Y, outcome X is preferred to Y, and if outcomes X and Y are assigned the same number, they are indifferent. Under certainty only preferences for outcomes enter into a person's choices, since each action is associated with a single outcome. But under uncertainty and risk, preferences for lotteries over outcomes must also enter into choice. If there is to be a measure of these preferences, such that we may interpret the person's choices as maximizing it, then two further conditions on preference, in addition to completeness and transitivity, must hold. Given these conditions, an interval measure over the outcomes and lotteries possible in a particular choice situation may be defined, such that the utility assigned to any lottery is its *expected utility*—that is, the sum of the products obtained by multiplying the utility of each of the prizes (or outcomes) of the lottery by its probability.

An example may be helpful. Suppose Bruce is to receive a fruit taken at random from the first of the bowls mentioned at the end of the last subsection—the bowl with two apples, five pears, and one peach. Then the probability of Bruce receiving an apple is 0.25, a pear 0.625, and a peach 0.125. If the utility, to Bruce, of an apple is 1, a pear 0.5, and a peach 0, then the expected utility of receiving a fruit taken at random from the bowl is $[(1 \times 0.25) + (0.5 \times 0.625) + (0 \times 0.125)]$, or 0.5625.

To say that the utility of a lottery is its expected utility, is to say that preferences over lotteries may be inferred from the expected utilities of the lotteries. If lottery X has greater expected utility than lottery Y, then lottery X is preferred to lottery Y. Given utility as an interval measure of Bruce's preferences over possible outcomes, we may then infer his preferences over lotteries with these outcomes as prizes by calculating their expected utilities.

The theory of rational choice identifies practical rationality with utility maximization. If the utility of a lottery is its expected utility, then in conditions of risk or uncertainty practical rationality is identified with *expected utility-maximization*. This is the central thesis of Bayesian decision theory.[14] Although the theory does not command universal assent, we shall not enter into its merits and defects here, but only assert (dogmatically) that we know no satisfactory alternative.

What are the further conditions on preference required for an interval measure? The first is *monotonicity*. Consider two lotteries, X and Y, that differ in only one respect—one of the prizes (or outcomes) in X, P, is replaced by another prize in Y, Q (with, of course, the same probability). Monotonicity requires that if Q is preferred to P, then Y is preferred to X.

Consider a simple example. Diana is to receive a fruit taken at random from a fruit bowl. Initially the bowl contains three apples, three pears, and four peaches. But before Diana gets her fruit, Mark removes one of the peaches and replaces it by an apple. If Diana prefers getting an apple to getting a peach, then monotonicity requires that she prefer the final lottery to the initial one.

The second condition is *continuity*. Consider three possible outcomes, X, Y, and Z, such that X is preferred to Y and Y to Z. Continuity requires that there is one and only one lottery, with X and Z as prizes, that is indifferent to Y. Or in other words, there is a unique probability p such that the lottery $[pX + (1-p)Z]$ is indifferent to Y.

Given that an individual's preferences satisfy completeness, transitivity, monotonicity, and continuity, there is an easy way (in principle) to assign utilities measuring his preferences over the members of any set of possible outcomes, such that the utility of any lottery taking members of the set as prizes will be its expected utility. Let the most preferred outcome(s) be assigned a utility of 1, and let X be such an outcome. Let the least preferred outcome(s) be assigned a utility of 0, and let Z be such an outcome. Then the utility of any other outcome Y is p, where Y is indifferent to the lottery $[pX + (1-p)Z]$. This assignment, it should perhaps be noted, is not unique; if U is a utility function providing an interval measure of an individual's preferences over the members of a set of possible outcomes, then any positive linear transform of U is also such a function. But we need not pursue these complications here.

We have not commented on the plausibility of monotonicity and continuity. Monotonicity in effect rules out preferences directed at

[14] See Harsanyi, *Rational Behavior*, p. 9.

lotteries themselves—preferences for or against risks—as opposed to preferences for the prizes (possible outcomes). We indicated at the beginning of this subsection that this must be done; the reader may, however, object that in many situations the requirement is unreasonable. If I prefer sunshine tomorrow to rain, then I must prefer a slight chance of sun (and otherwise rain) to rain for sure, if monotonicity is to hold. But surely, and quite reasonably, I may not; a slight chance of sun may only complicate my plans for the morrow in comparison with the certainty of rain. My preferences may be perfectly coherent even though I prefer sun for sure to rain for sure and rain for sure to a 10 per cent chance of sun.

Continuity may seem equally suspect. To borrow an example from one of the standard sources (Luce and Raiffa): I prefer $1 to 1c and 1c to death. If continuity holds, then there must be a lottery over $1 and death which I consider indifferent to 1c. But would I run any increased risk of death, in return for $1 if I do not die? If not, then I must prefer 1c to any lottery over $1 and death.[15]

There are seemingly easy responses to the objections revealed in these examples. The first, it may be noted, reflects misunderstanding of monotonicity and of the special features of the lotteries to which it applies. Suppose that I am indifferent between a holiday next year in Greece and a holiday next year in Mexico. If I am rational, must I be equally indifferent between either holiday for sure and a lottery with these as prizes? If the lottery is to be decided now, then it is plausible to hold that the answer is affirmative. But if the lottery is to be decided the day before the holiday commences, then the answer may well be negative; I do not care whether I take a holiday in Greece or Mexico but I want to know now where I shall go, so that I may make suitable plans. In this second case, the lottery introduces a period of epistemic risk that would otherwise be absent, and towards which I need not be indifferent.

Monotonicity entails indifference to risk or uncertainty as such. But it does not require indifference between the presence and the absence of a temporal period of uncertainty. It is a plausible requirement for coherent preference over lotteries in which the actual prize or outcome is determined immediately, so that the risk associated with the lottery does not affect the epistemic state of the participants. But real-life lotteries need not be decided immediately. Although I prefer sun tomorrow to rain tomorrow, I may prefer the

[15] Luce and Raiffa, p. 27.

certainty of rain to a small chance of sun because the weather 'lottery' will not be decided until tomorrow, leaving me in the subjectively undesirable state of not knowing what to expect. Such real-life lotteries do not undermine monotonicity as a condition on coherent preference, but they do reveal the limits of its applicability.

The second example, suggesting the failure of continuity, is perhaps best handled by limiting the contexts in which continuity is expected to hold by exempting extreme cases. But is there any precise way of distinguishing the extreme? Are we appealing to anything other than a gut response—usually continuity holds but sometimes our preferences turn out to be hierarchically or lexicographically ordered? With these questions unanswered, and further problems about monotonicity, amply represented in the literature of utility theory, unraised, we turn from our sketch of coherent preference, aware that the theory of rational choice is still an underdeveloped territory, to equally intractable but less technical concerns.[16]

4.1 The introduction of utility as a measure of preference is in itself an intellectual exercise that does not determine the role utility is to play. We have claimed that by relating it to considered preference, we could treat it as the norm for choice, identifying rational choice with the maximization of utility. This is to equate utility with value. Economists have been content to note this and to proceed with their study of decision-making. Philosophers must pause, to examine the conception of value implicit in equating it with utility.

Value on this conception is a measure of preference. A measure depends for its existence on what it measures—no preference, no value. Of course value may be ascribed to an object—an apple, for example—or more properly to a state of affairs involving an object—eating an apple—without supposing that the object or the related state of affairs does in fact enter into the preferences of any person. The apple may be sufficiently similar to others actually involved in human preferences to permit an inference to the hypothetical preferences of some person concerning states of affairs in which it might be involved. And in this way value may be assigned to those states of affairs. But objects or states of affairs may be ascribed

[16] Elster continues the passage quoted in note 14, ch. I, above, 'but many problems concerning its scope and resolving power remain to be settled'. He then offers 'a list of such problems'. It is not a short list.

value only in so far as, directly or indirectly, they may be considered as entering into relations of preference. Value is then not an inherent characteristic of things or states of affairs, not something existing as part of the ontological furniture of the universe in a manner quite independent of persons and their activities. Rather, value is created or determined through preference. Values are products of our affections.

To conceive of value as dependent on affective relationships is to conceive of value as *subjective*. The opposed, objective conception does not deny that values are affectively related, but it does deny that they are products of such relationships. To conceive of value as objective is to conceive of it as existing independently of the affections of sentient beings, and as providing a norm or standard to govern their affections. The subjectivist view denies the existence of such a norm.

Here one might ask whether a theological conception of value, treating it as dependent on the divine will, is objective or subjective.[17] Dependence on God's will, it may be urged, is the analogue to dependence on sentient affection. We may reply that on most theological conceptions, everything is dependent on the divine will, so that from the standpoint of finite, sentient creatures, value has the same objectivity as other aspects of the divine order. To conceive value as a divinely ordained norm or standard to govern our affections is to conceive it as objective.

The difference between subjective and objective conceptions of value is not a difference between the objects or states of affairs to which value may be ascribed. It might be thought that subjectivism implies that only what is itself subjective—only a state of sentient experience—could possess intrinsic value. But subjectivism concerns the ground of value, not its object. There is no restriction on the nature of those states of affairs that may be objects of preference, and so that may be valued. There may be some persons who reveal and express preferences only in relation to their own experience, but there are surely few whose preferences are so confined. We must not confuse the view that only what is preferred for its own sake is or can be intrinsically good, with the view that only what is experienced pleasurably can be intrinsically good.

An objective conception of value is equally neutral with respect to

[17] My colleague Shelly Kagan did ask just this, and numerous other questions leading to discussions and clarifications at many other points.

the nature of the objects of intrinsic value. It is quite compatible with, although certainly it does not require, the view that the only bearers of intrinsic value are states of sentient experience. One might suppose that contemplative activity was the sole, or more plausibly the supreme, intrinsically valuable state of affairs, and while one might claim that it was also most truly pleasurable and most appropriately preferred, these judgements of its affective character would derive from rather than determine its value, which on this view would depend on the cognitive nature of the experience.

Or consider a more mundane view—that individual conscious survival is the sole intrinsic good. A subjectivist might advance this position because he supposed that conscious beings capable of choice did in fact take conscious survival as their sole goal, at least given full consideration. An objectivist might advance this position even though he supposed that some conscious beings did not make survival their sole concern, but would insist that nevertheless it afforded the proper objective for rational choice. The subjectivist would base the value of conscious survival on its actual place in our concerns; the objectivist would determine its proper place on the basis of its value. But both would take sentient experience as affording the sole intrinsic value. If both are mistaken (as we should argue), their mistake is not one that offers any ground for choosing between subjectivist and objectivist conceptions of value.

Subjectivism is not to be confused with the view that values are arbitrary. As we have insisted, if utility is to be identified with value, it must be the measure of considered preference. Values are not mere labels to be affixed randomly or capriciously to states of affairs, but rather are registers of our fully considered attitudes to those states of affairs given our beliefs about them. Although the relation between belief and attitude is not itself open to rational assessment, it is not therefore arbitrary. We have noted our agreement with Hume's insistence that it is not contrary to reason to prefer the destruction of the world to the scratching of one's finger. A person who on full consideration held such a preference, would correctly assign to the destruction of the world a value greater than he would assign to the scratching of his finger. Although, as we have also noted, we might have grounds, independent of the content of this preference, for holding such a person to be mad, we should not have grounds for considering his preference arbitrary. Madness need not imply either a failure of reason or a failure of reflection. (Madness, we should hold, is primarily a disorder of the affections. But this does not imply that the affections are irrational, any more than a disorder of the stomach implies that it is irrational.)

Subjectivism is also not to be confused with the view that values are unknowable. Evaluation, as an activity of measurement, is cognitive. Preference, what is measured, is knowable. What the subjectivist denies is that there is a knowledge of value that is not ordinary empirical knowledge, a knowledge of a special realm of the valuable, apprehended through some form of intuition differing from sense-experience. Knowledge of value concerns only the realm of the affects; evaluation is cognitive but there is no unique 'value-oriented' cognition.

Value is the norm for choice. The objectivist considers value to be the norm for choice because it is also the norm for preference. For him, relating choice to preference does not show choice to be rational except in so far as preference itself may be related to value as its norm. The subjectivist considers value to be the norm for choice because it is the measure of considered preference. For him, relating choice to preference does show choice to be rational, provided preference is fully considered and is coherent, fixed in relation to reflection and experience and satisfying the conditions necessary to define an interval measure. For the objectivist preference mediates choice and value; for the subjectivist value mediates choice and preference.

4.2 Value is a measure of individual preference, on the conception we are defending. The value of a state of affairs for some person measures its place in his preferences. Each state of affairs is thus characterized, as we noted in the first section of this chapter, not by a single value, but by a set of values, one for each affective relationship into which it enters or may be thought of as entering. The relationship between the values of different persons, or between the different values ascribed to a particular state of affairs, is a matter for empirical investigation. It may be thought that divergent values reflect opposed beliefs, not all of which can be correct. Yet it may also be thought that convergent values reflect the uncritical acceptance by one individual or the members of one group of the ideas of others, to the exclusion of full individual consideration. We have no good reason to suppose that the fully considered preferences of different persons over the same states of affairs would give rise to equivalent measures, even if we suppose the persons fully informed, fully reflective and experienced, and similarly placed with respect to the states of affairs.

To conceive of value as dependent on each individual's own affective relationships is to conceive of value as *relative*. There are of course other relativist conceptions of value. Common to all forms of purely individualistic relativism is the view that each person has his own good (and bad), and that the goods of different persons are not parts of a single, overall good. Other, non-individualistic forms of relativism may suppose there to be a good common to a family, or to a class, or to a society, while denying that the goods of different families or classes or societies are parts of an overall good. Opposed to all forms of relativism is an absolute or universal conception of value. An absolutist conception holds that values are the same for all persons, or for all sentient beings. An absolutist may suppose that values are affectively determined, so that a state of affairs is good simply because it is preferred by some person, but then he must hold that the state of affairs is good, not only in relation to or from the standpoint of that person, but from the standpoint of every person. The individualistic relativist supposes that your good and my good are quite independent, and not parts of a single universal good; the absolutist insists that your good is simply that part of the single good which pertains to you.[18] If we were developing a full theory of value we should have to examine the nuances of both relativist and absolutist positions. We might find, not two opposed views, but a continuum of outlooks. But we shall remain with a simple opposition between a purely individualistic relativism and an undifferentiated absolutism.

On both the absolute and the relative conceptions it is possible to distinguish what is good *for* some person from what is straightforwardly good, and to suppose that a state of affairs that is good for some individual may be considered good from the standpoint of others. A state of affairs is good for someone if it contributes to his well-being. On the absolute view, if contributing to someone's well-being is a source of positive value, then it is such a source for everyone; a state of affairs that is good for—and perhaps only for—a single individual is then good from everyone's standpoint in being good for that individual. On the relative view, contributing to someone's well-being is a source of positive value for others if it

[18] See G. E. Moore, *Principia Ethica* (Cambridge, 1903), pp. 97–102, for a defence of this form of absolutism.

enters into their good, as it does on our particular relativistic position if those others prefer such a contribution. A state of affairs that is good for a single individual is then good from the standpoint of each person who prefers or would prefer the enhancement of that individual's well-being.

Perhaps the classic philosophic formulation of a conception of value both subjective and relative was offered in the seventeenth century by Thomas Hobbes. Writing in *Leviathan*, he says,

> But whatsoever is the object of any mans Appetite or Desire; that is it, which he for his part calleth *Good*: And the object of his Hate, and Aversion, *Evill* . . . For these words of Good, Evill . . . are ever used with relation to the person that useth them: There being nothing simply and absolutely so; nor any common Rule of Good and Evill, to be taken from the nature of the objects themselves; but from the Person of the man.[19]

And again he says,

> *Good*, and *Evill*, are names that signifie our Appetites, and Aversions; which in different tempers, customes, and doctrines of men, are different: And divers men, differ not onely in their Judgement, on the sense of what is pleasant, and unpleasant to the tast, smell, hearing, touch, and sight; but also of what is conformable, or disagreeable to Reason, in the actions of common life. Nay, the same man, in divers times, differs from himselfe; and one time praiseth, that is, calleth Good, what another time he dispraiseth, and calleth Evil.[20]

Hobbes links subjectivism with relativism—the view that value is dependent on appetite or preference with the view that value is relative to each individual. Natural as this linkage may seem, so that the two positions are easily confused, yet each may be held without the other. Indeed, a common, although surely mistaken, interpretation of Hobbes himself denies that he is a subjectivist, while granting that he is a relativist.[21] Hobbes supposes that the chief good from the standpoint of any person is his own survival. As we have noted, this may be given an objective interpretation—individual survival provides a norm for our affections and preferences, so that anyone who seeks his own destruction is irrational, even if on full consideration he prefers death to life. Were this Hobbes's view it

[19] Hobbes, *Leviathan*, ch. 6, p. 24.

[20] Ibid., ch. 15, p. 79.

[21] See B. Gert's introduction to Hobbes, *Man and Citizen* (New York, 1972), pp. 13–16.

would be difficult to relate it to the position expressed in the passages we have quoted, in which value is clearly linked to appetite in a subjectivist manner.

A position both subjectivist and absolutist seems implicit in the views of many defenders of one of the most influential modern moral theories, utilitarianism. John Stuart Mill suggests such a position in his attempt to offer a sort of proof for the principle of utility—subjectivist in saying that 'the sole evidence it is possible to produce that anything is desirable is that people do actually desire it', and absolutist in insisting 'that each person's happiness is a good to that person, and the general happiness, therefore, a good to the aggregate of all persons'.[22] But there is an evident awkwardness in this union of subjectivism and absolutism noticeable in Mill's own statement, which in passing from a seemingly relativist premiss (that each person's happiness is a good to that person) to an absolutist conclusion (that the general happiness is a good to all persons) has generally been held to exemplify the fallacy of composition.

Utilitarianism finds itself under pressure to move away from a conception of value at once subjective and absolute. The most plausible way to resist this pressure would seem to be to accept a universalistic conception of rationality, and to argue that since rationality is identified with the maximization of value, and rationality is universal, then what is maximized, value, must similarly be universal—the same from every standpoint. If however utilitarianism remains true to its roots in the economic conception of rationality, then either subjectivism or absolutism gives way. On the one hand value may be conceived as relative, but a special form of value, moral value, is introduced, which is the measure of those considered preferences held from a standpoint specially constrained to ensure impartiality. On the other hand value may be conceived as objective, as the measure of an inherent characteristic of states of experience—enjoyment—that affords a standard or norm for preference. This is not the place to embark on a discussion of these positions, so that we shall merely (but dogmatically) affirm that a hundred years of ever more sophisticated efforts to avoid Mill's fallacy have not advanced the cause of utilitarianism a single centimetre. But we shall of course give more serious attention, especially to the second of the above ways of defending utilitarianism, as we continue the exposition of our own theory.

22 John Stuart Mill, *Utilitarianism* (London, 1863), ch. iv, para. 3.

If there is pressure against a conception of value at once subjective and absolute, there is also pressure against a conception both objective and relative. The view that each individual is a member of some natural kind, and that each kind has its own characteristic perfection, quite different from that of other natural kinds, is, if not widespread in secular ethics today, yet of great historical importance. But this view has rarely, if ever, embraced a relative conception of value. For the objectivity of each characteristic perfection, its role as a norm or standard against which each individual member of the kind may be judged, has been supposed to depend on considering each perfection to be a manifestation, appropriate to its particular circumstances, of a single universal good. The seemingly relative goods of the several kinds are really facets of absolute good. The demands of objectivity thus force an apparently relative conception of value into an absolutist mould.

We shall therefore treat a relative conception of value as the natural counterpart of a subjective conception, even though the two are logically independent. But relativism may seem an absurd doctrine. A McIntosh is a good eating apple (indeed, I am enjoying one as I write these words). Were you to deny this you would be mistaken. Yet you may be no apple fancier, or your taste in apples may extend to the sweet Golden Delicious rather than to the tarter McIntosh. In calling a McIntosh a good eating apple the word 'good' is not 'ever used with relation to the person that useth' it; indeed, one would be wrong to claim that a McIntosh was a good eating apple if one's sole ground were one's own liking for it. Hence it would seem that the evaluation is not a relative one. Yet it is subjective; the goodness of McIntosh apples is independent of the taste of any particular individual, but not of taste in general. The value of a McIntosh is a measure of preference, but of common preference.

Plausible as this argument against relativism may seem, it exploits a confusion, present in Hobbes's thought and not uncommon in formulations of a relativist position, to advance a thoroughly mistaken objection. Hobbes is wrong to suppose that such words as 'good' are used in relation to the user; indeed, our typical evaluative terms presuppose a common standpoint which may or may not be shared by the evaluator. A good eating apple is thus one that is commonly or usually preferred for eating. But although committed to this standpoint by the language of evaluation, one is not committed to it either as a measure of one's own preferences or as a standard for one's own choices. In saying that a McIntosh is a good eating apple, you do not imply that you are an apple fancier, or that you enjoy McIntoshes more than most other apples, or that you would or should choose a McIntosh to eat. A McIntosh is good, relative to the standpoint presupposed in the use of 'good', but this value does not afford a norm for choice from any other standpoint.

The utility of a state of affairs is its value, to a person, as a possible outcome—as an alternative, therefore, to certain other possible states of affairs. Beginning from these utility values, subjective and relative as they are, we may move in two quite different directions. We may generalize from the utilities that measure a particular person's preferences over different states of affairs, to the kind of values held by that person. From these personal values we are not able directly to infer particular preferences, but rather the kinds of preference that the person will exhibit in different situations. We may assess these personal values in the ways discussed in previous sections of this chapter, determining how far they are considered and coherent.

But we may also generalize from the utilities that measure the preferences of particular individuals to the range of values exhibited by the different states of affairs into which a particular object, or kind of object, may enter. We find that in some cases the preferences of different persons proceed from shared or similar standpoints; this is revealed by parallel orderings in their utilities. The common language of value exploits these parallel orderings; we may talk of good eating apples because we find similarities in the tastes of those who eat apples.

A common language of value may however be established in a more systematic way without requiring parallel tastes. For we may conceive the objects, or at least some of the objects, that enter into the directly valued outcomes, as related to each other in a market. They are commodities, items of exchange among persons. So conceived, each object comes to possess a fixed value in exchange, relating it to all other commodities, and common to all of the persons whose exchange relationships are embraced by the market.

The standpoint for evaluation induced by a market is not only recognized by each person in his evaluations, but is actually shared by him. Parallel preferences among apple fanciers determine a common standpoint from which a McIntosh is evaluated as a good eating apple; you may recognize this evaluation without sharing the preference for McIntoshes. But if a McIntosh has greater market value than a Golden Delicious, if it commands 25c and a Golden Delicious only 20c, then, whatever your tastes, you would prefer a McIntosh, since you may exchange it for a Golden Delicious and 5c. To prefer a Golden Delicious to a McIntosh within the context of exchange would be to prefer 20c to 25c. But the common values and common standpoint of the market rest on individual utilities which are strictly relative. In understanding how the absolute or universal values of the market emerge from a given set of relative individual values and a given technology of production, we in fact understand the fallacy in the charge that value relativism ignores the common standards underlying ordinary evaluation. Since the theory of value in exchange is a commonplace of elementary economics we shall not expound it here, but it is to that theory that the reader should turn if she finds herself tempted by the most common objections to a relativist conception of value.

4.3 The defence of subjectivism is the primary task facing anyone who identifies value with the measure of considered preference. The defence of relativism is essentially a matter of detailed enquiry into the relation between individual and common norms. But the conflict between subjective and objective accounts of value lies at the very core of moral philosophy. No disagreement more seriously hinders the development of an adequate moral theory. We cannot expect to resolve this conflict in a way that all will find convincing or even plausible. Nevertheless we find the case for subjectivism compelling, and we shall endeavour to sketch our reasons—reasons which, we should note at the outset, owe much to the work of Gilbert Harman and John Mackie.[23]

Our first problem arises in formulating the opposed, objectivist position. We face the inevitable danger of erecting a straw man. In particular we must beware of ascribing to the objectivist ontological commitments that she believes unnecessary or avoidable, and then defending subjectivism by rejecting this ontology. Let us say that the objectivist holds that any adequate account of our experience or our environment must refer to value or to the valuable as being independent of sentient beings and their affections. In our view

[23] See G. Harman, *The Nature of Morality: An Introduction to Ethics* (New York, 1977), ch. 1; also J. L. Mackie, *Ethics: Inventing Right and Wrong* Harmondsworth, Middx., 1977) ch. 1.

this does commit the objectivist to an ontology of value but we shall not press this point in our argument.

We must immediately clarify what is implicit in the independence of value ascribed to objectivism. The objectivist may insist that there is a necessary linkage between sentient beings and value, holding that value provides the norm for our affections. The proper object of preference is, and is necessarily, the good. But this link, on the objectivist view, is not found within sentient affection, but ties that affection to something else which in itself affords the ground of the tie. This other terminal of the link (and we shall not impose on the objectivist a particular account of what it is) must be independent of sentient beings and their affections, even though linked to them. In our discussion, we shall designate this alleged other terminal, *objective value*.

How are we to decide whether any adequate account of our experience or environment must refer to objective value? The answer, in our view, is that we consider whether any reference to objective value occurs in *the best explanation* we can provide for our actions and choices.[24] Now we cannot embark here on a theory of explanation. So we shall only assert that the only serious candidate for an explanatory schema for human action is, as we noted previously: choice maximizes preference fulfilment given belief. Objective value plays no role in this account. The best explanation we can provide for our observations is that there are physical objects with properties that, given our sensory apparatus, cause those observations. We therefore accept physical properties as part of any adequate account of our experience and environment. But the best explanation we can provide for our choices is not that there are objects with values that, given our affective apparatus, cause those choices. We therefore reject objective values as part of any adequate account of our experience and environment. The difference between G. E. Moore's notorious simple properties, yellow and good, is that from the standpoint of explanation good is a fifth wheel.[25] Objective value, like phlogiston, is an unnecessary part of our explanatory apparatus, and as such is to be shaved from the face of the universe by Ockham's razor.

[24] Our approach is suggested by Harman, *The Nature of Morality*, pp. 6–9. The phrase 'the best explanation' comes from Harman, 'The Inference to the Best Explanation', *Philosophical Review* 74 (1965), pp. 88–95.

[25] See Moore, pp. 7–10, for his comparison of yellow and good.

John Mackie has argued that the best case against objective value turns on its ontological queerness.[26] It does not fit comfortably with our account of apprehension, or of knowledge; it does not relate happily to 'fact'. The objectivist may complain that Mackie is imposing ontological and epistemological requirements that are no part of her position. But objective value would be, if not queer, yet unique in the kind of force or power that it would exert. It must exercise a form of attraction as the proper object of preference that is very different from any other attraction we observe or experience. (Yet is this so? Might not the attraction of objective value resemble that exercised by certain persons? 'From the moment she entered the room, every man had eyes only for her. You could not say that her appearance, or her manner, or her attire, was in itself striking, but no one could ignore her.') However, we should not regard queerness as a disqualification for objective value, given the particles and forces to which our best physical explanations refer. What is queer about objective value is that it has no explanatory role to play, and that does disqualify it.

Mackie suggests that 'if the requisite theological doctrine could be defended', then a form of value objectivity would be true.[27] This seems correct. For the defence of such a theological doctrine would be, or would include, a defence of its explanatory role. And if we relate value to divine will, then in such a doctrine objective value would also play an explanatory role. We cannot deny that in principle, the best explanation for our actions and choices might require reference to objective value; indeed, our principal intellectual ancestors—the classical Greeks and medieval Europeans—advanced explanations with just this requirement. But our explanations are not their explanations. When Laplace doomed God to explanatory redundancy, stating that 'Je n'avais pas besoin de cet hypothèse', he implicitly doomed objective value as well.[28]

There is an evident objection to our claim that objective value has no explanatory role. Value-ascriptions frequently enter into the reasons offered for our choices and actions. 'Why did you send your son to Harvard?' 'Because it's a good university.' This is not a very

[26] See Mackie, pp. 38–42.

[27] Ibid., p. 48.

[28] See E. T. Bell, *Men of Mathematics*, 2 vols. (Harmondsworth, Middx., 1953), vol. i, p. 198.

illuminating explanation, but it is at least the beginning of an explanation, whereas 'Because I prefer Harvard' is not.

Part of the explanatory role of value-ascriptions may be understood on the basis of our discussion of the common language of value in the preceding subsection. We relate our choices and actions to what is commonly preferred, or to what is preferred in exchange. In so far as the criteria for such preference are generally known, then it is possible to infer from value-ascriptions to particular characteristics; a good carving knife is sharp and keeps its edge. The explanatory role of such value-ascriptions is readily accounted for on a subjective and relative conception of value.

We admit that value-ascriptions are thought to have a further explanatory role. For the belief in objective value is widely, if confusedly held, and those who believe in objective value appeal to it in accounting for their behaviour, just as those who believe in God appeal to Him in accounting for their behaviour. But although we must refer to belief in objective value in the explanation we provide for certain choices and actions, we are clearly not thereby committed to such belief. That we cannot understand what religious persons do without referring to their belief in God does not commit us to such a belief. (That we cannot explain what certain would-be geometers do without referring to their belief that it is possible to square the circle does not commit us to such a belief.) Among the beliefs that enter into the explanation of our choices are some that, were they true, would require references to objective value. What we deny is that such beliefs are true.

Our account of value must therefore include what Mackie calls an 'error theory'.[29] We suppose that persons objectify their preferences, and so come to consider their subjective attitudes and affections as properties characterizing the objects of their preferences. If we were to suppose that the correct conception of value could be discovered by an analysis of ordinary language, we should no doubt be led to an objective conception (or perhaps to a conception with objective and subjective elements intertwined in hopeless confusion). But if instead we suppose that the correct conception of value can be discovered only by an appeal to the best explanation of what value is supposed to affect, then we uncover the error present in ordinary views, and establish a subjective conception. To be sure, inference to the best explanation will not show that there is no objective value, any more

[29] See Mackie, pp. 35, 48–9.

than it will show that there are no fairies at the bottom of the garden. We are content to put objective value on a par with the fairies.

Value, then, we take to be a measure of individual preference—subjective because it is a measure of preference and relative because it is a measure of individual preference. What is good is good ultimately because it is preferred, and it is good from the standpoint of those and only those who prefer it. We have tried to fill in some of the qualifications and niceties for this view to be convincing, but we repeat that a full development and defence would require a full study and not merely our brief sketch. Our concern is to demonstrate the possibility and the characteristics of a rational morality, given that value is itself subjective and relative.

III

STRATEGY: REASON AND EQUILIBRIUM

1.1 Jane wants very much to go to Ann's party. But even more she wants to avoid Brian who may be there. Brian wants very much to avoid Ann's party. But even more he wants to meet Jane. If Jane expects Brian to be at Ann's party she will stay at home. If Brian expects Jane to stay at home so will he. If Jane expects Brian to stay at home she will go to the party. If Brian expects Jane to go so will he. If Jane . . . but this is where we began. Jane and Brian face—from opposed standpoints—a problem in interaction. If each knows not only his own preferences but the other's as well, then what expectation should he form, and which of his possible actions should he choose?

Our focus in this chapter is on strategic rationality—rationality in interaction. In our discussion of parametric rationality, where the actor takes his circumstances to be fixed so that his choice is the only variable element, we found that the definition of an interval measure of preference over possible outcomes enabled us to reduce the problem of rational choice to an exercise in maximizing expected utility. Interaction defies such straightforward treatment. Rational actors must determine their choices, not in fixed circumstances, but in terms of reciprocal expectations about those very choices. Both choices and expectations must rest on the actors' beliefs about the actions each may perform, the possible outcomes of these actions, and the utilities to each of these possible outcomes. In the ideal case—and however unlikely the full-blown ideal may be, it provides our point of departure in theorizing about rational choice—these are matters of common knowledge. Everyone knows that everyone knows them. But then each person's reasoning from these data to his own expectations and choices must be accessible to every other person. In effect individual choice must emerge from common reasoning. Each must view strategic choice both as a response to the choices of his fellows and as being responded to by those choices.

This ideal case will be the arena for our treatment of strategic rationality.[1] The complications occasioned by imperfect rationality

[1] The theory of games has focused primarily on this ideal case. See the discussion in R. D. Luce and H. Raiffa, *Games and Decisions* (New York, 1957), p. 49.

and incomplete knowledge conceal the logical structure of interaction, and it is this structure which serves as the foundation of moral theory. Our sole departure from the fully ideal case will be to make it subjective. That is, we shall examine interaction from the standpoint of an individual who assumes that ideal conditions prevail. She is rational, assumes her fellows to be rational, and believes that everyone's rationality is common knowledge. She assumes that everyone has perfect information about possible actions, possible outcomes, and all preferences over these outcomes, and that it is common knowledge that everyone has such perfect information. She introduces an interval measure for the preferences of each person, defines a utility function for each, and supposes that everyone else does the same. Thus she believes that her reasoning about interaction replicates, and is replicated by, everyone else's reasoning. Our analysis of strategic rationality proceeds from such an ideal standpoint, but it is irrelevant to that analysis whether the standpoint itself rests on correct beliefs and suppositions.

To make our analysis more precise, we formulate three conditions on strategically rational choice:

A: Each person's choice must be a rational response to the choices she expects the others to make.

B: Each person must expect every other person's choice to satisfy condition A.

C: Each person must believe her choice and expectations to be reflected in the expectations of every other person.

Condition A relates the rationality of the actor to the framework of interaction; it requires her to be strategically rational. Condition B makes explicit the assumption that all parties to the interaction are strategically rational and that this rationality is a matter of common knowledge. Condition C makes explicit the assumption that each person views the situation as if her knowledge of the grounds for choice were complete, shared by all, and known by all to be so shared. Each condition is necessary, but we do not claim at this point that they are severally sufficient for rational interaction.

We have left the phrase 'rational response' undefined in formulating the three conditions. Given the identification of rationality with individual utility-maximization, we might suppose that we should simply substitute 'utility-maximizing' for 'rational' in condition A. Let us do this, and relate the conditions so understood to our initial example.

Jane has two choices—to go to Ann's party, or to stay at home. Suppose she chooses to go. Then by condition A she must expect Brian to choose to stay at home. So by condition B she must expect Brian to expect her to stay at home. But then her choice is not reflected in what she believes to be Brian's expectations, so that condition C is violated. Suppose then she chooses to stay at home. Then by condition A she must expect Brian to choose to go to Ann's party. So by condition B she must expect Brian to expect her to go. But then her choice is not reflected in what she believes to be Brian's expectations, so that again condition C is violated. Neither of Jane's possible choices satisfies our three conditions. Nor does either of Brian's choices. How then is rational choice possible for Jane and Brian? How may we formulate a principle of strategic rationality satisfying conditions A, B, and C?

1.2 Before we can answer these questions, we must introduce some terminological and notational conventions.[2] These make dry reading, but are essential to the understanding of our argument, not only in this but also in subsequent chapters.

An action is the object of a choice. An outcome, as we defined it earlier, is the product of an action and a set of determinate circumstances. In choice under certainty each action is correlated with a single set of circumstances and so with a single outcome. In choice under risk or uncertainty each action is correlated with a probability distribution over several sets of circumstances and so may be treated as a lottery with possible outcomes as prizes. Throughout we have supposed that from the standpoint of an individual actor, each possible action has a distinct outcome for each set of circumstances to which he assigns non-zero probability.

We now modify this conception of an outcome. In interaction an outcome results, not from the choice of a single actor, but from the choices of several actors. Thus we initially modify our definition of an outcome, so that we say that an outcome is the product of several actions, one for each person involved in interaction, and a set of determinate circumstances. But this new definition is needlessly unwieldy. We further modify it by suppressing the last clause, so that we say simply that an outcome is the product of several actions, one for each person involved in interaction.

[2] These conventions are standard in the exposition of the theory of games. Our discussion here makes no claim to originality.

How do we justify removing all reference to the circumstances? A particular actor may of course assign non-zero probability to each of several sets of determinate circumstances correlated with an interaction. He supposes then that each set whose members are actions, one chosen by each of the persons interacting, may have several possible outcomes. But for each such set he determines a single utility, equal to his expected utility for the set considered as a lottery over these possible outcomes. We treat this single utility as if it were the utility of a single outcome, defining this outcome as the product of the members of the set of actions. In this way we eliminate reference to the circumstances.

It will be noted that in interaction particular choices or actions enter into two quite different relations. On the one hand, if we take one action for each of the interacting persons, then we have a set of compossible actions, and we have defined an outcome as the product of the members of such a set. On the other hand, if we take all of the actions possible for any one of the interacting persons, then we have a set of mutually exclusive actions, the possible choices of a given actor. An outcome is then the product obtained by taking one choice from each of these sets. The set of outcomes for any interaction is therefore the Cartesian product of the sets of choices possible for the actors.

We may conveniently represent any interaction involving only two persons by a matrix in which the rows represent the choices or actions of one person and the columns the choices or actions of the other. Each intersection of a row and a column thus represents an outcome, and we may show at this intersection the utility of the outcome for each person. By convention Row's utilities are given first. When we assume only an ordinal measure of preference we shall employ a ranking, so that the most preferred outcome is ranked first. But when we assume an interval measure we shall employ cardinal numbers for the utilities. It must be remembered that these numbers have only interval significance. Both the zero-point and the unit of measurement are selected arbitrarily. (Compare the measurement of temperature. The difference between 30 °C and 50 °C is twice that between 20 °C and 30 °C. But 40 °C is not twice as hot as 20 °C.) Furthermore, interval comparisons may be made only between utilities of the same individual; the measure provides no basis for interpersonal comparison.

We may illustrate the matrix representation of interaction using our initial example. A possible ordering of the preferences of Jane and Brian would be this:

		Brian	
		go	stay
Jane	go	4th, 1st	1st, 4th
	stay	2nd, 3rd	3rd, 2nd

Jane's first and fourth preferences should be clear from our story. Jane prefers staying at home if Brian goes to Ann's party to staying at home if he does not go, because in the latter case she would regret not going. Thus we have her second and third preferences. Brian's first and second preferences should be clear from our story. Brian also prefers going to the party if Jane stays at home to staying at home if Jane goes, even though the former affords him his least pleasant evening, because in the latter case he would severely regret not going. Thus we have his third and fourth preferences.

We may see from the matrix that if Brian goes to the party, Jane's utility-maximizing response is to stay at home. If she stays at home, Brian's utility-maximizing response is also to stay at home. If Brian stays at home, Jane's utility-maximizing response is to go to the party. And if she goes, Brian's utility-maximizing response is also to go. Thus if one person's action is a utility-maximizing response to the action of the other, the other's action is not a utility-maximizing response to the action of the first person. This is sufficient to ensure that conditions A, B, and C cannot be simultaneously satisfied.

As the first step to showing that rational choice is nevertheless possible in such situations as this, we must expand the scope of choice, so that each may choose not only an action, but also a lottery over possible actions. In the preceding chapter, we identified an action performed under risk or uncertainty as a lottery with possible outcomes as prizes. We are now introducing the idea of a choice as a lottery with possible actions as prizes. The two types of lottery must not be confused.

The enlargement of the scope of choice to include lotteries with actions as prizes would be pointless in parametric situations, but is essential to the very possibility of rational choice in strategic situations. Given the choice of a lottery, then the action actually performed is determined by a randomizing device programmed with the chosen distribution of prizes. Jane could choose a lottery that gave going to the party a probability of 1/4 and staying at home a probability of 3/4 by selecting a card randomly from a jokerless pack, and going to the party if and only if the card selected were a spade. We assume the universal availability of a randomizing device programmable to ensure the probability distribution required by any possible lottery, and we assume also that the device is costless to use. Again, these idealizing assumptions are made to simplify our analysis.

A lottery over possible actions is termed a *strategy*. A *pure strategy* assigns the probability 1 to one action and 0 to all others; it is a lottery with but one prize, and that prize always forthcoming. A *mixed strategy* assigns a non-zero probability to more than one action, the sum of probabilities assigned being of course 1; it is a lottery with several actions as prizes.

Expanding the scope of choice from actions to strategies does not expand the range of possible outcomes. Whatever strategy each actor chooses, he must perform one of his possible actions, and the product of the actions performed by each actor is one of the possible outcomes. However, this outcome is not determined with certainty by the choice of strategies, unless only pure strategies are chosen. Each strategy is a lottery over actions, and so each set of strategies, one for each interacting person, determines a lottery over outcomes. We define an *expected outcome* as such a lottery, as the product of the lotteries or strategies chosen by each person. The set of expected outcomes is thus the Cartesian product of the actors' sets of strategies. We shall henceforth use 'outcome' to mean 'expected outcome', except where this is clearly excluded by the context.

We may now define the key concept required by an account of strategic rationality, the concept of *equilibrium*. An (expected) outcome is in equilibrium, or is an equilibrium outcome, if and only if it is the product of strategies, each of which maximizes the expected utility of the person choosing it given the strategies chosen by the other persons. Simplifying this, we may say that an outcome is in equilibrium if and only if it is the product of mutually utility-maximizing strategies. Thus if we assume conditions A, B, and C, and interpret a rational response as a utility-maximizing response, each person must expect the outcome of his choice to be in equilibrium.

The proof of this requirement is straightforward. Let there be *n* persons, and let any person, whom we may designate person 1, choose a strategy s_1. By condition A, s_1 maximizes his utility given the strategies $s_2, \ldots, s_n$ which he expects the others to choose. By condition B, s_2 must maximize person 2's utility given the strategies $s_1', s_3', \ldots, s_n'$ which person 1 expects person 2 to expect. And s_3 must maximize person 3's utility given the strategies $s_1'', s_2'', s_4'', \ldots, s_n''$ which person 1 expects person 3 to expect, and so on. By condition C, person 1's choice and expectations must be reflected in his beliefs about others' expectations, so that $s_1 = s_1' = s_1''$ ... and $s_2 = s_2'' = \ldots$, and $s_3 = s_3' = \ldots$, and so on. Hence each strategy $s_1, s_2, \ldots, s_n$ must be utility-maximizing given the others, and so the expected outcome of choosing s_1 must be in equilibrium.

Important as this argument is in relating strategic rationality to equilibrium, we must bear in mind its assumptions and limitations. The proof depends both on treating rational responses as utility-maximizing, and on supposing that each person forms determinate expectations about the choices of others. And the proof does not show that the outcomes of rationally chosen strategies must in fact be in equilibrium; this would follow only if each person knew the utilities of his fellows so that all expectations were matters of common knowledge. Rationally chosen strategies may rest on mistaken expectations, so that the actual outcome need not be in equilibrium. But the fault is then with the expectations, and not the choice.

Let us return once again to our initial example. We may note that none of the outcomes afforded by pure strategies is in equilibrium. In order to introduce mixed strategies and to assign expected utilities to their outcomes, we need an interval measure of preference. This requires additional data; we must relate preferences intermediate in the orderings of Jane and Brian to lotteries over their extreme preferences. Let us suppose then that Jane is indifferent between her second preference (staying at home if Brian goes to the party) and a lottery with a 2/3 chance of her first preference (going to the party if Brian stays at home) and a 1/3 chance of her fourth preference (both going to the party). And let us suppose that she is indifferent between her third preference (both staying at home) and a lottery with a 1/3 chance of her first preference and a 2/3 chance of her fourth preference. Using the method of II.3.2, we may assign utilities of 1, 2/3, 1/3, and 0 to the four outcomes in order of Jane's preference. Let us suppose that Brian is indifferent between his second preference (both staying at home) and a lottery with a 1/2 chance of his first preference (both going to the party) and a 1/2 chance of his fourth preference (staying at home if Jane goes). And let us suppose that he is indifferent between his third preference (going if Jane stays at home) and a lottery with a 1/6 chance of his first preference and a 5/6 chance of his fourth preference. Then we may assign utilities of 1, 1/2, 1/6, and 0 to the four outcomes in order of Brian's preference. We have this representation of the situation, which we assume to be held by both Jane and Brian:

		Brian			
			go		stay
Jane	go	0,	1	1,	0
	stay	2/3,	1/6	1/3,	1/2

Suppose that Jane chooses a mixed strategy assigning a probability of 1/4 to going to the party, and 3/4 to staying at home. Then if Brian goes to the party his expected utility is $[(1/4 \times 1) + (3/4 \times 1/6)] = 3/8$. If Brian stays at home his expected utility is $[(1/4 \times 0) + (3/4 \times 1/2)] = 3/8$. Each action yields him the same expected utility. Therefore any lottery over the two actions must yield him the same expected utility. Whatever he chooses, his expected utility is 3/8.

Suppose that Brian chooses a mixed strategy assigning a probability of 1/2 to going to the party and 1/2 to staying at home. The reader may verify that whatever Jane chooses, her expected utility is 1/2. It follows that the outcome resulting from the choice of these two mixed strategies is in equilibrium. Each is utility-maximizing as a response to the other. Of course, each is not a uniquely utility-maximizing response, but our definition does not require this. (Given Jane's choice of strategy, any response by Brian would be utility-maximizing, and given Brian's choice, any response by Jane would be utility-maximizing.)

By extending their choices to include lotteries with actions as prizes, we have shown that Jane and Brian may arrive at an equilibrium outcome. We may of course verify that conditions A, B, and C are satisfied, taking a rational response to be utility-maximizing. Each choice is a utility-maximizing response to the expected choice of the other person. Each expects the other's choice to be a utility-maximizing response to the other's expectation of his choice. And each believes his choice and expectations to be reflected in the other's expectations.

Our example illustrates a general possibility. It has been demonstrated by J. F. Nash that in any situation with a finite number of persons (hardly a restrictive assumption), each with a finite number of pure strategies, and each with preferences satisfying the conditions for an interval measure, there must be at least one (expected) outcome in equilibrium.[3] There must be at least one set of mutually utility-maximizing strategies. Thus in any interaction it is possible for each person to relate his choice, his expectations about the choices of others, and his expectations about the expectations of others, to a set of mutually utility-maximizing strategies. It is always possible to satisfy conditions A, B, and C, taking a rational response as a utility-maximizing response. Nash would seem to have demonstrated that strategically rational choice is always possible in principle.

The principle for rational choice that emerges from this discussion is that in interaction, each person should relate his choice of strategy and expectations of others' choices to a set of mutually utility-maximizing strategies. This principle is not always a practical guide to action; there may be no feasible way to determine the appropriate strategy set. In a complex situation with many pure strategies for each of many persons, the cost of determining an equilibrium may be far greater than any benefit which could result were it known. But waiving this practical issue, there are several theoretical objections to the proposed principle. These relate to the premisses from which it is derived; they concern the alleged connection between a rational response and a utility-maximizing one, or the supposition that each person may form a determinate expectation about the strategy chosen by every other person.

2.1 We have interpreted condition A to require that each person choose a strategy that maximizes his expected utility, given his expectations of the choices of others. One may have several such strategies. Then condition A permits the choice of any one of them, treating each as a rational response. But this is incompatible with the requirement that preference be revealed in rational choice. If one has several strategies, each utility-maximizing given one's expectations, then one must be indifferent among their outcomes. This indifference is expressed behaviourally by choosing among them on an equiprobable basis. Were one to choose one strategy rather than another except as the result of such a lottery, this would reveal one's

[3] For the proof, see J. F. Nash, 'Non-cooperative Games', *Annals of Mathematics* 54 (1951), pp. 286–95.

preference for its outcome, and so would require one to assign that outcome an expected utility greater than one assigned to the outcomes of the rejected strategies. And this would be incompatible with the supposition that each strategy is equally utility-maximizing.[4]

If we accept this objection, then we must reformulate condition A to require that each person's choice be *the* rational response to the choices he expects the others to make, where *the* rational response is defined as the response determined by a lottery giving equal probability to all responses satisfying other rationality requirements. Given that we identify rationality with utility-maximization, we may say that each person's choice must be the *centroid utility-maximizing response* to the expected choices of the others. And so we must reformulate the proposed principle for strategically rational choice to require that each person relate his choice of strategy and expectations of others' choices to a set of mutually centroid utility-maximizing strategies.

But this principle fails in many situations where there are no mutully centroid utility-maximizing strategies. Recall the example discussed in the first section of this chapter. We found that an equilibrium results if Jane chooses a mixed strategy assigning a probability of 1/4 to going to Ann's party and 3/4 to staying at home and Brian chooses a mixed strategy assigning a probability of 1/2 to going to the party and 1/2 to staying at home. There is no other equilibrium in this situation. If Jane were to increase her probability of going to Ann's party, Brian's utility-maximizing response would be to go to the party, Jane's utility-maximizing response to that would be to stay at home—we should be back in the cycle with which the chapter began. If Jane were to decrease her probability of going to Ann's party, Brian's utility-maximizing response would be to stay at home, Jane's utility-maximizing response to that would be to go to the party—back in the cycle again. If Brian were to change his strategy, the result would be the same.

But as we noted, if Brian chooses a strategy, assigning equal probabilities to going to the party and staying at home, then any response by Jane is utility-maximizing for her. Her centroid utility-maximizing response is therefore her mixed strategy assigning equal

[4] For a statement of the position sketched here, see J. C. Harsanyi, *Rational Behavior and Bargaining Equilibrium in Games and Social Situations* (Cambridge, 1977), pp. 114–15.

probabilities to going to the party and staying at home. But Brian's strategy is then not a utility-maximizing response to Jane's new strategy; he should go to the party. In this situation there are no mutually centroid utility-maximizing strategies.

We have defined an outcome as in equilibrium if and only if it is the product of mutually utility-maximizing strategies. It is in *strong* equilibrium if and only if each strategy is the actor's only utility-maximizing response to other strategies. Otherwise the outcome is in *weak* equilibrium. If an outcome is in strong equilibrium, then it is trivially the product of a set of mutually centroid utility-maximizing strategies. But if an outcome is in weak equilibrium, then it need not be, and generally is not, the product of a set of mutually centroid utility-maximizing strategies. Since many situations, such as our example, lack a strong equilibrium, we consider the proposed reformulation to our conditions unacceptable. We are unwilling to leave rational choice undefined for situations with only weak equilibrium outcomes.[5]

We do not reject the requirement that preference be revealed in rational choice. But we do insist that it be applied with care to strategic rationality. Choice reveals preference given belief. In interaction belief includes expectation. A person may be genuinely indifferent among several strategies given his expectations. But these expectations may themselves reflect the choice of one and only one of the strategies among which he is indifferent. He must then choose that strategy in order to sustain his expectations. If Jane expects Brian to choose between going to the party and staying at home with equal probability then she is indifferent among her strategies. But by condition B, Jane must expect Brian's choice to maximize his utility, given his expectation of her strategy, and by condition C, Jane must expect Brian to expect the strategy she chooses. Going to the party and staying at home with equal probability maximizes Brian's utility only if he expects Jane to choose the strategy that assigns a probability of 1/4 to her going to the party and 3/4 to her staying at home. So among her indifferent strategies, only one sustains the

[5] Harsanyi's account of rational choice for such situations abandons strategic rationality based on expectations about the choices of others, for a 'maximin' approach. See Harsanyi, *Rational Behavior*, esp. pp. 116, 138. One might question the consistency of Harsanyi's acceptance of maximin strategies with his vehement rejection of Rawls's use of maximin arguments in ethical theory. See 'Can the Maximin Principle Serve as a Basis for Morality? A Critique of John Rawls's Theory', in *Essays on Ethics*, especially pp. 39–40.

expectation on which her indifference rests. The requirement that preference be revealed in rational choice is to be satisfied in the manner, and only in the manner, appropriate to the strategic character of interaction.

2.2 Nash proves that in any situation there is at least one set of mutually utility-maximizing strategies, or as we shall henceforth find convenient to say, at least one equilibrium set of strategies. But there may be more than one such set. Indeed we shall shortly give a matrix representation for a situation in which every set containing one strategy for each person is an equilibrium set, although the pattern of preferences giving rise to this may be uncommon. The principle of rational choice proposed at the end of the first section of this chapter requires only that each person relate her choice and expectations of others' choices to an equilibrium set. But if there are several such sets, how is one to choose among them? To which set shall one relate one's expectations of others' choices, so that one's own choice may be a rational response to them? One may not form expectations about others' choices simply at will; how then may one ground one's expectations?

If there is but one equilibrium set of strategies, then since only expectations relating to that set satisfy conditions A, B, and C (assuming that a rational response must be utility-maximizing), these expectations are sufficiently grounded. The first step in grounding expectations given several equilibrium sets is to consider the special case in which only one set yields an *undominated* equilibrium outcome. An equilibrium outcome is dominated if everyone disprefers it to some other equilibrium outcome. Since no outcome dominates itself and domination is a transitive relation, then an equilibrium outcome cannot be dominated only by other dominated equilibrium outcomes; if it is dominated, then there must be an undominated equilibrium outcome dominating it. A unique undominated equilibrium outcome must therefore be preferred by everyone to every other equilibrium outcome. It affords a natural focus for the expectations of persons who identify rationality with utility-maximization. Each would choose the strategy that belonged to the set yielding the unique undominated equilibrium outcome, expecting others to do the same. Although this is not required by conditions A, B, and C, it seems an unproblematic extension of the conception of rational choice they express.

The second step in grounding expectations given several

equilibrium sets is to consider the case in which only one set yields an undominated equilibrium outcome that no one disprefers to any other equilibrium outcome. If there is one and only one undominated equilibrium outcome, then as we have shown everyone must prefer it to every other equilibrium outcome. Now we consider the case in which there may be several undominated equilibrium outcomes, but only one that no one disprefers to any other. If we label this outcome Y, and compare it with any other undominated equilibrium outcome X, then some persons are indifferent between Y and X, some prefer Y to X, and none prefers X to Y. Again, it would seem that such an outcome affords a natural focus for expectations. Each would choose the strategy that belonged to the set yielding the unique equilibrium outcome not dispreferred by any person to any other equilibrium outcome, expecting others to do the same. But this proves to be a less unproblematic extension of the conception of rational choice expressed in conditions A, B, and C than might at first be thought.

Consider the situation presented in this matrix:

		Norman	
		does	doesn't
Noreen	does	1, 1	0, 1
	doesn't	1, 0	0, 0

Every expected outcome in this situation is in equilibrium. Every expected outcome in which either Noreen or Norman does whatever it is that they do is in undominated equilibrium. But only the outcome resulting if both do it is in undominated equilibrium and dispreferred by neither to any other equilibrium outcome. If we accept the argument of the preceding paragraph, this outcome is then a natural focus for the expectations of Noreen and Norman, and so they should each do it.

But it would seem that neither has reason to do it. Neither can affect the utility she obtains in this situation by her choice. The only effect of each person's choice is to determine the other's utility, and this affords persons who identify rationality with individual utility-maximization no reason for choice. In this situation the requirement that choice reveal preference would seem to entail that each choose a lottery affording equal probability to doing it and not doing it; in other words, that each choose her centroid utility-maximizing response. This would afford each an expected utility, not of 1, but of 0.5.

Deep issues in our account of rationality, and indeed of morality, come to the surface in this example. Utility is a measure of individual preference. Since no restriction has been placed on the content of preference, each person's exclusive concern with her own utility does not imply any material selfishness. But this example suggests that the structure of some interactions leads to a formal selfishness. Noreen and Norman could maximize each other's utility at no personal cost, but it would seem that neither has reason to do so.

In later chapters we shall develop an account of rational co-operation which may be applied to this situation, to show that it is rational for Noreen and Norman each to do it. But we cannot give that account yet. So we shall put the situation to one side, and return to the general problem of grounding expectations given several equilibrium sets of strategies.

Consider the situation represented by this matrix:

		Valerie	
		b_1	b_2
Victor	a_1	1, 1/3	0, 0
	a_2	1/3, 2/3	2/3, 1

It is clear by inspection that $(a_1 \times b_1)$ and $(a_2 \times b_2)$ are outcomes in strong equilibrium. There is a third outcome in weak equilibrium. If Victor chooses his mixed strategy assigning equal probabilities to a_1 and a_2, then Valerie receives an expected utility of 1/2 whatever she chooses. Similarly if Valerie chooses her mixed strategy assigning equal probabilities to b_1 and b_2, then Victor receives an expected utility of 1/2 whatever he chooses. These strategies therefore yield an equilibrium outcome, $[(1/2a_1 + 1/2a_2) \times (1/2b_1 + 1/2b_2)]$.

Victor's preference is clearly for $(a_1 \times b_1)$; Valerie's is for $(a_2 \times b_2)$. But were Victor to choose his first action (a_1) on the optimistic expectation that Valerie would choose b_1, and Valerie were to choose her second action on the optimistic expectation that Victor would choose a_2, then the actual outcome would be the disastrous $(a_1 \times b_2)$. Neither could do worse.

Suppose first that neither is able to form a determinate expectation about the other's choice of strategy. Neither is then able to determine his utility-maximizing response. Is there some other basis for a response that would be recognizably rational? *Faute de mieux*, each might seek to protect himself by choosing the strategy that would maximize the minimum utility he could receive, whatever choice the other might make. Victor would avoid a_1, since it would afford him 0 were Valerie to choose b_2, but he could do better than a_2, which would afford him 1/3 were Valerie to choose a_1, by the mixed strategy $(1/4a_1 + 3/4a_2)$ which affords him an expected utility of 1/2 whatever Valerie chooses. Valerie would avoid b_2, and could not do better than to choose b_1, which would afford her 1/3 were Victor to choose a_1, since any mixed strategy would afford her a lesser expected utility against a_1. Victor then is able to guarantee himself an expected utility of 1/2 and Valerie is able to guarantee herself an expected utility of 1/3; we call these their *maximin* utilities.

The resort to maximin may seem a counsel of despair. But in fact it offers a way of generating the expectations Victor and Valerie seek. Victor compares three prospects—the utility to him of his most favoured equilibrium (1), the utility to him of Valerie's most favoured equilibrium (2/3), and the utility to him of his maximin (1/2). Were he to concede Valerie's most favoured equilibrium, the cost to him taking his most favoured equilibrium as base would be a utility of 1/3; were he to throw up his hands in despair and settle for his maximin the cost would be 1/2. The ratio of these costs, 2/3, may be taken as a measure of his relative reluctance to concede to Valerie.

This measure of Victor's reluctance to concede does not depend on those features of the numerical measure of his utility—the zero-point and the unit—that are arbitrary. Any interval measure of Victor's preferences must yield this same degree of reluctance. And this gives us a basis for interpersonal comparisons. We may ask if Victor's reluctance to concede to Valerie is greater or smaller than her reluctance to concede to him.

She also compares three prospects—the utility to her of her most favoured equilibrium (1), the utility to her of Victor's most favoured equilibrium (1/3), and the utility to her of her maximin (1/3). Since these latter two are equal, it is evident that the cost to her of conceding his most favoured equilibrium is equal to the cost to her of settling for her maximin. And so her relative reluctance to concede to Victor—the ratio of these two costs—is 1.

We may now appeal to a principle deriving from the work of Frederik Zeuthen, which states that the person whose ratio between cost of concession and cost of deadlock is less must rationally concede to the other.[6] That person is more willing, or less unwilling, to concede. In our example Victor is that person. And so Victor and Valerie find that each has a basis for determinate expectations about the other's choice. Victor expects Valerie to hold firm in seeking her most favoured equilibrium and so he expects her to choose b_2; he chooses a_2. Valerie expects Victor to yield and so expects him to choose a_2; she chooses b_2. The third, weak equilibrium outcome does not enter our argument since each disprefers it to $(a_2 \times b_2)$.

In illustrating the use of maximin utilities and Zeuthen's principle of rational concession to ground determinate expectations about choices in situations with more than one equilibrium set of strategies, we intend only to introduce a complex and controversial subject which we cannot pursue here. The presence of several outcomes in equilibrium calls for *co-ordination* by the actors on one equilibrium. The interested reader may wish to pursue different approaches to the problem of co-ordination in the work of John Harsanyi and Thomas Schelling, and in my own paper 'Coordination'.[7] Our aim here is only to suggest that the requirement that one's choice be related to an equilibrium set of strategies is not restricted by its reliance on determinate expectations to situations with only one equilibrium outcome, or even only one undominated equilibrium outcome.

But before leaving this subject, we should note that the devices introduced in discussing the problem of co-ordination faced by Victor and Valerie will play a central role in the development of our moral theory. We shall find that the choice function that provides a principle of rational and impartial bargaining depends on a measure that is defined as a ratio of the differences between utilities, similar then to the ratio of costs employed here. And we shall then use an extended form of Zeuthen's procedure for rational concession. At that point we shall examine the rationale for Zeuthen's principle, a matter which, as the reader will have noted, we have ignored here.

3.1 Equilibrium is a rationality property of outcomes considered as products of strategies. But outcomes may also be considered as

[6] See F. Zeuthen, *Problems of Monopoly and Economic Warfare* (London, 1930), pp. 111–21.

[7] See Harsanyi, *Rational Behavior*, pp. 133–5, 273–88; T. C. Schelling, *The Strategy of Conflict* (Cambridge, Mass., 1960), pp. 54–8, 83–118; and my 'Coordination', *Dialogue* 14 (1975), pp. 195–221.

sets of utilities. Each person whose strategy is one of the inputs to an outcome receives a pay-off, which we express in terms of his utilities, as one of the outputs of the outcome. And we may define a rationality property of outcomes in terms of their outputs. This property, *optimality*, grounds a challenge to the identification of 'utility-maximizing response' with 'rational response' in conditions A, B, and C.[8]

An (expected) outcome is optimal (or, more fully, Pareto-optimal) if and only if there is no possible outcome affording some person a greater utility and no person a lesser utility. Alternatively, an outcome is optimal if and only if any other outcome affording some person a greater utility also affords some other person a lesser utility. We may characterize optimality in a manner that reveals a significant parallel with equilibrium. If an outcome is in equilibrium then each of its input strategies affords its actor his maximum utility, given that no other strategy is altered. If an outcome is optimal then each of its output pay-offs affords its recipient his maximum utility, given that no other pay-off is decreased. The two properties are not quite parallel; an outcome affording each person his maximum utility given that no other pay-off is altered may fail to be optimal if all pay-offs may simultaneously be increased. But each property represents a set of constrained maxima; the members of an equilibrium set of strategies, and the members of an optimal set of pay-offs, are both mutually utility-maximizing.

If an outcome is optimal, then no alternative to it is unanimously preferred. But if an outcome is not optimal, then there must be some alternative affording some person more utility and no person less—and perhaps some alternative affording every person more utility. A non-optimal outcome is inefficient in terms of its utility outputs for those engaged in interaction. Optimality is therefore an attractive property for the outcome of interaction.

But we must not overstate its claims. For any non-optimal outcome, there is some optimal alternative which benefits some at no cost to others. But not every optimal alternative to a given outcome affords only increased benefits. Consider once again our friends Jane and Brian. Every outcome that can result if Jane chooses to go to the

[8] The usual term is 'Pareto-optimality', after the Italian economist Vilfredo Pareto. But he spoke of the 'maximum ophelimity' enjoyed by the members of a collectivity. See his *Manual of Political Economy*, trans. Ann S. Schwier, ed. Ann S. Schwier and A. N. Page (New York, 1971), p. 261.

party—whatever Brian chooses—is optimal. And these are all of the optimal outcomes. Thus if we consider the outcome should each stay at home, we find that each would expect greater utility were Jane to go to the party, and were Brian to choose a mixed strategy assigning a probability of going to the party falling between 1/2 and 2/3. (A probability of more than 1/2 affords him an expected utility of more than 1/2, which is his utility if both stay at home; a probability of less than 2/3 affords Jane a utility of more than 1/3, which is her utility if both stay at home.) But if Brian chooses any other strategy, then the outcome, although optimal, affords either Jane or Brian an expected utility less than what she would receive were both to stay at home. If Brian chooses to go to the party (assuming that Jane chooses to go), then the outcome is optimal—every alternative affords him a lesser utility—but the worst possible for Jane.

The sole equilibrium outcome in this situation affords Jane an expected utility of 1/2 and Brian an expected utility of 3/8, as we showed in the first section. Note that it is not optimal. If Jane chooses to go to the party, and Brian chooses a mixed strategy assigning a probability of going to the party falling between 3/8 and 1/2, then each expects a utility greater than she would expect from the equilibrium outcome. That the equilibrium outcome(s) and the optimal outcome(s) in a particular situation may be mutually exclusive will be part of the core of our argument for a rational morality.

As this example shows, many situations possess a multiplicity of optimal outcomes. Not always—Noreen and Norman have but one optimal possibility; each must do it. Although we shall not attempt to demonstrate this here, Valerie and Victor have two sets of optimal outcomes—those resulting if Valerie chooses b_1 and Victor chooses any strategy assigning a probability greater than 1/2 to a_1, and the single outcome $(a_2 \times b_2)$. Both Victor's preferred equilibrium $(a_1 \times b_1)$ and Valerie's preferred equilibrium $(a_2 \times b_2)$ are optimal in this situation.

Given the usual multiplicity of optimal outcomes, and given also that an outcome that minimizes some individual's utility may nevertheless be optimal, we should not want to propose that the attainment of optimality be a sufficient condition for rational choice in interaction. It may however be proposed as a necessary condition. Thus it may be suggested that in conditions A, B, and C, 'rational response' should be read 'optimizing response'. An optimizing response is a strategy whose outcome, given the expected strategies of the other persons, is optimal. Only certain expectations are compatible with an optimizing response; only if Brian expects Jane to choose to go to the party can he choose a strategy whose outcome is optimal. But any situation, or at least any situation involving only a finite number of persons each of whom has only a finite number of pure strategies, must have at least one optimal outcome. Thus it is always possible to find a strategy and set of expectations satisfying conditions A, B, and C, if rationality be identified with optimization.

We have already noted that optimality and equilibrium are not always compatible. Thus we cannot require that a response be both utility-maximizing and optimizing, if we suppose that strategically rational choice is generally possible. Going to the party is Jane's optimizing response, whatever Brian chooses, but it cannot be combined with any strategy of Brian's to yield a pair of mutually utility-maximizing responses. How then may we reconcile or, failing reconciliation, decide between the claims of utility-maximization and optimization? This is the central problem for any theory of strategic rationality. As we shall show, moral theory is essentially the theory of optimizing constraints on utility-maximization.

But this is to anticipate. Given our account of practical rationality, deciding between the two claims may seem unproblematic. It may seem evident that the demands of utility-maximization must take precedence over any demands of optimization. Choice reveals preference. If one chooses a strategy and then claims to disprefer its expected outcome to the expected outcome of some other strategy that one might have chosen, then one's behavioural and expressed preferences are in conflict and one's utilities, if identified with one's values, are undefined. One is not in a position to act rationally. If one chooses a strategy and agrees that one does not disprefer its outcome to that of any alternative strategy, then the expected utility of its outcome must be at least equal to the utility of the outcome of any alternative. Hence one cannot rationally choose an optimizing strategy rather than a utility-maximizing strategy; in choosing a strategy one shows that, in so far as one's utilities are well defined, one considers it to be utility-maximizing.

If this argument is sound then optimization cannot override utility-maximization as a requirement for strategically rational choice, but at best can serve as a ground for choosing among utility-maximizing strategies. And many theorists of rational choice consider the argument sound.[9] We may not dismiss it by showing that only the choice of an optimizing strategy sustains the expectations on which the choice is based. We used that argument to defend the choice of a particular utility-maximizing strategy, but no similar argument will serve to defend the choice of a strategy that is not utility-maximizing. There may be a unique strategy compatible with a particular expectation, but if the strategy is not utility-maximizing given the expectation, then it may plausibly be argued that neither the choice of the strategy nor the expectation may be supposed rational.

We are not yet in a position to reply to this rejection of the rationality of optimization. Later we shall attempt to undermine the force of the demand that rational choice reveal preference by showing that its scope may be restricted by what is in effect a meta-choice, a choice about how to make choices. But to conclude this chapter, let us simply reflect on some of the consequences of requiring that a strategically rational outcome be in equilibrium—consequences that should make our unwillingness to acquiesce in the straightforward identification of rationality with utility-maximization more appealing.

3.2 The classic illustration of the untoward consequences of utility-maximization is the 'Prisoner's Dilemma', a story attributed to A. W. Tucker.[10] Fred and Ed have committed (the District Attorney is certain) a serious crime, but some of the evidence necessary to secure a conviction is, unfortunately, inadmissible in court (the District Attorney curses the law reformers who make her task more difficult). She is, however, holding Fred and Ed, and has been able to prevent them from being in a position to communicate one with the other. She has them booked on a lesser, although still serious, charge, and she is confident that she can secure their conviction for it. She then calls, separately, on Fred and Ed, telling each the same tale and making each the same offer. 'Confess the error of your ways—and the crime you have committed', she says, 'and if your former partner does not confess, then I shall convince the jury that you are a reformed man and your ex-partner evil incarnate; the judge will sentence you to a year and him to ten. Do not confess, and if your former partner does, then you may infer

[9] As Harsanyi says, 'under our theory ... efficiency considerations can operate only *within* the enforceable set [of strategies]', pp. 127–8, *Rational Behavior*.

[10] See Luce and Raiffa, p. 94.

your fate. And should neither of you choose to confess, then I shall bring you to trial on this other matter, and you may count on two years.' 'But what', says Fred (or Ed), 'if we both confess?' 'Then', says the District Attorney, 'I shall let justice take its natural course with you—it's a serious crime so I should estimate five years', and without further ado she leaves Ed (or Fred) to solitary reflection.

Both are quite single-mindedly interested in minimizing their time behind bars, and so both represent the situation in this simple way:

	He	
	confesses	does not confess
I confess	5 years each	1 year for me, 10 for him
do not confess	10 years for me, 1 for him	2 years each

So each reasons: 'If he confesses, then I had better confess—otherwise I'm in for ten years. If he doesn't confess, then if I confess I'm out in a year. So whatever he does, I should confess. Indeed' (each being a student of strategic rationality and the theory of games) 'in this situation there is but one outcome in equilibrium—the product of mutual confession. My course is clear.'

And the District Attorney (also a student of strategic rationality and the theory of games) returns to Fred and Ed on the following day, a smile on her face, to collect the confessions which she knows are forthcoming, and which will put Fred and Ed out of evil paths for five years—whereas, if they had kept their mouths shut (or their pens dry), they would have been back at their favourite occupations in but two years.

This may be a happy result of the appeal to mutually utility-maximizing rather than mutually optimizing strategies. (In this situation any outcome resulting from a decision by either or both not to confess is optimal; the symmetry of the situation however makes evident that a sufficient condition of choice based on optimization would require each not to confess.) But if we abstract from this particular story, we recognize the seriousness of the problem—in any situation with a structure parallel to that faced by Fred and Ed, supposedly rational utility-maximizers do much worse for themselves than could supposedly irrational optimizers.

Another illustration will suggest how unfortunate this is.[11] Con-

[11] The illustration is now familiar in the literature. See my 'Morality and Advantage', *Philosophical Review* 76 (1967), pp. 460–75.

sider two nations, which for convenience (and disclaiming any apparent reference to real nations as purely coincidental) we shall call the US and the SU. They are engaged in an arms race, the dangers of which are appreciated by both, for neither wants all-out war with the other. Mutual disarmament would remove the threat of war, and would not, let us suppose, have other disadvantages (such as depressing the economy), so that both strongly prefer mutual disarmament to continuation of the arms race. However, there is no way to ensure compliance with an agreement to disarm, and each knows that, were it alone to disarm, it would be at the other's mercy, whereas if it alone were to remain armed, it would be the world's dominant power. Each prefers the arms race, despite the risk of all-out war, to being at the mercy of the other, and each prefers the prospect of being top nation to mutual disarmament. Hence, before concluding an agreement to disarm, each represents the aftermath to itself thus:

		SU	
		violate	comply
US	violate	3rd, 3rd	1st, 4th
	comply	4th, 1st	2nd, 2nd

The structure of this situation precisely parallels that faced by Fred and Ed. Hence the reasoning is also parallel. Whatever the other does, violation maximizes one's own utility. The only outcome in equilibrium is mutual violation. Needless to say, the US and the SU do not conclude an agreement which would not be worth the paper on which it was written, but confine their negotiations either to enforceable agreements or to matters in which mutual compliance is (and is recognized to be) each nation's most preferred alternative.

We do not question the rationality of the US and the SU in the situation in which they in fact find themselves. For them mutual optimization is not a viable alternative to mutual utility-maximization. The world of nations is what Thomas Hobbes referred to as the natural condition of mankind, and in that natural condition there are no rational constraints on the endeavour of each individual person or nation to maximize his own utility.[12] But this, of course, is precisely what is wrong with the world of nations. The natural condition of mankind is an irrational condition, because it

[12] See Hobbes, *Leviathan*, ch. 13, p. 63.

condemns persons or nations to non-optimal outcomes that, in 'Prisoner's Dilemma-type' situations, may be little better than disastrous. No individual person or nation is able unilaterally to remove himself from the natural condition of mankind. But everyone would benefit from ending a state of affairs in which it is rational to interact only on the basis of mutual utility-maximization. What we shall show is the rationale, and very strictly the utility-maximizing rationale, for replacing 'utility-maximizing response' by 'optimizing response' in interpreting the conditions A, B, and C which govern strategic rationality.

IV

THE MARKET: FREEDOM FROM MORALITY

1 Economics is the pioneer study of rational interaction. And it celebrates an ideal of interaction free from all constraint. In two brief passages in *The Wealth of Nations*, Adam Smith formulated the canonical statement of this ideal:

> All systems . . . of restraint . . . being . . . completely taken away, the obvious and simple system of natural liberty establishes itself of its own accord. Every man, as long as he does not violate the laws of justice, is left perfectly free to pursue his own interest his own way, and to bring both his industry and capital into competition with those of any other man . . .[1]

And the outcome of this free and natural competition harmonizes the fulfilment of each person's private interest with that of the social interest. Generalizing from a particular instance, Smith argued:

> By preferring the support of domestic to that of foreign industry, he intends only his own security; and by directing that industry in such a manner as its produce may be of the greatest value, he intends only his own gain, and he is in this, as in many other cases, led by an invisible hand to promote an end which was no part of his intention. Nor is it always the worse for the society that it was no part of it. By pursuing his own interest he frequently promotes that of the society more effectually than when he really intends to promote it.[2]

Smith envisaged the 'system of natural liberty' as a perfectly competitive market. The idea of such a market illuminates our understanding of rational interaction by revealing a structure in which the divergent and seemingly opposed interests of different individuals fully harmonize. Conceived as an ideal type, the perfect market, as we shall see, guarantees the coincidence of equilibrium and optimality, and so its structure is the very antithesis of the Prisoner's Dilemma.

[1] Adam Smith, *An Enquiry into the Nature and Causes of the Wealth of Nations*, 1776, bk. iv, ch. ix; introduced by E. R. A. Seligman, 2 vols. (London, 1910), vol. 2, p. 180.

[2] Ibid., bk. iv, ch. ii; vol. 1, p. 400.

The market is a central concern of our study. Indeed, we shall argue in Chapter VIII that one of the clauses in the agreement that gives rise to a rational morality provides for the choice of a perfectly competitive market, or a near approximation, as a social institution in those circumstances in which such a market is a practicable alternative. But note that our claim is that the market is to be chosen where it is to be had. For one of our central themes is that the market is not always to be had, that it embodies a very special structure of interaction which cannot be all-embracing. The world might be a better place if it were, as the enthusiasts of *laissez-faire* economics have believed it to be, a perfectly competitive market. But it is not. And as we shall argue, because the world is not a market, morality is a necessary constraint on the interaction of rational persons.

Morality arises from market failure. The first step in making this claim good is to show that the perfect market, were it realized, would constitute a morally free zone, a zone within which the constraints of morality would have no place. In leaving each person free to pursue her own interest in her own way, the market satisfies the ideal of *moral anarchy*. We are more familiar with anarchy as a political ideal. The political anarchist offers us the picture of a human society that neither has nor needs external constraints—a society of peaceable, productive, and companionable persons whose interactions are blessedly free of all authority or compulsion. The political anarchist seeks to convince us of the possibility of an order in human affairs that does not require the artifice of politics. The moral anarchist offers us the comparable picture of a human society that neither has nor needs internal constraints—a society of peaceable, productive, and companionable persons who nevertheless are without conscience. The moral anarchist seeks to convince us of the possibility of an order in human affairs that does not require the deeper artifice of morality.

In this chapter we shall assess the claims of moral anarchy. We shall examine the perfectly competitive market as a structure for rational interaction, showing that its operation would need no constraints on individual utility-maximizing choice. Indeed we shall show why such constraints would be both rationally and morally unjustified. But our enquiry will reveal the limits of the market. In this way we shall prepare the ground for our subsequent examination of a quite different structure for rational interaction, which does require constraints on individual utility-maximizing choice. Understanding the nature, place, and limits of a morally free zone in human affairs will help us to understand the nature and necessity of a morally (and politically) constrained zone.

In defending the 'simple system of natural liberty' Smith himself noted that every man is free 'as long as he does not violate the laws of justice'. But justice, as the reader may recall, is conspicuously absent from Thomas Hobbes's account of the natural condition of mankind where 'Force, and Fraud, are ... the two Cardinall vertues'.[3] And the absence of force and fraud is essential to the workings of the market. Before Smith's invisible hand can do its beneficent work. Hobbes's war of every man against every man must first be exorcized. And this, as we shall see, means that the ideal of free interaction which Smith celebrates is not natural but artificial, arising, for rational persons, only within a framework of agreed constraints. In understanding the perfect market as a morally free zone we shall be led back to its underlying, antecedent morality.

2.1 The idealization of interaction represented by the perfectly competitive market includes the removal of both circumstantial uncertainty and strategic calculation. Market decision-making, although practically complex, is logically of the simplest kind. Each chooses parametrically, as if his actions were the sole variable factor, taking the actions of others as fixed circumstances. And each chooses as if he knew the outcome of each of his possible actions. The core of traditional economic theory, examining the workings of the market, is thus concerned with the analysis of rational choice under the assumption of certainty.[4]

We shall not enter into a full description of the familiar workings of the market, but note only those features relevant to our argument. The goods of the market are its products; the bads are the factor services used in production. Each person wants to consume as many products as possible, and as much of each as possible, although desire is assumed to diminish as consumption increases. Each also wishes to provide as few factor services, and as little of each, as possible, and here the desire not to provide such services is assumed to diminish as one's supply of those services diminishes. In addition to production and consumption the market is the locus of exchange.

[3] Hobbes, *Leviathan*, ch. 13, p. 63.

[4] See J. C. Harsanyi, 'Advances in Understanding Rational Behavior', in *Essays on Ethics, Social Behavior, and Scientific Explanation* (Dordrecht, 1976), p. 94.

The conditions for the optimality of production and exchange, for the conversion of factor services into consumption goods, are found in any standard elementary acount of economic theory, and need not delay us here.

The perfectly competitive market presupposes private ownership of all products and factors of production. Thus the market is specified, not only by the utility functions of those interacting in it, which determine demand, and the production functions reflecting existing technology, which determine supply, but also by an initial distribution of factors, affording each person his initial factor endowment. For our purposes each person may be defined by his utility function and his factor endowment. These fix his preferences and capacities, which alone are relevant to his activity in the market. The initial distribution of factors, and so the definition of each individual which in part depends upon it, will play a significant role in our discussion; we should note at the outset that from the perspective of market activity, of production and exchange, it is simply a given condition.

To say that a factor or product is owned by an individual is to say that he may use it as he pleases in the processes of production, exchange, and consumption. The right of ownership extends only to market use, but it extends fully to that use. Thus the market involves the entirely free activity of each individual, limited only by the factors and products that he owns, the production functions that determine the possibilities of transforming factors into products, and the utility functions of others that determine the possibilities of exchange. The presupposition of private ownership thus may be divided into two parts: *individual factor endowments*, and *free individual market activity*.

The perfectly competitive market presupposes a second form of privacy in the consumption of all products. Each unit good enters into the utility function of only one person. This has a twofold implication. On the one hand all goods must be strictly private in the sense that consumption of a unit by one person precludes its consumption by another. Food is a purely private good; what one person eats, no one else can. A roadway is not purely private; many persons may drive on it. On the other hand utility functions must be strictly independent; no person gains or loses simply from the utilities of others. Each person's utility is strictly determined by the goods he consumes and the factor services he provides. Or in other words, bundles of goods consumed and services provided are strictly discrete, and each person's utility is determined by and only by the size and composition of his bundle.

The restriction to private goods is of considerable significance in limiting the scope of the perfectly competitive market. In effect, the morally free zone is the zone of private goods. But important as this will be in later discussion, we shall focus in the present chapter more on the requirement that utility functions be independent. A happy expression of this idea is offered by John Rawls; people 'are conceived as not taking an interest in one another's interests'.[5] In fact his formulation is more restrictive than needed; the market requires only that persons be conceived as not taking an interest in the interests of those with whom they exchange. This is Wicksteed's requirement of 'non-tuism'; my preferences do not involve you, although they may involve some third person not party to our interaction.[6] Private consumption, like private ownership, is thus divided into two parts: *private goods*, and *mutual unconcern*.

The existence of unowned factors or products, or the presence of public goods or interdependent utilities, may give rise to economic externalities. The absence of *externalities*, however they might arise, is a further condition of perfect competition. An externality arises whenever an act of production or exchange or consumption affects the utility of some person who is not party, or who is unwillingly party, to it. Such an effect may of course be either beneficial or harmful; if beneficial we speak of a positive externality or external efficiency, if harmful we speak of a negative externality or external inefficiency.

An example of each may be helpful. Let us suppose that a group of shipowners agree to erect a lighthouse to aid the navigation of their ships. Given freedom of the seas, anyone may avail herself of the navigational aid afforded by the light. Those who erect it have no way of restricting access to the good they provide to those persons who share the costs of its provision. The effect on those shipowners who are not party to the construction of the lighthouse is then a positive externality.

[5] J. Rawls, *A Theory of Justice* (Cambridge, Mass., 1971), p. 13.

[6] See P. H. Wicksteed, *The Common Sense of Political Economy and Selected Papers and Reviews on Economic Theory*, ed. L. Robbins, 2 vols. (London, 1933); 'The specific character of an economic relation is not its "egoism" but its "non-tuism"', vol. 1, p. 180.

Let us now suppose that a factory owner disposes of the wastes from her factory by having them discharged into the atmosphere, thus causing pollution. If anyone may use the air as she pleases, so that it is a free good, then there is no way to require the factory owner to compensate others for the ill effects on them of her method of waste disposal. The effect on any person breathing the polluted air is then a negative externality.

Note that in these examples, the externality arises because of the existence of a free good—a good that is not privately owned by an individual or group of individuals, but is available for use by all. The existence of the sea as a free good enables anyone to take advantage of improvements to navigation. The existence of the atmosphere as a free good enables anyone to take advantage of its capacity as a sink. In showing that these give rise to externalities we are not suggesting that sea and air should be private possessions. We are however showing that they preclude the efficient workings of the market.

Essential to the operation of the perfectly competitive market is the marginal matching of supply and demand. Externalities upset this matching. Lighthouses tend to be undersupplied by a market; air pollution is over supplied. The explanation is straightforward. Demand is effective only as a willingness to pay the costs of supply. But those who benefit from the availability of lighthouses have little or no incentive to pay their costs. Given freedom of the seas, there is no way to channel their demand into a user's fee. And so demand is ineffective. Those who supply lighthouses do so only to the extent of their own demand—not to the extent of the further demand represented by the non-paying users. Supply therefore tends to fall short of full demand. To use the terminology of the previous chapter, the outcome is in equilibrium—each acts in a utility-maximizing way given the actions of the others, but it is not optimal—everyone would benefit, if the demand for lighthouses could be channelled to bring forth increased supply.

The situation is reversed with respect to air pollution. Those who create it, given that air is available for use freely, must pay only its direct costs to themselves, and not the costs their pollution imposes on others. Hence lack of demand, as it were, does not inhibit supply. Air pollution is supplied up to the point at which its marginal cost to the suppliers equals its marginal benefit to them; the additional costs to others have no effect in restraining that supply. Again the outcome is in equilibrium but not optimal—everyone could benefit if pollution were controlled at the point at which marginal cost to all equals marginal benefit to all (although whether everyone would benefit depends on the way in which costs and benefits are allocated).

Individual factor endowments and private goods, free market activity and mutual unconcern, and the absence of externalities—these are the presuppositions of a perfectly competitive market. In it both production and exchange are carried on under certainty. Certainty of production is assured by fixed production functions representing a known technology. Certainty of exchange is assured by known market prices, varying in accordance with aggregate supply and demand, but effectively independent of the behaviour of any individual. Although prices are determined by the preferences of those interacting in the market, yet they present themselves to each as objective data to which they must conform in their activities. We noted the emergence of these common, universal, and seemingly objective values in II.4.2. Marxist analysis suggests a useful term for this appearance of objectivity—it is a form of *fetishism*.[7]

Free activity under certainty is sufficient to ensure that the market constantly moves toward an equilibrium condition. And the economist now offers his triumphant demonstration that given perfect competition, the market equilibrium must also be optimal—no one could be made better off unless someone else were to become worse off.[8] We have seen that the presence of externalities may lead to a non-optimal equilibrium, but under perfect competition externalities are necessarily absent. In the outcome of the perfectly competitive market, no one could consume more products given the factor services she provides, or provide fewer services given the products she consumes, unless some other person were to consume fewer products while providing the same services, or were to provide more services without consuming more products. Adam Smith's invisible hand is thus made visible by the economist's analysis. In setting out the conditions for the perfectly competitive market we show those features that, if present in the structure of interaction, ensure that each individual, intending only her own gain, promotes the interest of society, in bringing about a mutually beneficial optimal outcome, even though this be no part of her intention.

[7] See Karl Marx, *Capital: A Critical Analysis of Capitalist Production*, vol. i, ch. i, sect. 4; trans. S. Moore and E. Aveling (London, 1889), pp. 41–55.

[8] For a brief account of this demonstration, emphasizing that perfect competition is sufficient for optimality but not necessary, see D. M. Winch, *Analytical Welfare Economics* (Harmondsworth, Middx., 1971), pp. 89–95.

The coincidence of equilibrium and optimality in the outcome of the perfectly competitive market is necessary to our argument that it would provide a morally free zone. In the equilibrium resulting after all voluntary exchanges have been made, individual gain is assured; each does as well as she can given the actions of the others. In optimality mutual benefit is assured; each does as well as she can given the pay-offs to the others. It is the failure of the equilibrium resulting from the pursuit of individual gain to be optimal that is the source of the complaints by Hobbes and others against the natural condition of humankind. The perfect market overcomes this failure, and in doing so, gives rise to Smith's panegyric to the invisible hand. But we must not simply dismiss from attention the other features of the market that we have noted; they are not merely conditions of the coincidence between equilibrium and optimality. Although this coincidence shows the full strategic rationality of market interaction, yet to argue that the ideal market would be a morally free zone, the presupposition of free activity is independently necessary. We must therefore ask what free activity is.

2.2 Consider the activity of a solitary being, a Robinson Crusoe as we shall call her. Crusoe is free to use her capacities in whatever way will best fulfil her preferences given the external circumstances in which she finds herself. Her capacities of course limit the extent of her fulfilment. Her preferences affect the use she makes of her capacities—not in limiting what she can do but what she finds worth doing. But neither of these limitations constrains Crusoe's freedom. A person is free in so far as she is able, without interference, to direct her capacities to the service of her preferences. Since Crusoe may do this, she enjoys the full benefit of her labours; what she consumes is what she produces. And since she may cease her productive efforts when the cost of further production exceeds the benefit of consuming the good produced, she has only herself to blame if the marginal costs and benefits of her activity are not equal. In so far as she is rational, the value to her of the last unit good she produces must equal the cost to her of the last unit factor service she supplies for its production.

The effect of the perfectly competitive market is to ensure, at the interpersonal level, the same freedom enjoyed by Robinson Crusoe in her solitude, while making possible the enormously expanded range of benefits afforded by exchange and the division of labour—and also, in the long run, by investment. As we have noted, the perfect market reduces strategic interaction to parametric choice; the production and demand functions in terms of which each chooses her utility-maximizing course of action are fixed circumstances. Thus although the use any particular individual may make of her talents or the fulfilment she may obtain for her preferences depends on considerations of aggregate supply and demand, and thus on the talents and preferences of all those interacting in the market, yet no one is in a position to control the terms of interaction for others.

Each person is thus a Robinson Crusoe, even in the market. Of course the existence of other persons, and the possibilities of exchange, affect the limits on each person's behaviour. Not only her own capacities, but also the capacities of others, limit the fulfilment any individual can provide for her preferences, and this in two ways. First, the overall productive capacity of a society is limited by the capacities of its members. And second, the return each person may expect for the use of her capacities in the provision of factor services depends on the relations of substitutability between her capacities and those of others. If the average person rose to the heights of an Aristotle, my philosophical talents would not be readily marketable.

Furthermore, not only one's own preferences, but also the preferences of others, affect the use one makes of one's capacities, in limiting what one finds worth doing. Wayne Gretzky's talents on ice would be of little benefit to him were there no audience for hockey. But these limitations are the interpersonal analogues of those experienced by Robinson Crusoe alone on her island. If her freedom is not constrained by her limited talents and particular interest, then it remains unconstrained when she leaves her island and comes to relate her talents and interests with those of others.

Robinson Crusoe enjoys the full benefit of her labours. Similarly those who engage in market interaction enjoy the full benefit of their labours. Under standard conditions, the value of total market output is equal to the sum of the marginal values each person contributes to that output—the sum of the marginal differences each person makes. In the free exchanges of the market each may expect a return equal in value to her contribution.[9] Thus the income each receives, or the value of the goods each is able to consume, is equal

[9] See Wicksteed; 'the economic forces . . . tend to secure to every kind of human effort a remuneration corresponding to its marginal worth to any member of the community', vol. 1, p. 338.

to the contribution she makes, or the marginal difference she adds to the value of the total product. And as with Robinson Crusoe, each person in the market has only herself to blame if the marginal costs and benefits of her activity are unequal. In so far as she is rational, the value to her of the last unit good she produces or obtains in exchange is equal to the cost to her of the last unit factor service she contributes to production or the last unit good she offers in exchange. Thus the market yields an optimal outcome in which returns to individuals equal contributions made by those same individuals. And this occurs, not through any deliberate intent on the part of the individuals interacting in the market, each of whom seeks only to maximize her gain, but as a result of the structure for interaction provided by the conditions of perfect competition.

3.1 *Laissez-faire* economists accept the coincidence of equilibrium and optimality in the outcome of free market activity as justifying the liberty of each person to pursue her own interest. Any restriction of this liberty, any interference with the natural functioning of the market, seems to them neither rationally nor morally acceptable. Many forms of interference would of course prevent the market outcome from being optimal, leaving some persons worse off than need be given the returns to the others. But even if optimality were preserved, interference would involve a redistribution of products leaving some persons better off and others worse off than they had been in free interaction. What, the defenders of the market ask, could entitle the beneficiaries to their gains, taken at the expense of their fellows? And what could reconcile those fellows to their losses? The sole activity affecting the market that could be either rational or right is simply to preserve it, to protect it from force or fraud, those cardinal virtues of Hobbes's natural condition of war that are the great enemies of free and mutually beneficial interaction.

The argument that the *laissez-faire* economists would advance for an end to political constraints is clearly also an argument for an end to moral constraints. If each is not morally free to pursue her own gain, then some must benefit at the expense of others. Where earlier thinkers saw in the unbridled pursuit of individual utility the ultimate source of conflict in human affairs, the defenders of the market see in it rather the basis of the true harmony resulting from the fullest compossible fulfilment of the preferences which utility measures. The traditional moralist is told that his services are not wanted.

That market interaction is rational may seem evident. The coincidence of equilibrium and optimality in the outcome ensures that the conditions for rational choice set out in the preceding chapter are satisfied, whether we suppose that a rational response to the choices of others is utility-maximizing or optimizing. The argument of the advocates of *laissez-faire* may then seem to require the claim that where choice is both utility-maximizing and optimizing, it must also be morally right. But a more profound interpretation of their argument, which we endorse, is that it rests on the claim that morality has no application to market interaction under the conditions for perfect competition. Choice is neither morally right nor wrong, because the coincidence of utility-maximization and optimization in free interaction removes both need and rationale for the constraints that morality provides, which enable us to distinguish choices as right or wrong. Moral constraints arise only in the gap created by conflict between the two rationality properties, when mutual benefit is not assured by the pursuit of individual gain. We assess outcomes as right or wrong when, but only when, maximizing one's utility given the actions of others would fail to maximize it given the utilities of others.

We shall defend this view, arguing from our conception of human beings as rational (or potentially rational) individual actors and our conception of morality as a constraint on the individual pursuit of utility. But we must emphasize that our argument does not entail defence of *laissez-faire* in economic practice. For its traditional advocates supposed, as we do not, that the perfectly competitive market is realized, or almost realized, or at least could be realized, in most of our economic transactions. They failed to appreciate the unavoidable presence of externalities in almost all contexts—or, if they recognized their presence, underestimated their magnitude. Hence they derived policy conclusions from their basic normative stance that in fact require empirical premisses that seem false or at best doubtful. Our concern is to show that there would be a morally free zone in ideal interaction, not to argue for its presence in most of our daily activities.

Furthermore the advocates of *laissez-faire* failed to appreciate the normative significance of some of the presuppositions of the market. We have noted that it presupposes private consumption, and this is a factual matter. Consumption of a unit good by one person either does or does not preclude its consumption by another, and the utilities of one person either are or are not independent of the utilities of another. But the market also presupposes private ownership of factors and goods, and this is a normative matter. The initial factor endowment of each person is taken as given, but why should it be so taken? Each product and each factor of production is owned by some individual who may use it as she pleases as far as production, exchange, and consumption are concerned, but why should individuals exercise this control?

The presupposition of private ownership would seem to raise questions, not only about the alleged non-morality of interaction within the market, but about the rationality and morality of accepting the market structure for interaction. And these questions are especially pressing since in any market there are many possible optimal outcomes, the actual one being determined by the initial factor endowments of the interacting individuals, given their preferences and the technology of production. The actual outcome yields each individual a return equal to her contribution, but the factor services that an individual contributes must depend on the factors she possesses, and so on her endowment. We have supposed that each person may be defined by her utility function and her factor endowment. But the second part of this definition may seem quite arbitrary, and a different definition of each person, all else remaining the same, leads to a different final distribution of goods.

In responding to these questions, we distinguish the *conditions* of the market from its *operation*. The operation of the market is to convert an initial situation specified in terms of individual factor endowments into a final outcome specified in terms of a distribution of goods or products among the same individuals. Since the market outcome is both in equilibrium and optimal, its operation is shown to be rational, and since it proceeds through the free activity of individuals, we claim that its rationality leaves no place for moral assessment. Given the initial situation of the market, its outcome cannot but be fully justified.

But neither the operation of the market nor its outcome can show, or can even tend to show, that its initial situation is also either rationally or morally acceptable. Nothing then in the argument we shall present about the inapplicability of moral assessment to the operation of the market can show that the initial factor endowments themselves raise no moral issues. In his analysis of the optimality of perfect competition, David Winch notes, 'The perfectly competitive system is dependent on private ownership of factors of production' so that 'the essence of the system is that distributive justice is an attribute of the inputs of the system, not the outputs'.[10] With this we are in full agreement. Any defence of particular market arrangements must include a defence of the inputs, of the particular factor endowments. But then as Winch insists, 'the acceptance of an initial distribution of factors . . . precludes our having value judgements about the distribution of utilities'. The operation of a market cannot in itself raise any evaluative issues. Market outcomes are fair if, but of course only if, they result from fair initial conditions. In later chapters we shall see what the standard of fairness is.

3.2 We shall now endeavour to defend the claim that the perfect market would create a morally free zone for individual activity, arguing from our initial conception of morality as an impartial constraint on the direct pursuit of individual utility. We ask whether the operation of the market exhibits any form of partiality that would justify from a moral standpoint the constraint needed to overcome it. Since we have already defended the claim that market interaction is rational, were we to find it to be partial, we should have established at least a prima-facie conflict between moral and rational requirements. We shall deny that there is such a conflict. But we must not simply assume that, because market interaction is rational and morality is not opposed to rationality, the market is therefore morally free. We must argue independently, from our conception of morality as an impartial constraint, if our conclusion is not to beg the question.

Perhaps the best way to decide whether market interaction exhibits partiality is to ask whether any individual could reasonably claim that the operation of the market affected her in any differential way, whether favourably or unfavourably, or whether she could enter any reasonable complaint or objection against the market outcome. We take for granted that no individual could reasonably object to any outcome she might bring about as a Robinson Crusoe. Since our present concern is with the operation of the market, we also take for granted, at least initially, the market definition of the individual. Later in this section we shall determine what in this definition may require further defence, if not only the operation but also the conditions of the market are to be shown as morally acceptable.

[10] Winch, p. 97.

First, then, we note that the presupposition of *free activity* ensures that no one is subject to any form of compulsion, or to any type of limitation not already affecting her actions as a solitary individual. Each chooses for herself what to produce, what to exchange, and what to consume, against a known technology of production and a known set of prices, which neither she nor any other individual is able to affect. If the market were to bring about an outcome, albeit optimal and in equilibrium, through the exercise of compulsion by some individual or group on others, then we might well suppose that the market affected persons differentially, and insist on the need for moral constraints to overcome such partiality. But given the freedom of market interaction, the introduction of moral constraints would be the introduction of the very compulsion that we suppose morality is intended to counteract. Since the market provides nothing to correct, the introduction of a corrective device would itself be a source of partiality.

Second, the *absence of externalities* ensures that no one is affected, whether beneficially or harmfully, by any market activity to which she has not chosen to be party. Not only has each acted freely, but also each has interacted freely. No one is then in the position of either a free-rider or a parasite. A free-rider obtains a benefit without paying all or part of its cost. A parasite in obtaining a benefit displaces all or part of the cost on to some other person. Recall our previous examples. The shipowners whose vessels take navigational advantage of a lighthouse although they have contributed neither to its erection nor to its maintenance are free-riders. Although they do not displace costs on to others, they do gain without paying any of the costs required to provide the gain. The factory owner who disposes of her gaseous wastes by polluting the atmosphere without compensating those who suffer the pollution she causes is a parasite, displacing part of the costs of her activities on to others. And note that she would remain a parasite even were others to pay her not to pollute, for she would then be charging them the costs of an alternative method of disposing of her wastes.

The free-rider does not make others worse off by her behaviour. Those who erect and maintain the lighthouse maximize their utility in so doing. But she obtains a benefit that they do not enjoy, so that the outcome affects her in a differentially favourable way. The parasite does make others directly worse off. His activity may seem more evidently unfair than that of the free-rider. Indeed, he directly violates the conditions of free activity in forcing others to interact with him in a manner not of their choosing. He benefits differentially, and others suffer differentially. But although the parasite is doubly at fault, both undermine the impartiality found in interaction in which each pays the costs of the benefits she obtains.

The equation of income with marginal contribution ensures just this impartiality. Not only does each interact freely with her fellows, but each benefits from and only from the contribution she makes. One might freely choose to enter into differentially unfavourable interaction with others because of the lack of better alternatives. Man Friday might be better off as a slave than as a Robinson Crusoe; given a choice between slavery and solitude he might choose slavery. But Man Friday does not benefit from interaction to the extent of his contribution. The market rules out all such biased forms of interaction. Despite propaganda to the contrary, wage slavery is not and cannot be a feature of the perfectly competitive market—a point to which we shall return in the last section of this chapter, where we examine a Marxist objection to our defence of the market.

Third, the *optimality* of the market outcome ensures that any alternative to it that was not worse for everyone would benefit some individuals at the expense of others. For every alternative must involve a diminution in some person's utility, and we may treat this as either a loss of benefits or an increase in costs. If the former, then the person will not receive some benefit for which in free interaction she paid the cost; if the latter, then the person must pay some costs in addition to those that in free interaction were sufficient to cover all of her benefits. In either case her interests are prejudicially affected, and she may reasonably complain, if someone else enjoys an increase in benefits or a reduction in costs, that the other person has benefited at her expense.

But this last point must be qualified. The market affords each person a return for the factor services she supplies. But this return may include two rather different components. First, and necessarily, the price paid in the market for a factor service must cover the cost of its supply. Each person, in bringing her abilities and materials to production and exchange, receives a return covering the costs of developing and maintaining those abilities, and obtaining those materials. Were this not so, interaction would not be voluntary. If each did not receive her cost of supply then she would supply factor services only under threat of coercive penalties. But second, to the extent to which certain factors are in fixed supply—to the extent to which certain abilities or materials are not freely substitutable in the market—there is the possibility that demand for the goods produced with the use of these abilities or materials will bring about a market price for their use that includes rent.[11] The recipient of rent benefits from the scarcity of the factors she controls—a scarcity which is of course entirely accidental from her standpoint, since it depends, not on the intrinsic nature of the factors, but on the relation between them and the factors controlled by others. She receives more than is needed to induce her to bring her factors to the market; rent is by definition a return over and above the cost of supply.

If the market outcome includes rent, then its optimality does not straightforwardly ensure that any alternative that was not worse for everyone would benefit some individuals at the expense of others. As long as each individual receives the full cost of supply for the factor services she provides, and as long as each individual also pays the full cost of supply for the factor services she obtains, then no one would seem to benefit at the expense of another. Whether the surplus represented by rent goes to the owner of the scarce factor, or is distributed in some other way, would seem to be left rationally and morally open by all that we have so far said. We shall return to the subject of rent, in considering the establishment of the perfectly competitive market as one of the terms of agreement among rational persons. For the present, we should note that our argument in support of the claim that the perfect market would create a morally free zone has not been shown to apply to those parts of market transactions that involve rent. We may however conclude that free activity, the absence of externalities, and optimality are together sufficient to defeat all charges of partiality in the operation of the market—and ensure that, rent aside, any alternative to the market outcome would either leave everyone worse off or be partial in

[11] For a brief discussion of economic rent in relation to market returns, see S. Gordon, *Welfare, Justice, and Freedom* (New York, 1980), pp. 98–9. Readers unfamiliar with economic terminology should not suppose that what is here called 'rent' is identical with the price paid for leasing property. This price may contain not a penny of economic rent. Leasing property is similar to any other purchase; the buyer in the market must pay the cost of the service supplied. Rent controls are generally used to ensure that the buyer does not pay the full cost of supply; the property owner is coerced into the loss of at least opportunity costs, if not others as well. Rent controls typically are unrelated to the distribution of the surplus that constitutes economic rent.

enabling some to benefit at the expense of others. The idea of a morally free zone is upheld.

Or at least, it is upheld for persons defined by their utility functions and factor endowments. Let us say that these constitute a person's *market self*; then in so far as an individual identifies with his market self he will of course find the market impartial. Now an individual can hardly fail to identify with his utility function, the measure of his considered preferences, but he may not identify with his factor endowment, considering it purely arbitrary. Indeed, one may reject the very idea of an endowment, and claim that there is no justification for the presuppositions of the market.

In market societies the process of socialization unsurprisingly encourages each person to identify with his market self. Carrying this to its extreme, we may imagine a society in which the outcome of interaction, whatever it may be, is treated as optimal, and the members of the society are shaped to fit that outcome—to have the preferences and to be endowed with the factors that are required if the outcome is to be an optimal equilibrium. This inversion of market society, in which individuals serve the market rather than vice versa, is a matter of serious concern, both theoretical and practical. We shall return to it in the last two chapters of this study, and show that our moral theory requires its rejection.

We do not then claim that an individual may reasonably identify with his market self, however that self may be established. We do want to argue that each person is defined in part by an appropriately-based factor endowment. Indeed, this is presupposed even in our account of Robinson Crusoe and the freedom she enjoys to direct her capacities to the service of her preferences. Although Robinson Crusoe's natural endowment is in one sense arbitrary, in that she would have no ground for complaint were it quite other than it is, yet in another sense it is not at all arbitrary. In the solitary condition in which Crusoe finds herself, her endowment is whatever she can put to use. It thus affords a natural and determinate starting point for her behaviour.

Extending this conception of natural endowment to situations involving interaction may seem problematic. If we suppose that each person's endowment is whatever he can use, then endowments overlap, so that as Hobbes insists, every person 'has a Right to every thing; even to one anothers body'.[12] On the other hand, if we

[12] Hobbes, *Leviathan*, ch. 14, p. 64.

suppose that each person's endowment is what he alone can use, then endowments vanish, so that no one has a right to any thing, not even to his own body. But we may resolve this problem by modifying the conception. Even though Robinson Crusoe is in fact solitary, we may define her *basic endowment* as what she can make use of, and what no one else could make use of in her absence. And we may extend this notion from solitude to the market. Each person's basic endowment is what he can make use of simply in virtue of his presence in a situation, and what no one else can make use of in his absence. It thus comprises his physical and mental capacities. And so it is related to the liberty that both Crusoe and those interacting in the market enjoy.

A person's endowment may include other factors of production, and indeed must do so for perfect competition to be possible. In Chapter VII we shall show how such an endowment may arise, and how even the basic endowment may be rationally grounded. But for present purposes, we need suppose only that each person includes in his conception of himself both his physical and mental capacities, and that this conception, of a basic endowment applicable both to Robinson Crusoes and to market men and women, is not arbitrary. For each then has a sufficient reason to consider interaction with his fellows to be impartial only in so far as it affords him a return equal to the services he contributes through the use of his capacities.

3.3 The activities of a perfect market exhibit mutual unconcern among the actors. And this conception, of persons as taking no interest in one another's interests, is fundamental not only to economics, but also to moral theory. For we agree with Kant that moral constraints must apply in the absence of other-directed interests, that indeed they must apply whatever preferences individuals may happen to have.[13] Where we differ with Kant is in recognizing an ideal of human interaction free from such constraints.

The assumption of mutual unconcern may be criticized because it is thought to be generally false, or because true or false, it is held to reflect an unduly nasty view of human nature, destructive not only of morality but of the ties that maintain any human society. But such criticism would misunderstand the role of the assumption. Of course persons exhibit concern for others, but their concern is

[13] See Immanuel Kant, *Groundwork of the Metaphysic of Morals*, 1785, in *Kants Gesammelte Schriften*, 22 vols. (Berlin, 1900–42), vol. 4, pp. 397–8, 444.

usually and quite properly particular and partial. It is neither unrealistic nor pessimistic to suppose that beyond the ties of blood and friendship, which are necessarily limited in their scope, human beings exhibit little positive fellow-feeling. Where personal relationships cease only a weak negative concern remains, manifesting itself perhaps in a general willingness to refrain from force and fraud if others do likewise, and in a particular willingness to offer assistance in extreme situations—for example, in the desire to aid victims of disasters, even at greater cost than would have been needed to prevent the disaster. But this limited concern is fully compatible with the view that each person should look after herself in the ordinary affairs of life, with a helping hand to, and from, friends and kin.

We treat utility functions as independent in analysing the possibility and characteristics of moral and social relationships in the limiting but practically important case in which particular ties among persons are either absent or, if present, too weak to sustain such relationships. One of the problems facing most human societies is the absence of any form of effective and mutually beneficial interaction among persons not linked by some particular bond. Thus the fundamental importance of kinship systems; one co-operates with one's kin because there is a bond of trust, of assurance that those with whom one interacts will not prove unmindful of one's interests. But other persons are potential enemies; the absence of any determinate bond implies a lack of concern that is thought to make any co-operative relationship impossible. Thus the traffic in women (to use Gayle Rubin's label for the practice documented by Lévi-Strauss), exemplified particularly in exogamous marriage in patrilocal societies, is needed to create a network of hostages as a safeguard against the eruption of the hostility latent among groups that are not kin.[14] The fundamental distinction between 'us' and 'them', between blood-brothers and strangers, has limited the scope of co-operation (and contributed to the subjection of women) among much of humankind. We invoke the assumption of mutual unconcern to determine if that limitation is an inescapable evil of the human condition.

The superiority of market society over its predecessors and rivals

[14] See Gayle Rubin, 'The Traffic in Women: Notes on the "Political Economy" of Sex', in Rayna R. Reiter (ed.), *Toward an Anthropology of Women* (New York, 1975), esp. pp. 173-7 As Rubin notes, the phrase 'the traffic in women' comes from Emma Goldman.

is manifest in its capacity to overcome this limitation and direct mutual unconcern to mutual benefit. If human interaction is structured by the condition of perfect competition, then no bond is required among those engaged in it, save those bonds that they freely create as each pursues his own gain. The impersonality of market society, which has been the object of wide criticism, and at the root of charges of *anomie* and alienation in modern life, is instead the basis of the fundamental liberation it affords. Men and women are freed from the need to establish more particular bonds, whether these be affective or coercive, in order to interact beneficially. The division between siblings and strangers disappears, and is not replaced by a new division in which subjects co-operate only so long as they remain under the watchful eye of Big Brother. Against the market background of mutual unconcern, particular human relationships of trust and affection may flourish on a voluntary basis. Those who hanker after the close-knit relationships of other and earlier forms of human society are in effect seeking to flee from the freedom to choose the persons in whose interests they will take an interest.

But liberation brings attendant dangers. Market society frees individuals from particular affective and coercive bonds. In real quasi-market societies there is a temptation, manifest both in thought and practice, to see the entire social world as falling within the scope of the market, and thus as free from all forms of constraint. On the one hand the ideal of a morally free zone is extended to embrace all social interaction, and on the other hand all human relationships are interpreted as self-interestedly contractual, lacking in interpersonal concern. Thus neither the need for moral and political constraints nor the possibility of genuinely affective human ties is sufficiently recognized.

As we have already insisted, one of our fundamental themes is that the morally free zone created by the market can arise only within a deeper moral framework. We shall show that moral constraint is not only compatible with mutual unconcern, but indeed rationally required given this unconcern and the typical structures of interaction. Thus we propose to defend the liberating idea of a society that imposes no affective bonds on its members, while distinguishing affective liberty from moral and political anarchy, and a free society from an all-embracing market.

Morality, as a system of rationally required constraints, is possible if the constraints are generated simply by the understanding that they make possible the more effective realization of one's interests, the greater fulfilment of one's preferences, whatever one's interests or preferences may be. One is not then able to escape morality by professing a lack of moral feeling or concern, or a lack of some other particular interest or attitude, because morality assumes no such affective basis. Hume believed the source of morality to lie in the sympathetic transmission of our feelings from one person to another.[15] But Kant, rightly, insisted that morality cannot depend on such particular psychological phenomena, however benevolent and humane their effect, and however universally they may be found.[16] The Kantian insistence that morality binds independently of the nature and content of our affections is thus at least partially captured in the insistence that it be based on the assumption of mutual unconcern.

From this standpoint the market is necessarily non-moral. For in the operation of a system of perfect competition there are no constraints that mutually unconcerned persons must or rationally would acknowledge. Constraints would be not merely pointless, but positively inimical to their interaction. The essence of the market is to afford an area of freedom rationalized by its optimality. The early defenders of *laissez-faire* may be forgiven for the enthusiasm with which they welcomed this idea, an enthusiasm which led them to apply it without considering how far perfect competition could be realized in human affairs. We do not suppose that actual quasi-market societies have realized, or could have realized, the ideal of free and optimal interaction. And while we may believe that those societies that have professed the market ideal have come closer to its realization than those that have pursued other objectives, yet in the absence of an adequate theory of the second-best we may not even assert this lesser claim with confidence.

In the next chapters we shall consider interaction among persons in circumstances that preclude the harmony of equilibrium and optimality under free activity which the market affords. We shall turn to contexts structured by the Prisoner's Dilemma, and there, without abandoning the assumption of mutual unconcern, we shall find a place for morality as a set of constraints on the pursuit of

[15] See Hume, *Treatise*, ii. i. xi, pp. 316–20, and iii. iii. i, pp. 575–8.

[16] See, in addition to reference in note 13 above, Kant, *Critique of Practical Reason*, in *Kants Gesammelte Schriften*, vol. 5, pp. 22–6.

maximum utility that every rational person must acknowledge. But in preserving mutual unconcern, it may seem that we are ignoring a second danger attendant on the liberation from affective bonds that it affords.

We have already referred to this danger, in noting that in real quasi-market societies there is a tendency to interpret all human relationships as lacking in interpersonal concern. A society that frees individuals from the need to develop affective bonds in order to engage in social interaction may encourage its members to conceive themselves as unrelated individual atoms lacking the potential for developing genuinely affective ties. Market man is a maximizer of non-tuistically based utilities; our account, it may seem, gives market man a morality but denies him any other-directed concern. The particular affective ties that we acknowledged at the beginning of this subsection may be only the residue of an image of human beings that we have rejected.

The critic need not deny that individuality, except as the privilege of a numerically insignificant élite, has emerged only in quasi-market societies, to argue that nevertheless this individuality proves self-destructive, so that the liberation achieved by a society that encourages mutual unconcern ends in alienation. But we have hope of a happier ending, and we shall conclude our study with a sketch of the liberal individual who, we shall suggest, enjoys the free affectivity that a society based on purely rational constraints allows. With this promissory note we leave mutual unconcern. But before we move on from market interaction, we should briefly examine the flaws in two classic theories that would reject the defence of the market as a morally free zone that we have offered: utilitarianism and Marxism.

4.1 The utilitarian relates morality to society as we relate rationality to the individual; morality is identified with *collective* maximization. The moral actor seeks to maximize a measure which we shall call *welfare*, defined as a strictly increasing function of all individual utilities. In our present discussion we need no more precise specification of the welfare function. Utilitarians generally treat it as an additive function of individual utilities, assuming a measure of individual preference with interpersonal significance. But nothing in our argument turns on the possibility of such an additive measure.

Maximization of the welfare function must yield an optimal outcome. But there is no reason to expect that this outcome, which we shall call the *welfare optimum*, will coincide with the optimal equilibrium that would be reached through the operation of a perfectly competitive market. Indeed the two cannot always coincide, since the welfare optimum depends only on the individual utility functions and the technology of production, whereas the market outcome depends also on the initial distribution of the factors of production. Different initial endowments yield different market outcomes without affecting the welfare optimum.

The utilitarian is therefore led to reject the outcome of perfect competition. If the utilitarian principle, requiring maximization of the welfare function, is applied in a market society, there must, it seems, be a redistribution of products from that realized in market equilibrium. But as we have shown, such a redistribution can satisfy neither our criteria for rational interaction nor our conception of morality. The utilitarian, in redistributing goods, necessarily imposes costs on some persons in addition to those that have fully paid for the benefits they received in free interaction, and confers benefits on others who have not paid their costs. A society that maximizes welfare thus creates free-riders and parasites.

Utilitarianism and *laissez-faire* economics were products of the same revolution in social enquiry. But the two theories soon found themselves in conflict. The utilitarian, who began as the ally of the economist in criticizing the political and moral constraints still present in the society of his day, turned against the new market society and became the advocate of the welfare state—the state that redistributes goods to achieve the welfare optimum. The utilitarian has not been fully successful in his advocacy. And this is hardly surprising, for the attempt to marry the welfare state to the free market is in principle incoherent, involving the simultaneous application of two incompatible standards of assessment. The utilitarian looks to the outcome, but as David Winch insists, 'We cannot judge a perfectly competitive system by the equity of the outcome, for the essence of the system is that distributive justice is an attribute of the inputs of the system, not the outputs.'[17]

Why then should the utilitarian not shift the point of his concern from outputs to inputs? Why should he not seek to reconcile the maximization of welfare with acceptance of the operation of the market by applying the utilitarian principle to the determination of

[17] Winch, p. 97

the initial distribution of the factors of production? This is precisely what is implicit in John Stuart Mill's very brief account of the utilitarian basis of rights. 'To have a right, then, is, I conceive, to have something which society ought to defend me in the possession of. If the objector goes on to ask why it ought, I can give him no other reason than general utility.'[18] We may interpret Mill as saying that each person's factor endowment, those things that he may use as he sees fit in market activity, and which therefore society must protect from the forcible or fraudulent intervention of others, are to be determined by considering what distribution of factors will best serve general utility, or in our terminology, best serve to maximize welfare.

In this brief passage Mill seeks to institute a major conceptual shift in our understanding of rights (which for present purposes we may identify with factor endowments). To reduce rights to general utility or welfare is, it may seem, to mistake the core of the conception of right—of that to which one is entitled and welfare be damned! Rights seem to carve out a moral space for each individual which appeals to the maximization of welfare deny. But we may now see that this is too simplistic a criticism of Mill's position; it does not take into account what he is trying to accomplish.

Mill applies the welfare function, or more specifically the greatest happiness principle, directly to the factor endowments of individuals. He claims that persons should have those rights that lead them to interact in such a way that the market outcome is also the welfare optimum. As we have noted, given fixed production and demand functions, the market equilibrium is determined by the factor endowments. We are therefore to begin with the welfare function, apply it to determine the possible outcome of market interaction that would maximize welfare, and then work backwards to determine the set of initial rights that would yield that outcome. The welfare function is taken as the independent variable and individual rights or factor endowments as the dependent variables.

Mill's account alters but does not abandon the traditional understanding of rights. An individual's rights, however conceived, must afford him a moral space within which he may engage in market activity. Mill's account fully recognizes and allows this. Having solved the problem of relating initial endowments to the welfare optimum, we may not then meddle further with these endowments

[18] Mill, ch. v, para. 25.

or with the market interaction proceeding from them by applying the utilitarian principle yet again to the market outcome. Winch's insistence that the perfectly competitive system not be judged by its outputs is respected. We must allow interaction to proceed from the assigned rights if we are to claim that the outcome satisfies the requirements both of rational interaction and of welfare maximization.

The welfare state appears now not as the agent of redistribution upsetting the rational market outcome in the name of an irrational moral ideal, but rather as the determinant of one of the givens in market activity. There is no basis for criticizing the activity of the state, where this is limited to the determination of factor endowments, from within the market itself, or from the standpoint of the individuals engaged in market interaction. The state does not interfere with the operation of the market, but simply sets its conditions. We noted at the conclusion of 3.1 that market arrangements are fair if and only if they result from fair initial conditions. Utilitarianism provides the standard of fairness. The maximization of welfare is reconciled with the operation of the perfectly competitive market.

But before we join the utilitarian celebration in this happy prospect, we must turn to certain complications in the determination of factor endowments that have no counterpart in Mill's simple account of rights, but which become evident once we recall the other elements which contribute to the market outcome—the production functions, reflecting technology, and the demand function or the individual utility functions on which it rests. In a changing and dynamic economy there is a continuing and essentially unpredictable change in the production functions. Technology is not static, and market competition accelerates its growth. This implies that a fixed assignment of factor endowments will not continue over time to yield the same market outcome. Technological changes alter the productivity of the factors in unpredictable ways, and hence alter the final rights to commodities. A distribution of factors that under a given technology yields relatively equal benefits to persons with different endowments may, under technological change, yield highly unequal benefits to those persons. It is unlikely that both outcomes can maximize welfare.

We may identify certain types of change as having characteristic effects, even though other types are less predictable. An example, discussed by Winch, may be illuminating to the reader unfamiliar with the economic literature.[19] Rising productivity in agriculture depresses the utility levels of the owners of land and livestock, and of agrarian labourers, because of the relative inelasticity of demand for agricultural products. On the other hand, rising productivity in manufacturing tends to increase the utility levels of factory owners and of industrial workers, because of the relatively high elasticity of demand for manufactured products. In so far as individuals come to correlate utility levels, or commodity distributions, with factor endowments, and to suppose that their right to the latter affords a correlative right to the former, changes in technology that bring about rising productivity in both agriculture and manufacturing will have adverse effects on social stability, as farmers find themselves in an increasingly less favourable position relative to industrial owners and workers, and suppose that they are being denied their just rewards. This problem has constituted an enduring theme in American history since the late nineteenth century.

The welfare economist may try to cope with the problem of industrial boom and agrarian depression by measures that artificially inflate the value of factor endowments in agriculture—farm price supports, limits on production, and the like. Such measures bring about an ever-increasing misallocation of social resources, and an ever-increasing overall inefficiency in production given real demand. And these measures, correctly perceived as upsetting the effects of market interaction, are then resented by the industrial sector of the economy, although this resentment may be relatively weak because it involves a slower rate of gain rather than actual loss. Efficiency can be restored only by reallocating resources, including persons, from agriculture to manufacturing. In the absence of welfare-state interference this reallocation will occur under economic pressures, restoring efficiency at severe short-term costs to the individuals displaced. And this cost they may be especially unwilling to bear because they see, rightly, that their way of life is being undermined. The market is not a respecter of life-styles.

In order to minimize inefficiency in a manner compatible with maximizing welfare, it is necessary to change factor endowments—to reallocate rights. But this undermines the fixity that rights must have. Once we recognize that to maintain the correct utilitarian relationship between factor endowments and the distribution of

[19] See Winch, p. 193.

commodities we must continually adjust those endowments in the light of technological change, we must conclude that so-called rights in a dynamic utilitarian society must be evanescent.

Changes in the demand function, reflecting changed individual preferences, have the same consequence. Certain factors increase or decrease in usefulness as demand changes. Typically, changes in demand accompany changes in technology—the classic example, of demand for the services of blacksmiths, illustrates this. Thus we must replace our initial picture of fixed endowments determined by their maximization of welfare by a new picture, in which endowments constitute only a temporary barrier against direct redistribution, but are themselves subject to adjustment as changes occur in production or exchange or demand.

This new picture should give us pause before we join the utilitarian celebration. Under static conditions basing rights on the utilitarian principle may seem acceptable. But the speciousness of this acceptability becomes apparent when we examine the dynamics of a society in which rights become subject to continual readjustment. It becomes apparent that, to quote Winch once more, 'The rights to factors are then vested in the government and their association with individuals is a temporary matter of convenience.'[20] Although this vesting is implicit in the utilitarian account, it is concealed if the changes in rights resulting from economic development are ignored.

Utilitarianism denies to individuals in society the freedom enjoyed by Robinson Crusoe, who was able to direct her capacities to the service of her preferences. For the utilitarian supposes that even a person's natural attributes, her physical and mental capacities, are vested in her only in so far as this proves socially convenient. It may be claimed that welfare is almost certainly maximized if each person is given a right to what she can naturally make use of, and what no one else can use in her absence—to what we have called each person's basic endowment. For it may seem evident that the efficient use of these capacities is achieved by making the person with natural or direct access to them also the rightholder. Imagine a scheme such as *demoktesis*, as sketched by Robert Nozick, in which each is owned by all, so that the right to the use of each person's physical and mental capacities is divided and sold in equal portions to every member of society.[21] Under this scheme the costs of decision-making

[20] Ibid., p. 99.

[21] See R. Nozick, *Anarchy, State, and Utopia* (New York, 1974), pp. 280–90.

would rapidly become prohibitive, so that we might expect the consortium which owned me to agree to empower me to make the relevant decisions about the best use of my talents and powers. Or at least, I should be allowed to make the lower-level decisions. But were I the world's ablest heart surgeon my executive right might not be so willingly granted. We must expect the utilitarian to welcome the idea, suggested by John Rawls, that the talents of the naturally most favoured are to constitute a common asset for the benefit of all.[22]

If each person's identification with her basic endowment is not arbitrary, as we claimed in 3.2, then the utilitarian determination of each person's rights to factors on the basis of welfare-maximization denies free activity to the individual. We reject, therefore, the utilitarian attempt to reconcile the maximization of welfare with the operation of the perfectly competitive market, as providing an unacceptable way of determining individual factor endowments—as indeed denying each person her basic endowment of physical and mental capacities. But utilitarianism is a Protean theory, and we shall find it opposing our argument again, when we consider the nature of the moral constraints to which persons must rationally agree.

4.2 Marxism offers a direct challenge to our account of the operation of the market which, if sustained, would refute the claim that market interaction is impartial. For the Marxist insists that private ownership of the means of production, a fundamental presupposition of the market, is necessarily exploitative. The argument is simple.[23] Under private ownership, nothing can prevent the emergence of a situation in which some individuals (capitalists) own the means that others (workers) need if they are to engage in productive activity. These others are then compelled to sell their labour power to the owners of the material means that production requires. This sale is exploitative. For the essential and distinctive characteristic of labour is that it produces more than the cost of its own production; labour thus reproduces itself and in addition produces what in Marxist thought is called *surplus value*. Now labour power is bought and sold, as any other commodity, at a price sufficient to cover its cost of production. Hence the buyer of labour power necessarily receives the surplus value, since he pays the

[22] See Rawls, *A Theory of Justice*, pp. 101–2.

[23] See Marx, *Capital*, vol. i, ch. vii, sect. 2, pp. 166–80.

worker a wage equal to the cost of producing the labour power sold, and receives a price equal to the value of what that labour power produces. The market systematically favours the buyer of labour power over the seller; hence its operation is in principle partial to the capitalist.

In the form in which Marxists present this argument it depends on the labour theory of value, which holds that the value of a commodity is determined by the quantity of socially necessary labour required for its production.[24] This is of course incompatible with our identification of value with utility. But we may discuss the claim that surplus value goes to the buyer rather than to the seller of labour without first refuting the Marxist theory of value. For Marxists on the whole agree that whatever the value of a commodity, its market price is determined by supply and demand. So we may simply ask whether the seller of labour power is prejudicially affected by the terms of sale, whether the price she receives for her labour power affords systematic advantage to the buyer.

Let us begin from the claim that the market price of what labour produces is greater than the cost of its own production. Suppose that labour power sells at a price equal to the cost of producing it. Then obviously there will be a demand for more labour, since buyers profit from the difference between what they pay for labour power and what they receive for its product. This demand will continue until the price received for the marginal product of an additional unit of labour power is equal to the marginal cost of producing that additional unit. But at this point the wage—the price paid for labour power—is equal to the price received for its product. There is no surplus value when the supply of labour is brought into equilibrium with the demand for it. The worker receives a wage equal to the marginal difference her labour power adds to the total product.

The Marxist avoids this conclusion by denying that supply and demand come to equilibrium. He insists that the buyer of labour power is able to keep the wage below the price he receives for its product because the supply of labour exceeds the demand for it, since there is always the 'reserve army of unemployed'.[25] But we have just shown that if the wage is below the price received for the

[24] See ibid., vol. i, ch. i, sect. 1, p. 6.

[25] Frederick Engels, 'The Housing Question', in Karl Marx and Frederick Engels, *Selected Works*, 2 vols. (Moscow, 1951), vol. 1, p. 527. The usual phrase is 'industrial reserve army', as in Marx, *Capital*, vol. i, ch. xxv, sect. 3, p. 642.

product of labour, then there will be an effective demand for more labour—demand will exceed supply. The Marxist is thus caught in a contradiction. The buyer of labour power is able to extract surplus value—to pay a wage lower than the price he receives for the product of labour—only if the supply of labour exceeds the demand. But if there is surplus value to extract, this creates a demand for labour in excess of the existing supply. Or to put the matter another way, if the supply of labour exceeds the demand for it, this can only be because the cost of producing labour exceeds the price that can be received for its product. So there can be surplus value only if supply exceeds demand but if supply exceeds demand there can be no surplus value.

The operation of the perfectly competitive market must bring about an equilibrium between the supply of labour power and the demand for it, if—as Marxists suppose—labour power is a commodity brought into existence by the market. At equilibrium, there can be no surplus value for the buyer to extract and hence no exploitation of the seller. Now this proves nothing about the operation of imperfectly competitive markets. It proves nothing about a situation in which labour power comes into being as a by-product of other activities in which people engage for reasons quite other than meeting the market demand for labour. This could give rise to a permanent excess of labour power from which the owner of the means of production might benefit. And this might raise questions about the propriety of factor endowments that put some persons in a position to benefit from this over-supply of labour.

The appearance of market exploitation may be brought about by the very real exploitation actually occasioned by non-market features of society, or by features, such as the initial distribution of factors, taken as given in market interaction. And this may help to explain why the Marxist argument has convinced so many people, even though it is in fact incoherent and misdirected. But if it is a misdirected argument, which has nothing to do with the operation of perfectly competitive markets, then the Marxist theory of surplus value and exploitation serves only as a smoke-screen, concealing the very real exploitation that actual social arrangements, including of course those in 'Marxist' societies, may embody.

V

CO-OPERATION: BARGAINING AND JUSTICE

1.1 Reason, which increases the costs of natural interaction among human beings, offers not only a remedy for the ills it creates, but also the prospect of new benefits achieved mutually, through co-operation. Where the invisible hand fails to direct each person, mindful only of her own gain, to promote the benefit of all, co-operation provides a visible hand. In this chapter we begin our examination of co-operation as the rational response to market failure.

Where market interaction, with its pre-established harmony between equilibrium and optimum, is beyond good and evil, and natural interaction, in the presence of free-riders and parasites, degenerates into force and fraud, co-operative interaction is the domain of justice. Justice is the disposition not to take advantage of one's fellows, not to seek free goods or to impose uncompensated costs, provided that one supposes others similarly disposed. We shall show that in satisfying the conditions of practical rationality, co-operation ensures the elimination of the free-ridership and parasitism endemic to our natural condition, so that we may identify justice with the rational disposition to co-operative behaviour. Thus we find ourselves in agreement with the most influential contemporary theorist of justice, John Rawls, when he says, 'The circumstances of justice may be described as the normal conditions under which human cooperation is both possible and necessary.'[1]

David Hume, whose account of the circumstances of justice is followed by Rawls, supposes that the need for co-operation arises from the conjunction of scarcity, characterizing our 'outward circumstances', and a bias in favour of the self, characterizing our 'natural temper'.[2] The mutual unconcern presupposed by the market is an extreme form of self-bias, although the structure of market interaction makes it an innocuous one. If nature were to provide in

[1] J. Rawls, *A Theory of Justice* (Cambridge, Mass., 1971), p. 126.

[2] Hume, *Treatise*, iii. ii. ii, pp. 486–8; see also *Enquiry*, iii. i, pp. 183-6.

abundance the goods needed to satisfy our desires, or if benevolence were to lead each person to regard her fellows' concerns as her own, there would be no free-riders or parasites to be restrained by the visible hand of co-operation. All would seek naturally to co-ordinate their actions for the common good, without putting forward opposed claims to the fruits of their endeavours, which justice must resolve.

But scarcity and self-bias are not sufficient warrant for co-operative interaction. Were the scarcity faced by each person not aggravated by the presence of her fellows, then however self-biased she might be, her activities would bear little relation to those of others, and neither conflict nor co-operation would result. And could this scarcity not be alleviated by joint activities, then the domain of justice would extend only to the avoidance of mutually destructive conflicts, and not to the co-operative provision of mutual benefits. Thus among the circumstances necessary to justice we must include the variability of scarcity. The sources of satisfaction and dissatisfaction are not in fixed supply, so that by appropriate interaction overall costs may be lessened, and overall benefits increased.

Yet strictly speaking, it is not the fact of variable supply, but awareness of the fact, which is important. This awareness has both its negative and positive effects. On the one hand we become aware of each other as competitors for scarce goods, and this awareness exacerbates our competition, increasing our costs. It is to this awareness that we refer when we say that reason adds to the disadvantages of nature. On the other hand we become aware of each other as potential co-operators in the production of an increased supply of goods, and this awareness enables us to realize new benefits. Thus we note also that reason offers advantages unobtainable in nature.

Different theorists vary in the emphasis which they place on these aspects of our awareness. Thomas Hobbes focuses on the effect of recognizing one's fellows as competitors.[3] He argues that given scarcity and total mutual unconcern, each must view all other persons as in at least potential competition for the goods that she needs for survival or for greater well-being. But this creates in each person an actual preference for dominating her fellows; if she is able to establish her dominance now, then she may expect to be more

[3] See Hobbes, *Leviathan*, ch. 13, pp. 60–2.

successful in any future struggle for scarce goods. In this way potential conflict is converted into actual hostility, leading to the war of every man against every man, a war from which everyone must expect to suffer, yet from which no one dare abstain. To avoid this unending war each must agree to constrain her behaviour, provided others similarly agree, to the end that all may live peaceably. Justice, for Hobbes, lies in adherence to such agreement.

Hobbes's account reveals with stark clarity the role of reason in adding to the costs of natural interaction. For it is only a reasoning being, seeking to maximize her utility, who will adopt a pre-emptive strategy in interacting with her fellows. Those who are unaware of the prospect of bettering themselves by imposing costs on others will not find themselves in the peculiarly unpleasant condition which Hobbes describes. But Hobbes's account equally reveals the role of reason in enabling us to overcome this condition, for reason suggests the 'convenient Articles of Peace', agreement to which leads us out of the natural condition of humankind and eventually into society.[4]

Little in Hobbes's argument suggests a more positive role for co-operation. We are aware of each other as competitors, and so we come to co-operate in order to avoid mutually destructive conflict, but we are less aware of each other as potential sources of mutual benefit. Indeed, the world described by Hobbes resembles in some respects that which is said (with what accuracy I know not) to obtain among those South Pacific islanders, the Dobu.[5] Since it is the idea and not the reality which concerns us, we may ignore anthropological data which may or may not confirm our story, and suppose that the Dobu believe that the world offers only a fixed supply of the goods they treasure—primarily yams. The more yams in my garden, the fewer in yours. There is no place in the Dobuan scheme of things for co-operation directed at an increase of benefits, for more yams cannot be grown. At most, the costs of Hobbesian conflict can be avoided or alleviated. For even if each person is bent on acquiring, by the appropriate magical devices, the yams in her neighbours' gardens, it may still be better for each if no one seeks to pre-empt her fellows by designs, magical or otherwise, on their lives.

The Dobuan world may have its sophisticated defenders. Indeed, if we consider interaction among social classes rather than indivi-

[4] Ibid., ch. 13, p. 63.

[5] See Ruth Benedict, *Patterns of Culture* (Boston and New York, 1934), pp. 139–40, 146–8.

duals, the Marxists are foremost among them, for they suppose that in a class-based society, the more yams for the bourgeoisie, the fewer for the proletariat. And this leads some Marxists, insufficiently mindful of Hobbes, to deny the possibility of co-operation and the relevance of justice in class-based societies. But we shall suppose that the Dobuan view of the world is false. And given variable supply we may be aware of others as potential co-operators in increased production. It is this awareness which is emphasized by Hume and Rawls.

But recognition of the possibilities of increased production implicit in the idea of variable supply is also the basis of the market. And Hume and Rawls are insufficiently mindful of the role of the market in limiting the need for co-operation. Market interaction takes place under conditions of variable supply among persons who are mutually unconcerned. But given perfect competition they have no use for co-operative interaction as a visible hand, since the optimality of the market outcome excludes any alternative that would reduce overall costs or increase total benefits. Thus among the circumstances of justice, in addition to awareness of variable scarcity and individual bias, we must include recognition of the presence of externalities. Justice is concerned with both the inefficiencies occasioned by the imposition of costs without the provision of corresponding benefits, and those occasioned by the failure to provide benefits due to the inability to recover costs. Since externalities presuppose variable supply, we may then say that the fundamental circumstances of justice, those features of the human situation that give rise to co-operation, are awareness of externalities in our environment, and awareness of self-bias in our character.

1.2 When the market fails, each person, seeking to maximize her utility given the strategies she expects others to choose, fails to maximize her utility given the utilities those others receive. The equilibrium outcome of mutually utility-maximizing responses is not optimal. The dilemma of strategic rationality, posed starkly in the structure of the Prisoner's Dilemma, comes to possess our interactions, turning them away from the ends we seek. It can be exorcized only by changing the mode of interaction. Heretofore we have supposed that each person forms expectations about the choices of others to which she responds in choosing her own strategy, but that she considers only the costs and benefits to herself in making that choice. Externalities, unchosen third-party costs and benefits, are ignored. And so in many situations the outcome brought about by the independent choices of those interacting is sub-optimal. In order to take effective account of externalities, each person must choose her strategy to bring about a particular outcome determined by prior agreement among those interacting. This agreement, if rational, will ensure optimality. It may of course be implicit rather than explicit, an understanding or convention rather than a contract. But it is not a mere fiction, since it gives rise to a new mode of interaction, which we identify as co-operation. In nature each person faces a separate strategic problem which must be solved in choosing her strategy. As co-operators, all persons face a common strategic problem which must be solved to determine every individual's choice of strategy.

As a preliminary characterization, to be modified in the next subsection, let us say that in co-operative interaction the primary object of choice is a set of strategies, one for each person. If co-operation is voluntary, as we shall assume unless we explicitly state otherwise, then each individual participates in, or agrees to, this primary choice. Since the product of a set of strategies, one for each interacting person, is an outcome, we may also say that in co-operative interaction the object of agreement is an outcome, which then determines each person's choice of strategy. In this chapter we shall determine the conditions for rational co-operative choice, or rational agreement on an outcome.

We have already stated one such condition: the object of rational co-operative choice must be an optimal outcome. We noted in Chapter III that an outcome may be considered either as a product of strategies or as set of utilities. We should expect that if each person selects her strategy independently of the others, as in natural interaction or in the market, then the first of these conceptions would take precedence. But if each selects her strategy as a result of agreement with the others, then since each in reaching agreement will be concerned with her utility, not her strategy, we should expect that the second conception would come to the fore. Now this suggests that in non-co-operative interaction the core rationality property is equilibrium, whereas in co-operative interaction the core rationality property is optimality. The three conditions on rational interaction introduced in Chapter III are therefore to be read in one way for the non-co-operative interaction of nature and the market, and in another way for co-operative interaction. Condition A, that each person's choice must be a rational response to the choices she expects the others to make, must be read as requiring a utility-maximizing response in non-co-operative interaction, and as requiring an optimizing response in co-operation. Or in other words, in the absence of agreement on an outcome or set of strategies, it is rational for each person to seek to maximize her utility given the strategies she expects the others to choose, whereas in the context of agreement it is rational for each to seek an optimal outcome given the agreed strategies of the others. The first part of this proposition is a direct corollary of the identification of practical rationality with individual utility-maximization, but the corollary may seem so direct that the second part of the proposition is refuted. Our task is to show that this is not so, that co-operation is a rational mode of interaction.

In the two preceding paragraphs we have identified two quite distinct problems. Suppose we are to agree on an outcome or set of strategies; under what conditions is our agreement rational? This is the first problem; it concerns what we may call the internal rationality of co-operation, the rational way of making a co-operative choice. We shall solve this problem by finding a principle that rationalizes agreement in the way that the principle of expected utility-maximization rationalizes individual choice.

Under what conditions is it rational to agree to an outcome or set of strategies and act on that agreement? This is the second problem; it concerns the external rationality of co-operation. We must show when it is rational to act co-operatively rather than non-co-operatively. In resolving the first problem we take co-operation for granted; in turning to the second problem, we call co-operation into question and demand its rationale as a mode of interaction. The problems are of course related, but in this chapter we shall be concerned with the second only in so far as it bears on the first. Our resolution of it will come in Chapters VI and VII.

A third problem concerns the morality of co-operation. Under what conditions is co-operative interaction fair or impartial? And here, as with the market, we may distinguish the operation of co-operative practices from their conditions. In this chapter we shall examine the impartiality of the operation of co-operative practices and institutions in the light of our account of the internal rationality of co-operation, asking whether the principle of rational co-operative choice is an impartial principle. Thus there is a significant parallel between the argument of this chapter and that of the preceding one; we must exhibit the rationality and impartiality of co-operative interaction just as we exhibited the rationality and impartiality of market interaction. But we shall find that co-operation does not create a morally free zone; rather it requires moral constraints on maximizing behaviour.

In the next subsection we shall clarify the characteristics of co-operative interaction, showing how it can extend the range of available strategies and of (expected) outcomes. In section 2 we discuss alternative approaches to determining the conditions that co-operative choice must satisfy to be rational. In section 3 we set out in detail our own answer; we develop a principle for rational agreement. And in section 4 we examine the impartiality of rational co-operation.

1.3 Ernie and Bert want to meet. Ernie would prefer that they meet at the library, Bert at the cinema. Each is indifferent as to where he is should they fail to meet. So that we may provide an interval measure of their preferences, let us suppose that Ernie is indifferent between meeting at the cinema, and a lottery with equal chances of meeting at the library and not meeting, and that Bert is indifferent between meeting at the library, and a lottery with an equal chance of meeting at the cinema and not meeting. Calculating their utilities in accordance with the method of II.3.2, we arrive at this matrix representation of their situation:

	Bert goes to the	
	library	cinema
Ernie goes to the library	1, 1/2	0, 0
Ernie goes to the cinema	0, 0	1/2, 1

There are exactly two optimal outcomes; both must go to the same place. These outcomes are also in equilibrium. Unfortunately, the symmetry of the situation makes it impossible for Ernie and Bert to co-ordinate on one of these outcomes using Zeuthen's principle, as Victor and Valerie were able to do in III.2.2. If each chooses to go to his favoured meeting place they will fail to meet. If each, baffled, decides where to go by tossing a coin (that is adopting the mixed strategy which assigns a probability of 1/2 to each of his possible actions), then the expected outcome will be a lottery with a probability of 1/4 that they meet at the library, 1/4 that they meet at the cinema, and 1/2 that they do not meet, and the expected utility to each will be 3/8.

But suppose Ernie and Bert adopt a co-operative approach to

their interaction. Then a whole new range of possibilities opens up. For they can make a single, joint strategy choice rather than independent strategy choices. And the symmetry of their situation singles out a unique joint strategy, assigning a probability of 1/2 to both going to the library and 1/2 to both going to the cinema. Instead of each tossing a coin, they toss but one coin, agreeing that both will abide by the result. The expected outcome is then a lottery with a probability of 1/2 that they meet at the library and 1/2 that they meet at the cinema, and the expected utility to each is 3/4. This outcome is optimal, as indeed is the outcome of any joint mixed strategy that consists of a lottery with both going to the library and both going to the cinema as the only prizes. But none of these strategies, and so none of these outcomes, was available to Ernie and Bert in non-co-operative interaction.

As this example illustrates, co-operation may extend the range of strategies and outcomes. (It does not always do so; Noreen and Norman (III.2.2) could not extend their prospects by co-operating.) Let us define a *joint pure strategy* as the product of the members of a set of pure strategies, one for each person involved in interaction. A joint pure strategy is then simply a possible outcome (where we exclude merely expected outcomes). A *joint mixed strategy* is then a lottery with joint pure strategies, or possible outcomes, as prizes. An expected outcome is then simply a joint mixed strategy, or a lottery over possible outcomes. In co-operative interaction every lottery over possible outcomes determines an expected outcome. This need not be the case in non-co-operative interaction, where the set of expected outcomes is a subset (sometimes proper, sometimes improper) of the set of lotteries over possible outcomes.

In extending the range of strategies from individual to joint, we have implicitly altered our previous characterization of co-operative interaction, as having a set of strategies, one for each person, as the object of agreement. We should now say that the primary object of choice or agreement is a joint strategy. Since a set of strategies, one for each person, may always be represented by a joint strategy, but not conversely, this new characterization broadens our initial conception of co-operation.

We may conveniently represent any co-operative interaction involving only two persons in graphic form. We let the horizontal axis represent the utility scale of one person and the vertical axis represent the utility scale of the other. Each possible outcome is represented by taking its utilities as co-ordinates. The closed, convex figure obtained by joining the points representing the possible outcomes then represents the range of lotteries over possible outcomes, or expected outcomes. Each point on or within this figure corresponds to an expected outcome, and each expected outcome corresponds to such a point. We call this figure the *outcome-space*. The upper right bound of this space then represents the range of optimal outcomes. Figures 1 and 2 illustrate two of our examples—Ernie and Bert, and Jane and Brian from Chapter III. We also show in Fig. 2 the point representing the unique outcome in equilibrium; its non-optimality is evident.

Although graphic treatment becomes difficult, this mode of representation may be extended to co-operative interactions involving any number of persons by employing an n-dimensional utility space with one dimension for each person's utilities. The outcome-space remains a closed, convex figure—although in n-dimensions rather than two—and its upper bound, generally n-1-dimensional, represents the range of optimal outcomes.

Although we shall not pursue a mathematical treatment here, we may sketch the formal problem that we seek to solve informally in this chapter. We want to define a choice function, which we call the *co-operation function*. Its domain is a set of outcome-spaces. Its values are the members of a set of points in utility space. The idea, of

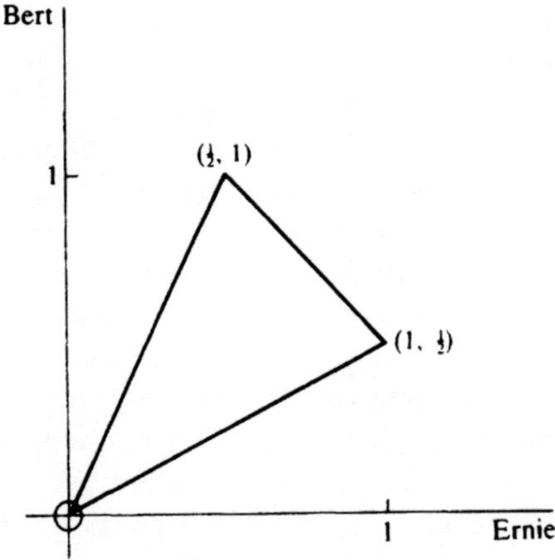

Figure 1

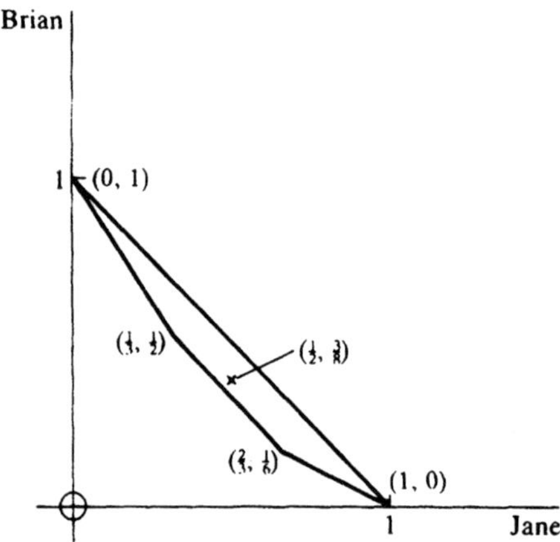

Figure 2

course, is that for an outcome-space, representing the outcomes of a possible co-operative interaction, the function determines a point, representing the particular outcome that determines the co-operators' joint strategy. One condition that we should want to impose on the co-operation function is that its domain be complete, including every possible outcome-space. A second condition is that for every member of its domain, the function determine a unique point as its value. We may specify this more closely; the point must be included in the outcome-space (so that it represents an outcome of the interaction) and indeed must fall on the upper bound of the outcome-space (so that it represents an optimal outcome). These are only necessary conditions, too weak to determine a unique function. We shall pursue the task of stating, although only informally, a sufficiently strong set of conditions in section 3. But we shall begin by considering three ways in which one might propose to arrive at a co-operation function.

2.1 Several persons are to agree on an outcome which is then to be brought about by a joint strategy determining each person's action. Under what conditions is their agreement rational? Individual choice is rational in so far as it is utility-maximizing. Is there an analogue to utility-maximization for agreement or co-operative choice? Since it is to be voluntary, it must reflect, and in some sense reflect equally, the preferences of each person. A first proposal, therefore, would be that we derive, from the individual preference orderings of the co-operators, a social preference ordering. We then define a measure of social preference, and identify rational co-operative choice with the maximization of this measure.

The reader familiar with the literature of social choice will recognize the problem facing this proposal. Kenneth Arrow has demonstrated that it is not possible to derive a social preference ordering from every configuration of individual preference orderings without violating one of the following conditions:[6]

(1) If each individual prefers outcome X to outcome Y, then society prefers X to Y;
(2) There is no individual whose preferences are automatically society's preferences, whatever the preferences of the others;
(3) Social preference over any outcomes depends only on individual preferences over those outcomes.

Since we require that co-operative choice select an optimal outcome, we cannot reject condition (1). Since we require that co-operative choice reflect the preferences of each person, we cannot reject condition (2). And since on this proposal social preference is based on and only on individual preferences, we surely must require it to be based on relevant individual preferences, so that we cannot reject condition (3). Hence we cannot derive a social preference ordering for every configuration of individual preference orderings and the first suggestion would seem to be a non-starter.

But let us not proceed too hastily. We suppose that an interval measure, utility, can be defined over the preferences of each co-operator. A modified proposal, then, is that we derive, from these interval measures, a social interval measure, and identify rational co-operative choice with the maximization of this measure. However, this modified proposal does not enable us to escape from Arrow's demonstration. Recall that we have introduced no basis for comparing the utilities of different persons. Given interpersonal incomparability, Arrow's demonstration may be reproduced for the problem of defining a social interval measure on the basis of individual interval measures.[7]

A more promising modification is suggested by the formal state-

[6] See K. J. Arrow, 'Values and Collective Decision-Making', in P. Laslett and W. G. Runciman (eds.), *Philosophy, Politics and Society*, 3rd series (Oxford, 1967), pp. 225–6.

[7] See R. D. Luce and H. Raiffa, *Games and Decisions* (New York, 1957), pp. 344–5.

ment of our problem in the preceding section. We seek a function that determines an outcome for every outcome-space, or in effect, an outcome for every set of outcomes on the basis of the individual utilities assigned to the members of the set. Why not bypass a social preference ordering or social interval measure and go directly from the individual measures to the chosen outcome? This may seem to be a dodge, but it is a dodge that works; we may derive a social choice from every configuration of individual preference orderings and satisfy these conditions:

(1′) If each individual prefers outcome X to outcome Y, then society does not choose Y if X is available;
(2′) There is no individual whose utility is automatically maximized by society's choices, whatever the utilities of the others;
(3′) Social choice over any outcomes depends only on individual utilities for those outcomes.

The revised proposal, then, is that we derive, from the individual preference orderings of the co-operators, a social choice, by a function including all configurations of individual orderings in its domain and satisfying conditions (1′), (2′), and (3′). But the only plausible way to satisfy our conditions is to include, in the social choice, the entire range of optimal outcomes.[8] Rather than picking out a single outcome, we find ourselves with no basis for selecting among those that survived our previous statement of necessary conditions on co-operative choice.

But again, let us not proceed too hastily. In the literature of social choice, lotteries are generally ignored; outcomes are treated as possible outcomes, excluding expected outcomes that are lotteries with possible outcomes as prizes. Since we have no objection to lotteries, why should we not suppose that, if our function for determining social choice selects all optimal outcomes, then operationally it selects the lottery that assigns equal probability to all of the optimal possible outcomes, and which must itself be an expected outcome? There is an immediate problem with this new proposal; the expected outcome determined by a lottery that assigns equal probability to each of the optimal possible outcomes need not be

[8] See discussion in A. K. Sen, *Collective Choice and Social Welfare* (San Francisco, 1970), pp. 47–50. Our claim is stronger than anything defended by Sen, and relies in part on work in progress.

itself optimal.[9] Perhaps a further modification would accommodate this problem. But since our concern is not to examine formal issues in the theory of social choice, we shall not pursue this here. We have shown that, despite Arrow's notorious demonstration of the impossibility of deriving a social preference ordering from individual preference orderings, it may be feasible to relate co-operative choice to individual preferences in such a way that the choice in any situation depends only on the individual utilities for the outcomes of the situation.

But feasible as it may be, we reject the view that agreement or co-operative choice should rest only on individual utilities, because it leads to treating all optimal outcomes as rationally indifferent. This may be appropriate if we think of social choice as choice, by some person in authority, or some authoritative body, taking into account the preferences of those affected by the choice, and excluding all other considerations. Those affected are treated as passive. The outcome cannot be affected by any interaction among them. They are recipients or consumers of the goods (and, perhaps, bads) to be provided; they are not producers of those goods.

The context of co-operative choice is quite different. Although co-operators are concerned with the utility outputs rather than the strategic inputs of the outcomes among which they must choose, yet they are not passive in the process of agreement, and its strategic character may not be ignored in our analysis. Given a range of optimal outcomes, each person has a definite preference ordering over the members of the range, and since the outcomes are optimal, each preference of each person must conflict with some preference of some other person. As rational, each seeks to maximize her own utility, and so to exert herself to secure that outcome or those outcomes that she favours. To suppose that the optimal outcomes are to be taken as indifferent, so that selection among them proceeds simply by lot, is to treat the process of agreement quite apart from its actual dynamic character. And in this process some outcome or outcomes may be singled out in ways that do not depend directly and solely on the preference orderings of the individual co-opera-

[9] The proof is simple and proceeds by example. Consider a situation with three optimal possible outcomes, represented by the points (0.1, 1), (0.7, 0.7), and (1, 0.1), and a fourth possible outcome at (0, 0). A lottery assigning equal probabilities to each of the optimal points determines the expected outcome represented by the point (0.6, 0.6), which is evidently sub-optimal.

tors. Co-operative choice must reflect the preferences of each person, if it is to be rational, but how it reflects their preferences must depend on the structure of their interaction, on the consequences for everyone of what each is able to do. We shall show presently how several persons may choose an outcome to be brought about by a joint strategy, taking into account their status as actors. Social choice, in ignoring this status (quite reasonably, given its context of application) proves irrelevant to the co-operative choice of a joint strategy.

2.2 Defeated in its assault on the market, utilitarianism returns to the battle in offering itself as a guide to rational agreement.[10] We asked at the beginning of the preceding subsection whether there is an analogue to utility-maximization for co-operative choice. The utilitarian replies that there is indeed an analogue, *welfare-maximization*, where welfare is defined as the sum of individual utilities. The utilitarian differs in his approach from that considered in 2.1, in insisting on the possibility of an interpersonally comparable measure of individual utility, which enables us to sum the utilities of different persons, and thus determine social welfare. The utilitarian proposal identifies rational co-operative choice with the maximization of this sum.

Since co-operative choice assumes a fixed group of co-operators, the proposal that the sum of individual utilities be maximized is equivalent to the proposal that the *average* of individual utilities be maximized. (The average is simply the sum divided by the number of persons.) This enables the utilitarian to enlist the support of John Harsanyi, who has demonstrated that if social welfare meets the same rationality requirements as individual utility (if, in other words, it affords an interval measure defined over the outcomes), and if the welfare of an outcome is positively related to the individual utilities of that outcome, then welfare must be a weighted average of those utilities.[11] Furthermore, if the weighting is not

[10] The terminology is not his, but the view is that of Harsanyi. He claims that 'the updated version of classical utilitarianism is the only ethical theory which consistently abides by the principle that moral issues must be decided by rational tests and that moral behaviour itself is a special form of rational behaviour', 'Morality and the theory of rational behaviour', p. 40.

[11] The demonstration may be found in J. C. Harsanyi, 'Cardinal Welfare, Individualistic Ethics, and Interpersonal Comparisons of Utility', in *Essays on Ethics*, pp. 10–15; also in *Rational Behavior and Bargaining Equilibrium in Games and Social Situations* (Cambridge, 1977), pp. 64–9.

arbitrary, but reflects a common measure of utility, then social welfare must be simply the average of individual utilities. The utilitarian may then claim that his proposal is the uniquely rational method of taking into account the preferences of each in choosing an outcome to be brought about by a joint strategy.

Superficially, the utilitarian proposal may seem very different from those examined in the preceding subsection. There we found that all optimal outcomes were rationally indifferent. The utilitarian provides a measure that distinguishes among them. But this contrast conceals a deeper affinity between utilitarianism and the approach of social choice. Both suppose that the choice of an outcome is to be based on and solely on the preferences of those affected. Both ignore the process of agreement among persons each of whom is concerned to maximize her own utility. The utilitarian proposal, applied to co-operation, treats the co-operators as passive recipients of goods, not as actively engaged in producing them and agreeing on their distribution. In their interaction, no one need take an interest in the outcome which maximizes average utility, except that particular no one who is the average person. But even should the average person be one of the co-operators, he is but one among the many who must participate in co-operative choice.

In examining the market we noted that the welfare optimum does not in general coincide with the optimal outcome achieved through perfect competition. The redistribution that would be required to bring the outcome of market interaction into accord with utilitarian requirements could not be viewed as rational by some of the persons in the market. We may suppose that similarly the welfare optimum would not in general coincide with the outcome achieved through co-operation. For the utilitarian ignores, as his principles require him to ignore, the structure of interaction. From the perspective of co-operation, utilitarianism as a proposal for choosing the outcome seems to have nothing to recommend it.

We have, of course, no quarrel with Harsanyi's demonstration; one does not quarrel with proofs. We agree that an interval measure defined over outcomes and positively based on the individual interval measures of preference must be utilitarian. If an interpersonally comparable measure of utility can be defined, then utilitarianism would seem to provide the rationally required method of social choice. But we deny the relevance of Harsanyi's demonstration to our problem. Rational co-operative choice must reflect the preferences of the co-operators, but their preferences as actors. We turn without further ado to an approach to co-operative choice that takes interaction, as well as preference, fully into account.

2.3 Co-operation arises from the failure of market interaction to bring about an optimal outcome because of the presence of externalities. We may then think of co-operative interaction as a visible hand which supplants the invisible hand, in order to realize the same ideal as the market provides under conditions of perfect competition. In market exchange, costs and benefits are related in a manner that is not only optimal, but that affords each person a return equal in value to her marginal contribution. The joint strategy selected for co-operative interaction should bring about the same relation of costs and benefits under conditions in which the provision of a benefit may not directly result in the recovery of its costs, or the imposition of a cost may not directly require the provision of a compensating benefit. In accepting the joint co-operative strategy as the basis for her own actions, each individual forgoes the opportunities for free-ridership or parasitism that imperfect competition affords, in return for others forgoing their similar opportunities. But of course each endeavours to have the joint strategy chosen that is most favourable to herself, minimizing the costs of her restraint and maximizing the benefits she receives from the restraint of others. In reaching agreement on a joint strategy, then, each individual sees herself engaged in a process of *bargaining* with her fellows. Through bargaining, individuals arrive at a basis for co-operative interaction that enables them to relate costs and benefits, despite the presence of externalities, in the way automatically brought about by the market in the absence of those externalities.

The idea of a bargain enables us to incorporate into our account of rational co-operative choice what is missing from the perspectives of social choice and utilitarianism—the active involvement of the co-operators. It also enables us to capture the requirement that agreement on a joint strategy be voluntary. A rational bargain ensures the participation of each in reaching an agreed outcome. As we noted at the beginning of this chapter, not all co-operation is based on actual agreement. We may not then suppose that every joint strategy is chosen by a bargaining procedure in which all of those basing their actions on the strategy participated. But for co-operation to be rational, we must suppose that the joint strategy would have been chosen through such a procedure, so that each person, recognizing this, may voluntarily accept the strategy. Each is then able to view the distribution of the benefits realized from co-operation as acceptable to her as an actor, a full participant in the co-operative process.

Before turning to our account of rational bargaining, we should guard against one possible misunderstanding of our argument. Co-operative interaction is not itself bargaining. Co-operative interaction results from, and is determined by, the choice of a joint strategy. Each then chooses her own actions as required by that strategy; in so doing she is not bargaining with her fellows. Rather, choosing this joint strategy involves bargaining. Bargaining thus gives rise to co-operative interaction but is itself non-co-operative. This distinction is of great importance in subsequent discussion, for as we shall see, in co-operating persons must at times constrain their utility-maximizing behaviour, but in bargaining itself persons accept no such constraint. The constraints required by co-operation are arrived at through bargaining, but are no part of the bargaining process. To refer back to what should be a familiar distinction at this point in our argument, in bargaining, each person's behaviour must be a utility-maximizing response to her expectations of others' behaviour, whereas in co-operating each person's behaviour must be an optimizing response to the expectations she forms of others' behaviour on the basis of their joint strategy.

3.1 The general theory of rational bargaining is underdeveloped territory. Whether there are principles of rational bargaining with the same context-free universality of application as the principle of expected utility maximization has been questioned, notably by Alvin Roth.[12] John Harsanyi insists that there is a general theory, and claims to have constructed it, building on earlier work of Frederik Zeuthen and John Nash.[13] Although the Zeuthen–Nash–Harsanyi approach has commanded widest support among those who accept the possibility of a general theory, it is not without competitors. Undaunted both by Roth's scepticism and by Harsanyi's

[12] See A. E. Roth, M. W. K. Malouf, and J. K. Murnighan, 'Sociological versus Strategic Factors in Bargaining', *Journal of Economic Behavior and Organization* 2 (1981), pp. 174–7.

[13] See F. Zeuthen, *Problems of Monopoly and Economic Welfare* (London, 1930), ch. 4; J. F. Nash, 'The Bargaining Problem', *Econometrica* 18 (1951), pp. 155–62, and 'Two-person Cooperative Games', *Econometrica* 21 (1953), pp. 128–40; Harsanyi, *Rational Behavior*.

dogmatism, we shall outline our own theory.[14] Interested readers will find our reasons for preferring it to the Zeuthen–Nash–Harsanyi theory in 3.4.

In any bargain it is necessary first to specify the initial position of the parties—the *initial bargaining position*, as we shall call it. We may think of this initial position as an outcome, or as a set of utilities, one for each bargainer. A bargaining situation then consists of a set of outcomes, any one of which may be realized by the bargainers through agreement on the appropriate joint strategy, and a specially designated outcome, the initial bargaining position. In 1.3 we introduced the representation of the set of outcomes graphically, as a closed, convex figure in utility space. The initial bargaining position is of course represented by a point in that space. Fig. 3 depicts a typical two-person bargaining situation.

The initial bargaining position fixes a base point from which bargaining proceeds. The utility it affords each person represents, in effect, what she brings to the bargaining table, and is not part of what she seeks to gain at the table from the bargain. In agreeing to a joint strategy the bargainers are concerned with the distribution of only the utility that each may receive over and above what she obtains in the initial bargaining position. We shall say that the bargainers are concerned with the distribution of the gains which co-operation may bring them, or with the co-operative *surplus*. The initial bargaining position identifies that part of each person's utility that is not part of the co-operative surplus.

In 1.3 we introduced the idea of a co-operation function. There we

[14] The underlying idea of our theory appears in 'Rational Co-operation', *Noûs* 8 (1974), pp. 53–65. A brief sketch appears in 'Economic Rationality and Moral Constraints', *Midwest Studies in Philosophy* 3 (1978), pp. 92–3, and a fuller account in 'The Social Contract: Individual Decision or Collective Bargain?', in C. A. Hooker, J. J. Leach and E. F. McClennen (eds.), *Foundations and Applications of Decision Theory*, 2 vols. (Dordrecht, 1978), vol. 2, pp. 47–67. An informal account is found in 'Bargaining Our Way Into Morality: A Do-It-Yourself Primer', *Philosophic Exchange* 2, no. 5 (1979), pp. 14–27. More recently still, see 'Justified Inequality?', *Dialogue* 21 (1982), pp. 431–43, and 'Justice as Social Choice', in D. Copp and D. Zimmerman (eds.), *Morality, Reason and Truth: New Essays on the Foundations of Ethics* (Totowa, N J, 1985), pp. 251–69. For two-persons situations, our account yields solution G, discussed in A. E. Roth, *Axiomatic Models of Bargaining* (Berlin, 1979), pp. 98–108, and axiomatized by E. Kalai and M. Smorodinsky, 'Other Solutions to Nash's Bargaining Problem', *Econometrica* 43 (1975), pp. 513–18. But for situations involving more than two persons, our account departs from solution G in those cases in which G fails to be Pareto-optimal. See my paper 'Bargaining and Justice', appearing in *Social Philosophy and Policy* 2, no. 2.

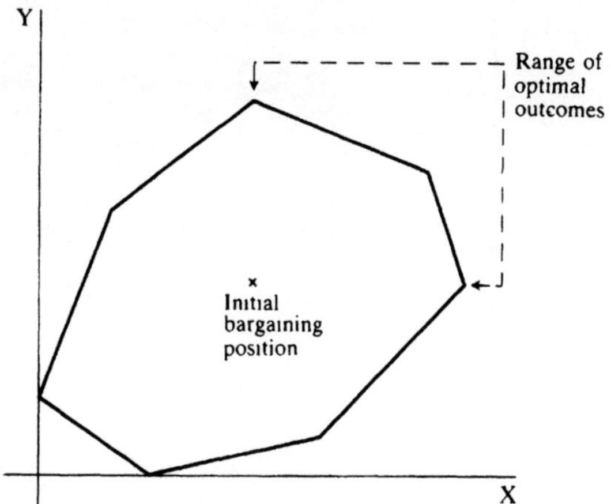

Figure 3

suggested that its domain was a set of outcome-spaces, each space representing the outcomes of a possible co-operative interaction. We must now revise that account to accommodate the initial bargaining position. The domain of the co-operation function is a set of (representations of) bargaining situations, that is, a set of outcome-spaces each with its specially designated point representing the initial bargaining position. For each bargaining situation, the co-operation function determines a point representing the outcome to be realized through co-operative interaction. In 1.3 we stated that this point must fall on the upper bound of the outcome-space, since it must represent an optimal outcome. We may now add that this point must represent an outcome affording each person a utility no less than her utility in the initial bargaining position. In Figure 4 we illustrate the effect of this requirement, in determining what we shall call the range of *admissible* optimal outcomes.

The inclusion of the initial position in the bargaining situation formally distinguishes our account of the co-operation function from those proposed on the basis of social choice or of utilitarianism. On both of these views, nothing but the preferences of those concerned (or the measure of those preferences) is relevant to the choice of an outcome. On our view, preferences with respect to a particular state of affairs are singled out for special consideration.

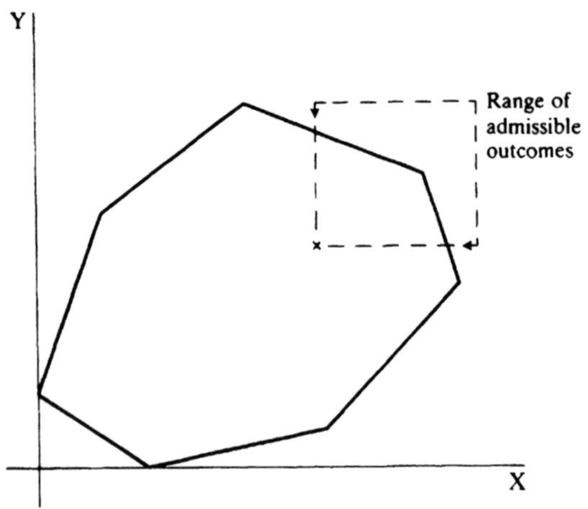

Figure 4

Neither social choice nor utilitarian treatments allow such preferences to restrict the range of optimal outcomes available for selection. And as we shall see, the initial bargaining position has further effects on the procedure of bargaining.

But how is the initial bargaining position to be determined? If we suppose co-operation to parallel market interaction in its structure, then we might propose to identify the initial position with the initial distribution of the factors to be used in co-operation, treating it as the set of pay-offs or utilities directly realizable from the initial factor endowments. But this identification would seem to ignore the place of co-operation in our argument. We have introduced it as an alternative to natural and market interaction, entered into because of their failure to provide optimal outcomes in the face of externalities. The co-operative surplus, we might then suppose, is what may be gained over and above what would result from non-co-operative interaction. Thus we might propose to identify the initial bargaining position with the non-co-operative outcome.

But non-co-operative interaction is marred by force and fraud, by the presence of free-riders and parasites. Co-operation is intended to eliminate all of these. Is it then rational for each bargainer to enter into agreement with her fellows if they may bring to the bargaining table whatever they might obtain from free-ridership and parasitism, or more correctly the utility equivalent, and to consider the distribution only of the additional goods which co-operation provides?

We must here distinguish two quite different issues. On the one hand, we may ask what each person may bring to the bargaining table, if co-operation is to be rational. On the other hand, we may ask what each person must take from the bargaining table, if co-operation is to be rational. We may agree that each person must take from the bargain the expectation of a utility at least equal to what she would expect from non-co-operative interaction, if she is to find it rational to co-operate. It does not follow that she must bring such a utility to the bargain, as determining her share of the base point from which bargaining proceeds.

The determination of the initial bargaining position raises some of the most complex issues that we must examine. But we need not examine them here; indeed, we shall defer them to Chapter VII. They concern the external rationality of co-operation. The initial bargaining position must be fixed in such a way that it is rational for persons to enter into co-operation, agreeing to a joint strategy and acting on their agreement. Here our concern is with the internal rationality of co-operation, the rational way of choosing the joint strategy for interdependent interaction. Thus in this chapter we shall examine the initial bargaining position only in terms of its role in the selection of the co-operative strategy.

3.2 The procedure of bargaining may be divided into two principal stages. First, each party advances a claim—proposes an outcome or joint strategy for mutual acceptance. In general the claims of the parties are incompatible. Hence second, each party—or at least some party—offers a concession by withdrawing some portion of his original claim and proposing an alternative outcome. Barring deadlock the process of concession continues until a set of mutually compatible claims is reached. We may simplify this second stage if we suppose that after each party advances his initial claim, agreement is reached in a single round of concessions. What claims, and what concessions, will rational bargainers make?

Each person expects that what he gets will be related to what he claims. Each wants to get as much as possible; each therefore claims as much as possible. But in deciding how much is possible, each is constrained by the recognition that he must neither drive others away from the bargaining table, nor be excluded by them. Hence each person's claim is limited by the overall co-operative surplus, and more specifically by the portion of the surplus that it is possible for him to receive. To claim more would be to propose that others give up some of what they brought to the bargaining table, some of their pay-off in the initial bargaining position. Since no rational person can expect any other rational person to do this, to claim more than one's largest possible portion of the co-operative surplus would be idle, or worse since if one were to press such a claim, one would only drive others away or face exclusion oneself. Since one wants to benefit from a share of the co-operative surplus, one has no interest in causing the process of bargaining to fail, as its failure would result in no co-operation and so no surplus. Each person, seeking to maximize his own utility and aware that others are seeking to maximize theirs, thus claims the outcome or joint strategy that would maximize the utility he can receive from the co-operative surplus. Or in other words, each person proposes, from among the admissible outcomes, the one that maximizes his utility. In Fig. 5 we show the claims that rational individuals would advance in several bargaining situations. Inspection makes it apparent that in two-person bargaining, claim points are easily determined from the outcome-space and the point representing the initial bargaining position.

However, we must beware lest consideration of two person bargaining lead us to misunderstand the determination of claims. In a situation involving more than two persons, each person may not always claim all of the co-operative surplus that he might receive, but only that part of the surplus to the production of which he would contribute. Each person's claim is bounded by the extent of his participation in co-operative interaction. For if someone were to press a claim to what would be brought about by the co-operative interaction of others, then those others would prefer to exclude him from agreement.

Given the claims of the bargainers, what concessions is it rational for them to make? To answer this question we must first consider how concessions are to be measured. The absolute magnitude of a concession, in terms of utility, is of course the difference between the utility one would expect from the outcome initially claimed and the utility one would expect from the outcome proposed as a concession. But this magnitude offers no basis for relating the concessions of different bargainers, since the measure of individual utility does not permit interpersonal comparisons. However, we may introduce a

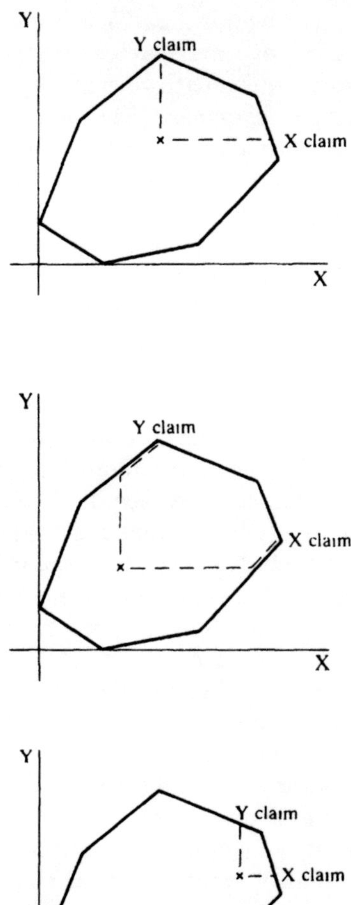

Figure 5

measure of *relative concession* which does enable us to compare the concessions of different bargainers, and which thus gives us a basis for determining what concession each must rationally make.

Suppose one were to receive one's claim. Then one would make no concession whatsoever. Suppose on the other hand one were to end up in the initial bargaining position. Then one would in effect make a complete concession; one would receive no more than what one brought to bargaining, no more than what one had been allotted in the claims of the other bargainers. The *relative magnitude* of any concession may be expressed as the proportion its absolute magnitude bears to the absolute magnitude of a complete concession. If the initial bargaining position affords some person a utility u^*, and he claims an outcome affording him a utility u^*, then if he concedes an outcome affording him a utility u, the absolute magnitude of his concession is $(u^* - u)$, of complete concession $(u^* - u^*)$, and so the relative magnitude of his concession is $[(u^* - u)/(u^* - u^*)]$.

Relative concession is a proportion of two utility-differences or intervals. Now an interval measure, such as utility, fixes these proportions independently of its arbitrary features—the zero-point and the unit. Consider three temperatures, as shown on both the Celsius and Fahrenheit scales: let them be 10 °C = 50 °F, 20 °C = 68 °F, and 25 °C = 77 °F. Measured on the Celsius scale, the difference or interval between the first and second is 10 °C, between the second and third 5 °C. Measured on the Fahrenheit scale, the intervals are 18 and 9 °F. But the proportion between the two intervals, 10/5 and 18/9, is 2, independent of the choice of scale. This illustrates for temperature what holds for all interval measures and so for utility. Relative concession is independent of the choice of utility scale. Each person's relative concessions are fixed no matter how we choose to measure his utilities.

Furthermore, we have introduced relative concession so that for each person, the relative magnitude of no concession is always 0, and the relative magnitude of complete or full concession is always 1. Thus we have a measure of relative concession which, without introducing any interpersonal comparison of utility (for we do not suppose that equal relative concessions have equal utility costs), nevertheless enables us to compare the concessions advanced by different persons in a bargaining situation.

We now represent each outcome in the admissible range, not in terms of the utilities it affords to each person, but in terms of the concessions that would be required from each, were the outcome to be chosen as determining the joint strategy for co-operative interaction. Zeuthen's principle may then be employed to provide a rule deciding what concessions must rationally be made and so what outcome must be accepted. It will be remembered from III.2.2 that this principle states that the person whose ratio between cost of concession and cost of deadlock is less must concede to the other. Or in terms of our present discussion, the principle states that the person with a lesser relative concession must concede. Extending this rule to bargaining among several persons, we claim that the principle should state that given a range of outcomes, each of which requires concessions by some or all persons if it is to be selected, then an outcome be selected only if the greatest or *maximum* relative concession it requires, is as small as possible, or a *minimum*, that is, is no greater than the maximum relative concession required by every other outcome. We call this the principle of minimum-maximum, or *minimax relative concession*.

Let us return to a familiar example—Jane and Brian. Suppose that we identify the initial bargaining position with the unique equilibrium outcome they might expect to result from non-co-operative interaction; it affords Jane a utility of 1/2 and Brian a utility of 3/8. We illustrate this situation in Fig. 6. The admissible outcomes are those optimal outcomes affording Jane a utility of at least 1/2 and Brian a utility of at least 3/8; the points representing them fall on the line joining (0, 1) and (1, 0), between the points (1/2, 1/2) and (5/8, 3/8) inclusive. It is evident that Jane claims the latter and Brian the former. The outcome with utility to Jane 9/16 and utility to Brian 7/16 requires from Jane a relative concession of $[(5/8-9/16)/(5/8-1/2)]=1/2$, and from Brian a relative concession of $[(1/2-7/16)/(1/2-3/8)]=1/2$. Any admissible outcome more favourable to Jane will clearly demand a larger relative concession from Brian and any outcome more favourable to Brian will demand a larger relative concession from Jane. Hence by the principle of minimax relative concession, Jane and Brian should agree on this outcome, affording her 9/16 and him 7/16; if they co-operate, she should go to the party and he should follow a mixed strategy assigning a probability of 7/16 to going to the party and 9/16 to staying at home.

A second example illustrates how certain seemingly plausible objections to the principle of minimax relative concession, taken as a basis for co-operation, may be answered. Adelaide and Ernest have the opportunity to co-operate in a mutually profitable way if they can first agree on how to share their gains. Let us suppose that their utilities are linear with monetary values, so that we may give the payoffs in dollars. Adelaide would receive a net benefit of $500 from their joint venture, provided she receives all of the gains after

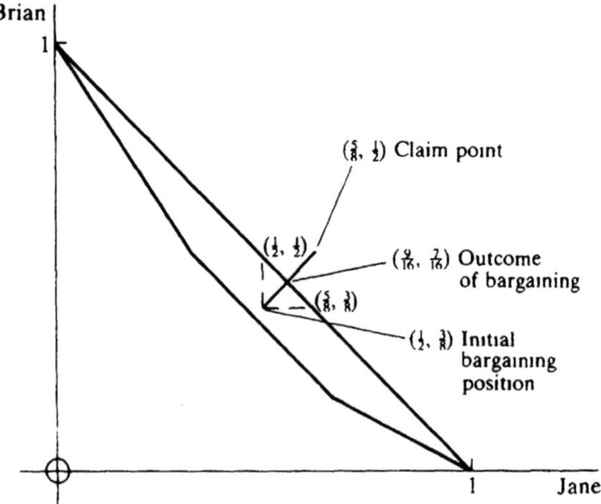

Figure 6

Ernest's costs are fully covered; Ernest however would receive only \$50 if all of the gains go to him after Adelaide's costs are covered. Since their present goods are not in contention, and since they have no alternative sources of gain, we may set the pay-offs to each in the initial bargaining situation at \$0. We suppose that the admissible optimal outcomes fall on the curve shown in Fig. 7.

Each claims as much as affords the other only marginal inducement to co-operate, so that Adelaide's claim approaches \$500 and Ernest's, \$50. From Fig. 7, we see that agreement is possible if each makes a relative concession of nearly 0.3, yielding an outcome affording Adelaide \$353 and Ernest \$35, to the nearest dollar. We see also that agreement on any other outcome would require one to make a greater relative concession. Hence Adelaide should concede \$147 of her possible gain and accept \$353; Ernest should concede \$15 of his possible gain and accept \$35.

Suppose that Ernest complains that Adelaide is getting far more than he—\$353 as opposed to a mere \$35. Adelaide will reply that Ernest is conceding far less than she—a mere \$15 as opposed to \$147. If Ernest were to argue that his gain should be increased because it is so much smaller than Adelaide's, Adelaide would reply that his concession should be increased because it is so much smaller

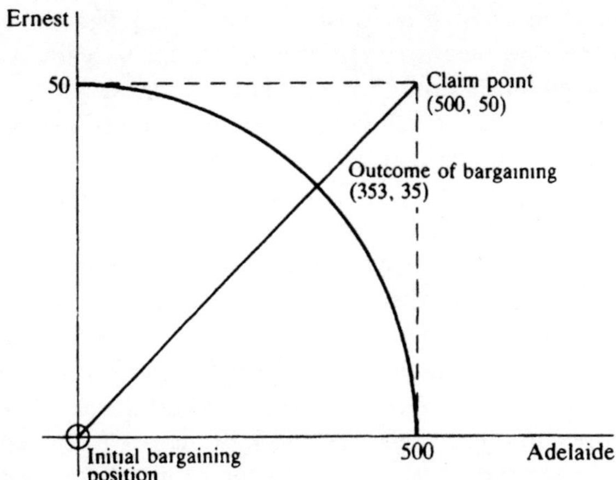

Figure 7

in dollars than hers. If Adelaide were to argue that Ernest should care relatively little about how much he concedes, Ernest would reply that he cares equally little about reaching agreement. His smaller potential benefit reduces the pressure on him to refuse a concession, but equally it reduces the pressure on him to reach agreement and so to make a concession. Her larger stake increases the pressure on her to reach agreement, but equally it increases the pressure on her to hold out against a concession comparable in relative magnitude.

The fundamental rationale for the principle of minimax relative concession does not require even the rough interpersonal comparisons of benefit that we have used in this example. Rather, the rationale turns on an interpersonal comparison of the proportion of each person's potential gain that he must concede. However, were we to assume a measure of utility permitting interpersonal comparisons, and were we then to be tempted by some principle of equal gain, we should remind ourselves that any such temptation could be countered by a principle of equal loss, in relation to one's claim. The unique acceptability of minimax relative concession is made evident when we balance gain in relation to non-co-operation with loss in relation to claim or potential gain.

The two examples we have discussed may suggest that the

principle of minimax relative concession is in fact a principle of minimum equal relative concession—that it requires the smallest equal concessions, measured relatively, from the bargainers. I have indeed claimed this in print, but mistakenly. In most cases, minimax relative concession will result in equal relative concessions, but Alvin Roth has demonstrated that this is not always so.[15]

What we may show is that, if there is an optimal outcome requiring equal relative concessions from each person, then the principle of minimax relative concession selects that outcome. For if an outcome is optimal, then every other outcome in the situation must afford some person a lesser utility. But to accept an outcome with lesser utility, one must make a greater concession—greater in absolute magnitude, since the difference between the utility of one's claim and the utility of one's concession is increased, and so greater in relative magnitude, since the proportion this difference bears to complete concession must also be increased. Thus if there is an optimal outcome requiring equal relative concessions from each person, every other outcome requires a greater concession from some person, and so every other outcome requires a concession greater than the minimax.

There is a simple graphic representation of the outcome required by minimax relative concession, given that there is an optimal outcome requiring equal relative concessions from each. Let the claim point be that point in utility space representing a utility, to each person, equal to what he would expect from his claim. Then all points on the line joining the point representing the initial bargaining position to the claim point, represent outcomes requiring equal relative concession. If this line intersects the upper right bound of the outcome-space, then the point of intersection represents the outcome requiring minimum equal relative concessions, which is the outcome selected by the principle of minimax relative concession. We show this in Figs. 6 and 7.

A third example relates the principle of minimax relative concession to the obvious supposition that in a partnership, each should benefit in proportion to investment. Abel and Mabel agree to pool their resources, finding this advantageous because over the range of their contributions there is a linear increase in returns to scale on investment. Their pooled resources have a value of 1, and they expect a return at rate k. (As in the preceding example, we assume

[15] Roth, pp. 105–7.

utilities are linear with monetary values.) If Abel contributes r, and so Mabel $(1-r)$ to their combined resources, and if Abel would expect a return at rate c were he to invest independently, then by the assumption of a linear increase in returns to scale, Mabel must expect a return at rate $[(k - 2kr + cr)/(1 - r)]$ were she to invest independently. Abel would receive cr from independent investment, and Mabel would receive $(k - 2kr + cr)$. We let these returns be their pay-offs from the initial bargaining position. Abel's claim is then k less Mabel's initial pay-off, or $(2kr - cr)$, and Mabel's claim similarly is $(k - cr)$.

In this situation the principle of minimax relative concession will require equal relative concessions from Abel and Mabel. If we let the return from co-operation to Abel be x, then his absolute concession in his claim $(2kr - cr)$ less x; his full concession is his claim less his initial pay-off; so his relative concession is $[(2kr - cr - x)/(2kr - 2cr)]$. Similarly, Mabel's relative concession is $[(x - cr)/(2kr - 2cr)]$, since her return from co-operation must be $(k - x)$. Since their relative concessions are equal, we may equate them and solve for x. We find $x = kr$. Abel's return kr is equal to the total return k multiplied by the proportion his investment r bears to the total investment 1. And Mabel's return $k(1 - r)$ is equal to the total return multiplied by the proportion her investment $1 - r$ bears to the total investment. These results are of course what we should expect if minimax relative concession does, as we claim, provide the rational basis for co-operation.

3.3 We now present a more formal account of the theory of rational bargaining sketched in the preceding subsections. We begin with some definitions:

(1) The *initial bargaining position* is an outcome, the utilities of which constitute the bargaining endowments of the prospective co-operators. (Thus each bargainer has an entitlement to his utility in the initial bargaining position which is not at stake in the bargaining process.)

(2) The *co-operative surplus* is a set of utility-differences, one for each co-operator, each non-negative in value and equal to the difference between his utility from co-operation and his utility in the initial bargaining position. (The distribution of the co-operative surplus, that is the selection of a particular set of utility-differences constituting such a surplus, is at stake in the bargaining process.)

(3) A *bargaining situation* is a set of outcomes, represented in utility space by a closed, convex figure, the *outcome-space*, and an initial bargaining position, represented by a point of the outcome-space.
(4) A *claim* is a demand by a prospective co-operator for a particular co-operative surplus, made initially in bargaining.
(5) The *claim point* is the point in utility space representing the (possibly hypothetical) outcome that would afford each person a utility equal to that of his claim; it is *feasible* if and only if it is a point of the outcome-space.
(6) A *concession* is an offer by a prospective co-operator to accept a particular utility less than that of his claim.
(7) A *concession point* is a point in utility space representing the (possibly hypothetical) outcome that would result from a set of concessions, one from each prospective co-operator (but possibly including null concessions); it is *feasible* if and only if it is a point of the outcome-space.
(8) A person is willing to *entertain* a concession point if and only if he is willing to make the concession it requires from him provided others are willing to make the concessions it requires from them. The person is then willing to entertain the concession in relation to the concession point.
(9) The *absolute magnitude* of a concession is the difference between the utility of the person's claim and the utility of the concession.
(10) The *relative magnitude* of a concession is the proportion its absolute magnitude bears to the difference between the utility of the person's claim and his utility in the initial bargaining position. Alternatively, the relative magnitude of a concession is the proportion its absolute magnitude bears to the utility-difference for the person of the co-operative surplus that he claimed.
(11) A *maximum concession* for any concession point is the concession (or one of the concessions) with greatest relative magnitude required to bring about the outcome represented by the point.
(12) A *minimax concession* in any bargaining situation is the maximum concession (or one of the maximum concessions) with least relative magnitude required to bring about an outcome represented by a feasible concession point. (Thus in any

bargaining situation, each outcome represented by a feasible concession point must require a concession with relative magnitude at least equal to that of the minimax concession.)

We now formulate the conditions on rational bargaining:

(i) *Rational claim.* Each person must claim the co-operative surplus that affords him maximum utility, except that no person may claim a co-operative surplus if he would not be a participant in the interaction required to provide it.

(ii) *Concession point.* Given claims satisfying condition (i), each person must suppose that there is a feasible concession point that every rational person is willing to entertain.

(iii) *Willingness to concede.* Each person must be willing to entertain a concession in relation to a feasible concession point if its relative magnitude is no greater than that of the greatest concession that he supposes some rational person is willing to entertain (in relation to a feasible concession point).

(iv) *Limits of concession.* No person is willing to entertain a concession in relation to a concession point if he is not required to do so by conditions (ii) and (iii).

The rationale for these conditions turns on the benefit each person seeks to realize from the co-operative surplus. Each can increase his utility by co-operating; hence as a utility-maximizer each must find it rational to co-operate. And each recognizes that everyone else must find it rational to co-operate.

Condition (i) is a straightforward application of utility-maximization to the context of bargaining. Each seeks to maximize his return from co-operation so each claims as much as possible, but no person seeks to exclude other co-operators or to be excluded himself, and so each limits his claim to avoid this.

Condition (ii) follows from the fact that, for co-operation to occur, all must agree on an outcome (or joint strategy) represented by a feasible point in outcome-space. Any person who supposes that there is no feasible concession point on which rational persons can agree is denying that there is any way in which those rational persons can co-operate. But each recognizes that everyone finds it rational to co-operate.

Condition (iii) expresses the equal rationality of the bargainers. Since each person, as a utility-maximizer, seeks to minimize his concession, then no one can expect any other rational person to be willing to make a concession if he would not be willing to make a similar concession.

Finally, condition (iv) is again a straightforward application of utility-maximization, given that the other conditions suffice to require concessions leading to an outcome represented by a feasible point. No rational person can be willing to make unnecessary, or unnecessarily large, concessions. We now demonstrate that conditions (ii) and (iii) do suffice to bring about agreement on a feasible point.

We noted in the parenthetical remark to definition (12) that each outcome represented by a feasible concession point must require a concession with relative magnitude at least equal to the minimax concession. Since by condition (ii) each person must suppose that there is a feasible concession point that every rational person is willing to entertain, then each must suppose that every rational person is willing to entertain a concession point requiring someone to make a concession with relative magnitude at least equal to the minimax concession. But then each must suppose that some rational person is willing himself to entertain a concession with relative magnitude at least equal to the minimax concession, in relation to this concession point. It follows from condition (iii) that each person must himself be willing to entertain a concession with relative magnitude at least equal to the minimax concession, in relation to a feasible concession point.

But in every situation there is a feasible concession point requiring no concession greater in relative magnitude than the minimax concession. By conditions (ii) and (iii), then, every person must be willing to entertain this point. But then condition (ii) cannot require any person to suppose that there is a feasible concession point that every rational person is willing to entertain and that requires a concession greater in relative magnitude than the minimax concession. And so condition (iii) cannot, either itself or on the basis of condition (ii), require any person to be willing himself to entertain a concession greater in magnitude than the minimax concession, in relation to any feasible concession point. Hence by condition (iv) no person is willing to entertain a concession point requiring him to make a concession greater in magnitude than the minimax concession. And so each person must be willing to entertain those and only those feasible concession points that require concessions with relative magnitudes as great as, but no greater than, the minimax concession.

Let us say that claims that satisfy condition (i) are *maximal*. Then from conditions (i) to (iv) we have established the *Principle of Minimax Relative Concession*: in any co-operative interaction, the rational joint strategy is determined by a bargain among the co-operators in which each advances his maximal claim and then offers a concession no greater in relative magnitude than the minimax concession.

The principle of minimax relative concession plays a threefold role in our argument. First, it expresses the principle of expected utility-maximization in the context of bargaining. Rational bargainers, each seeking to maximize his own utility, determine their claims and concessions by an appeal to the principle. Second, it determines the formal content of a rational bargain; rational bargainers agree on that joint strategy affording each person an expected utility no less than he would expect from his maximal claim and minimax concession. Thus the principle governs both the process and the object of rational choice in bargaining situations.

Third, the principle of minimax relative concession is the principle of rational behaviour in co-operative interaction—interaction based on the joint strategy agreed to in bargaining. Each person acts, not to maximize his own utility, but to bring about the outcome that is the object of the bargain, affording each person an expected utility no less than he would expect from his maximal claim and minimax concession. We have yet to demonstrate that such action is rational—that each person should rationally comply with the joint strategy to which he has rationally agreed. This will be our task in the next chapter. It is this third role which establishes the distinctively moral character of the principle, and of co-operation. For applied to co-operative interaction, the principle of minimax relative concession constitutes a constraint on the direct pursuit of individual utility. Thus if we can show it to be a rational and impartial basis for co-operative interaction, we shall have established its credentials as a moral principle.

Rational persons, faced with the costs of natural or market interaction in the face of externalities, agree to a different, co-operative mode of interaction. They agree to act, not on the basis of individual utility-maximization, but rather on the basis of optimization, where the particular optimal outcome is determined by the principle of minimax relative concession. In reaching this agreement, of course, each seeks to maximize his own utility. The same principle, minimax relative concession, serves rational persons both in reaching agreement, and in complying with the agreement reached—both as a principle of choice in bargaining, and as a principle of choice in co-operating. In bargaining minimax relative concession directly expresses the demands of utility-maximization; this we have argued in the present section. In co-operation minimax relative concession constrains and so overrides the demands of utility-maximization. This will be the theme of the next chapter.

3.4 A brief discussion of the principal alternative to our account of rational bargaining, the Zeuthen–Nash–Harsanyi theory, will complete our treatment of this subject.[16] It may be omitted by readers whose interests do not extend to infighting among bargaining theorists, as it contains nothing of positive importance to the development of our argument.

Consider two persons, Ann and Adam, who find themselves in a bargaining situation. Let the initial bargaining position afford Ann a utility u^* and Adam a utility v^*. Ann claims an outcome affording her a utility u_1 and Adam v_1; Adam claims an outcome affording him a utility v_2 and Ann u_2. Assuming their claims to be incompatible, so that (u_1, v_2), the point affording them their claimed utilities, is not feasible, at least one must offer a concession. If Ann were to accept Adam's claim she would give up $(u_1 - u_2)$; if they were to deadlock on the initial bargaining position she would give up $(u_1 - u^*)$. If Adam were to accept Ann's claim he would give up $(v_2 - v_1)$; if they were to deadlock on the initial bargaining position he would give up $(v_2 - v^*)$. The ratio $[(u_1 - u_2)/(u_1 - u^*)]$ measures Ann's loss from accepting Adam's claim as a proportion of her loss from deadlock; the ratio $[(v_2 - v_1)/(v_2 - v^*)]$ similarly measures Adam's loss from accepting Ann's claim as a proportion of his loss from deadlock. We may compare the ratios and suppose, applying Zeuthen's principle, that the person whose ratio is smaller risks more by not making a concession, or alternatively, loses proportionately less by making a concession.

But he need not make a full concession, accepting the other's

[16] See, in addition to the references to Nash and Zeuthen in note 13 above, Luce and Raiffa, pp. 124–37. Harsanyi gives a brief account of earlier work in *Rational Behavior*, pp. 143–53.

claim, if, by making a lesser concession, he may increase his ratio sufficiently so that it is larger than that of the other bargainer. Suppose that Ann must concede; $[(u_1 - u_2)/(u_1 - u^*)]$ is smaller than $[(v_2 - v_1)/(v_2 - v^*)]$. But suppose she can propose an outcome affording her a utility u_3 and Adam v_3, where u_3, although less than her original claim u_1, is greater than what she would receive by accepting Adam's claim, u_2, and also where $[(u_3 - u_2)/(u_3 - u^*)]$ is larger than $[(v_2 - v_3)/(v_2 - v^*)]$. Adam's risk is now greater than Ann's so he must offer a concession.

We suppose that this process of concession continues until their proposals coincide. It can be shown that given this procedure for bargaining, the outcome selected must afford Ann a utility u' and Adam a utility v' such that, for any feasible point (u, v), the product $(u' - u^*)$ $(v' - v^*)$ is at least as great as the product $(u - u^*)$ $(v - v^*)$. Thus on the Zeuthen–Nash–Harsanyi theory, rational agreement maximizes the product of the individual utility-differences in the co-operative surplus.

In some situation this procedure will yield the same outcome as the one we have proposed. But we show in Fig. 8 a bargaining situation where the procedures differ. The possible outcomes are represented by the points (0, 0), (1/2, 1), and (1, 0); (0, 0) is (we suppose) the initial bargaining position. The optimal outcomes are represented by the points on the line joining (1/2, 1) and (1, 0). The

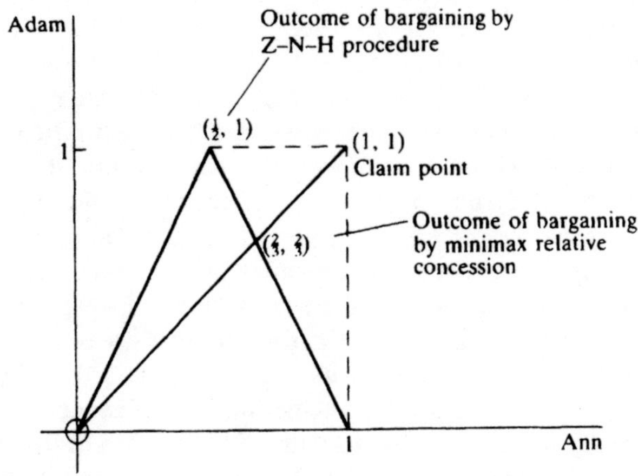

Figure 8

bargaining outcome, by the procedure just sketched, must be represented by that point on the optimal line maximizing the value of $(u - 0)\ (v - 0)$; this is the point (1/2, 1).

Following our procedure, it is clear that both Ann and Adam must claim a utility of 1; the point (2/3, 2/3) on the optimal line requires each to make a concession with relative magnitude $[(1 - 2/3)/(1 - 0)]$, or 1/3, and any other point, since it affords either Ann or Adam a utility less than 2/3, requires one of them to make a concession with greater relative magnitude. Therefore by the principle of minimax relative concession the bargaining outcome is represented by the point (2/3, 2/3).

We do not suppose that intuition should have the final word in deciding questions in the theory of rational choice. But if it has any word at all, it is surely not spoken here in support of the Zeuthen–Nash–Harsanyi approach, which gives Adam his claim, leaving it to Ann to make all the concessions.

But let us raise deeper objections. The outcome of the Zeuthen–Nash–Harsanyi procedure is determined by maximizing the product of the individual utility-differences in the co-operative surplus. The only constraint that need be placed on the bargainers' claims, to ensure this outcome, is that they specify outcomes that are admissible in the sense of 3.1, and that afford the claimant no less than he would receive from the bargaining outcome. Whereas in our procedure each person has an interest in advancing his maximal claim, on this alternative no one has such an interest, since one cannot expect more by claiming more. There is no rationale for determining the size of one's claim.

At each stage in the process of bargaining a minimum concession is made, in accordance with the requirements of maximizing rationality. But a concession from what? From a claim that has no significance. It is not possible to determine, at the end of the bargaining process, whether one party has conceded more than the other, since concessions are measured only at each stage in the process and are relative to that stage. And even if there be but one stage, we can say that one party has conceded more only in relation to initial claims that, as we have seen, are quite arbitrarily made. Surely then we must question whether the idea of concession retains any real significance on this account of bargaining. In treating the magnitude of claims as arbitrary, the magnitude of concessions also becomes arbitrary.

We might of course suppose that the bargainers were to begin by making real claims—claims satisfying our condition (i). Although they would have no reason to do this, yet if they did, it would enable us to attach meaning to the measure of each person's concessions, by taking these claims as a starting point. But we should then face the obvious and unpalatable consequence that so measured, concessions need not be minimal. Since the outcome of the Zeuthen–Nash–Harsanyi bargaining procedure need not be the outcome yielded by our procedure, we may be certain that it does not always satisfy the principle of minimax relative concession. We may then ask why rational bargainers would employ a procedure that might require greater concessions from one of them than anyone need make.

The core of this alternative theory of bargaining is found in one of Nash's postulates, usually labelled 'independence of irrelevant alternatives'. The postulate, expressed in terms of the representation of the bargaining situation in utility space, states that restricting the outcome-space can affect the bargaining outcome only if it makes the point representing the original outcome unfeasible, outside the restricted outcome-space, or if it affects the initial bargaining position. Alternatively, expanding the outcome-space can affect the bargaining outcome only if the new outcome falls outside the original outcome-space, or again if it affects the initial bargaining position. This postulate makes very explicit the irrelevance of the bargainers' claims, since restricting or expanding the outcome-space may clearly affect the possible claims without affecting the bargaining outcome. Nash's postulate thus denies what we affirm, that the outcome of rational bargaining depends on the claims advanced by the bargainers.

Harsanyi employs a different set of postulates, among which he includes the plausible requirement that the bargaining outcome must not depend (or be expected to depend) on factors whose relevance cannot be established on the basis of the other postulates.[17] In itself this is surely acceptable. But Harsanyi is able to use it to conclude that only those factors that enter into the choice between one's own claim and the other person's claim—between not making and making a concession—are relevant, because of the way in which he describes the bargaining process. If one supposes that fully rational persons proceed by a series of claims (or offers) and concessions leading to new claims, treating each step as involving a

[17] See Harsanyi, *Rational Behavior*, pp. 118, 153–62.

comparative assessment of immediate risks, then unsurprisingly one is led to Harsanyi's conclusion. But if one supposes that rational persons proceed by making maximal claims, and then a single set of concessions, one obtains our result. For what is relevant to bargaining varies between the two descriptions of the process.

One might suppose that the serial character of bargaining, as Harsanyi represents it, is in fact a better account of the true nature of bargaining than we provide. But as we have seen, if one supposes that the serial character of claim–concession–claim is central, then it turns out that from a rational point of view the process is a dummy. What one claims does not matter, and so what one concedes is based on something that does not matter. The outcome of the Zeuthen–Nash–Harsanyi procedure is entirely independent of the serial process that the account purports to capture. On our view, although there is but one claim and one concession on the part of each person, yet the claim does matter, and the concession is then based on something that matters. The process is not a dummy. And this, we insist, more adequately captures the nature of bargaining. We surely suppose that each bargainer's initial claim must be significant, and that his overall concession from that claim must be of central concern. Our account of bargaining satisfies these suppositions. It represents rational persons who are actually bargaining.

4.1 Justice has been silent throughout our long discussion of the internal rationality of co-operation. But as we shall now show, justice and reason coincide in a single ideal of co-operative interaction. The principle of minimax relative concession serves not only as the basis for rational agreement, but also as the ground of an impartial constraint on each person's behaviour. And justice is the disposition to abide by this constraint.

In treating co-operative interaction as the domain of justice we make a twofold claim. The first is that like the market, rational co-operation excludes all partiality. The second is that unlike the market, this exclusion requires each co-operator to constrain her maximizing activity. Interaction that achieves impartiality without constraint constitutes a morally free zone, from which the externalities are absent that lead utility-maximizers into free-ridership and parasitism. But co-operative interaction faces these externalities; co-operation is the visible hand restraining persons from taking advantage of their fellows, but restraining them impartially and in a way beneficial to all. Such restraint commands rational acceptance; this is the idea underlying morals by agreement.

Our argument in this chapter will be limited in two quite different ways. First, since we have examined only the process of bargaining, leaving aside the initial bargaining position, we shall consider only the impartiality or fairness of this process. Given the initial position, co-operation is just if the joint strategy on which it is based is the outcome of a fair bargain among the co-operators. But the fairness of the bargaining process does not correct any partiality that may be present in the initial position; indeed, it would simply transmit the partiality from the initial position to the joint strategy selected. In Chapter VII we shall examine the conditions under which the inital bargaining position is impartial.

Second, we shall address impartiality, as we have addressed rationality, from the standpoint of the individual actually involved in bargaining. But we noted in Chapter I that other theorists have attempted to link reason and morals by addressing impartiality in an apparently different perspective, considering what principles of interaction would be chosen by any individual occupying a specially conceived, impartial standpoint. Although we shall show in Chapter VIII that this perspective harmonizes with our own, it is not our concern here. We focus on the co-operative choice of a joint strategy, which is impartial because it is acceptable from every standpoint, by every person involved.

Note that no constraint on maximizing behaviour is involved in this choice. Bargaining is a straightforwardly maximizing activity leading to agreement on a joint strategy. Constraint enters in co-operative interaction, which requires adherence to this strategy even though the outcome is not in general an equilibrium. Our concern in this section is to show that if co-operation results from rational agreement, the constraint it imposes is just. But one may still ask, with Hobbes's Foole, whether it is rational to be just, to adhere to the constraint to which one has rationally agreed.[18] This question, of compliance, will be addressed in Chapter VI.

4.2 Recall that co-operation is intended to afford an optimal outcome in situations in which the presence of externalities would make the outcome of natural or of market interaction sub-optimal. The moral significance of externalities is found in the possibility that

[18] See Hobbes, *Leviathan*, ch. 15, pp. 72–3.

one person may take advantage of another, either as a free-rider, obtaining some benefit cost free as a spin-off from the other's activities, or as a parasite, transferring the cost of some benefit to the other. Co-operation, to avoid this possibility, must ensure that the ratio between the benefit the co-operator receives and the contribution she makes is, so far as possible, constant, the same for all. But how is this to be done?

Let us begin with a simple example, in which we shall suppose that the fruits of co-operation—the co-operative surplus, distribution of which is at stake in the bargaining process—may be treated as a single, transferable good.[19] The quantity of this good produced through co-operative interaction is fixed; it may be distributed in any way among the co-operators, and its quantity is not affected. Each person's utilities must be linear with respect to her share of this good, but no interpersonal comparison of utilities is assumed. In our example we shall suppose that this good is money.

Our example is the partnership between Abel and Mabel introduced at the end of 3.2. They expect a return of k on their joint investment. But k is not their co-operative surplus. That surplus is k, less the sum of the return each would expect from independent investment, which for Abel is cr and for Mabel $(k - 2kr + cr)$. So the co-operative surplus is $(2kr - 2cr)$.

How is this surplus divided between Abel and Mabel? Abel, we showed in 3.2, receives kr from co-operation; subtracting his initial pay-off cr we find that his share of the co-operative surplus is $(kr - cr)$, or exactly one-half. Mabel receives $k(1 - r)$ from co-operation; subtracting her initial pay-off $(k - 2kr + cr)$ we find that her share of the co-operative surplus is, of course, also $(kr - cr)$. If each receives a total return proportionate to contribution, then each receives half of the co-operative surplus. Since we suppose that returns are divided between Abel and Mabel on the basis of their contributions, this shows that both contribute equally to providing the co-operative surplus.

Our discussion has revealed what must surely appear a very surprising result. If Abel and Mabel are to engage in a partnership in which their returns are proportionate to their contributions, then they must divide the co-operative surplus brought about by their partnership equally. An equal division of the surplus may not seem surprising in itself. For since neither can gain any part of this surplus

[19] For an account of a transferable good, see Luce and Raiffa, pp. 168–9.

without the other, then each is equally responsible for making it available, and so each is entitled to an equal share of it. What is surprising is that this egalitarian view of co-operation proves to be fully compatible with the reasonable insistence that overall returns be proportionate to (differing) overall contributions.

This egalitarian view of co-operation is indeed implicit in our analysis. The co-operative surplus is in the fullest sense the joint product of the co-operators. No one may reasonably or fairly expect more, and no one should reasonably or fairly accept less, than an equal share of the co-operative surplus, where equal shares may be determined. If there is a single transferable good, produced in fixed quantity and divisible in any way among the co-operators, then rationality and impartiality require its equal division. It is evident that this is the outcome required by our theory of bargaining, for given a fixed good, fully divisible, each claims all of it, and maximum concession is then minimized if and only if each person receives an equal share of the good.

But, it may be objected, this result is absurd. Ms Macquarrie, the pharmaceutical chemist, requires a laboratory assistant to aid her in carrying out her experiments, and hires Mr O'Rourke. When as a result of her experiments, Ms Macquarrie discovers a wonder drug that makes her a millionaire, must she divide her royalties with O'Rourke? Of course not. Her experiments were not carried out as a co-operative venture with her assistant. Although she required an assistant, she did not require O'Rourke. Her relationship with him was strictly a market transaction; she hired him at (presumably) the going rate for laboratory assistants. Macquarrie would be ungenerous not to give O'Rourke a handsome bonus, but she does not owe him anything.

Consider, on the other hand, the plight of Sam McGee, the prospector, who discovers the richest vein of gold in the Yukon, but lacks the necessary cash (say $100) to register a claim to it.[20] If Grasp, the banker, is the only man in Dawson City with the ready cash to lend to McGee, then poor Sam will (rationally) have to offer Grasp a half-share in the claim. For although Grasp's $100 is worth only $100 in the absence of McGee's discovery, yet McGee's discovery is worthless to him without Grasp's money. Of course, if there are other sources of funds, Sam is in a position comparable to

[20] For S. McGee, see 'The Cremation of Sam McGee', in R. W. Service, *Songs of a Sourdough* (Toronto, 1907).

Ms Macquarrie; he needs money but not Grasp's money, so he can borrow at the going rate. But in the Dawson City of our example there is, alas, no going rate.

4.3 What if there is no single, transferable good, produced in fixed quantity and divisible at will among the co-operators? How may we determine fair shares of the co-operative surplus? Recall the significance of the claim each person makes. Each claims as much of the surplus as it is possible for him to receive, but only for those co-operative interactions in which he participates. Thus no contribution yields no claim; some contribution yields full claim. A full claim is a claim to the entire surplus in so far as the claimant can receive it. Let us then equate the full claims of the bargainers; each makes a claim equivalent to that of every other person. Suppose that all receive the same proportion of their claims. Then since their claims are equivalent, they receive equivalent shares of the co-operative surplus.

We suggested in the preceding subsection that each person who contributes to a co-operative interaction is equally responsible for the resulting surplus. We may modify this, if co-operation does not result in a fixed quantity of a fully transferable good, to say that each person has a responsibility equivalent to what he can receive of the co-operative surplus. Each then has an equal entitlement to the surplus in so far as the products of co-operation are available to him. Although we have no measure enabling us to divide the surplus into equal shares, yet we can divide it (in general) into shares which are equivalent in terms of the full claims, and so entitlements, of the bargainers. Thus if a fair or impartial distribution of the co-operative surplus relates the benefit each person receives to the contribution he makes, each person's fair share of the surplus is determined by making shares proportional to claims.

We are now in a position to set out a principle of fair bargaining. Suppose, as in 3.2, that the initial bargaining position affords some person a utility u^*, and he claims an outcome affording him a utility $u^{\#}$. Then his claim for the co-operative surplus is $(u^{\#} - u^*)$. Suppose the joint strategy chosen for co-operative interaction affords him an expected utility u; then his expected share of the co-operative surplus is $(u - u^*)$. The proportion of his claim to the co-operative surplus that he receives is then $[(u - u^*)/(u^{\#} - u^*)]$; we shall call this his *relative benefit*. Note that relative benefit must fall between 0, which is the relative benefit of the initial bargaining position $[(u_*-u_*)/u^*-u_*)]$, and 1, which is the relative benefit of the claim $[(u^*-u_*)/(u^*-u_*)]$. If we are to make shares proportional to claims, then we must divide the co-operative surplus so that each person receives maximum equal relative benefit.

This may not always be possible. Or rather, it may be that if each person receives the maximum equal relative benefit, then not all of the co-operative surplus will be distributed among the co-operators. In such a case, it would seem reasonable to maximize minimum relative benefit. Since this is equivalent to maximizing equal relative benefit when the latter uses up the co-operative surplus, we may say that a fair or impartial distribution of the co-operative surplus—and so a fair or impartial choice of the joint strategy for co-operative interaction—must accord with the *Principle of Maximin* (maximum-minimum) *Relative Benefit*.

But this is our old friend, minimax relative concession, in a new guise. For relative benefit and relative concession sum to unity. $[(u-u_*)/(u^*-u_*)] + [(u^*-u)/(u^*-u_*)]=1$. One maximizes minimum relative benefit by minimizing maximum relative concession. Impartiality and rationality coincide in bargaining.

We should not find this result surprising. For those considerations that might justifiably lead us to question the fairness of many instances of everyday bargaining cannot arise in the context of full rationality. In ordinary bargaining persons may conceal significant features of their circumstances, or the full range of their options, may misrepresent their preferences, or the strengths of their preferences. But we suppose each person to be fully informed—to know the possible actions available to every person, the possible outcomes that may result from those actions, and the utility pay-offs to every person of each possible outcome. In ordinary bargaining persons may bluff, especially if they are also able to conceal or misrepresent factors, so that others have uncertain or mistaken expectations about what the bluffers are willing to do. But here there is no place for bluffing; not only is each person fully informed but he is a rational utility-maximizer who knows his fellows to be also rational utility-maximizers. In ordinary bargaining persons may make threats, but among fully rational persons threats are useless; no one will believe anyone who claims that he will act in a non-utility-maximizing way should others not comply with his threat, and to say that one will act in a utility-maximizing way is not to threaten.[21] Our bargainers have no psychological strengths to exploit, or psychological weaknesses to be exploited. And we assume that bargaining is cost free, in terms of both utility and time, so that no one need come to a decision without full consideration; bargaining is unpressured. Thus each bargainer can employ only his own rationality to appeal to the equal rationality of his fellows. In addition to rationality, there are only each person's preferences and possible actions to consider, and it is about these that everyone bargains.

We might suppose that even granting the ideal nature of our bargainers, their circumstances might nevertheless give rise to significant partiality. But problems about circumstances concern the initial bargaining position, not the process of bargaining. We shall turn to these in Chapter VII. Certainly, if the ideal of co-operative interaction is to eliminate the free-ridership and parasitism of natural interaction, then some constraint on identifying the initial position with the non-co-operative outcome will be required, since that outcome may incorporate the effects of the very activities co-operation would eliminate. But here our concern is with the choice of a basis for co-operative interaction taking an initial position for granted, and our argument is that in affording equal or equivalent shares of the co-operative surplus to all persons, the principle of minimax relative concession ensures that bargaining impartially relates each person's contribution to co-operation to the benefit he receives from it.

Let us conclude this discussion by noting that many of our actual moral principles and practices are in effect applications of the requirements of minimax relative concession to particular contexts. We may suppose that promise-keeping, truth-telling, fair dealing, are to be defended by showing that adherence to them permits persons to co-operate in ways that may be expected to equalize, at least roughly, the relative benefits afforded by interaction. These are among the core practices of the morality that we may commend to each individual by showing that it commands his rational agreement.

[21] We shall argue in VI.3.2 that threats are compatible with rationality, but not in the context of co-operation. In effect, threat behaviour would be proscribed by the constraint on the initial bargaining position, to be developed in Chapter VII.

VI

COMPLIANCE: MAXIMIZATION CONSTRAINED

1.1 The just person is disposed to comply with the requirements of the principle of minimax relative concession in interacting with those of his fellows whom he believes to be similarly disposed. The just person is fit for society because he has internalized the idea of mutual benefit, so that in choosing his course of action he gives primary consideration to the prospect of realizing the co-operative outcome. If he is able to bring about, or may reasonably expect to bring about, an outcome that is both (nearly) fair and (nearly) optimal, then he chooses to do so; only if he may not reasonably expect this does he choose to maximize his own utility.

In order to relate our account of the co-operative person to the conditions on rational interaction stated in Chapter III, let us define a fair optimizing strategy (or choice, or response) as one that, given the expected strategies of the others, may be expected to yield an outcome that is nearly fair and optimal—an outcome with utility pay-offs close to those of the co-operative outcome, as determined by minimax relative concession. We speak of the response as nearly fair and optimal because in many situations a person will not expect others to do precisely what would be required by minimax relative concession, so that he may not be able to choose a strategy with an expected outcome that is completely fair or fully optimal. But we suppose that he will still be disposed to co-operative rather than to non-co-operative interaction.

A just person then accepts this reading of condition A : A′: Each person's choice must be a fair optimizing response to the choice he expects the others to make, provided such a response is available to him; otherwise, his choice must be a utility-maximizing response. A just person is disposed to interact with others on the basis of condition A′.

A just person must however be aware that not all (otherwise) rational persons accept this reading of the original condition A. In forming expectations about the choices of others, he need not suppose that their choices will satisfy A′. Thus as conditions of strategic interaction, we cannot dispense with the original conditions A, B, and C; 'rational response' remains (at least until our theory has gained universal acceptance) open to several interpretations.

Our task in this chapter is to provide a utility-maximizing rationale for condition A′. We shall do this by demonstrating that, given certain plausible and desirable conditions, a rational utility-maximizer, faced with the choice between accepting no constraints on his choices in interaction, and accepting the constraints on his choices required by minimax relative concession, chooses the latter. He makes a choice about how to make further choices; he chooses, on utility-maximizing grounds, not to make further choices on those grounds.

In defending condition A′, we defend compliance with agreements based, explicitly or implicitly, on the principle of minimax relative concession. Indeed, we defend compliance, not just with agreements, but with practices that would be agreed to or endorsed on the basis of this principle. If our defence fails, then we must conclude that rational bargaining is in vain and that co-operation, although on a rationally agreed basis, is not itself rationally required, so that it does not enable us to overcome the failings of natural and market interaction. Indeed, if our defence fails, then we must conclude that a rational morality is a chimera, so that there is no rational and impartial constraint on the pursuit of individual utility.

In defending condition A′, we uphold the external rationality of co-operation against the objections of the egoist. Whatever else he may do, the egoist always seeks to maximize his expected utility. Recognizing that co-operation offers the prospect of mutual benefit, he nevertheless denies that it is rational to behave co-operatively, where this would constrain maximization. This egoist makes his philosophical début as the Foole in Thomas Hobbes's *Leviathan*, where we shall now observe him.

1.2 Hobbes begins his moral theory with a purely permissive conception of the right of nature, stating what one may do, not what one must be let do, or what must be done for one. The permission is rational, for as Hobbes says, 'Neither by the word *right* is anything else signified, than that liberty which every man hath to make use of his natural faculties according to right reason.'[1] And Hobbes claims that in the natural condition of humankind this liberty is unlimited,

[1] Hobbes, *De Cive*, ch. I, para. 7; in *Man and Citizen*, p. 115.

so that 'every man has a Right to every thing; even to one anothers body.'[2] In so treating the right of nature, Hobbes expresses a straightforwardly maximizing view of rational action, subject to the material condition, central to his psychology, that each seeks above all his own preservation. For Hobbes each person has the initial right to do whatever he can to preserve himself, but there is no obligation on others, either to let him do or to do for him what is necessary to his preservation.

The condition in which this unlimited right is exercised by all persons is, Hobbes claims, one in which 'there can be no security to any man, (how strong or wise soever he be,) of living out the time, which Nature ordinarily alloweth men to live.'[3] Persons who seek their own preservation find themselves locked in mortal combat. But if reason brings human beings to this condition of war, it can also lead them out of it. Hobbes says, 'Reason suggesteth convenient Articles of Peace, upon which men may be drawn to agreement. These Articles ... are called the Lawes of Nature.'[4] Laws of nature are precepts, 'found out by Reason, by which a man is forbidden to do, that, which is destructive of his life, or taketh away the means of preserving the same; and to omit, that, by which he thinketh it may be best preserved.'[5]

Since war is inimical to preservation, the fundamental or first law of nature is, 'That every man, ought to endeavour Peace, as farre as he has hope of obtaining it', to which Hobbes adds, 'and when he cannot obtain it, that he may seek, and use, all helps, and advantages of Warre.'[6] From this Hobbes immediately derives a second law, setting out, as the fundamental means to peace, 'That a man be willing, when others are so too, as farre-forth, as for Peace, and defence of himselfe he shall think it necessary, to lay down this right to all things; and be contented with so much liberty against other men, as he would allow other men against himselfe.'[7] Since the unlimited right of nature gives rise to war, renouncing some part of this right is necessary for peace. The renunciation must of course be mutual; each person expects to benefit, not from his own act of renunciation, but from that of his fellows, and so no one has reason to renounce his rights unilaterally. What Hobbes envisages is a rational bargain in which each accepts certain constraints on his

[2] Hobbes, *Leviathan*, ch. 14, p. 64.
[3] Ibid.
[4] Ibid., ch. 13, p. 63.
[5] Ibid., ch. 14, p. 64.
[6] Ibid.
[7] Ibid., ch. 14, pp. 64–5.

freedom of action so that all may avoid the costs of the natural condition of war.

The defence of this second law is perfectly straightforward. Hobbes needs to say only that 'as long as every man holdeth this Right, of doing any thing he liketh; so long are all men in the condition of Warre.'[8] And the mutuality required by the law is defended in an equally simple way: 'if other men will not lay down their Right, as well as he; then there is no Reason for any one, to devest himselfe of his: For that were to expose himselfe to Prey, (which no man is bound to) rather than to dispose himselfe to Peace.'[9] It is directly advantageous for each to agree with his fellows to a mutual renunciation or laying down of right, and so a mutual acceptance of constraint. Hobbes conceives such constraint as obligation, arising only through agreement, for there is 'no Obligation on any man, which ariseth not from some Act of his own; for all men equally, are by Nature Free.'[10] Hobbes's theory, as our own, introduces morals by agreement.

Hobbes recognizes that it is one thing to make an agreement or covenant, quite another to keep it. He does not suppose that the second law of nature, enjoining us to agree, also enjoins us to compliance. Thus he introduces a third law of nature, 'That men performe their Covenants made', which he considers to be the 'Originall of JUSTICE'.[11] A just person is one who keeps the agreements he has rationally made.

Hobbes's defence of this third law lacks the straightforwardness of his defence of the second. As he recognizes, without it 'Covenants are in vain, and but Empty words; and the Right of all men to all things remaining, wee are still in the condition of Warre.'[12] But this does not show that conformity to it yields any direct benefit. Each person maximizes his expected utility in making a covenant, since each gains from the mutual renunciation it involves. But each does not maximize his expected utility in keeping a covenant, in so far as it requires him to refrain from exercising some part of his previous liberty. And this opens the door to the objection of the Foole.

We shall let him speak for himself.

The Foole hath sayd in his heart, there is no such thing as Justice; and sometimes also with his tongue; seriously alleaging, that every mans

[8] Ibid., ch. 14, p. 65.
[9] Ibid.
[10] Ibid., ch. 21, p. 111.
[11] Ibid., ch. 15, p. 71.
[12] Ibid.

conservation, and contentment, being committed to his own care, there could be no reason, why every man might not do what he thought conduced thereunto: and therefore also to make, or not make; keep, or not keep Covenants, was not against Reason, when it conduced to ones benefit. He does not therein deny, that there be Covenants; and that they are sometimes broken, sometimes kept; and that such breach of them may be called Injustice, and the observance of them Justice: but he questioneth, whether Injustice . . . may not sometimes stand with that Reason, which dictateth to every man his own good. . . .[13]

The Foole does not seriously challenge the second law of nature, for Hobbes assumes that each person will make only those covenants that he expects to be advantageous, and such behaviour the Foole does not question. What the Foole challenges is the third law, the law requiring compliance, or adherence to one's covenants, for let it be ever so advantageous to make an agreement, may it not then be even more advantageous to violate the agreement made? And if advantageous, then is it not rational? The Foole challenges the heart of the connection between reason and morals that both Hobbes and we seek to establish—the rationality of accepting a moral constraint on the direct pursuit of one's greatest utility.

1.3 In replying to the Foole, Hobbes claims that the question is, given sufficient security of performance by one party, 'whether it be against reason, that is, against the benefit of the other to performe, or not'.[14] On the most natural interpretation, Hobbes is asking whether keeping one's covenant is a rational, that is utility-maximizing, response to covenant-keeping by one's fellows. If this is indeed Hobbes's view, then he is endeavouring to refute the Foole by appealing, in effect, to condition A for strategically rational choice, taking a rational response to be simply a utility-maximizing response. We may not be very hopeful about Hobbes's prospect of success.

Hobbes's first argument reminds the Foole that the rationality of choice depends on expectations, not actual results. It need not detain us. His second argument joins issue with the Foole at a deeper level.

He . . . that breaketh his Covenant, and consequently declareth that he thinks he may with reason do so, cannot be received into any Society, that unite themselves for Peace and Defence, but by the errour of them that receive him; nor when he is received, be retayned in it, without seeing the

[13] Ibid., ch. 15, p. 72.

[14] Ibid., ch. 15, p. 73.

danger of their errour; which errours a man cannot reasonably reckon upon as the means of his security.[15]

A person disposed to violate his covenants cannot be admitted as a party to co-operative arrangements by those who are both rational and aware of his disposition, and so such a person cannot rationally expect to reap the benefits available to co-operators. Even if his particular breaches of covenant would benefit him, yet the disposition that leads him to such breaches does not.

In effect Hobbes moves the question from whether it be against reason, understood as utility-maximization, to keep one's agreement (given sufficient security of others keeping their agreements), to whether it be against reason to be disposed to keep one's agreement. The disposition to decide whether or not to adhere to one's covenants or agreements by appealing to directly utility-maximizing considerations, is itself disadvantageous, if known, or sufficiently suspected, because it excludes one from participating, with those who suspect one's disposition, in those co-operative arrangements in which the benefits to be realized require each to forgo utility-maximization—or in Hobbes's terminology, require each to lay down some portion of his original, unlimited right of nature. The disposition to keep one's agreement, given sufficient security, without appealing to directly utility-maximizing considerations, makes one an eligible partner in beneficial co-operation, and so is itself beneficial. This will prove to be the key to our demonstration that a fully rational utility-maximizer disposes himself to compliance with his rationally undertaken covenants or agreements.

But for Hobbes to take full advantage of this response to the Foole, he must revise his conception of rationality, breaking the direct connection between reason and benefit with which he began his reply. Hobbes needs to say that it is rational to perform one's covenant even when performance is not directly to one's benefit, provided that it is to one's benefit to be disposed to perform. But this he never says. And as long as the Foole is allowed to relate reason directly to benefit in performance, rather than to benefit in the disposition to perform, he can escape refutation.

Hobbes does suggest a revision in his conception of rationality in his discussion with Bishop Bramhall. Agreeing with Bramhall that 'moral goodness is the conformity of an action with right reason', he

[15] Ibid.

does not claim that what is morally good is conducive to one's benefit, but instead holds that

> All the real good ... is that which is not repugnant to the law ... for the law is all the right reason we have, and ... is the infallible rule of moral goodness. The reason whereof is this, that because neither mine nor the Bishop's reason is ... fit to be a rule of our moral actions, we have therefore set up over ourselves a sovereign governor, and agreed that his laws shall ... dictate to us what is really good.[16]

To the Foole's contention that injustice may 'sometimes stand with that Reason, which dictateth to every man his own good',[17] Hobbes can reply that injustice may not stand with that reason that is constituted by the law of the sovereign. Just as it is unprofitable for each man to retain his entire natural right, so it is unprofitable for each man to retain his natural reason as guide to his actions. But Hobbes does not suppose that each man internalizes the right reason of the sovereign. His egoistic psychology allows the internalization of no standard other than that of direct concern with individual preservation and contentment. And so it is only in so far as the sovereign is able to enforce the law that compliance with it is rationally binding on the individual. But this is to propose a political, not a moral, solution to the problem posed by the Foole.

If the market acts as an invisible hand, directing the efforts of each person intending only his own benefit to a social optimum, the sovereign acts as a very visible foot, directing, by well-placed kicks, the efforts of each to the same social end. Each device performs the same task, ensuring the coincidence of an equilibrium in which each person maximizes his expected utility given the actions of his fellows, with an optimum in which each person gains the maximum utility compatible with the utilities of his fellows. Each device affects the conditions under which interaction occurs, leaving every individual free to maximize his utility given those conditions. Of course, the sovereign appears as a constraint on each person's freedom whereas the market does not, but this is the difference between visibility and invisibility; the sovereign visibly shapes the conditions that reconcile each person's interest with those of his fellows, whereas the market so shapes these conditions simply in virtue of its structure.

[16] Hobbes, *The Questions Concerning Liberty, Necessity, and Chance*, 1656, no. xiv; in Sir William Molesworth (ed.), *The English Works of Thomas Hobbes*, 11 vols. (London, 1839–45), vol. 5, pp. 193–4.

[17] Hobbes, *Leviathan*, ch. 15, p. 72.

The sovereign makes morality, understood as a constraint on each person's endeavour to maximize his own utility, as unnecessary as does the market. Our moral enquiry has been motivated by the problems created for utility-maximizers by externalities. Adam Smith reminds us of the conditions in which externalities are absent, so that the market ensures that each person's free, maximizing behaviour results in an optimal outcome. Thomas Hobbes introduces the sovereign, who constrains each person's options so that maximizing behaviour results in a seemingly optimal outcome even when externalities are present. We may retain the idea of justice as expressing the requirement of impartiality for principles that regulate social interaction, but it no longer expresses a constraint on individual maximization. It would seem that between them, economics and politics resolve our problem with no need for morality.

But Hobbes's sovereign lacks the appeal of the market, and for good reason. The invisible hand is a costless solution to the problems of natural interaction, but the visible foot is a very costly solution. Those subject to the Hobbesian sovereign do not, in fact, attain an optimal outcome; each pays a portion of the costs needed to enforce adherence to agreements, and these costs render the outcome sub-optimal. Even if we suppose that power does not corrupt, so that the sovereign is the perfect instrument of his subjects, acting only in their interests, yet each would expect to do better if all would adhere voluntarily to their agreements, so that enforcement and its costs would be unnecessary. We pay a heavy price, if we are indeed creatures who rationally accept no internal constraint on the pursuit of our own utility, and who consequently are able to escape from the state of nature, in those circumstances in which externalities are unavoidably present, only by political, and not by moral, devices. Could we but voluntarily comply with our rationally undertaken agreements, we should save ourselves this price.

We do not suppose that voluntary compliance would eliminate the need for social institutions and practices, and their costs. But it would eliminate the need for some of those institutions whose concern is with enforcement. Authoritative decision-making cannot be eliminated, but our ideal would be a society in which the coercive enforcement of such decisions would be unnecessary. More realistically, we suppose that such enforcement is needed to create and maintain those conditions under which individuals may rationally expect the degree of compliance from their fellows needed to elicit their own voluntary compliance. Internal, moral constraints operate to ensure compliance under conditions of security established by external, political constraints. But before we can expect this view to be accepted we must show, what the Foole denies, that it is rational to dispose oneself to co-operate, and so to accept internal, moral constraints. Hobbes's argument that those not so disposed may not rationally be received into society, is the foundation on which we shall build.

2.1 The Foole, and those who share his conception of practical reason, must suppose that there are potentialities for co-operation to which each person would rationally agree, were he to expect the agreement to be carried out, but that remain unactualized, since each rationally expects that someone, perhaps himself, perhaps another, would not adhere to the agreement. In Chapter V we argued that co-operation is rational if each co-operator may expect a utility nearly equal to what he would be assigned by the principle of minimax relative concession. The Foole does not dispute the necessity of this condition, but denies its sufficiency. He insists that for it to be rational to comply with an agreement to co-operate, the utility an individual may expect from co-operation must also be no less than what he would expect were he to violate his agreement. And he then argues that for it to be rational to agree to co-operate, then, although one need not consider it rational to comply oneself, one must believe it rational for the others to comply. Given that everyone is rational, fully informed, and correct in his expectations, the Foole supposes that co-operation is actualized only if each person expects a utility from co-operation no less than his non-compliance utility. The benefits that could be realized through co-operative arrangements that do not afford each person at least his non-compliance utility remain forever beyond the reach of rational human beings—forever denied us because our very rationality would lead us to violate the agreements necessary to realize these benefits. Such agreements will not be made.

The Foole rejects what would seem to be the ordinary view that, given neither unforeseen circumstances nor misrepresentation of terms, it is rational to comply with an agreement if it is rational to make it. He insists that holders of this view have failed to think out the full implications of the maximizing conception of practical rationality. In choosing one takes one's stand in the present, and looks to the expected utility that will result from each possible action. What has happened may affect this utility; that one has agreed may affect the utility one expects from doing, or not doing, what would keep the agreement. But what has happened provides in itself no reason for choice. That one had reason for making an agreement can give one reason for keeping it only by affecting the utility of compliance. To think otherwise is to reject utility-maximization.

Let us begin our answer to the Foole by recalling the distinction introduced in V.1.3 between an individual strategy and a joint strategy.[18] An individual strategy is a lottery over the possible actions of a single actor. A joint strategy is a lottery over possible outcomes. Co-operators have joint strategies available to them.

We may think of participation in a co-operative activity, such as a hunt, in which each huntsman has his particular role co-ordinated with that of the others, as the implementation of a single joint strategy. We may also extend the notion to include participation in a practice, such as the making and keeping of promises, where each person's behaviour is predicated on the conformity of others to the practice.

An individual is not able to ensure that he acts on a joint strategy, since whether he does depends, not only on what he intends, but on what those with whom he interacts intend. But we may say that an individual bases his action on a joint strategy in so far as he intentionally chooses what the strategy requires of him. Normally, of course, one bases one's action on a joint strategy only if one expects those with whom one interacts to do so as well, so that one expects actually to act on that strategy. But we need not import such an expectation into the conception of basing one's action on a joint strategy.

A person co-operates with his fellows only if he bases his actions on a joint strategy; to agree to co-operate is to agree to employ a joint rather than an individual strategy. The Foole insists that it is rational to co-operate only if the utility one expects from acting on the co-operative joint strategy is at least equal to the utility one would expect were one to act instead on one's best individual strategy. This defeats the end of co-operation, which is in effect to substitute a joint

[18] Our answer to the Foole builds on, but supersedes, my discussion in 'Reason and Maximization', *Canadian Journal of Philosophy* 4 (1975), pp. 424–33.

strategy for individual strategies in situations in which this substitution is to everyone's benefit.

A joint strategy is fully rational only if it yields an optimal outcome, or in other words, only if it affords each person who acts on it the maximum utility compatible in the situation with the utility afforded each other person who acts on the strategy. Thus we may say that a person acting on a rational joint strategy maximizes his utility, subject to the constraint set by the utilities it affords to every other person. An individual strategy is rational if and only if it maximizes one's utility given the *strategies* adopted by the other persons; a joint strategy is rational only if (but not if and only if) it maximizes one's utility given the *utilities* afforded to the other persons.

Let us say that a *straightforward* maximizer is a person who seeks to maximize his utility given the strategies of those with whom he interacts. A *constrained* maximizer, on the other hand, is a person who seeks in some situations to maximize her utility, given not the strategies but the utilities of those with whom she interacts. The Foole accepts the rationality of straightforward maximization. We, in defending condition A′ for strategic rationality (stated in 1.1), accept the rationality of constrained maximization.

A constrained maximizer has a conditional disposition to base her actions on a joint strategy, without considering whether some individual strategy would yield her greater expected utility. But not all constraint could be rational; we must specify the characteristics of the conditional disposition. We shall therefore identify a constrained maximizer thus: (i) someone who is conditionally disposed to base her actions on a joint strategy or practice should the utility she expects were everyone so to base his action be no less than what she would expect were everyone to employ individual strategies, and approach what she would expect from the co-operative outcome determined by minimax relative concession; (ii) someone who actually acts on this conditional disposition should her expected utility be greater than what she would expect were everyone to employ individual strategies. Or in other words, a constrained maximizer is ready to co-operate in ways that, if followed by all, would yield outcomes that she would find beneficial and not unfair, and she does co-operate should she expect an actual practice or activity to be beneficial. In determining the latter she must take into account the possibility that some persons will fail, or refuse, to act co-operatively. Henceforth, unless we specifically state otherwise, we shall understand by a constrained maximizer one with this particular disposition.

There are three points in our characterization of constrained maximization that should be noted. The first is that a constrained maximizer is conditionally disposed to act, not only on the unique joint strategy that would be prescribed by a rational bargain, but on any joint strategy that affords her a utility approaching what she would expect from fully rational co-operation. The range of acceptable joint strategies is, and must be left, unspecified. The idea is that in real interaction it is reasonable to accept co-operative arrangements that fall short of the ideal of full rationality and fairness, provided they do not fall too far short. At some point, of course, one decides to ignore a joint strategy, even if acting on it would afford one an expected utility greater than one would expect were everyone to employ an individual strategy, because one hopes thereby to obtain agreement on, or acquiescence in, another joint strategy which in being fairer is also more favourable to oneself. At precisely what point one decides this we make no attempt to say. We simply defend a conception of constrained maximization that does not require that all acceptable joint strategies be ideal.

Constrained maximization thus links the idea of morals by agreement to actual moral practice. We suppose that some moral principles may be understood as representing joint strategies prescribed to each person as part of the ongoing co-operative arrangements that constitute society. These principles require each person to refrain from the direct pursuit of her maximum utility, in order to achieve mutually advantageous and reasonably fair outcomes. Actual moral principles are not in general those to which we should have agreed in a fully rational bargain, but it is reasonable to adhere to them in so far as they offer a reasonable approximation to ideal principles. We may defend actual moral principles by reference to ideal co-operative arrangements, and the closer the principles fit, the stronger the defence. We do not of course suppose that our actual moral principles derive historically from a bargain, but in so far as the constraints they impose are acceptable to a rational constrained maximizer, we may fit them into the framework of a morality rationalized by the idea of agreement.

The second point is that a constrained maximizer does not base her actions on a joint strategy whenever a nearly fair and optimal outcome would result were everyone to do likewise. Her disposition to co-operate is conditional on her expectation that she will benefit in comparison with the utility she could expect were no one to co-operate. Thus she must estimate the likelihood that others involved in the prospective practice or interaction will act co-operatively, and calculate, not the utility she would expect were all to co-operate, but the utility she would expect if she co-operates, given her estimate of the degree to which others will co-operate. Only if this exceeds what she would expect from universal non-co-operation, does her conditional disposition to constraint actually manifest itself in a decision to base her actions on the co-operative joint strategy.

Thus, faced with persons whom she believes to be straightforward maximizers, a constrained maximizer does not play into their hands by basing her actions on the joint strategy she would like everyone to accept, but rather, to avoid being exploited, she behaves as a straightforward maximizer, acting on the individual strategy that maximizes her utility given the strategies she expects the others to employ. A constrained maximizer makes reasonably certain that she is among like-disposed persons before she actually constrains her direct pursuit of maximum utility.

But note that a constrained maximizer may find herself required to act in such a way that she would have been better off had she not entered into co-operation. She may be engaged in a co-operative activity that, given the willingness of her fellows to do their part, she expects to be fair and beneficial, but that, should chance so befall, requires her to act so that she incurs some loss greater than had she never engaged herself in the endeavour. Here she would still be disposed to comply, acting in a way that results in real disadvantage to herself, because given her *ex ante* beliefs about the dispositions of her fellows and the prospects of benefit, participation in the activity affords her greater expected utility than non-participation.

And this brings us to the third point, that constrained maximization is not straightforward maximization in its most effective disguise. The constrained maximizer is not merely the person who, taking a larger view than her fellows, serves her overall interest by sacrificing the immediate benefits of ignoring joint strategies and violating co-operative arrangements in order to obtain the long-run benefits of being trusted by others.[19] Such a person exhibits no real

[19] Thus constrained maximization is not parallel to such strategies as 'tit-for-tat' that have been advocated for so-called iterated Prisoner's Dilemmas. Constrained

constraint. The constrained maximizer does not reason more effectively about how to maximize her utility, but reasons in a different way. We may see this most clearly by considering how each faces the decision whether to base her action on a joint strategy. The constrained maximizer considers (i) whether the outcome, should everyone do so, be nearly fair and optimal, and (ii) whether the outcome she realistically expects should she do so affords her greater utility than universal non-co-operation. If both of these conditions are satisfied she bases her action on the joint strategy. The straightforward maximizer considers simply whether the outcome he realistically expects should he base his action on the joint strategy affords him greater utility than the outcome he would expect were he to act on any alternative strategy—taking into account, of course, long-term as well as short-term effects. Only if this condition is satisfied does he base his action on the joint strategy.

Consider a purely isolated interaction, in which both parties know that how each chooses will have no bearing on how each fares in other interactions. Suppose that the situation has the familiar Prisoner's Dilemma structure; each benefits from mutual co-operation in relation to mutual non-co-operation, but each benefits from non-co-operation whatever the other does. In such a situation, a straightforward maximizer chooses not to co-operate. A constrained maximizer chooses to co-operate if, given her estimate of whether or not her partner will choose to co-operate, her own expected utility is greater than the utility she would expect from the non-co-operative outcome.

Constrained maximizers can thus obtain co-operative benefits that are unavailable to straightforward maximizers, however far-sighted the latter may be. But straightforward maximizers can, on occasion, exploit unwary constrained maximizers. Each supposes her disposition to be rational. But who is right?

2.2 To demonstrate the rationality of suitably constrained maximization we solve a problem of rational choice. We consider what a rational individual would choose, given the alternatives of adopting straightforward maximization, and of adopting constrained maximization, as his disposition for strategic behaviour. Although this

maximizers may co-operate even if neither expects her choice to affect future situations. Thus our treatment of co-operation does not make the appeal to reciprocity necessary to Robert Axelrod's account; see 'The Emergence of Co-operation among Egoists', *American Political Science Review* 75 (1981), pp. 306–18.

choice is about interaction, to make it is not to engage in interaction. Taking others' dispositions as fixed, the individual reasons parametrically to his own best disposition. Thus he compares the expected utility of disposing himself to maximize utility given others' expected strategy choices, with the utility of disposing himself to co-operate with others in bringing about nearly fair and optimal outcomes.

To choose between these dispositions, a person needs to consider only those situations in which they would yield different behaviour. If both would be expressed in a maximizing individual strategy, or if both would lead one to base action on the joint strategy one expects from others, then their utility expectations are identical. But if the disposition to constraint would be expressed in basing action on a joint strategy, whereas the disposition to maximize straightforwardly would be expressed in defecting from the joint strategy, then their utility expectations differ. Only situations giving rise to such differences need be considered. These situations must satisfy two conditions. First, they must afford the prospect of mutually beneficial and fair co-operation, since otherwise constraint would be pointless. And second, they must afford some prospect for individually beneficial defection, since otherwise no constraint would be needed to realize the mutual benefits.

We suppose, then, an individual, considering what disposition to adopt, for situations in which his expected utility is u should each person act on an individual strategy, u' should all act on a co-operative joint strategy, and u'' should he act on an individual strategy and the others base their actions on a co-operative joint strategy, and u is less than u' (so that he benefits from co-operation as required by the first condition) and u' in turn is less than u'' (so that he benefits from defection as required by the second condition).

Consider these two arguments which this person might put to himself:

Argument (1): Suppose I adopt straightforward maximization. Then if I expect the others to base their actions on a joint strategy, I defect to my best individual strategy, and expect a utility, u''. If I expect the others to act on individual strategies, then so do I, and expect a utility, u. If the probability that others will base their actions on a joint strategy is p, then my overall expected utility is $[pu'' + (1-p)u]$.

Suppose I adopt constrained maximization. Then if I expect the others to base their actions on a joint strategy, so do I, and expect a utility u'. If I expect the others to act on individual strategies, then so do I, and expect a utility, u. Thus my overall expected utility is $[pu' + (1-p)u]$.

Since u'' is greater than u', $[pu'' + (1-p)u]$ is greater than $[pu' + (1-p)u]$, for any value of p other than 0 (and for $p = 0$, the two are equal). Therefore, to maximize my overall expectation of utility, I should adopt straightforward maximization.

Argument (2): Suppose I adopt straightforward maximization. Then I must expect the others to employ maximizing individual strategies in interacting with me; so do I, and expect a utility, u.

Suppose I adopt constrained maximization. Then if the others are conditionally disposed to constrained maximization, I may expect them to base their actions on a co-operative joint strategy in interacting with me; so do I, and expect a utility u'. If they are not so disposed, I employ a maximizing strategy and expect u as before. If the probability that others are disposed to constrained maximization is p, then my overall expected utility is $[pu' + (1-p)u]$.

Since u' is greater than u, $[pu' + (1-p)u]$ is greater than u for any value of p other than 0 (and for $p = 0$, the two are equal). Therefore, to maximize my overall expectation of utility, I should adopt constrained maximization.

Since these arguments yield opposed conclusions, they cannot both be sound. The first has the form of a dominance argument. In any situation in which others act non-co-operatively, one may expect the same utility whether one is disposed to straightforward or to constrained maximization. In any situation in which others act co-operatively, one may expect a greater utility if one is disposed to straightforward maximization. Therefore one should adopt straightforward maximization. But this argument would be valid only if the probability of others acting co-operatively were, as the argument assumes, independent of one's own disposition. And this is not the case. Since persons disposed to co-operation only act co-operatively with those whom they suppose to be similarly disposed, a straightforward maximizer does not have the opportunities to benefit which present themselves to the constrained maximizer. Thus argument (1) fails.

Argument (2) takes into account what argument (1) ignores—the difference between the way in which constrained maximizers interact with those similarly disposed, and the way in which they interact with straightforward maximizers. Only those disposed to keep their agreements are rationally acceptable as parties to agreements. Constrained maximizers are able to make beneficial agreements with their fellows that the straightforward cannot, not because the latter would be unwilling to agree, but because they would not be admitted as parties to agreement given their disposition to violation. Straightforward maximizers are disposed to take advantage of their fellows should the opportunity arise; knowing this, their fellows would prevent such opportunity arising. With the same opportunities, straightforward maximizers would necessarily obtain greater benefits. A dominance argument establishes this. But because they differ in their dispositions, straightforward and constrained maximizers differ also in their opportunities, to the benefit of the latter.

But argument (2) unfortunately contains an undefended assumption. A person's expectations about how others will interact with him depend strictly on his own choice of disposition only if that choice is known by the others. What we have shown is that, if the straightforward maximizer and the constrained maximizer appear in their true colours, then the constrained maximizer must do better. But need each so appear? The Foole may agree, under the pressure of our argument and its parallel in the second argument we ascribed to Hobbes, that the question to be asked is not whether it is or is not rational to keep (particular) covenants, but whether it is or is not rational to be (generally) disposed to the keeping of covenants, and he may recognize that he cannot win by pleading the cause of straightforward maximization in a direct way. But may he not win by linking straightforward maximization to the appearance of constraint? Is not the Foole's ultimate argument that the truly prudent person, the fully rational utility-maximizer, must seek to appear trustworthy, an upholder of his agreements? For then he will not be excluded from the co-operative arrangements of his fellows, but will be welcomed as a partner, while he awaits opportunities to benefit at their expense—and, preferably, without their knowledge, so that he may retain the guise of constraint and trustworthiness.

There is a short way to defeat this manœuvre. Since our argument is to be applied to ideally rational persons, we may simply add another idealizing assumption, and take our persons to be *transpar-*

ent.[20] Each is directly aware of the disposition of his fellows, and so aware whether he is interacting with straightforward or constrained maximizers. Deception is impossible; the Foole must appear as he is.

But to assume transparency may seem to rob our argument of much of its interest. We want to relate our idealizing assumptions to the real world. If constrained maximization defeats straightforward maximization only if all persons are transparent, then we shall have failed to show that under actual, or realistically possible, conditions, moral constraints are rational. We shall have refuted the Foole but at the price of robbing our refutation of all practical import.

However, transparency proves to be a stronger assumption than our argument requires. We may appeal instead to a more realistic *translucency*, supposing that persons are neither transparent nor opaque, so that their disposition to co-operate or not may be ascertained by others, not with certainty, but as more than mere guesswork. Opaque beings would be condemned to seek political solutions for those problems of natural interaction that could not be met by the market. But we shall show that for beings as translucent as we may reasonably consider ourselves to be, moral solutions are rationally available.

2.3 If persons are translucent, then constrained maximizers (CMs) will sometimes fail to recognize each other, and will then interact non-co-operatively even if co-operation would have been mutually beneficial. CMs will sometimes fail to identify straightforward maximizers (SMs) and will then act co-operatively; if the SMs correctly identify the CMs they will be able to take advantage of them. Translucent CMs must expect to do less well in interaction than would transparent CMs; translucent SMs must expect to do better than would transparent SMs. Although it would be rational to choose to be a CM were one transparent, it need not be rational if one is only translucent. Let us examine the conditions under which the decision to dispose oneself to constrained maximization is rational for translucent persons, and ask if these are (or may be) the conditions in which we find ourselves.

As in the preceding subsection, we need consider only situations in

[20] That the discussion in 'Reason and Maximization' assumes transparency was pointed out to me by Derek Parfit. See his discussion of 'the self-interest theory' in *Reasons and Persons* (Oxford, 1984), esp. pp. 18–19. See also the discussion of 'Reason and Maximization' in S. L. Darwall, *Impartial Reason* (Ithaca, NY, 1983), esp. pp. 197–8.

which CMs and SMs may fare differently. These are situations that afford both the prospect of mutually beneficial co-operation (in relation to non-co-operation) and individually beneficial defection (in relation to co-operation). Let us simplify by supposing that the non-co-operative outcome results unless (i) those interacting are CMs who achieve mutual recognition, in which case the co-operative outcome results, or (ii) those interacting include CMs who fail to recognize SMs but are themselves recognized, in which case the outcome affords the SMs the benefits of individual defection and the CMs the costs of having advantage taken of mistakenly basing their actions on a co-operative strategy. We ignore the inadvertent taking of advantage when CMs mistake their fellows for SMs.

There are then four possible pay-offs—non-co-operation, co-operation, defection, and exploitation (as we may call the outcome for the person whose supposed partner defects from the joint strategy on which he bases his action). For the typical situation, we assign defection the value 1, co-operation u'' (less than 1), non-co-operation u' (less than u''), and exploitation 0 (less than u'). We now introduce three probabilities. The first, p, is the probability that CMs will achieve mutual recognition and so successfully co-operate. The second, q, is the probability that CMs will fail to recognize SMs but will themselves be recognized, so that defection and exploitation will result. The third, r, is the probability that a randomly selected member of the population is a CM. (We assume that everyone is a CM or an SM, so the probability that a randomly selected person is an SM is $(1-r)$.) The values of p, q, and r must of course fall between 0 and 1.

Let us now calculate expected utilities for CMs and SMs in situations affording both the prospect of mutually beneficial co-operation and individually beneficial defection. A CM expects the utility u' unless (i) she succeeds in co-operating with other CMs or (ii) she is exploited by an SM. The probability of (i) is the combined probability that she interacts with a CM, r, and that they achieve mutual recognition, p, or rp. In this case she gains $(u''-u')$ over her non-co-operative expectation u'. Thus the effect of (i) is to increase her utility expectation by a value $[rp(u''-u')]$. The probability of (ii) is the combined probability that she interacts with an SM, $1-r$, and that she fails to recognize him but is recognized, q, or $(1-r)q$. In this case she receives 0, so she loses her non-co-operative expectation u'.

Thus the effect of (ii) is to reduce her utility expectation by a value $[(1-r)qu']$. Taking both (i) and (ii) into account, a CM expects the utility $\{u'+[rp(u''-u')]-(1-r)qu'\}$.

An SM expects the utility u' unless he exploits a CM. The probability of this is the combined probability that he interacts with a CM, r, and that he recognizes her but is not recognized by her, q, or rq. In this case he gains $(1-u')$ over his non-co-operative expectation u'. Thus the effect is to increase his utility expectation by a value $[rq(1-u')]$. An SM thus expects the utility $\{u' + [rq(1-u')]\}$.

It is rational to dispose oneself to constrained maximization if and only if the utility expected by a CM is greater than the utility expected by an SM, which obtains if and only if p/q is *greater* than $\{(1-u')/(u''-u') + [(1-r)u']/[r(u''-u')]\}$.

The first term of this expression, $[(1-u')/(u''-u')]$, relates the gain from defection to the gain through co-operation. The value of defection is of course greater than that of co-operation, so this term is greater than 1. The second term, $\{[(1-r)u']/[r(u''-u')]\}$, depends for its value on r. If $r = 0$ (i.e. if there are no CMs in the population), then its value is infinite. As r increases, the value of the expression decreases, until if $r = 1$ (i.e. if there are only CMs in the population) its value is 0.

We may now draw two important conclusions. First, it is rational to dispose oneself to constrained maximization only if the ratio of p to q, i.e. the ratio between the probability that an interaction involving CMs will result in co-operation and the probability that an interaction involving CMs and SMs will involve exploitation and defection, is greater than the ratio between the gain from defection and the gain through co-operation. If everyone in the population is a CM, then we may replace 'only if' by 'if and only if' in this statement, but in general it is only a necessary condition of the rationality of the disposition to constrained maximization.

Second, as the proportion of CMs in the population increases (so that the value of r increases), the value of the ratio of p to q that is required for it to be rational to dispose oneself to constrained maximization decreases. The more constrained maximizers there are, the greater the risks a constrained maximizer may rationally accept of failed co-operation and exploitation. However, these risks, and particularly the latter, must remain relatively small.

We may illustrate these conclusions by introducing typical numerical values for co-operation and non-co-operation, and then considering different values for r. One may suppose that on the whole, there is no reason that the typical gain from defection over co-operation would be either greater or smaller than the typical gain from co-operation over non-co-operation, and in turn no reason that the latter gain would be greater or smaller than the typical loss from non-co-operation to exploitation. And so, since defection has the value 1 and exploitation 0, let us assign co-operation the value 2/3 and non-co-operation 1/3.

The gain from defection, $(1-u')$, thus is 2/3; the gain through co-operation, $(u''-u')$, is 1/3. Since p/q must exceed $\{(1-u')/(u''-u') + [(1-r)u']/[r(u''-u')]\}$ for constrained maximization to be rational, in our typical case the probability p that CMs successfully co-operate must be more than twice the probability q that CMs are exploited by SMs, however great the probability r that a randomly selected person is a CM. If three persons out of four are CMs, so that $r = 3/4$, then p/q must be greater than 7/3; if one person out of two is a CM, then p/q must be greater than 3; if one person in four is a CM, then p/q must be greater than 5. In general, p/q must be greater than $2 + (1-r)/r$, or $(r + 1)/r$.

Suppose a population evenly divided between constrained and straightforward maximizers. If the constrained maximizers are able to co-operate successfully in two-thirds of their encounters, and to avoid being exploited by straightforward maximizers in four-fifths of their encounters, then constrained maximizers may expect to do better than their fellows. Of course, the even distribution will not be stable; it will be rational for the straightforward maximizers to change their disposition. These persons are sufficiently translucent for them to find morality rational.

2.4 A constrained maximizer is conditionally disposed to co-operate in ways that, followed by all, would yield nearly optimal and fair outcomes, and does co-operate in such ways when she may actually expect to benefit. In the two preceding subsections, we have argued that one is rationally so disposed if persons are transparent, or if persons are sufficiently translucent and enough are like-minded. But our argument has not appealed explicitly to the particular requirement that co-operative practices and activities be nearly optimal and fair. We have insisted that the co-operative outcome afford one a utility greater than non-co-operation, but this is much weaker than the insistence that it approach the outcome required by minimax relative concession.

But note that the larger the gain from co-operation, $(u'' - u')$, the smaller the minimum value of p/q that makes the disposition to constrained maximization rational. We may take p/q to be a measure of translucency; the more translucent constrained maximizers are, the better they are at achieving co-operation among themselves (increasing p) and avoiding exploitation by straightforward maximizers (decreasing q). Thus as practices and activities fall short of optimality, the expected value of co-operation, u'', decreases, and so the degree of translucency required to make co-operation rational increases. And as practices and activities fall short of fairness, the expected value of co-operation for those with less than fair shares decreases, and so the degree of translucency to make co-operation rational for them increases. Thus our argument does appeal implicitly to the requirement that co-operation yield nearly fair and optimal outcomes.

But there is a further argument in support of our insistence that the conditional disposition to co-operate be restricted to practices and activities yielding nearly optimal and fair outcomes. And this argument turns, as does our general argument for constraint, on how one's dispositions affect the characteristics of the situations in which one may reasonably expect to find oneself. Let us call a person who is disposed to co-operate in ways that, followed by all, yield nearly optimal and fair outcomes, *narrowly compliant*. And let us call a person who is disposed to co-operate in ways that, followed by all, merely yield her some benefit in relation to universal non-co-operation, *broadly compliant*. We need not deny that a broadly compliant person would expect to benefit in some situations in which a narrowly compliant person could not. But in many other situations a broadly compliant person must expect to lose by her disposition. For in so far as she is known to be broadly compliant, others will have every reason to maximize their utilities at her expense, by offering 'co-operation' on terms that offer her but little more than she could expect from non-co-operation. Since a broadly compliant person is disposed to seize whatever benefit a joint strategy may afford her, she finds herself with opportunities for but little benefit.

Since the narrowly compliant person is always prepared to accept co-operative arrangements based on the principle of minimax relative concession, she is prepared to be co-operative whenever co-operation can be mutually beneficial on terms equally rational and fair to all. In refusing other terms she does not diminish her prospects for co-operation with other rational persons, and she ensures that those not disposed to fair co-operation do not enjoy the benefits of any co-operation, thus making their unfairness costly to themselves, and so irrational.

In the next chapter we shall extend the conception of narrow compliance, so that it includes taking into account not only satisfaction of minimax relative concession, but also satisfaction of a standard of fairness for the initial bargaining position. We shall then find that for some circumstances, narrow compliance sets too high a standard. If the institutions of society fail to be both rational and impartial, then the narrowly compliant person may be unable to effect any significant reform of them, while depriving herself of what benefits an imperfect society nevertheless affords. Then—we must admit—rationality and impartiality can fail to coincide in individual choice.

But we suppose that among fully rational persons, institutions, practices, and agreements that do not satisfy the requirements of minimax relative concession must prove unstable. There would, of course, be some persons with an interest in maintaining the unfairness inherent in such structures. But among the members of a society each of whom is, and knows her fellows to be, rational and adequately informed, those who find themselves with less than they could expect from fair and optimal co-operation can, by disposing themselves to narrow compliance, effect the reform of their society so that it satisfies the requirements of justice. Reflection on how partiality sustains itself shows that, however important coercive measures may be, their effectiveness depends finally on an uncoerced support for norms that directly or indirectly sustain this partiality, a support which would be insufficiently forthcoming from clear-headed constrained maximizers of individual utility.

2.5 To conclude this long section, let us supplement our argument for the rationality of disposing ourselves to constrained maximization with three reflections on its implications—for conventional morality, for the treatment of straightforward maximizers, and for the cultivation of translucency.

First, we should not suppose that the argument upholds all of conventional morality, or all of those institutions and practices that purport to realize fair and optimal outcomes. If society is, in Rawls's words, 'a cooperative venture for mutual advantage', then it is rational to pay one's share of social costs—one's taxes. But it need not be rational to pay one's taxes, at least unless one is effectively coerced into payment, if one sees one's tax dollars used (as one may believe) to increase the chances of nuclear warfare and to encourage both corporate and individual parasitism. If tax evasion seems to many a rational practice, this does not show that it is irrational to comply with fair and optimal arrangements, but only, perhaps, that it is irrational to acquiesce willingly in being exploited.

Second, we should not suppose it is rational to dispose oneself to constrained maximization, if one does not also dispose oneself to exclude straightforward maximizers from the benefits realizable by co-operation. Hobbes notes that those who think they may with reason violate their covenants, may not be received into society except by the error of their fellows. If their fellows fall into that error, then they will soon find that it pays no one to keep covenants. Failing to exclude straightforward maximizers from the benefits of co-operative arrangements does not, and cannot, enable them to share in the long-run benefits of co-operation; instead, it ensures that the arrangements will prove ineffective, so that there are no benefits to share. And then there is nothing to be gained by constrained maximization; one might as well join the straightforward maximizers in their descent to the natural condition of humankind.

A third consideration relates more closely to the conceptions introduced in 2.3. Consider once again the probabilities p and q, the probability that CMs will achieve mutual recognition and co-operate, and the probability that CMs will fail to recognize SMs but will be recognized by them and so be exploited. It is obvious that CMs benefit from increasing p and decreasing q. And this is reflected in our calculation of expected utility for CMs; the value of $\{u'+[rp(u''-u')]-(1-r)qu'\}$ increases as p increases and as q decreases.

What determines the values of p and q? p depends on the ability of CMs to detect the sincerity of other CMs and to reveal their own sincerity to them. q depends on the ability of CMs to detect the insincerity of SMs and conceal their own sincerity from them, and the ability of SMs to detect the sincerity of CMs and conceal their own insincerity from them. Since any increase in the ability to reveal one's sincerity to other CMs is apt to be offset by a decrease in the ability to conceal one's sincerity from SMs, a CM is likely to rely primarily on her ability to detect the dispositions of others, rather than on her ability to reveal or conceal her own.

The ability to detect the dispositions of others must be well developed in a rational CM. Failure to develop this ability, or neglect of its exercise, will preclude one from benefiting from constrained maximization. And it can then appear that constraint is irrational. But what is actually irrational is the failure to cultivate or exercise the ability to detect others' sincerity or insincerity.

Both CMs and SMs must expect to benefit from increasing their ability to detect the dispositions of others. But if both endeavour to maximize their abilities (or the expected utility, net of costs, of so doing), then CMs may expect to improve their position in relation to SMs. For the benefits gained by SMs, by being better able to detect their potential victims, must be on the whole offset by the losses they suffer as the CMs become better able to detect them as potential exploiters. On the other hand, although the CMs may not enjoy any net gain in their interactions with SMs, the benefits they gain by being better able to detect other CMs as potential co-operators are not offset by corresponding losses, but rather increased as other CMs become better able to detect them in return.

Thus as persons rationally improve their ability to detect the dispositions of those with whom they interact, the value of p may be expected to increase, while the value of q remains relatively constant. But then p/q increases, and the greater it is, the less favourable need be other circumstances for it to be rational to dispose oneself to constrained maximization. Those who believe rationality and morality to be at loggerheads may have failed to recognize the importance of cultivating their ability to distinguish sincere co-operators from insincere ones.

David Hume points out that if 'it should be a virtuous man's fate to fall into the society of ruffians', then 'his particular regard to justice being no longer of use to his own safety or that of others, he must consult the dictates of self-preservation alone'.[21] If we fall into a society—or rather into a state of nature—of straightforward maximizers, then constrained maximization, which disposes us to justice, will indeed be of no use to us, and we must then consult only the direct dictates of our own utilities. In a world of Fooles, it would not pay to be a constrained maximizer, and to comply with one's

[21] Hume, *Enquiry*, iii. i, p. 187.

agreements. In such circumstances it would not be rational to be moral.

But if we find ourselves in the company of reasonably just persons, then we too have reason to dispose ourselves to justice. A community in which most individuals are disposed to comply with fair and optimal agreements and practices, and so to base their actions on joint co-operative strategies, will be self-sustaining. And such a world offers benefits to all which the Fooles can never enjoy.

Hume finds himself opposed by 'a sensible knave' who claimed that '*honesty is the best policy*, may be a good general rule, but is liable to many exceptions; and he ... conducts himself with most wisdom, who observes the general rule, and takes advantage of all the exceptions.'[22] Hume confesses candidly that 'if a man think that this reasoning much requires an answer, it would be a little difficult to find any which will to him appear satisfactory and convincing'.[23] A little difficult, but not, if we are right, impossible. For the answer is found in treating honesty, not as a policy, but as a disposition. Only the person truly disposed to honesty and justice may expect fully to realize their benefits, for only such a person may rationally be admitted to those mutually beneficial arrangements—whether actual agreements or implicitly agreed practices—that rest on honesty and justice, on voluntary compliance. But such a person is not able, given her disposition, to take advantage of the 'exceptions'; she rightly judges such conduct irrational. The Foole and the sensible knave, seeing the benefits to be gained from the exceptions, from the advantageous breaches in honesty and compliance, but not seeing beyond these benefits, do not acquire the disposition. Among knaves they are indeed held for sensible, but among us, if we be not corrupted by their smooth words, they are only fools.

3.1 In defending constrained maximization we have implicitly reinterpreted the utility-maximizing conception of practical rationality. The received interpretation, commonly accepted by economists and elaborated in Bayesian decision theory and the Von Neumann–Morgenstern theory of games, identifies rationality with utility-maximization at the level of particular choices. A choice is rational if and only if it maximizes the actor's expected utility. We identify rationality with utility-maximization at the level of dispositions to choose. A disposition is rational if and only if an actor holding it can expect his choices to yield no less utility than the choices he would

[22] Ibid., ix. ii, pp. 282–3. [23] Ibid., ix. ii, p. 283.

make were he to hold any alternative disposition. We shall consider whether particular choices are rational if and only if they express a rational disposition to choose.

It might seem that a maximizing disposition to choose would express itself in maximizing choices. But we have shown that this is not so. The essential point in our argument is that one's disposition to choose affects the situations in which one may expect to find oneself. A straightforward maximizer, who is disposed to make maximizing choices, must expect to be excluded from co-operative arrangements which he would find advantageous. A constrained maximizer may expect to be included in such arrangements. She benefits from her disposition, not in the choices she makes, but in her opportunities to choose.

We have defended the rationality of constrained maximization as a disposition to choose by showing that it would be rationally chosen. Now this argument is not circular; constrained maximization is a disposition for strategic choice that would be parametrically chosen. But the idea of a choice among dispositions to choose is a heuristic device to express the underlying requirement, that a rational disposition to choose be utility-maximizing. In parametric contexts, the disposition to make straightforwardly maximizing choices is uncontroversially utility-maximizing. We may therefore employ the device of a parametric choice among dispositions to choose to show that in strategic contexts, the disposition to make constrained choices, rather than straightforwardly maximizing choices, is utility-maximizing. We must however emphasize that it is not the choice itself, but the maximizing character of the disposition in virtue of which it is choiceworthy, that is the key to our argument.

But there is a further significance in our appeal to a choice among dispositions to choose. For we suppose that the capacity to make such choices is itself an essential part of human rationality. We could imagine beings so wired that only straightforward maximization would be a psychologically possible mode of choice in strategic contexts. Hobbes may have thought that human beings were so wired, that we were straightforwardly-maximizing machines. But if he thought this, then he was surely mistaken. At the core of our rational capacity is the ability to engage in self-critical reflection. The fully rational being is able to reflect on his standard of deliberation, and to change that standard in the light of reflection. Thus we suppose it possible for persons, who may initially assume that it is rational to extend straightforward maximization from parametric to strategic contexts, to reflect on the implications of this extension, and to reject it in favour of constrained maximization. Such persons would be making the very choice, of a disposition to choose, that we have been discussing in this chapter.

And in making that choice, they would be expressing their nature not only as rational beings, but also as moral beings. If the disposition to make straightforwardly maximizing choices were wired in to us, we could not constrain our actions in the way required for morality. Moral philosophers have rightly been unwilling to accept the received interpretation of the relation between practical rationality and utility-maximization because they have recognized that it left no place for a rational constraint on directly utility-maximizing behaviour, and so no place for morality as ordinarily understood. But they have then turned to a neo-Kantian account of rationality which has led them to dismiss the idea that those considerations that constitute a person's reasons for acting must bear some particular relationship to the person.[24] They have failed to relate our nature as moral beings to our everyday concern with the fulfilment of our individual preferences. But we have shown how morality issues from that concern. When we correctly understand how utility-maximization is identified with practical rationality, we see that morality is an essential part of maximization.

3.2 An objector might grant that it may be rational to dispose oneself to constrained maximization, but deny that the choices one is then disposed to make are rational.[25] The objector claims that we have merely exhibited another instance of the rationality of not behaving rationally. And before we can accuse the objector of paradox, he brings further instances before us.

Consider, he says, the costs of decision-making. Maximizing may be the most reliable procedure, but it need not be the most cost-effective. In many circumstances, the rational person will not maximize but satisfice—set a threshold level of fulfilment and choose the first course of action of those coming to mind that one expects to meet this level. Indeed, our objector may suggest, human beings, like other higher animals, are natural satisficers. What

[24] See, for example, T. Nagel, *The Possibility of Altruism* (Oxford, 1970), pp. 90–124.

[25] The objector might be Derek Parfit; see *Reasons and Persons*, pp. 19–23. His book appeared too recently to permit discussion of his arguments here.

distinguishes us is that we are not hard-wired, so that we can choose differently, but the costs are such that it is not generally advantageous to exercise our option, even though we know that most of our choices are not maximizing.

Consider also, he says, the tendency to wishful thinking. If we set ourselves to calculate the best or maximizing course of action, we are likely to confuse true expectations with hopes. Knowing this, we protect ourselves by choosing on the basis of fixed principles, and we adhere to these principles even when it appears to us that we could do better to ignore them, for we know that in such matters appearances often deceive. Indeed, our objector may suggest, much of morality may be understood, not as constraints on maximization to ensure fair mutual benefit, but as constraints on wish-fulfilling behaviour to ensure closer approximation to maximization.

Consider again, he says, the benefits of threat behaviour. I may induce you to perform an action advantageous to me if I can convince you that, should you not do so, I shall then perform an action very costly to you, even though it would not be my utility maximizing choice. Hijackers seize aircraft, and threaten the destruction of everyone aboard, themselves included, if they are not transported to Havana. Nations threaten nuclear retaliation should their enemies attack them. Although carrying out a threat would be costly, if it works the cost need not be borne, and the benefit, not otherwise obtainable, is forthcoming.

But, our objector continues, a threat can be effective only if credible. It may be that to maximize one's credibility, and one's prospect of advantage, one must dispose oneself to carry out one's threats if one's demands are not met. And so it may be rational to dispose oneself to threat enforcement. But then, by parity of reasoning with our claims about constrained maximization, we must suppose it to be rational actually to carry out one's threats. Surely we should suppose instead that, although it is clearly irrational to carry out a failed threat, yet it may be rational to dispose oneself to just this sort of irrationality. And so similarly we should suppose that although it is clearly irrational to constrain one's maximizing behaviour, yet it may be rational to dispose oneself to this irrationality.

We are unmoved. We agree that an actor who is subject to certain weaknesses or imperfections may find it rational to dispose himself to make choices that are not themselves rational. Such dispositions may be the most effective way of compensating for the weakness or imperfection. They constitute a second-best rationality, as it were. But although it may be rational for us to satisfice, it would not be rational for us to perform the action so chosen if, cost free, the maximizing action were to be revealed to us. And although it may be rational for us to adhere to principles as a guard against wish-fulfilment, it would not be rational for us to do so if, beyond all doubt, the maximizing action were to be revealed to us.

Contrast these with constrained maximization. The rationale for disposing oneself to constraint does not appeal to any weakness or imperfection in the reasoning of the actor; indeed, the rationale is most evident for perfect reasoners who cannot be deceived. The disposition to constrained maximization overcomes externalities; it is directed to the core problem arising from the structure of interaction. And the entire point of disposing oneself to constraint is to adhere to it in the face of one's knowledge that one is not choosing the maximizing action.

Imperfect actors find it rational to dispose themselves to make less than rational choices. No lesson can be drawn from this about the dispositions and choices of the perfect actor. If her dispositions to choose are rational, then surely her choices are also rational.

But what of the threat enforcer? Here we disagree with our objector; it may be rational for a perfect actor to dispose herself to threat enforcement, and if it is, then it is rational for her to carry out a failed threat. Equally, it may be rational for a perfect actor to dispose herself to threat resistance, and if it is, then it is rational for her to resist despite the cost to herself. Deterrence, we have argued elsewhere, may be a rational policy, and non-maximizing deterrent choices are then rational.[26]

In a community of rational persons, however, threat behaviour will be proscribed. Unlike co-operation, threat behaviour does not promote mutual advantage. A successful threat simply redistributes benefits in favour of the threatener; successful threat resistance maintains the status quo. Unsuccessful threat behaviour, resulting in costly acts of enforcement or resistance, is necessarily non-optimal; its very *raison d'être* is to make everyone worse off. Any person who is not exceptionally placed must then have the *ex ante* expectation

[26] See 'Deterrence, Maximization, and Rationality', *Ethics* 94 (1984), pp. 474–95; also in D. MacLean (ed.), *The Security Gamble: Deterrence Dilemmas in the Nuclear Age* (Totowa, NJ, 1984), pp. 101–22.

that threat behaviour will be overall disadvantageous. Its proscription must be part of a fair and optimal agreement among rational persons; one of the constraints imposed by minimax relative concession is abstinence from the making of threats. Our argument thus shows threat behaviour to be both irrational and immoral.

Constrained maximizers will not dispose themselves to enforce or to resist threats among themselves. But there are circumstances, beyond the moral pale, in which a constrained maximizer might find it rational to dispose herself to threat enforcement. If she found herself fallen among straightforward maximizers, and especially if they were too stupid to become threat resisters, disposing herself to threat enforcement might be the best thing she could do. And for her, carrying out failed threats would be rational, though not utility-maximizing.

Our objector has not made good his case. The dispositions of a fully rational actor issue in rational choices. Our argument identifies practical rationality with utility-maximization at the level of dispositions to choose, and carries through the implications of that identification in assessing the rationality of particular choices.

3.3 To conclude this chapter, let us note an interesting parallel to our theory of constrained maximization—Robert Trivers' evolutionary theory of reciprocal altruism.[27] We have claimed that a population of constrained maximizers would be rationally stable; no one would have reason to dispose herself to straightforward maximization. Similarly, if we think of constrained and straightforward maximization as parallel to genetic tendencies to reciprocal altruism and egoism, a population of reciprocal altruists would be genetically stable; a mutant egoist would be at an evolutionary disadvantage. Since she would not reciprocate, she would find herself excluded from co-operative relationships.

Trivers argues that natural selection will favour the development of the capacity to detect merely simulated altruism. This of course corresponds to our claim that constrained maximizers, to be successful, must be able to detect straightforward maximizers whose offers to co-operation are insincere. Exploitative interactions between CMs and SMs must be avoided.

Trivers also argues that natural selection will favour the development of guilt, as a device motivating those who fail to reciprocate to

[27] See R. L. Trivers, 'The Evolution of Reciprocal Altruism', *Quarterly Review of Biology* 46 (1971), pp. 35–57.

change their ways in future.[28] In our argument, we have not appealed to any affective disposition; we do not want to weaken the position we must defeat, straightforward maximization, by supposing that persons are emotionally indisposed to follow it. But we may expect that in the process of socialization, efforts will be made to develop and cultivate each person's feelings so that, should she behave as an SM, she will experience guilt. We may expect our affective capacities to be shaped by social practices in support of co-operative interaction.

If a population of reciprocal altruists is genetically stable, surely a population of egoists is also stable. As we have seen, the argument for the rationality of constrained maximization turns on the proportion of CMs in the population. A small proportion of CMs might well suffer more from exploitation by undetected SMs than by co-operation among themselves unless their capacities for detecting the dispositions of others were extraordinarily effective. Similarly, a mutant reciprocal altruist would be at a disadvantage among egoists; her attempts at co-operation would be rebuffed and she would lose by her efforts in making them.

Does it then follow that we should expect both groups of reciprocal altruists and groups of egoists to exist stably in the world? Not necessarily. The benefits of co-operation ensure that, in any given set of circumstances, each member of a group of reciprocal altruists should do better than a corresponding member of a group of egoists. Each reciprocal altruist should have a reproductive advantage. Groups of reciprocal altruists should therefore increase relative to groups of egoists in environments in which the two come into contact. The altruists must prevail—not in direct combat between the two (although the co-operation possible among reciprocal altruists may bring victory there), but in the indirect combat for evolutionary survival in a world of limited resources.

In his discussion of Trivers's argument, Jon Elster notes two points of great importance which we may relate to our own account of constrained maximization. The first is, 'The altruism is the more efficient because it is *not* derived from calculated self-interest.'[29] This is exactly our point at the end of 2.1—constrained maximization is not straightforward maximization in its most effective guise. The

[28] Ibid., p. 50.

[29] J. Elster, *Ulysses and the Sirens: Studies in rationality and irrationality* (Cambridge, 1979), p. 145.

constrained maximizer genuinely ignores the call of utility-maximization in following the co-operative practices required by minimax relative concession. There is no simulation; if there were, the benefits of co-operation would not be fully realized.

The second is that Trivers's account 'does not purport to explain specific instances of altruistic behaviour, such as, say, the tendency to save a drowning person. Rescue attempts are explained by a general tendency to perform acts of altruism, and this tendency is then made the object of the evolutionary explanation.'[30] In precisely the same way, we do not purport to give a utility-maximizing justification for specific choices of adherence to a joint strategy. Rather we explain those choices by a general disposition to choose fair, optimizing actions whenever possible, and this tendency is then given a utility-maximizing justification.

We do not, of course, have the competence to discuss whether or not human beings are genetically disposed to utility-maximizing behaviour. But if human beings are so disposed, then we may conclude that the disposition to constrained maximization increases genetic fitness.

[30] Ibid., pp. 145–6.

VII

THE INITIAL BARGAINING POSITION: RIGHTS AND THE PROVISO

1 Once upon a time, long ago and far away, there was a society of masters and slaves. Unlike many such societies, this one rested on no false ideological appeals to the natural masterliness of masters and the natural slavishness of slaves. What distinguished the masters from the slaves, as both well knew, was power. Given half a chance, the slaves would happily have changed places with their masters, who therefore were careful never to give them that half chance.

But one day, as a group of masters were taking their customary leisurely mid-afternoon gin and tonics together, one of the younger men, recently returned from the university, interrupted the desultory remarks of his elders and held forth thus:

'Gentlemen, we have been fools these many years. The meagre pleasures that have consoled us [and here he snapped his fingers that his glass might be refilled] have been but shadows of the luxuries we might have enjoyed, had we not squandered our resources in coercing our slaves. And those slaves have performed their tasks grudgingly and carelessly (dammit, boy, where's the *lime* in my drink?) under the threat of our whips and chains, instead of freely and cheerfully serving us. To use the language of my professors, we've interacted non-co-operatively and ended up with a sub-optimal outcome.

'Now we can change all this. What we need is a bargain with our slaves—we'll free them, dismantling all the coercive apparatus that slavery involves, and in return they will voluntarily be our servants. We'll benefit—better service, less expense, money saved for other uses, and they'll benefit—no more beatings and chainings, and better living conditions, since from the money we'll save in doing away with coercion and the increased productivity we'll get from their willing service, we can pay them wages better than the living allowance we have to provide now, and still have the resources to put some *real* pleasures into our lives. I've figured it all out—there's this professor who's developed what he calls the principle of minimax relative concession for rational bargains. This deal with our slaves ought to fit it just about perfectly. And he's shown—this professor—that it's rational to comply voluntarily with such deals. So we shouldn't have any worries about doing away with coercion—our slaves are rational so they'll become willing servants.'

The older men shook their heads. Not only did a university education cost a lot of money, but it left one with the damnedest fool ideas—anyone with half an eye would see through a scheme like that. Take away the chains and you'd never get willing servants. But the younger men, impressed with the prospect of rational co-operation, were not to be put off by old fogies who thought that grandfather's way of doing things was best. At the very next election (for the masters were quite democratic among themselves) a reform administration carried the day, and within a few years the institutions of slavery were dismantled, an emancipation proclamation issued, and a solemn Bargain of Mutual Benefit enshrined in the constitution.

And did it all happen as the young man had said? Not at all. The older men had been quite right. As one of the ex-slaves explained, after he was sworn in as prime minister of an administration pledged to repeal the Bargain of Mutual Benefit, 'What those young men never understood was that this bargain was coercively based. It was only because of the power they held over us that it seemed a rational deal. Once that power was taken away, it became obvious that the fruits of co-operation weren't being divided up in accordance with that fancy principle of minimax relative concession. And so there wasn't any reason to expect voluntary compliance—we weren't about to become willing servants. Still, they saved themselves a revolution—so in the end it probably was a sensible move for them to make, even if they did it because of their mistaken expectations.'

This tale sets the scene for our discussion of the initial bargaining position—or indeed more generally, of the initial position whether for co-operative or market interaction. In Chapters IV and V we saw that both market competition and agreed co-operation begin from a specification of the factor endowments and prior utility expectations of the parties to interaction. We established the procedural rationality and fairness of these forms of interaction. But we noted explicitly that fair procedures yield an impartial outcome only from an impartial initial position. And it is equally true that rational procedures yield a rationally acceptable outcome only from a rationally acceptable initial position. Implicit in the prime minister's remarks in our cautionary tale is the claim that it is rational to comply with a bargain, and so rational to act co-operatively, only if its initial position is non-coercive.

In section 2 we shall develop this claim, examining two views that permit coercion in the initial position, and arguing that they do not provide a basis for rational compliance. The first view identifies the non-co-operative outcome of natural interaction with the initial bargaining position; the second view identifies the threat point—the outcome yielded by each person's maximally effective threat strategy—with the initial position. We shall deny the relevance of threat behaviour to rational interaction, and argue that, if the non-co-operative outcome involves coercion, then it must be constrained by removing the effects of that coercion if it is to serve as an initial position for bargaining to a joint strategy that rationally commands individual compliance.

But removing the effects of coercion from the non-co-operative outcome does not afford an adequate positive characterization of the initial position. The principal claim that we shall advance and defend in the present chapter is that whether we assess the rational acceptability of the outcome of interaction from the standpoint of each individual utility-maximizer, or the moral acceptability of the outcome as benefiting each individual impartially, we find that all effects of taking advantage must be removed from the initial position. We shall therefore argue that it is both rational and just for each individual to accept a certain constraint on natural interaction, and on the determination of his initial factor endowment, as a condition of being voluntarily acceptable to his fellows as a party to co-operative and market arrangements—to social interaction. This constraint is part of morals by agreement, not in being the object of an agreement among rational individuals, but in being a precondition to such agreement.

In developing this argument, we shall proceed from a characterization of this constraint to the demonstration of its moral and rational grounds. We begin then in section 3 with the statement of a form of the Lockean proviso, that there be 'enough, and as good left . . . for others'.[1] We show how the proviso functions as a constraint,

[1] The term 'Lockean proviso' comes from R. Nozick, *Anarchy, State, and Utopia* (New York, 1974), who discusses it on pp. 175–82. The proviso is stated in John Locke, *Two Treatises of Government* (London, 1690), second treatise, ch. v, paras. 27, 33.

but we do not show in section 3 that it actually determines initial factor endowments, that it is impartial, or that it is rational to adhere to it. In section 4 we turn to the first two of these tasks, showing how adherence to the proviso introduces a structure of rights into a previously non-moral state of nature, and arguing that this structure satisfies the core moral standard of impartiality. And then in section 5 we show that it is rational for utility-maximizers to accept the proviso as constraining their natural interaction and their individual endowments, in so far as they anticipate beneficial social interaction with their fellows.

This last point is essential. We may say that the proviso moralizes and rationalizes the state of nature—but only in so far as we conceive the state of nature as giving way to society. Although it is irrational for human beings to remain in a state of nature, accepting no constraints on their interactions, yet no individual can benefit from unilaterally constraining his behaviour. Adherence to the proviso is the equivalent of the requirement in Hobbes's first law of nature, 'That every man, ought to endeavour Peace, as farre as he has hope of obtaining it'.[2] But without such hope, of passing from nature to society, then every man 'may seek, and use, all helps, and advantages of Warre'. Without the prospect of agreement and society, there would be no morality, and the proviso would have no rationale. Fortunately, the prospect of society is realized for us; our concern is then to understand the rationale of the morality that sustains it.

2.1 The identification of the initial bargaining position with the non-co-operative outcome has been defended by James M. Buchanan in his convincing outline of a contractarian theory of rational interaction.[3] Since we agree with much of Buchanan's approach we must consider his argument carefully.

Buchanan supposes for simplicity a two-person world with one scarce good. This good is not produced by the inhabitants; it 'falls down' on them in fixed quantities. They cannot benefit from trade with each other, or from investment in production. Nevertheless we may suppose some interaction between them, dictated by the desire each has to consume as much of the good as possible. Each may have, or believe that she has, reason to invest effort in obtaining some portion of the good that originally fell down on the other. In

[2] Hobbes, *Leviathan*, ch. 14, p. 64.

[3] See J. M. Buchanan, *The Limits of Liberty: Between Anarchy and Leviathan* (Chicago, 1975).

other words one or both may invest in predation. And this investment may give one or both reason to make a counter-investment in defence. The eventual result of this predatory/defensive interaction is the emergence of what Buchanan calls the natural distribution, a condition of stability in which the predatory/defensive mix of each individual is the utility-maximizing response to the other's mix. This natural distribution is, in our terminology, the non-co-operative outcome.[4]

But now there is a basis for agreement. The natural distribution 'serves to establish an identification, a definition, of the individual persons *from which* contractual agreements become possible. Absent such a starting point, there is simply no way of initiating meaningful contracts, actually or conceptually.'[5] We may say that the natural distribution affords each person an explicit bargaining endowment; it determines what each may bring to the table and thus constitutes an initial bargaining position. Of course, the mere existence of a natural distribution is not sufficient for contracts to emerge. It must be sub-optimal—there must be the possibility of mutual improvement. But its sub-optimality is hardly in doubt, since the effort expended in predation and defence is largely wasteful. Both parties stand to benefit from an agreement that relieves them of the necessity of engaging in these non-productive activities. (If it be pointed out that under Buchanan's simplifying assumptions, there is no place for production, we may reply that there is place for leisure.)

Let us then suppose that agreement is reached, proceeding from the natural distribution, and let us also suppose that, in accordance with our argument in Chapter V, this agreement is based on the principle of minimax relative concession. (The search for a principle of agreement is no part of Buchanan's concern.) Then each person will receive her share in the natural distribution, or its equivalent in utility, plus a proportion of her potential benefit from co-operation, in general equal to that of the other person. Is this rationally acceptable to each party?

The answer is surely negative. In Buchanan's example, the sub-optimality of the natural distribution results from investment in predation and counter-investment in defence. Each imposes costs on the other by these activities. Although pure predation, in the form of unhindered seizure, need not be wasteful, yet the cost imposed on the predator by the defensive response her predation elicits, and the

[4] See ibid., pp. 23–5. [5] Ibid., p. 24.

cost of that defensive response, are both unproductive. Agreement ends this unproductive activity. It yields an optimal outcome in which predatory/defensive efforts are absent. But the effect of these efforts remain present, since each party brings to the bargaining table the fruits of her predatory/defensive activity, and takes them (or their utility equivalents) away from the table as part of the overall outcome. They do not enter into the co-operative surplus, which is constituted (in Buchanan's example) entirely by the agreement of each party to cease imposing costs on the other. Only this comes under the sway of the principle of minimax relative concession.

But clearly an individual would be irrational if she were to dispose herself to comply, voluntarily, with an agreement reached in this way. Someone disposed to comply with agreements that left untouched the fruits of predation would simply invite others to engage in predatory and coercive activities as a prelude to bargaining. She would permit the successful predators to reap where they had ceased to sow, to continue to profit from the effects of natural predation after entering into agreements freeing them from the need to invest further predatory effort. Co-operative compliance is not compliant victimization. We do not deny that, as long as her cost in resisting actual predation exceeds any benefit such resistance would bring her, the victim rationally must acquiesce. But if predatory activity is banned, then she no longer has reason to behave in a way that would maintain its effects. Agreement reached by minimax relative concession from the natural distribution therefore does not elicit the rational, voluntary compliance of both (or all) parties, if the natural distribution is in part the result of coercion.

Our initial tale is intended to illustrate this argument. The masters employ coercion to keep the slaves obedient. Coercion is costly to both. Masters and slaves would both benefit were coercion removed and the slaves continued to serve voluntarily. But ex-slaves would not comply with an agreement to this effect. The slaves provide their services because the costs of their resistance exceed the benefits it would afford them, given their masters' power. But only the maintenance of this power rationally induces them to continue their services. Without coercion, ex-slaves might accept and adhere to some form of co-operation, but not one based on the outcome of coercive interaction. If it were otherwise, then why should not an agreement, of the type proposed by the young master, be concluded—and adhered to—by whites and blacks in South Africa, or by the government of Poland and the members of Solidarity?

Buchanan is not unmindful of this problem. He asks 'Why will persons voluntarily comply with the rules and institutions of order that are in being?', where voluntary compliance excludes that based on coercion and punishment.[6] He insists, 'This question can only be answered through an evaluation of the existing structure, *as if* it were the outcome of a current contract, or one that is continuously negotiated. Individuals must ask themselves how their own positions compare with those that they might have expected to secure in a renegotiated contractual settlement.' And these positions are determined, at least in part, by considering 'imagined shifts in the natural distribution in anarchistic equilibrium which always exists "underneath" the observed social realities'.[7]

Buchanan supposes that one should comply with those rules (or, we might say, with that joint strategy) that would command agreement were the present underlying natural distribution to be realized. In deciding whether to comply one asks, 'Were agreement to lapse, then what might I expect?' Buchanan depends on the threat implicit in the natural distribution to elicit compliance. But a return to the natural distribution benefits no one. The threat is unreal. What motivates compliance is the absence of coercion rather than the fear of its renewal.

Consider once again the simple two-person world Buchanan discusses, and which we represent graphically in Fig. 9 (see p. 228). An agreement from the point I_n, the natural distribution or non-co-operative outcome, would lead to the optimal point B_n. But B_n requires individual V to make an unproductive transfer to person U, corresponding to U's net predatory gain from natural interaction. V would have to give U, quite voluntarily, some of the good that, in Buchanan's example, falls down on him. We have argued that in the absence of coercion V has no reason to do this. If he refuses, keeping the good for himself, then the effect is to move the outcome along the frontier, or upper right bound of the outcome-space, to B_c, the optimal point representing the outcome of agreement from the non-coercive initial position I_c. If U objects, seeking to compel a transfer from V, then she must reintroduce coercion, and so the outcome moves along the line joining B_c to the natural distribution I_n, a move which is costly to both parties and so irrational for U. Hence we

[6] Ibid., p. 75.

[7] Ibid., p. 79.

must suppose that a stable agreement ends at B_c even if the parties actually begin at I_n. The eventual outcome is as if I_c were the initial bargaining position.

In Buchanan's simple world, each will simply enjoy the good falling down on her, and devote to leisure the effort previously invested in predation and defence. But in a more complex world, we may suppose that this effort may be put to productive use, so that the two parties enter either into market arrangements or into co-operative production in which they obtain goods previously unavailable. The expected gains from their agreement are then considerably increased. And so if V refuses to make an unproductive transfer and U seeks to enforce it, then U must not only reintroduce coercion, but also give up the goods achieved from the productive use of the efforts that agreement had enabled her to divert from predation and defence. The cost to U, and so the irrationality of seeking to compel an unproductive transfer from V, becomes even more evident.

To relate this elementary analysis to our society of masters and slaves, we note that the point I_n corresponds to the situation at the beginning of our tale. B_n represents the outcome of agreement as naïvely imagined by the young master, in which without coercion the ex-slaves continue to serve their ex-masters. Provision of this service is the unproductive transfer required by this agreement from the ex-slaves, which of course they refuse. Their refusal moves society from B_n to B_c, the eventual outcome after the repeal of the so-called Bargain of Mutual Benefit. And this outcome is as if agreement had been reached from a non-co-operative but also non-coercive initial position, represented by the point I_c.

We have argued that it would be irrational for an individual to dispose herself to comply voluntarily with a joint strategy agreed to from a coercive initial position. In the light of our analysis we may reformulate our claim to say that it would be irrational for an individual to dispose herself voluntarily to make unproductive transfers to others. An unproductive transfer brings no new goods into being and involves no exchange of existing goods; it simply redistributes some existing goods from one person to another. Thus it involves a utility cost for which no benefit is received, and a utility gain for which no service is provided.

It is rational to make an unproductive transfer only if it is directly utility-maximizing to do so. Since the transfer itself is costly, it can be utility-maximizing only in so far as it is coercively exacted. It cannot, then, be part of any co-operative interaction, since such interaction involves mutual benefit. The presence of unproductive transfers in otherwise co-operative arrangements is evidence of residual natural predation.

In our examples residual predation may easily be detected. But in our world it readily disguises itself. Unproductive transfers parade in spurious moral and ideological trappings. If we are no longer taken in by the blandishments of nobility, we are all too ready to succumb to the plaints of inequality. But ideally rational persons are not so moved, recognizing unproductive transfers for what they are. They may coerce and be coerced, but they do not confuse coercion with co-operation.

Since the outcome of the co-operative joint strategy is not in equilibrium it lacks natural stability. Compliance provides an artificial but weaker stability where the stronger natural stability is not to be had. If we were to take the natural distribution as the initial bargaining position, then in some cases we should find that unproductive transfers were necessary to bring about the co-operative outcome. Even if particular transfers could be coercively exacted within co-operative arrangements, yet the arrangements themselves ultimately depend on voluntary compliance. And this would not be forthcoming from those called on to make the transfers. The co-operative outcome would then lack both natural and artificial stability. Hobbes's Foole would be able to show that, even though it might seem rational to enter into co-operative interaction, it would not be rational to comply with its demands.

We conclude that the initial bargaining position, as the starting point for rational co-operation, may not be identified with the natural distribution, or non-co-operative outcome. The natural distribution represents the effects of power. Now we have not shown, and we shall not show, any basis, rational or moral, for criticizing the effects of power considered in themselves. But if we consider the natural distribution in relation to market or co-operative interaction, then we assess it, not in itself, but for its suitability as determining what each person brings to the market or to the bargain underlying co-operative arrangements. We assess it as determining each person's endowment. And here we have found a basis for criticizing it, and indeed rejecting it in so far as it is coercive. If we think of each person's endowment as constituting her rights (a view we shall develop in 4.1 of this chapter), then we may say that to accept the natural distribution as the initial bargaining position would be to accept might as making right.[8] No doubt right is often invoked to maintain what might has made. But the right so invoked is an impostor, unable to pass the scrutiny of utility-maximizing rationality.

2.2 In the theory of rational bargaining developed by John Nash and generalized by John Harsanyi, the initial bargaining position is identified with the *threat point*, representing the outcome that would be realized were each person to act on her maximally effective threat strategy.[9] What are these strategies?

We saw in V.3.4. that on the Zeuthen–Nash–Harsanyi view, if the initial bargaining position for two persons, Ann and Adam, is represented by the point (u^*, v^*), then the outcome must be represented by that point (u', v') such that for any point (u, v) in the outcome-space, the product $(u' - u^*)\ (v' - v^*)$ is at least as great as the product $(u - u^*)\ (v - v^*)$. In this way we may correlate each point in the outcome-space, considered as an initial bargaining position, with a point on the upper right bound of the outcome-space, as the bargaining outcome for that initial position.

Conversely, we may correlate each point on the upper right bound of the outcome-space with that set of points in the outcome space each member of which (taken as initial bargaining position) determines it as the bargaining outcome. It is clear that each point in the outcome-space belongs to one and only one such set; two points belonging to the same set determine the same outcome; two points belonging to different sets determine different outcomes. Let us call these *outcome-equivalent sets*.

It is clear that in choosing a point to serve as the initial bargaining position, Ann and Adam are both indifferent between all points belonging to the same outcome-equivalent set, but have strictly opposed preferences between any two points belonging to different sets, corresponding to their strictly opposed preferences between any two optimal outcomes. In choosing a point to serve as the initial bargaining position, Ann and Adam are concerned with, and only with, the outcome-equivalent set to which it belongs.

[8] Buchanan insists that the initial bargaining position 'cannot properly be classified as a structure of *rights*, since no formal agreement is made' (ibid., p. 24). But we think of rights as providing the basis rather than the object of agreement; see 4.3 *infra*.

[9] See J. F. Nash, 'Two-person Cooperative Games', *Econometrica*, 21 (1953); Luce and Raiffa, pp. 140–3; J. C. Harsanyi, *Rational Behavior and Bargaining Equilibrium in Games and Social Situations* (Cambridge, 1977), pp. 167–9.

Suppose that, although the strategies available to Ann and Adam remain unchanged, the pay-offs of the outcomes are changed, so that what we shall call the utility^e of each outcome is a measure of preference for the outcome-equivalent set to which it belongs. (Preference for each set is of course determined by preference for its associated bargaining outcome.) Then it turns out that Ann and Adam face a strictly competitive situation, in which each has a strategy, utility^e-maximizing against the other's strategy, and so leading to an outcome in equilibrium^e, which is also optimal^e. These are their maximally effective threat strategies; if they were acting to determine an initial bargaining position, these are the strategies they should rationally choose.

This very neat analysis cannot be applied directly to our solution to the bargaining problem, but fortunately we need not face the problem of determining maximally effective threat strategies. For consider what these strategies signify. They play a purely hypothetical role in the Nash–Harsanyi analysis, since Ann and Adam do not actually choose them, but merely appeal to them to determine the costs that each could impose on the other in a strict competition for bargaining advantage. Maximally effective threat strategies would not be chosen by Ann and Adam were they to find themselves unable to co-operate; the threat point bears no particular relationship to the non-co-operative outcome. But if Ann and Adam would not choose these strategies, then they cannot credibly threaten with them. Maximally effective threat strategies prove to be idle.

Bargaining theorists generally suppose that individuals are in a position to make their threats binding.[10] But this is an unrealistic supposition in most situations. And we have already seen that in co-operation, threat behaviour would be proscribed. Thus, even apart from the irrationality of complying voluntarily with an agreement that took the threat point as the initial bargaining position, we conclude that potential co-operators would not dispose themselves to threat enforcement. We may dismiss the threat point from further consideration.

3.1 The initial bargaining position must be non-coercive. But must we go further in constraining natural interaction, in so far as it determines the basis of market or co-operative interaction? We shall argue that the terms of fully rational co-operation include the

[10] Harsanyi, however, distinguishes situations with and without binding threats. See *Rational Behavior*, p. 168.

requirement that each individual's endowment, affording him a base utility not included in the co-operative surplus, must be considered to have been initially acquired by him without taking advantage of any other person—or, more precisely, of any other co-operator. Otherwise those who consider themselves taken advantage of in initial acquisition will perceive society as unfair, in demanding payments from them without offering a compensating return, and will lack sufficient reason to accept market arrangements or to comply voluntarily with co-operative joint strategies.

Our concern in this and most of the fourth section will be to understand the requirement. We shall consider what is meant by the taking of advantage, and show how not taking advantage constrains the acquisition of an endowment for market and co-operative interaction. In our discussion we shall seek to make plausible the claim that not taking advantage is a reasonable and fair constraint that natural interaction must satisfy in so far as its outcome provides an initial position for bargaining. Thus we shall understand not taking advantage to exclude free-riders and parasites, so that as a constraint it extends to the state of nature the impartiality satisfied by the market and by co-operation. But plausibility is not proof; after we examine the effects of not taking advantage of others in natural interaction we shall seek to demonstrate that it is a moral and rational requirement. And we must emphasize again that nothing in our discussion should be taken to imply that it would be rational to refrain from taking advantage of others, or to adhere to any other constraint on straightforward maximization, from the strict standpoint of interaction in a state of nature. Throughout, we envisage not taking advantage as constraining natural interaction only in order to facilitate the emergence of society.

The first great attempt to rationalize and moralize the Hobbesian state of nature—that condition of unlimited predation—is John Locke's theory of property.[11] The principle of acquisition that constitutes the core of this theory suggests a preliminary formulation of the requirement that advantage not be taken. But we shall extend Locke's own position so that we may express his constraint on acquisition as a proviso that simultaneously licenses and limits the exclusive rights of individuals to objects and powers. Its effect is to afford each person a sphere of exclusive control by forbidding others from interfering with certain of his activities. This exclusive

[11] See Locke, second treatise, ch. v, and first treatise, ch. ix.

sphere constitutes a moral space, which defines the individual in his market and co-operative relationships.

According to Locke one acquires exclusive title to that with which one mixes one's labour, provided one uses, or at least does not waste, what one so acquires, and provided also that 'enough, and as good' is left, 'more than the yet unprovided could use'.[12] The initial bargaining position determined by this principle thus involves a distribution of factors of production and other goods based on each person's natural labour, in so far as this labour is related to use, and in so far as each person's acquisition leaves a surplus. Labour, use, and surplus are the three key concepts in understanding Locke's account, and each may seem deeply problematic.

Locke's theory of acquisition moralizes the Hobbesian state of nature. But how is this possible? How does my labour, to which I have only a liberty according to Hobbes, serve as the basis of my rights? How is Locke able to show that I have a right to my body and its powers, except by presupposing it and so begging the question of establishing a rational and impartial bargaining position? To resolve these difficulties we must approach the idea of initial or original acquisition in terms of the surplus constraint, which we shall find to be its core. The acquisition of one's body and its powers, the role of labour, and the demand that one put to use what one acquires, will all fall into place, given a suitable reading of the Lockean proviso expressed in the words 'enough, and as good', which constrains natural interactions in order to make society possible.

Taken literally these words might seem to defeat our enterprise from the outset. If one must leave enough and as good for others, then may one claim anything at all for one's factor endowment? Even the acquisition of one's body may seem to be precluded, for if you are abler and stronger than I, then your claim to your body and its powers will not leave enough and as good for me. I should do better with a half-share in our joint capacities than with a full share in mine and none in yours. And beyond this, to require enough and as good to be left would surely forbid the acquisition not only of what is actually scarce, but also of what is merely potentially in insufficient supply. There cannot be enough of what is scarce, so that if one person takes sufficient for himself, what is left for others is not as good. This literalistic reading of Locke's proviso would simply

[12] Locke, second treatise, ch. v, para. 33.

fail to define persons for the purposes of bargaining—or the market. The world and all of its inhabitants would be and remain a commons.

We are therefore led to consider the interpretation of the proviso offered by Robert Nozick. 'Locke's proviso that there be "enough and as good left in common for others" . . . is meant to ensure that the situation of others is not worsened.'[13] Natural interaction, if it is to determine the initial bargaining position, must exclude activities that worsen the situation of any person, whether by predation or in other ways. Each person's endowment includes whatever he acquires without worsening the situation of his fellows; this endowment then affords him a basis for applying minimax relative concession and so determines the expected outcome of co-operation. Each is free to use the resources in his endowment to increase what he brings to the bargaining table, and also, of course, to engage in market competition.

But simply to forbid worsening the situation of others is too strong. For there are situations in which one could avoid this only by worsening one's own position. Following Locke who allows one's own preservation to take justifiable precedence over that of others in one's deliberations, we modify Nozick's interpretation of the proviso, so that it prohibits worsening the situation of others except where this is necessary to avoid worsening one's own position. It is clear that any stronger proviso would fail as a possible constraint for determining the initial bargaining position among utility-maximizers.

How are we to understand worsening—and, conversely, bettering—someone's situation, where that someone may be oneself or another? We may treat 'better' and 'worse' as unproblematic; one situation is better for some person than another, if and only if it affords him a greater expected utility. Now one's situation is bettered or worsened only in relation to some base point. This base point cannot be that of the initial bargaining position itself, since that position is to be determined by the application of the proviso forbidding worsening the situation of another except to avoid worsening one's own. We must ask what, in natural interaction, may be taken as a base point for determining what effects the actions of one person have on the situation of another, or on his own situation.

[13] Nozick, p. 175.

The crucial distinction that we must establish is between worsening someone's situation and failing to better it, since the proviso prohibits only the former, not the latter.

To aid our enquiry at this point, let us consider an example beloved of philosophers. You are drowning in the river, and I, passing by on the river bank, leave you to drown. This is an outcome; consider two ways in which it might have come about. First, you fall into the water. I come along, hear your cries for help, but ignore them and continue on my way. Second, you are standing on the bank. I come along, push you into the water, and, ignoring your cries for help, continue on my way. In the first case, although certainly I fail to better your unhappy situation, I do not worsen it. In the second case, although the outcome is the same, I clearly do worsen your situation. Why this difference?

Suppose that I had not come along. Then in the first case you would likely have drowned; in the second case you would have remained safely on the bank. The outcome in the first case is no worse for you than it would have been in my absence; hence I have not worsened your situation. However, on the assumption that I might have been able to save you, or to help save you, from drowning, the outcome in the first case might have been better for you than it would have been in my absence, had I acted differently; hence I have failed to better your situation. (Were I, for whatever reason, completely incapable of doing anything to help you, then I should not have bettered your situation, but I should not have failed to better it.) The outcome in the second case is worse for you than it would have been in my absence; hence I have worsened your situation.

In this simple example, the base point for determining how I affect you, in terms of bettering or worsening your situation, is determined by the outcome that you would expect in my absence. Worsening, and equally bettering, are judged by comparing what I actually do with what would have occurred, *ceteris paribus*, in my absence. Failing to better, and equally failing to worsen, are judged by comparing what I might have done, but did not do, with what would have occurred without me. I push you in; you would not have fallen in without me; I worsen your situation. I could have saved you; you would not have been saved without me; I fail to better your situation.

There are complications to the determination of the appropriate base point which this example does not capture. If you are drowning, and I am a life-guard on duty, then by ignoring your cries for help I do worsen your situation. For here my behaviour is to be judged against what would have happened in my absence on a normally life-guarded beach, not on a beach that in lacking me also lacked a life-guard. But note that failure to provide a life-guard, assuming no prior requirement or commitment, could not worsen or contribute to worsening the situation of users of the beach, even though, once a life-guard is provided, her inattention to duty may worsen their situation. Complications such as this indicate the importance of considering the institutional framework and the nature of practices within which actions occur, in order to determine the base point appropriate for judging bettering or worsening.

To this point we have considered only the effect of one person on the situation of another. But what if a person affects her own situation? Here we cannot appeal to her absence in order to fix the base point. A determinate context for bettering or worsening one's own situation is however provided by the assumption of interaction. Although we may speak of someone bettering her situation in so far as she prefers its outcome both to her previous position and to some alternative that she might have brought about, yet this is not relevant to our present discussion. Rather, just as I better your situation in so far as you prefer the outcome of interaction with me to what you would have expected otherwise, in my absence, so I better my own in so far as I prefer the outcome of interaction with you to what I should have expected otherwise, in your absence or unavailability for interaction. And I worsen my own situation in interaction with you in so far as I prefer what I should have expected in your absence to the outcome that I actually bring about. Again, this abstracts from any institutional framework.

We interpret the Lockean proviso so that it prohibits worsening the situation of another person, except to avoid worsening one's own through interaction with that person. Or, we may conveniently say, the proviso prohibits bettering one's situation through interaction that worsens the situation of another. This, we claim, expresses the underlying idea of not taking advantage.

3.2 The proviso is intended to apply to interaction under the assumptions of individual utility-maximizing rationality and mutual unconcern. Each person is supposed to choose a strategy that maximizes his expected utility, unless specifically forbidden by the proviso to do so. Each is then free to better his own situation as he chooses, provided that he does not thereby worsen the situation of another. To require that, as a condition of bettering one's own situation, one must better that of others, would be to require that one give free rides. But no one is free to better his own situation through interaction worsening the situation of another. To allow that, in order to better one's own situation, one may worsen that of others, would be to allow one to be a parasite. Thus a stronger constraint on natural interaction than the proviso would license free-ridership, a weaker constraint would license parasitism. Navigating between these, the proviso constrains natural interaction to make rational, fair, and free co-operation possible.

A person who accepts the proviso as a constraint on his maximizing behaviour may be supposed to reason about the choice of a strategy in interaction in the following way:

(1) He divides his strategies into three groups:
A: those that afford each person an expected utility no less than she could expect in the absence of interaction;
B: those that afford him an expected utility no less than he could expect in the absence of interaction, but afford some other person an expected utility less than she could expect in the absence of interaction;
C: those that afford him an expected utility less than he could expect in the absence of interaction.

(2) If Group A is not empty, then he chooses from it a strategy maximizing his expected utility. He betters, or at least does not worsen his situation, without worsening that of anyone else.

(3) If Group A is empty and Group B is not empty, then he chooses from Group B a strategy minimizing the loss to others of expected utility in comparison to what they could expect in the absence of interaction. He does not worsen his own situation, and compatibly with this he minimizes worsening the situation of others. The proviso forbids unnecessary worsening.

(4) If Groups A and B are empty, then he chooses from Group C a strategy maximizing his expected utility. He minimizes worsening his situation when interaction is unprofitable to him.

Consider an example of interaction constrained by the proviso. Joanna and Jonathan find themselves castaways on a small and otherwise uninhabited island. Concerned to establish a basis for co-operation, each resolves to comply with the proviso. Thus Jonathan does not force Joanna to submit to his sexual desires, even though it might better his situation (in relation to her absence), because it would worsen hers (in relation to his absence). But when Joanna expresses her willingness, Jonathan maximizes his gratification without concern for her arousal. He betters himself without worsening her situation. Later, of course, they may agree to enhance each other's sexual enjoyment, finding this mutually beneficial. But such mutual enhancement is co-operative.

Each takes whatever food he or she pleases, without concern for the other. Since in the other's absence each would have access to all the food the island provides, each would worsen his or her situation by refraining from taking whatever food he or she wants and can get. However, when Joanna begins to cultivate a garden and grows a greater supply of fruits and vegetables, Jonathan refrains from seizing what he pleases, since he would then be bettering himself (for in her absence there would be no garden) by worsening her situation (since in his absence she would enjoy the garden alone). And when Jonathan makes a fishing rod and catches a greater supply of seafood, Joanna, for like reason, refrains from seizing what she pleases.

Of course, by this time we should expect Joanna and Jonathan to have reached an agreement to co-operate—and a good thing, too, given the pronounced swelling in Joanna's abdomen. But only such an agreement—explicit or implicit—can bring them to an optimal state of affairs. In natural interaction, even constrained by the proviso, each assesses every situation separately in deciding what to do, so that only immediate reciprocity can be taken into account. In co-operation, they may extend their horizon of concern, accepting costs now for expected benefits later.

In natural interaction it would be irrational for Joanna to run any risk whatsoever to save Jonathan from the sharks in the lagoon—assuming, of course, mutual unconcern. Were she to worsen her situation by bettering his in this way, she would in effect allow him to be a parasite. But an understanding to co-operate may place each of them under a rational and moral obligation to endeavour to save the other even at real risk to oneself. For both Joanna and Jonathan stand to benefit from a practice imposing certain costs on each in order to confer greater benefits on the other. Each insures himself or herself against being left to whatever perils there may be by agreeing to seek to rescue the other.

The proviso, then, does not incorporate the demands of fair optimality into the state of nature. It merely constrains natural interaction to determine an initial position from which a fair and optimal outcome may be attained. Or so we claim—for remember that we have yet to show that the proviso satisfies the standards of morals and reason.

4.1 Locke introduces the proviso to constrain a particular activity, the acquisition or appropriation of external objects. He argues that the exercise of this activity in conformity with the proviso affords the actor an exclusive right to the land or goods appropriated. In this way the actor obtains the material endowment in the factors of production that is required fully to define him for the purposes of market and co-operative interaction. But Locke assumes that each person begins with an exclusive right to his body and its powers, a right which is extended through labour to what he acquires.

For us the proviso plays a wider and more basic role. We treat it as a general constraint, by which we may move from a Hobbesian state of nature, in which there are no exclusive rights whatsoever but only liberties, to the initial position for social interaction. We begin by considering what each person may do with that body and those powers to which he has direct access, and what others may and may not do with that body and those powers. We show that each person has certain rights to his body and powers, constituting his basic endowment as we defined it in IV.3.2. We then consider how these rights, which Locke assumes but which we derive, lead to further rights in land and other goods. These arise, not simply from acts of appropriation conformable to the proviso, but jointly from what a person may do and from what others in consequence may not do—from the way in which an individual may use certain goods and the consequent restrictions that preclude others both from using the goods and from interfering with his use.

In this way we show that the proviso introduces a rudimentary structure of rights into natural interaction. It converts the predatory natural condition described by Hobbes into the productive natural condition supposed by Locke. But its primary role is to make possible the further structures required for the forms of social interaction, both competitive and co-operative. Of course we could imagine other ways of making social interaction possible, other ways of establishing a structure of rights determining each person's initial endowment. Our claim is that the proviso accomplishes this in a way both rational and impartial.

In the Hobbesian state of nature one may use one's body and powers as one pleases. Although the proviso constrains this use, it does so without affecting the core of the liberty manifested. For in exercising one's powers one need not interact with others, and so one need neither better one's situation in relation to what one would expect in their absence, nor worsen their situation in relation to what they would expect were one absent oneself. Any constraint arising from the proviso affects the manner in which one exercises one's powers, but not the mere fact of that exercise.

In the Hobbesian state of nature one may also use the bodies and powers of others as one pleases. Within the bounds of what one is able to do there is nothing one may not do. But this liberty is directly affected by the proviso. For in using the powers of others one betters, or expects to better, one's situation through interaction with them, and in so far as one's use must interfere with their own exercise of their powers, one worsens their situation by that interaction.

Each person, in the absence of his fellows, may expect to use his own powers but not theirs. This difference is crucial. For it provides the base point against which the proviso may be applied to interaction. Continued use of one's own powers in the presence of others does not in itself better one's situation; use of their powers does better one's own situation. Refraining from the use of one's own powers worsens one's situation; refraining from the use of others' powers fails to better one's situation but does not worsen it. Continued use of one's own powers may fail to better the situation of others but does not in itself worsen their situation; use of others' powers, in interfering with their own use, does worsen their situation. Thus the proviso, in prohibiting each from bettering his situation by worsening that of others, but otherwise leaving each free to do as he pleases, not only confirms each in the use of his own powers, but in denying to others the use of those powers, affords to each the exclusive use of his own. The proviso thus converts the unlimited liberties of Hobbesian nature into exclusive rights and duties. Each person has an exclusive right to the exercise of his own powers without hindrance from others, and a duty to refrain from the use of others' powers in so far as this would hinder their exercise by those with direct access to them.

We have provided the justification, promised in IV.3.2, of the *basic endowment*. We suppose that each person identifies with those capacities, physical and mental, to which he has direct access, and we see that this identification affords each person a normative sense of self, expressed in his right to those capacities. By appealing to the proviso we show that this identification is not arbitrary, but rather fully justified by the (yet to be shown) rationality and impartiality of the proviso.

The first step in the conversion of the state of nature is now complete; application of the proviso affords each person exclusive right to the use of his body and its powers, his physical and mental capacities. The next step is to extend this right to the effects of exercising one's powers. Here Locke's concern with labour and use enter the argument. But as we shall see, this second step does not afford an exclusive right to the fruits of one's labour, even if one puts those fruits to use.

Suppose that in the state of nature I cultivate a plot of land, intending to consume its produce. Here my exercise of my powers is quite independent of any other person, and so I do not better myself through interaction. Even if I worsen the situation of someone who would otherwise have cultivated the land, this worsening is incidental to the benefit I receive. My activity cannot violate the proviso. Now suppose that some other person seizes the produce of the land which I have cultivated. Then she does better herself as a result of my activity, and furthermore worsens my situation from what it would have been in her absence, by depriving me of the fruits of my labour. Her activity does violate the proviso. Thus we see more clearly what we claimed in the example of 3.2; Jonathan must not seize Joanna's fruits and vegetables, and Joanna must not seize Jonathan's fish.

Note that to establish a violation of the proviso, we appeal both to my labour in producing the good that the other person takes, and my intended use of that good. She betters her position through my labour, and worsens my position by depriving me of the expected use. The proviso would not be violated were she to take a windfall that I had thought to use but not laboured to produce, nor would it be violated were she to take produce for which I could find no use whatsoever.

By this argument we demonstrate a right in the effects of one's labour, but not an exclusive right to their possession. For we have not shown that the proviso would be violated were someone to seize the fruits of my labour while compensating me for my effort and intended use. If the benefit I receive is no less, in terms of my utilities, than what I expected from my labour in the absence of intervention, then my situation has not been worsened.

Thus the proviso requires what, following Nozick, we term *full compensation*, and not *market compensation*.[14] Full compensation leaves a person without any net loss in utility. Market compensation affords her a share of the benefit realized by the other individual who seizes the good and pays compensation—the share that could be expected from voluntary exchange. One worsens the situation of another in not giving her full compensation for the effects of one's actions on her. One would better the situation of another in giving her market compensation (where this exceeds full compensation); the gain from exchange is a benefit she could receive only through interaction. The proviso prohibits worsening but does not require bettering another's position, in bettering one's own. It does not then require that the person who seizes the fruits of another's labour share her gains; it requires only that she compensate for costs. Thus the proviso affords a right *in* the fruits of one's labour and so to full compensation, not a right *to* those fruits and so to market compensation.

This second step, from a right to one's body and its powers to a right in one's products, completes the conversion of the pure state of nature. The remaining steps concern the transition from natural interaction to market and co-operative interaction. The first of these constitutes the internalization of costs necessary to the emergence of the market.

Suppose that we live as fisherfolk along the banks of a river. If you compel me to fish for you then you violate the proviso in preventing me from exercising my powers as I see fit. If you seize the fish I catch then you violate the proviso unless you compensate me for my labour and my intended use of the fish. But if you, living upstream from me, merely use the river for the disposal of your wastes, then even though you thereby kill many of the fish in my part of the stream, you do not violate the proviso. For although you worsen my situation in relation to what I should expect in your absence, you do

[14] See ibid., pp. 57, 63–5.

not better your own situation through interaction with me. You are no better off than you would be were no one to live downstream from you. The cost you impose on me is not necessary to the benefit you receive; it is not a *displaced cost*. Rather, the cost is occasioned solely by my presence, which from your point of view may be simply unwanted.

But suppose now that we cease to live as independent fisherfolk. Instead of consuming all of the fish you catch, you use some in trades with or involving me. My willingness to trade—my desire for fish and the terms on which I accept fish—are of course affected by the supply of fish directly available to me, and so by your polluting activity. Exchanging with me betters your situation; from your point of view interaction with me is profitable. But it may not better my situation, taking as base point your absence. Although I benefit by trading with you when the alternative is not trading, yet I may do less well than I would were I alone, fishing in an unpolluted stream. Taking all of the ways in which we interrelate into account, you better your situation through interaction that worsens mine. And so your use of the river for waste disposal, because of its effect on the terms of trade between us, violates the proviso.

Suppose however that taking our interaction as a whole, each of us improves his situation. Our exchanges would then seem to compensate me—fully—for the pollution you cause. Does this free you from the charge of violating the proviso? No; the absence of global worsening does not show that no part of our interaction violates the proviso. You dispose of your wastes in a way that kills the fish in my part of the river. You thereby impose a cost on me that betters the terms of trade for you and correspondingly worsens them for me. The cost you impose on me is now necessary to some part of the benefit you receive, and so it is a displaced cost. You benefit from polluting my water; you better your situation through interaction that worsens mine.

Our exchanges do not constitute compensation to me for your pollution. You do not trade with me in order to compensate me. You do not trade with me because you have polluted my water; your method of waste disposal is not a necessary condition of our being able to trade. Indeed, our exchanges, far from compensating me for your pollution, are less beneficial to me than they would have been, were it not for your pollution. If you talk of compensation here, you add insult to injury. You impose uncompensated costs on me by your method of waste disposal, and given our interdependence, you benefit from imposing those costs and so violate the proviso.

The proviso is violated by an action that betters the actor's situation through worsening the situation of another person. An action performed in one context may be entirely innocent; it may benefit the actor and impose costs on another person, but benefit and cost are quite unrelated. The same action performed in another context may be clearly guilty; it may benefit the actor and impose costs on another person, and the benefit, at least in part, may depend on the cost.

By polluting the water in the stream in which I fish, you increase my demand for your fish, and so improve, from your standpoint, the terms of trade between us. But this need not be the only benefit you gain at my expense. Suppose that we are no longer simple fisherfolk, but two industrialists. We need pure water in our manufacturing activities, and we produce waste which is most cheaply disposed of by discharging it into water, thereby rendering the water impure. If each of us produces only for his own use, your use of the stream for waste diposal, although increasing my costs of production (since I must now install water-purifying equipment in my plant), does not decrease yours in relation to what they would be in my absence. But suppose each of us produces to sell to a third party. Now you put yourself at an advantage by keeping your waste disposal costs down in a way that raises my production costs. In this market situation, any costs of your activity that fall on me are displaced costs, benefiting you by worsening my competitive position, and so, if uncompensated, constitute violations on the proviso.

We may generalize from this argument to conclude that in both market and co-operative interaction, all of the costs of one person's activities that fall on others within the sphere of interaction are displaced costs,. requiring compensation if the proviso is not to be violated. For even if, narrowly conceived, some of these costs may seem unnecessary to the particular benefits received, yet in so far as the framework of the market or of co-operative institutions and practices is required for those activities, all costs occurring within that framework are necessary. To be sure, no displacement of costs can occur within the perfectly competitive market, or within co-operative interaction governed by the principle of minimax relative concession, but their initial positions are the outcome of natural interaction that must satisfy the proviso if no one is to take initial advantage. Thus in so far as natural interaction leads to market or co-operative interaction, the full internalization of costs among those interacting is required by the proviso. Even if in the state of nature itself, certain costs arise only because of the presence of others who do not affect the benefit received, yet in so far as these others enter into social interaction, costs imposed on them in the state of nature must be compensated in determining their market and co-operative endowments.

Because of the importance of this point to our analysis, we reiterate it. In a pure state of nature, the imposition of costs on those incidental to one's activity can in no way violate the proviso. Such costs are strictly incidental and unnecessary to the benefits one receives. One does not then better one's situation through interaction, even though one does worsen the situation of those on whom the costs fall. But if one views those persons as potential partners in social relationships, in market competition and in co-operation, then the proviso forbids the imposition of any costs upon them without appropriate compensation. For now the costs falling on them put them at a disadvantage with respect to the envisaged relationships, and so betters one's situation by worsening theirs.

Full, not market, compensation is required. Although our concern is with preconditions of the market, it is not with market interaction. The fisherfolk have a right in their stream, but not—yet—a right to it. Such rights emerge only in the final step by which the state of nature is converted into society. The effect of the first three steps in rationalizing and moralizing the state of nature is the creation of a framework of common use among interacting persons, in which full compensation is required should one person interfere with the use another makes or proposes to make of certain material goods, but in which there are no exclusive rights of possession to external objects. The fourth, and final step, which defines the full endowment of each individual, introduces exclusive rights to land and other goods.

Suppose that several persons inhabit an island. The land and its resources comprise in effect a commons available to all. But use is individual; each person provides primarily for her own needs, and interaction is non-co-operative. To make our account more realistic we should think not of individual persons but of families. The idea of a family is of a group the members of which take an interest one in another; hence internal interaction within the family is not treated directly in our analysis. We suppose then that each family provides for its own needs, interacting non-co-operatively with other families. But one individual, or head of a family, aware that planned, intensive cultivation would make the land more productive, proposes to take a certain area of the island for her exclusive use, so that she (and her family) may benefit by maximizing its productivity. She seeks an exclusive right to a certain portion of the island.

How may we assess this proposed right? First we must ask whether someone, in seeking exclusive use of land or other goods, violates the proviso, bettering her situation through worsening that of others. If not, then we must ask whether some other person, in interfering with a claim to exclusive use, violates the proviso. If so, then the proposed right is established. The right-holder, and no one else, may use the land or goods without violating the proviso. And if the proviso is violated, the compensation required will be, not full, but market compensation, for the right-holder is entitled to as much as she could have obtained by voluntary exchange, as compensation for any use made of her land or goods. A right *to* land or goods is a right not only to the fruits of use, but also to the fruits of exchange.

We begin then by considering the effects of granting a claim to exclusive control. On the one hand it is evident that the person, whom we shall call Eve, intends to better her situation by her appropriation of land for herself. And she intends to better it in relation to the base point set by the terms of the problem—that is, in relation to the system of common use. She seeks the security of tenure that a right to market compensation, rather than merely full compensation, confers. Thus she intends to better her situation in relation to her fellows. And this conclusion is reinforced by noting that a system of rights determines the endowments for prospective market and co-operative interaction; exclusive right to a portion of land therefore affords Eve a more favourable basis for such interaction than she would otherwise enjoy.

But although Eve intends to better her situation in relation to her fellows, she need not seek to bring this about by worsening their situation. They are, it is true, to lose their right to use in common the land that she appropriates. They are to be obliged to enter into exchanges with her that she voluntarily accepts, rather than merely paying her full compensation, should they use what she produces. Now we might suppose that Eve seeks a part of the island so large that she would leave her fellows worse off than before; the land remaining in common might support them less well than the entire island supported everyone. Eve's claim would then violate the proviso. But she need not seek such a large appropriation. Planned intensive cultivation made possible by her security of tenure may well make it possible for her to live better on a part of the island sufficiently small that the others would also be better off, living without her on the remaining land, than they were when all used the entire island in common. For of course, in seeking a private holding, Eve proposes to give up her right in the remaining commons.

Furthermore, the other inhabitants of the island may also benefit from new opportunities to trade their products for some of the goods resulting from Eve's more intensive cultivation. She may produce sufficient food to meet the needs of several families, so that others, who formerly grew their own food, may become specialist craftsmen and craftswomen, with benefits to all. Hence her appropriation may enable everyone to improve her situation, in relation to the base point set by use in common, so that it does not violate the proviso.

Given that the effects of exclusive use would be mutually beneficial, we may now consider the effects of interference with Eve's claimed right. This interference must take one of two forms; it may tend to restore common use, or it may involve only a transfer of exclusive use. Given the benefits of Eve's appropriation, the restoration of common use could not but worsen the situation of most persons. The benefits brought about by Eve's security of tenure would no longer be forthcoming. Any benefits that the person seeking to restore common use might hope to obtain would be purchased at the expense of most of his fellows, in clear violation of the proviso. The transfer of exclusive use—the seizure of the land from the original appropriator—is even more evidently in violation. The person seizing the right is bettering himself by worsening Eve's situation, and may avoid this only by paying market compensation, negotiating with Eve for the right to the land on mutually acceptable terms. But then Eve's right is recognized. If she does not violate the proviso by her claim, then anyone subsequently interfering with that claim would violate the proviso.

Eve's right is thus vindicated. Exclusive rights of possession may afford benefits to all, because they give individuals the security needed for it to be profitable to themselves to use the resources available to human beings in more efficient and productive ways.

They transform a system in which each labours on a commons to meet her own needs into a system in which each labours on her own property and everyone's needs are met through market exchange. Individual self-sufficiency gives way to role specialization. The division of labour opens up new ways of life, with opportunities and satisfactions previously unimagined. Thus the mutually beneficial nature of exclusive rights of possession provides a sufficient basis for their emergence from the condition of common use which is the final form of the state of nature. These rights depend on the proviso, which allows individual appropriation and forbids subsequent interference. Each person stands fully individuated and defined in relation to her fellows, her right to her own body and powers now extending to a right to material goods. Where the market fails, co-operative modes of interaction are available to achieve optimality in the face of externalities. Eve, the first appropriator of property, is the great benefactress of humankind, although in this she is led by an invisible hand to promote an end which was no part of her intention.

Different persons will of course benefit differentially from the emergence of a system of exclusive rights. We may assume that Eve, who first takes land for her exclusive use, will take the best portion; no other person is then able to make an equally advantageous appropriation. Eve does not leave her fellows 'as good' to appropriate, although in taking for herself she leaves them as well off, and indeed better off, than before. The proviso ensures that at every stage in interaction, each person is left as much as she could expect from the previous stage. Advantage is thus not taken, but equality is not assured. We must show, then, that the inequality allowed by the proviso is no indication of partiality.

4.2 Is the proviso an impartial constraint on interaction? What might lead us to question its impartiality? Does it go too far, in prohibiting persons from bettering themselves through interaction that worsens the situation of others? Does it not go far enough, in leaving persons free to better themselves as long as they do not gain from worsening the situation of others? Or in leaving persons free to worsen the situation of others, if the only alternative would be to worsen their own? Or does the proviso fail to be impartial, because it is based on considerations about bettering and worsening? It is this last question which raises the serious issues we must address. It is the relevance of bettering and worsening which is challenged, in questioning the impartiality of the proviso.

For, it will be urged, the proviso says nothing about equalizing. Or, it will also be urged, the proviso says nothing about meeting needs. The rich man may feast on caviar and champagne, while the poor woman starves at his gate. And she may not even take the crumbs from his table, if that would deprive him of his pleasure in feeding them to his birds.

Distressing as we may find this situation, we should not be misled by it. We think of rich and poor within a social context, and we think that his wealth and her poverty are in some way related. If so, then in examining how the situation came about, we may well find a violation, if not of the proviso, then of the principle of minimax relative concession. We should begin with a quite different example—one that we shall adapt to our purposes from Robert Nozick's *Anarchy, State, and Utopia.*[15]

There are sixteen Robinson Crusoes, each living on a different island. Each is either clever or stupid, either strong or weak, either energetic or lazy. Each lives on an island either well or ill supplied to meet human needs and desires. No two Robinson Crusoes are alike in their characteristics and circumstances (so given sixteen of them, all possible combinations are realized). There is a clever, strong, energetic Crusoe living very comfortably on a well-supplied island. There is a stupid, weak, lazy Crusoe barely surviving on an ill-supplied island. In between are fourteen other Crusoes.

Each is equipped with a two-way radio, putting him in communication with the other Robinson Crusoes. Each knows how his situation compares with that of each of the others. Each is also able to build small rafts, not large enough to carry a man or woman, but sufficient to carry provisions of various kinds. The ocean currents will take these rafts from one island to another, but only in a single direction, so that trade is impossible.

Suppose now that the clever, strong, energetic Crusoe, on the well-supplied island, could send provisions by raft to the stupid, weak, lazy Crusoe, on the ill-supplied island. It would no doubt be generous of her to do so. She might want to do so; there is nothing in our story to require that she takes no interest in the other Crusoes' interests. But suppose she does not want to do so; she knows about the others, but does not care about them. Is she under an obligation to supply the stupid, weak, lazy Crusoe? Is it unfair of her not to do so? Is the principle that allows each Crusoe to use his own capacities

[15] See ibid., p. 185.

and the resources of the island on which he finds himself for his own benefit, an unfair principle, or one which expresses partiality to some persons? Would an impartial principle require the better situated Crusoes to contribute to the worse situated ones, or the able Crusoes to the less able ones, where the ocean currents made such contributions possible? Would it require equalizing contributions when possible? Or would it set out needs and require that these be met when possible? No; any principle other than the one allowing each Crusoe to benefit himself would be unfair and partial, in requiring some to give free rides to others, or to be hosts for their parasitism.

Time passes; the Crusoes learn how to make larger rafts, making migration (in the direction of the currents) a possibility. If we follow the proviso, each has a right to his physical and mental capacities but only a right in the resources of the island he inhabits. (Given the difference between well-supplied and ill-supplied islands, once migration is possible some would better themselves by an exclusive right to an island in a way that would worsen the situation of others.) Hence the Crusoes may migrate, and each may use the resources of any island on which he lands, although he must compensate (fully) any other Crusoe if he takes the fruits of the other's labour. The clever, strong, energetic Crusoe on the ill-supplied island may (currents permitting) move to the well-supplied island occupied by a stupid, weak, lazy Crusoe and, ignoring the latter, make himself as comfortable as his counterpart who began her life on a well-supplied island. Of course some migrations may lead to co-operation—the clever but weak and lazy Crusoe supplying the brain for the strong and energetic but stupid Crusoe's brawn, for example. But they need not. Is the principle which allows each Crusoe to use his own capacities and the resources of any island he can reach for his own benefit an unfair one? Would an impartial principle require abler Crusoes to move (currents permitting) in order to assist less able ones? No; such a requirement would be unfair, as again requiring giving free rides or hosting parasites.

John Rawls insists, 'There is no more reason to permit the distribution of income and wealth to be settled by the distribution of natural assets than by historical and social fortune.'[16] We should rather 'regard the distribution of natural talents as a common asset and . . . share in the benefits of this distribution whatever it turns out to be. Those who have been favored by nature, whoever they are,

[16] J. Rawls, *A Theory of Justice*, (Cambridge, Mass., 1971), p. 74.

may gain from their good fortune only on terms that improve the situation of those who have lost out. . . . No one deserves his greater natural capacity nor merits a more favorable starting place in society.'[17] It is clear that Rawls would require persons to bargain from a position of equality, not only with respect to initial rights to goods, but also with respect to initial rights to personal powers and capacities. Those who are more capable or more fortunate than their fellows must not only refrain from taking advantage of others, as the proviso requires, but they must give advantage to others as a condition of benefiting themselves. For Rawls morality demands the giving of free rides; no other interpretation can be put on the insistence that talents be treated as a common asset.

We may agree with Rawls that no one deserves her natural capacities. Being the person one is, is not a matter of desert. But what follows from this? One's natural capacities determine what one gets, given one's circumstances, in a condition of solitude. One's natural capacities are what one brings to society, to market and co-operative interaction. Why should they not determine, or contribute to determining, what one gets in society? How could a principle determine impartially how persons are to benefit in interaction, except by taking into account how they would or could benefit apart from their interaction?

Rawls talks of the 'distribution of natural talents' and of the 'natural lottery'.[18] He falls prey to the dangers that lurk in this talk. There is no natural lottery; our talents are not meted out to us from a pool fixed to guarantee winners and losers. And if there is a distribution, there is no distributor—unless we assume a theistic base foreign to Rawls's argument. The proviso determines the initial endowments of interacting persons, taking into account the real differences among those persons as actors. But the proviso is not itself an actor or a distributor; it enters into the agency of persons in so far as they respect it. If there were a distributor of natural assets, or if the distribution of factor endowments resulted from a social choice, then we might reasonably suppose that in so far as possible shares should be equal, and that a larger than equal share could be justified only as a necessary means to everyone's benefit. But this would be to view persons as the creatures of a distributor—a God or a non-instrumental Society—and not as rational and individual

[17] Ibid., pp. 101–2.

[18] Ibid., pp. 101, 74.

actors. In agreeing with Rawls that society is a co-operative venture for mutual advantage, we must disagree with his view that natural talents are to be considered a common asset. The two views offer antithetical conceptions of both the individual human being and society.

Each human being is an actor with certain preferences and certain physical and mental capacities which, in the absence of her fellows, she naturally directs to the fulfilment of her preferences. This provides a basis, in no way arbitrary, from which we may examine and assess interaction, introducing such conceptions as bettering and worsening. A principle that abstracted from this basis would not relate to human beings as actors. A principle that did not take this basis as normatively fundamental would not relate impartially to human beings as actors.

If sixteen Robinson Crusoes lived, each on a separate island, and if each used his capacities to provide for himself from the resources of the island, then the outcome, whatever it might be, could not be unjustified. No more can it be unjustified if each person brings her capacities, and what she has realized through them without worsening the situation of others, as her individual endowment for the competitive and co-operative endeavours that constitute society. The proviso, in determining the rights persons have on the basis of what they do, and in treating what persons do from the standpoint of the individual actor, ensures the impartiality of interaction.

4.3 Human beings have rights. Moral theory has not been notably successful in providing an account of these rights. Utilitarianism, as we saw in IV.4.1, leads inexorably to the view that 'rights . . . are . . . vested in the government and their association with individuals is a temporary matter of convenience'.[19] If this view were not unacceptable on other grounds, we should have to ask how governments come to acquire or possess rights, a question not easily answered if one supposes governments to be instruments rather than masters of their citizens, but we may draw a decent veil of obscurity over this embarrassment to utilitarians. Forthright defenders of individual rights have on occasion been content to put the task of grounding rights to one side, 'following the respectable tradition of Locke, who does not provide anything remotely resembling a satisfactory explanation of the status and basis of the law of

[19] Winch, p. 99.

nature'.[20] Locke, indeed, unlike his modern-day disciples, did not suppose that a secular grounding of individual rights was possible; his moral theory, unlike Hobbes's, is overtly theistic.

Contractarianism offers a secular understanding of rights. But the idea of morals by agreement may mislead, if it is supposed that rights must be the product or outcome of agreement. Were we to adopt this account, we should suppose that rights were determined by the principle of minimax relative concession. But as we have seen, the application of this principle, or more generally, the emergence of either co-operative or market interaction, demands an initial definition of the actors in terms of their factor endowments, and we have identified individual rights with these endowments. Rights provide the starting point for, and not the outcome of, agreement. They are what each person brings to the bargaining table, not what she takes from it.

Market and co-operative practices presuppose individual rights. These rights are morally provided in the proviso. And the rights so grounded prove to be the familiar ones of our tradition—rights to person and to property. That they are also rationally grounded remains to be shown in section 5.

We must however recognize that these rights are not inherent in human nature. In defining persons for market competition and for co-operation, they assert the moral priority of the individual to society and its institutions. But they do not afford each individual an inherent moral status in relation to her fellows. In a pure state of nature, in which persons interact non-co-operatively and with no prospect of co-operation, they have no place. Rawls speaks of society as 'a cooperative venture for mutual advantage'.[21] It is only that prospect of mutual advantage which brings rights into play, as constraints on each person's behaviour. It is that prospect which enables rights to coexist with the assumption of mutual unconcern. The moral claims that each of us makes on others, and that are expressed in our rights, depend, neither on our affections for each other, nor on our rational or purposive capacities, as if these commanded inherent respect, but on our actual or potential partnership in activities that bring mutual benefit.

Each person acts rationally in seeking to maximize her utility, subject to two levels of constraint. First, each is constrained by the rights of her fellows, as determined by the proviso. If each respects

[20] Nozick, p. 9. [21] Rawls, p. 4.

the rights of others, then no one takes advantage of anyone else. The initial conditions for fair and rational market competition, and for the bargaining—explicit or implicit—that sets the terms for fair and rational co-operation, are satisfied. Second, each is constrained by the requirements of minimax relative concession, within co-operative institutions and practices. The error of some defenders of individual rights is to suppose that rights alone, the first level of constraint, are sufficient, and indeed, that further moral constraints on individual utility-maximization must be rejected as incompatible with rights. They would be correct if persons who adhered to the proviso found themselves always interacting with their fellows under conditions of perfect competition. For as we showed in Chapter IV, the market is a morally free zone. But the externalities that plague our interactions lead us to recognize that rights, although necessary, are morally insufficient. The compatibility of the two levels of constraint, respect for rights and adherence to co-operative practices, is a theme basic to the idea of morals by agreement.

5.1 Why should an individual seeking to maximize his utility not take advantage of his fellows? Why does his interest in market and co-operative arrangements, in itself an expression of his concern with utility-maximization, afford him reason to accept the proviso as limiting his rights in market and co-operative interaction? To bring our questions into sharper focus, let us consider once again the fisherfolk. You, the upstreamer, discharge your wastes into the running water of the river, thus causing pollution, and so costs for me, the downstreamer. This benefits you in interaction with me, and so brings the proviso into play; you lack the right to pollute.

There are two alternatives to consider—either your use of the river for waste disposal is the most efficient method overall, or it is not. If it is, then you should continue to pollute but compensate me for my resulting costs. If it is not, then you should adopt and pay for some other method of waste disposal that minimizes total costs. In each case optimality is achieved. But an optimal outcome may be realized in a quite different way. If using the river for waste disposal is efficient then you should simply continue to use it. If it is not, then I should pay you the difference in your costs necessary to induce you to adopt the most efficient method, since this payment must be less than the cost to me of your pollution. Again an optimal outcome is realized, although of course costs and benefits are distributed very differently between us.

When you and I agree to co-operate in a single society, you will no doubt contend that existing practices be continued, and I shall argue that those who create wastes should pay disposal costs. You will consider the pollution you bring about to be a simple consequence of natural interaction, and see no reason to refrain from it as a condition of co-operation—although you will refrain if I induce you to do so. I shall treat the effects of your pollution as a cost displaced on to me in natural interaction, and see no reason to accept it as a condition of co-operation—although I shall accept it if you compensate me. How may we resolve these opposed views? Appeal to the proviso would beg the question, since we are seeking its rationale. The proviso denies you, the upstreamer, the right to pollute, and awards me, the downstreamer, compensation should pollution occur. But do not the facts of the situation suggest a quite different assignment of rights? You do not coerce me by your method of waste disposal; you do not exact an unproductive transfer from me by predatory means. You simply dump your wastes in the river; if I object, then is not the onus on me to do something about it? The ban on coercion would seem to favour you, if anyone. Hence as a rational utility-maximizer you have no reason to change your method of waste disposal, and certainly no reason to make me a transfer payment, itself unproductive, as 'compensation'—unless I coerce you to pay. It may seem that reason and the proviso part company, and so, since the proviso ensures impartiality, do reason and morals.

But we deny this. Let us begin our rejoinder by recalling that co-operation has, as its sole and sufficient rationale, the maximization of expected utility. Thus in bargaining, the claim advanced and the concession offered by each person depend on his endeavour to maximize his utility, together with his recognition of the similar endeavour of every other person. The principle of minimax relative concession determines the outcome of co-operative interaction in such a way that shares in the co-operative surplus are related to contributions to its production in the same way for all. Of course, not every particular interaction, considered apart from a practice of co-operation, will benefit each party to it proportionately to his contribution. Everyone may expect to gain from certain arrangements for mutual assistance even though on any given occasion the recipient of assistance gains and the donor loses. It is the practice, and not the occasion, that must satisfy minimax relative concession.

Think now of the fisherfolk. I take a net loss if you dump your wastes in the river. Disposing of wastes by the method least costly to the disposer, ignoring all effects on others, is not a practice offering expected benefit to each member of society. The particular interaction cannot then be defended by relating it to a practice that satisfies minimax relative concession. Hence it violates the requirement, fundamental to rational co-operation, of mutual benefit proportionate to contribution.

If interaction is to be fully co-operative, it must proceed from an initial position in which costs are internalized, and so in which no person has the right to impose uncompensated costs on another. For if not, the resulting social arrangements must embody one-sided interactions benefiting some persons at cost to others. Even if each were to receive some portion of the co-operative surplus, yet each could not expect to benefit in the same relation to contribution as his fellows. Interactions based on displaced costs would be redistributive, and redistribution cannot be part of a rational system of co-operation.

But why should rational utility-maximizers interact in a fully co-operative manner? More generally, why should rational individuals enter fully into society, the locus of both market and co-operative interaction, rather than accepting particular market and co-operative practices within an enduring state of nature? Indeed, is not the state of nature the underlying reality of the human condition? These questions take us back to the position of the Foole. And here, as before, our answer to him turns on exhibiting the conditions for rational compliance with co-operative practices. In Chapter VI the Foole, appealing to the straightforward maximization appropriate to the state of nature, challenged the rationale for compliance with agreed joint strategies. There we showed that a rational individual will dispose himself to such compliance. Here the Foole challenges the rationale for limiting the effects of natural interaction in determining the individual rights from which social interaction proceeds. We must show that without limitations that exclude the taking of advantage, a rational individual would not dispose himself to co-operative compliance.

In VI.2.4 we distinguished broad and narrow compliance. A person disposed to broad compliance compares the benefit she would expect from co-operation on whatever terms are offered with what she would expect from non-co-operation, and complies if the former is greater. Were persons so disposed, then no one would have reason to accept the proviso, or any other constraint, on natural interaction. The non-co-operative outcome would serve as base-point, and any improvement on it would elicit voluntary co-operation. But broad compliance is not a rational disposition for utility-maximizers. Not only does a broadly compliant person invite others to take advantage of her in setting terms of co-operation, but if some persons are broadly compliant, then others, interacting with them, will find it advantageous not to be broadly, or even so much as narrowly, compliant. If you will comply for any benefit whatsoever, then in interacting with you I should dispose myself to comply with a joint strategy only if it offers me, not a fair share, but the lion's share of the co-operative surplus. So it is not and cannot be rational for everyone to be disposed to broad compliance. But since no one chooses to constrain his behaviour for its own sake, no person finds it rational to be more compliant than his fellows. Equal rationality demands equal compliance. Since broad compliance is not rational for everyone, it is not rational for anyone.

A person disposed to narrow compliance compares the benefit he would expect from co-operation with what he would expect from a fair and optimal outcome, and complies with a joint strategy only if the former approaches the latter. An outcome is fair in satisfying the standards of impartiality, which as we have shown are set by the proviso and the principle of minimax relative concession. Thus a person disposed to narrow compliance expects others to adhere, and to consider it rational to adhere, to the proviso as a condition of co-operation. But then, given equal rationality, he must consider it rational to adhere himself to the proviso as a condition of co-operation. The disposition to narrow compliance thus includes the disposition to accept the proviso as constraining natural interaction, in so far as one has the expectation of entering into society, into market and co-operative practices.

The rationality of disposing oneself to narrow compliance, and so to acceptance of the proviso, follows from the advantageousness of society and the equal rationality of its members. If all persons are less than narrowly compliant, refusing to act voluntarily on joint strategies leading to fair and optimal outcomes, then co-operation is not possible. If some persons are less than narrowly compliant, then co-operation is possible only if others are more compliant. But this violates equal rationality. If some persons are more than narrowly compliant, then others would find it advantageous, and so rational, to be less compliant. But this again violates equal rationality. It is rational for each person to be sufficiently compliant that society is possible if others are equally compliant; it is not rational for anyone to be so compliant that society is possible if others are less compliant; therefore it is rational for each person to be narrowly compliant.

Each person endeavours to maximize his own utility. In so doing, each seeks to take what benefits he can from the actions of others, and to displace what costs he can from his own actions to theirs. But also, each seeks to avoid interactions with others that afford them benefits for which he pays the costs. In purely natural interaction, the desire to avoid costly interaction has no independent force to constrain the desire to benefit oneself without regard to others. But in social interaction, requiring voluntary constraint, the desire to avoid costly interaction can be balanced with the desire to take benefits and displace costs. The proviso, forbidding the taking of advantage, represents the weakest constraint rationally acceptable to persons who would avoid costly interaction with others, and the strongest constraint rationally acceptable to persons who would be free to benefit themselves. Thus the proviso reflects the equal rationality of persons who must constrain their natural interaction in order to enter into mutually beneficial social relationships.

As we have seen, interaction constrained by the proviso generates a set of rights for each person, which he brings to the bargaining table of society as his initial endowment. He brings a right to his person, a right in the fruits of his labour, and a right to those goods, whose exclusive individual possession is mutually beneficial, that he has acquired either initially or through exchange. Where goods are not suitable for or capable of such possession, he brings a right of use on terms that internalize all costs. Without these rights, persons would not be rationally disposed, either to accept the prohibition on force and fraud needed for market competition, or to comply voluntarily with the joint strategies and practices needed for co-operation.

5.2 But is our reconciliation of reason and morals not too good to be true? Recall the tale of masters and slaves with which this chapter began. We introduce here Fig. 9, intepreted as illustrating the story, and Fig. 10, representing a significant variant of the tale. In both figures, I_n corresponds to the initial situation of masters

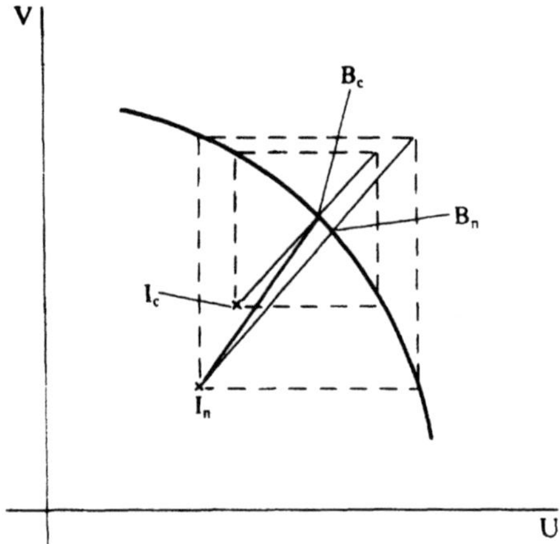

Figure 9

and slaves, B_n to the outcome of agreement as imagined by the young master, in which the ex-slaves voluntarily continue to serve, B_c to the real outcome in which the ex-slaves refuse to comply with the unproductive transfer involved in continued service, and I_c to the hypothetical situation, non-co-operative but non-coercive, that is determined by the proviso as the initial position for bargaining. The difference between the two variants of the tale is evident. If events occur as illustrated in Fig. 10, the final outcome for the ex-masters, represented by B_c, affords them a lesser expectation of utility than their initial situation, I_n. They lose by co-operation, if the initial bargaining position is constrained by the proviso.

Surely the masters, if rational and able to foresee the outcome, would never agree to co-operate on terms that would prove disadvantageous to them. We cannot suppose that Fig. 10 illustrates a real possibility. Rather, we must surely suppose either that no co-operation takes place, so that masters and slaves remain at I_n, or that co-operation takes place on terms affording mutual benefit to both, leading to a point such as B_a in Fig. 10, where the ex-slaves continue to serve the ex-masters to an extent sufficient to make the masters better off than at I_n.

Neither alternative seems palatable. The first enables us to hold fast to our insistence that it is rational to dispose oneself to comply

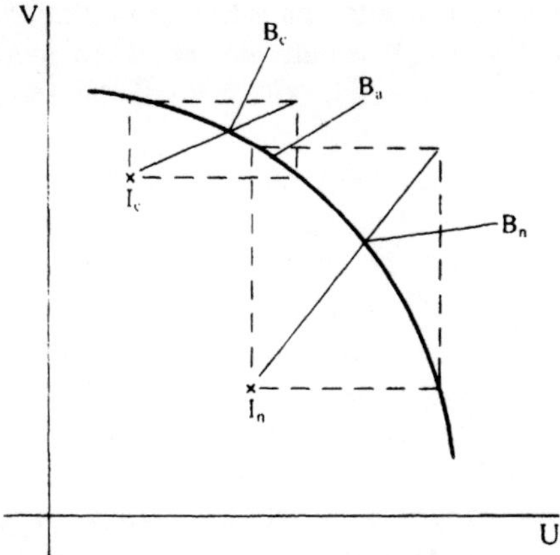

Figure 10

with co-operative arrangements only if they are (nearly) fair and optimal. Then the slaves are unwilling to accept any outcome that affords some portion of the co-operative surplus to the masters. We must deny that there can be any rational improvement on the sub-optimal non-co-operative outcome. The second alternative requires us to weaken the proviso and strengthen the disposition to comply. The masters' rights in the initial bargaining position allow them to take some advantage of the slaves. The slaves are willing to comply with a joint strategy leading to an optimal outcome that is as fair as is consistent with affording both parties mutual benefit. The link between rationality and impartiality is broken. (A third alternative, that the masters should accept the constraints of the proviso and co-operate even though they lose in relation to non-co-operation, we dismiss as clearly incompatible with a utility-maximizing conception of rationality, however constrained.)

For utility-maximizers, the link between co-operation and mutual benefit must take precedence over the link between co-operation and impartiality or fairness. But this does not require us to sever the second link. The proviso constrains the initial bargaining position to the extent, but only to the extent, that such constraint is compatible with the co-operative outcome affording each person the expectation of a utility greater than that afforded by the non-co-operative outcome. It is rational to comply with a co-operative joint strategy if and only if its expected outcome is (nearly) optimal and as fair as is compatible with mutual benefit. We abandon neither the proviso nor narrow compliance, but we subordinate them to the requirement of mutual benefit.

We should distinguish between compliance, as the disposition to accept fair and optimal co-operative arrangements, and *acquiescence*, the disposition to accept co-operative arrangements that are less than fair, in order to ensure mutual benefit. A person who acquiesces in a joint strategy does not consider her own greatest utility on the particular occasions when she follows the strategy. She constrains her utility-maximizing endeavours. But she does not ignore the advantage that she concedes to others in acquiescence, and she remains ready to withhold it, and to demand a joint strategy more favourable to herself, if she supposes that such a strategy would not make co-operation unprofitable to others. Here we suppose that each person does appeal to the natural distribution or non-co-operative outcome which underlies existing social realities, as Buchanan argues.[22] As this underlying equilibrium changes, the conditions of acquiescence also change.

Co-operation on terms less than fair is therefore less stable, in failing to gain the whole-hearted acceptance of all participants. Fair co-operation invites a full compliance which each does not stand ready to withdraw because of shifts in the natural distribution. For although no one is prepared to concede advantage to others in order to bring about this stability, each is willing to accept it, as enhancing the benefits of co-operative institutions and practices, when it is not costly to herself to do so.

We suppose that the link between reason and morals is loosened because of the role that three quite different considerations play in affecting interaction. First, there are ideological factors—beliefs that affect the terms of co-operation in ways that are unfair, sometimes to those who share the beliefs but typically to those who do not. If it is generally held that a woman's place is in the home, then a woman who does not find the home-maker's role satisfying may find it impossible to interact with others in a way that affords her a fair share of the co-operative surplus. Second, and often linked with ideology, are historical factors—institutions and practices that effec-

[22] See Buchanan, pp. 74–82, esp. p. 79.

tively determine the rights persons can exercise in interaction, whether these satisfy the proviso or not. If it is customary to pay women lower wages than men, no particular woman may reasonably expect to be recognized as entitled to equal pay for equal work.

These factors may, ultimately, depend on irrational beliefs—although the irrationality may be strongly ingrained in social practices and institutions that individuals are not effectively able to ignore. But this irrationality makes them less disturbing to our argument linking reason and morals than the third, technological factor. Technology is power; those with a more advanced technology are frequently in a position to dictate the terms of interaction to their fellows. Without their guns, a small number of Spaniards would never have been able to overcome the Indian civilizations of the Americas. To be sure, the Spaniards preferred to dominate rather than to co-operate, but it is clear that their technological superiority ensured that any co-operation must have proceeded from an initial position in violation of the proviso.

A superior technology enables its possessors rationally to maintain, and requires others rationally to acquiesce in, arrangements that rest on differential rights in clear violation of the proviso. And we may not suppose, as with ideology and its institutionalized effects, that the basis of this technology is irrational. On the contrary, it constitutes the most fully rational application of belief to practice. We may say that those possessing a superior technology are more rational than their fellows, in being better able to relate and devise means to their ends. And this reveals why technological factors weaken the link between rationality and impartiality. Our argument in support of the proviso, and in support of narrow compliance, rests on an assumption of equal rationality among persons which differences in technology deny.

Nevertheless, we suppose that the unequal rationality brought about by technological differences between societies is accidental. It does not reflect underlying differences in the capacities of the persons constituting those societies. Freed from false views of the world and the practices and institutions to which such false views give rise, human beings tend toward technological equality. They tend, then, toward a state of affairs in which the proviso, the principle of minimax relative concession, and the disposition to narrow compliance, come fully into play in linking the requirements of reason to the demands of impartiality or morals.

In reconciling reason and morals, we do not claim that it is never rational for one person to take advantage of another, never rational to ignore the proviso, never rational to comply with unfair practices. Such a claim would be false. We do claim that justice, the disposition not to take advantage of one's fellows, is the virtue appropriate to co-operation, voluntarily accepted by equally rational persons. Morals arise in and from the rational agreement of equals.

VIII

THE ARCHIMEDEAN POINT

1.1 'Embedded in the principles of justice there is an ideal of the person that provides an Archimedean point for judging the basic structure of society.'[1] Moral theory offers an Archimedean point analysis of human interaction. But what is an Archimedean point? The reader will recall that Archimedes supposed that given a sufficiently long lever and a place to stand, he could move the earth. We may then think of an Archimedean point as one from which a single individual may exert the force required to move or to affect some object. In moral theory, the Archimedean point is that position one must occupy, if one's own decisions are to possess the moral force needed to govern the moral realm. From the Archimedean point one has the moral capacity to shape society. We characterize the point in terms of its occupant, for it is the characteristics intrinsic to a person, and not her external contrivances or circumstances, which afford her moral force.

What ideal of the person does the Archimedean point express? How does that ideal lead to a judgement of the structure of society, or of the basic principles that underlie social interaction? And what is the import of this judgement for reason and for morals? Briefly, we suppose that the ideal presents a rational actor freed, not from individuality but from the content of any particular individuality, an actor aware that she is an individual with capacities and preferences both particular in themselves and distinctive in relation to those of her fellows, but unaware of which capacities, which preferences. Such a person must exhibit concern about her interactions with others, and this concern leads her to a choice among possible social structures. But her concern is necessarily impartial, because it is based on the formal features of individual rational agency without the biasing content of a particular and determinant set of individual characteristics.

We may think of the choice of this ideal person as proceeding at two levels. Abstractly it is a choice among principles of interaction; concretely it is a choice among social structures embodying these

[1] J. Rawls, *A Theory of Justice* (Cambridge, Mass., 1971), p. 584.

principles. Since we suppose the ideal actor to be fully rational and her standpoint impartial, then her choice among principles must express the norms of justice. Since we suppose her to be fully informed, not of course about her own particular capacities and preferences, but about human capacities, preferences, and circumstances, then her choice among social structures must be the choice of the just society. To articulate her reasoning is to reveal, as an internally rational system, the morality of persons who take no interest in one another's interests. Her choice expresses whatever demands morality makes on the institutions and practices of society.

But her choice expresses also the demands made, by the equal rationality of all persons, on society conceived as a framework of interaction into which each individual is born. Although society is the instrument of its members, yet it not only pre-exists each member, but also shapes to a considerable extent the realization of her capacities and the nature of her preferences, so that it determines in part the use she will seek to make of it. If we then ask what social structure, what institutions and practices, would command the rational agreement of all individuals, as determining the social conditions for their existence, we find the answer in the choice of an actor from the Archimedean point. For that choice, as we shall show, reflects all capacities and preferences in the only way possible prior to the determination of actual, particular individuals. We may thus identify the moral capacity to shape society with the capacity to determine the social contract into which all rational persons must enter.

In preceding chapters we have examined strategic choice from the perspective of the individual actor. We have derived a principle of co-operative interaction, minimax relative concession, from general maximizing considerations together with an account of the formal structure of strategic situations. We have shown that rational persons will dispose themselves to comply with the constraints on straightforward utility-maximization that this principle entails—provided that the endowments or rights that persons bring to interaction are constrained by another principle, the proviso. Thus we have derived internal constraints on utility-maximization within the framework of maximizing choice itself. We have identified the principles so established with the requirements of justice by testing them for impartiality, again from the perspective of the individual engaged in strategic interaction.

We now begin from impartiality, characterizing a standpoint that directly expresses its requirements. Given this moral perspective we then employ the device of rational choice to afford a direct derivation of principles embodying the norms of just interaction. These principles express the requirements of equal rationality on social institutions and practices conceived as prior to the individual actors who use them as a framework for their interactions. If morality and rationality are in harmony, then these principles must be those found in our earlier analysis. Archimedean choice must select individual expected utility-maximization, constrained by the proviso and minimax relative concession. The impartial perspective of the ideal actor must cohere with the perspectives of rational individuals actually engaged in strategic choice.

In the next sub-section we expand our account of the ideal actor, distinguishing her from other possible personae. We then examine the two principal rival accounts of choice from the Archimedean point, the utilitarian theory of John Harsanyi and the Kantian theory of John Rawls, showing our reasons for rejecting both.[2] We then develop our own positive account, establishing the full coherence of the ideal perspective afforded by the Archimedean point with the particular perspectives of individual rational actors. The theory of morals by agreement will then be fully in place.

1.2 The appeal to the choice of an ideal person, aware of her individuality but not of its particular content, reflects a certain conception of the moral enterprise and the ideal of impartiality on which it is founded. Morality is concerned with actors, persons considered as doing and choosing, and as implicated in the consequences of their deeds and choices. As an actor the ideal person is a utility-maximizer, seeking her greatest benefit. Her utilities may be independent of the utilities of others; the Archimedean point is compatible with the supposition of mutual unconcern. What is ideal is in large part determined by what is absent rather than by what is present; the ideal actor is of course rational and generally informed, but she seeks her greatest utility without being aware of the particular circumstances in which she acts, the particular capacities with which she acts, and the particular preferences for whose fulfilment she acts.

But the ignorance of the ideal actor extends only to her inability to

[2] The Kantian character of Rawls's theory comes increasingly to the fore in his more recent writings. See 'Kantian Constructivism in Moral Theory', p. 515.

identify herself as a particular person within society. About the nature of society and its members her knowledge is as complete as can be. She knows the limits and variations of human capacities and interests. She knows the range of feasible social structures, and the individual roles afforded by each. She knows how social structures and particular circumstances affect the manifestation of capacities and interests. Thus she knows the ways in which persons, defined by their capacities and utilities, and societies, defined by their structures and roles, can and cannot fit together. But all of this knowledge, together with the ability to use it in choice, she possesses only as an occupant of the Archimedean point. As in the myth of Er she must drink the waters of Lethe when she has chosen.[3] But unlike those who stand before Lachesis, she chooses not a life, but rather a society in ignorance of the life she will find in it, and she chooses not on the basis of antecedent preferences, for these would afford her a particular identity in choosing, but only by considering the ways in which preferences, capacities, and circumstances can fit within the feasible societies.

Is such choice possible? And if possible, can it have any rational basis? We must show that the ideal actor's concern to maximize the utilities of whatever person she proves to be affords a determinate basis for choice from the Archimedean point. Furthermore, we must show that this concern enables each person to identify with the ideal actor. For although ignorance of one's identity precludes any display of positive partiality in one's choice, this is insufficient to guarantee equal rationality. Impartiality in choice is found, not in the absence of concern for those affected, but in the presence of equal concern, And this is assured by the ideal actor's maximizing aim. Although she may identify with no one, everyone may identify with her. The impartiality of the ideal actor is thus exhibited in the fully representative character of her choice.

To sharpen our account we may distinguish the ideal actor from other ideal personae who have been thought relevant to morality, but whose credentials we reject. First, we must note that in moving to the Archimedean point we in no way abandon Hume's insistence that reason is and ought to be only the slave of the passions. The Kantian ideal of a pure reason which is practical despite its utter indifference to passion is entirely foreign to our argument.[4] The

[3] See *Republic* 620d–621b.

[4] For this ideal see Kant, *Groundwork of the Metaphysic of Morals*, pp. 425–6.

imperatives of reason remain assertoric. And they remain imperatives of individual reason. Whether it is fair to Kant to find in his theory a deep conflict between rationality and individuality is a question we need not explore, since we claim no affinity with his view of practical reason. But we must emphasize that the Archimedean point nullifies the biasing effects of individuality while retaining the idea, not merely of individual choice, but of choice by an individual concerned to advance his own interests. Rawls supposes that he follows Kant in treating the principles of justice in 'independence from the contingencies of nature'.[5] In our view human individuality cannot be separated from these contingencies, and moral principles must not deny but reflect them.

In addition to the Kantian ideal expressed in the noumenal self,[6] we should introduce three other personae—the ideal observer, the ideal sympathizer, and one who might be called the ideal proprietor. The first of these is characterized by his complete detachment from the social structures he assesses, and among which he is to choose.[7] As a pure observer he records what is present for observation, and records it correctly. He records the values, and the evaluations, of those whom he observes. But this record is not itself an evaluation. His detachment robs him of any basis for choice. If we suppose that he will choose principles of interaction that maximize the utilities realized by those who follow the principles, then we are importing into his choice a standard not present in observation itself. Observation is neutral between satisfaction and frustration, between maximizing utility and minimizing it.

The ideal sympathizer is quite the opposite of the ideal observer—totally involved rather than entirely detached. But she is affected only at one remove, by the affections of others. She has no personal concern with a choice among principles of interaction or the social structures that embody them. It is then only in so far as she takes an interest in others' interests—which of course is central to the conception of a sympathizer—that she has a basis for choice. But this is to require of the ideal persona what need not be present, and is not supposed, in her real self. The principles of justice afford a moral basis for interaction among persons who take no interest in one

[5] Rawls, *A Theory of Justice*, p. 256.

[6] Ibid., pp. 255–6, relates the noumenal self to the idea of a rational actor.

[7] Defenders of 'ideal observer' theories ignore this point, supposing that observation triggers reaction. See for example the account in R. B. Brandt, *Ethical Theory* (Englewood Cliffs, NJ, 1959), pp. 173–4.

another; to derive these principles from the idea of a person who necessarily is interested in her fellows would be fundamentally incoherent. The moral demands on persons must be directly intelligible to them, quite apart from whether they are also requirements of reason. But principles established from the standpoint of an ideal sympathizer would lack this intelligibility; they would appear completely alien to the interaction of persons lacking her sense of sympathy. The Archimedean point must idealize the person who finds himself in the circumstances of justice.

In rejecting the ideal sympathizer as the appropriate embodiment of moral choice we express our distance from Hume. Rejecting reason as the basis of morality, Hume saw no alternative but to find that basis in some feeling or effect that afforded a direct identification with others.[8] Here we agree with Kant that morality makes demands on us that are and must be quite independent of any fellow-feelings we may have.[9] Thus we must carefully exclude any appeal to such feelings from choice in the Archimedean point.

An ideal proprietor, in the sense in which we use the term, is someone with a prior right in the social structure—a god who may determine the conditions of interaction for his creatures. But with an ideal proprietor, as with an ideal observer, no standard for choice is afforded by the conception itself. The ideal proprietor's concern is found solely in his right of possession, but this determines no form of interaction among his creatures. No doubt we may import benevolence into our account of the ideal proprietor, but it is no part of that account. The demands of a theistic morality, in its pure form, must appear to beings who view themselves as rational and independent actors in the way expressed by Hobbes—'there is no kicking against the pricks.'[10] Only the power of the proprietor makes his demands relevant to utility-maximizers, and we, unlike Hobbes, reject might as the basis of right.

2 How may we characterize choice from the Archimedean point? A first suggestion, adapted from the moral theory of John Harsanyi, is that such choice involves a simple extension of the procedure for rational choice under risk and uncertainty.[11] What is

[8] See Hume's discussion of sympathy in *Treatise*, ii. i. xi, pp. 316–20.

[9] See Kant, *Groundwork of the Metaphysic of Morals*, p. 398.

[10] Hobbes, *De Cive* xv. 7, p. 294.

[11] See J. C. Harsanyi, 'Cardinal Utility in Welfare Economics and in the Theory of Risk-Taking', in *Essays on Ethics*, pp. 3–5. Harsanyi's theory is discussed at length in my 'On the Refutation of Utilitarianism', in H. B. Miller and W. H. Williams (eds.), *The Limits of Utilitarianism* (Minneapolis, 1982), pp. 144–63.

peculiar to the Archimedean point is only the form of uncertainty—only that, in choosing, one is uncertain, not about one's circumstances, but about one's identity. One must select basic principles of interaction or the social structures that embody them without knowing either the role one will occupy or the personal characteristics that will define one in the structure chosen. But this does not complicate the choice from a theoretical point of view, however difficult it may make it in practice.

The choice of the ideal actor must be impartial. Let us consider Harsanyi's own statement of how this impartiality is to be operationalized. He states that

> this requirement of impersonality and impartiality would always be satisfied if he [the individual choosing] had to choose between the . . . alternatives *without knowing*—or at least by voluntarily *disregarding*—what his own personal social position would be in the resulting social system. More specifically, these requirements would be satisfied if he had to choose between the . . . alternatives on the assumption that he had the *same probability* of occupying any of the existing social positions, from the very highest to the very lowest. (This model I shall call the *equiprobability model* of moral value judgments.)
>
> According to modern decision theory, a rational individual placed in this hypothetical choice situation would always choose the alternative yielding him the higher *expected utility*—which, under this model, would mean choosing the alternative yielding the higher *average utility level* to the individual members of society. Thus . . . making a moral value judgment involves trying to maximize the arithmetic mean of all individual utilities.[12]

Harsanyi supposes that, although impartiality precludes knowing who one is, yet one knows who are the persons in each of the social structures among which one must choose. For each such person one may determine an expected utility—the pay-off he would expect given the principles of interaction embodied in the society. Being completely uncertain of one's own identity, one must suppose that were one to choose a particular society, one would have an equal chance of being each of the persons in it. Thus for each society one weights the expected utility of each person by the probability $p = 1/n$, where n is the number of persons in the society, and one then sums the weighted expected utilities to yield a single expected utility, which is of course the average of the expected utilities of the members of the society. One then chooses those principles of interaction, or that social structure, yielding the greatest average

[12] Harsanyi, 'Rule Utilitarianism and Decision Theory', *Erkenntnis* 11 (1977), p. 28.

expected utility. One chooses in accordance with the principle of average-utilitarianism. Once again the utilitarian alternative is with us, now as an account of Archimedean choice.

Harsanyi supposes that the utilities of different persons are comparable, so that a meaningful average may be determined. We might object to this supposition, but instead we shall suggest a way in which utility comparisons might be made. For we shall argue that even if a meaningful average utility may be determined, maximizing this average is not, as Harsanyi states in the passage quoted, maximizing the expected utility of a rational individual who does not know her preferences and place in society—not, then, maximizing the expected utility of the ideal actor in the Archimedean point. Thus we shall argue that Harsanyi is mistaken in supposing that his choice procedure is a simple extension of rational choice under uncertainty.

How then may the utilities of different persons be compared? In II.3.2 we introduced a convenient way of assigning numerical utilities representing an individual's preferences over the members of any set of possible outcomes, by assigning a utility of 1 to the most preferred outcome and 0 to the least preferred outcome, and equating the utility of any other outcome Y to the expected utility of the lottery L over the most and least preferred outcomes such that L is indifferent to Y. Suppose however that we assign a utility of 1, not to the most preferred among possible outcomes, but to that hypothetical outcome (only rarely a real possibility) that would be completely satisfying, meeting the maximal consistent set of one's desires, aims, and interests, so that it would be most preferred among logically possible outcomes. And suppose that we assign a utility of 0 correspondingly to that hypothetical outcome that would be completely frustrating, so that it would be least preferred among logically possible outcomes. We should then use lotteries over these outcomes to determine the utilities of all actually possible outcomes. Measured on this scale, the utility of any outcome would indicate the extent to which it met or fulfilled one's preferences. We should have a measure of overall preference fulfilment.

The utilities of different persons may now seem fully comparable. The greater the utility, the greater the degree of preference fulfilment, whether one is comparing the utilities of a single person, or the utilities of different persons. If we determine the expected utilities of each person in each feasible social structure on this scale, then the average of the expected utilities of the persons in any social structure will represent the average level of preference fulfilment in that structure. We may then identify average-utilitarianism with the maximization of the average level of preference fulfilment. In choice from the Archimedean point, the maximization of expected utility under uncertainty is simply extended to the maximization of expected average utility, where the expected utility of each individual is a measure of the extent to which his preferences are fulfilled.

If Harsanyi's argument were sound, then the ideal actor, by maximizing average utility, would maximize the expected utility of the person she turns out to be, since the expected utility of each person, ignorant of his identity in society, is simply the average expected utility. Each person would then be able to identify with the ideal actor; each would consider that his own expected utility was being maximized in the unusual circumstances of Archimedean choice. Equally representing each rational person, the ideal actor would determine the terms of the social contract by her choice.

But the argument is not sound. Consider the choice envisaged. Each social structure may be characterized as a lottery, in which all prizes have equal probability, and each prize comprises being a person, with determinate capacities and preferences, in a particular social situation. We may represent such a prize by an ordered pair (a,x), where a is a determinate person and x is a particular situation. To the prize (a,x) we assign a utility—the expected utility for person a in situation x—which we may represent as $U_a(x)$. Harsanyi then claims that for any person i, unaware of what characteristics he will have and what social situation he will occupy, the expected utility of the social structure is the average of the utilities of the prizes. If a social structure consists of persons a, b, and c respectively in situations x, y, and z, then its expected utility, for any person i, is $1/3[U_a(x) + U_b(y) + U_c(z)]$.

But this is obviously false. When person i considers the prize (a,x), he will assign it, not $U_a(x)$, which is person a's utility for being in x, but $U_i(a,x)$, person i's utility for being person a in x. The expected utility of the simple social structure introduced in the preceding paragraph is $1/3[U_i(a,x) + U_i(b,y) + U_i(c,z)]$. For Harsanyi's argument to survive, we must assume that whenever utilities are interpersonally comparable, $U_a(x) = U_i(a,x)$, for all persons i and a, and all situations x. But this need not be so. It holds if and only if the extent to which person i's preferences are fulfilled by being person a in situation x is the same as the extent to which person a's preferences are fulfilled by being in situation x.

Consider, to take an example made famous by John Stuart Mill, Socrates dissatisfied and the fool satisfied.[13] Socrates' dissatisfaction reflects the low ranking his situation receives in terms of his 'wise' preferences, and the fool's satisfaction reflects the high ranking his situation receives in terms of his 'foolish' preferences. But wise or foolish, we may not incorporate into our interpersonal measure of preference any evaluation of the preferences; if they are the true, considered preferences of the persons concerned then they must be taken at face value. Hence we must assign a greater utility to the fool in his situation than to Socrates in his; U_{fool} (*satisfied*) must be greater than $U_{Socrates}$ (*dissatisfied*). Does it follow, reader, that you must prefer to be the satisfied fool to the dissatisfied Socrates, or in other words, that U_{reader} (*fool, satisfied*) must be greater than U_{reader} (*Socrates, dissatisfied*)? Mill leaves us in no doubt that he would prefer being Socrates dissatisfied to the satisfied fool. Not all may agree, but his preference is clearly not irrational.

In choosing between Socrates and the fool, Mill takes into account, not just the preferences they have, and the extent to which they are fulfilled, but his own preferences for having certain personal characteristics, and the extent to which they would be fulfilled. Harsanyi leaves these latter preferences out of account.[14] But they are surely important. Choosing as an average-utilitarian, we might expect the ideal actor to select Aldous Huxley's 'brave new world', in which each person's preferences fit perfectly his social role (apart from the particular failure of fit needed to generate an interesting novel), so that maximum preference fulfilment is guaranteed. If preference fulfilment were all that mattered, we should endorse that choice. But we do not. We must conclude that the ideal actor, if she maximizes average utility, need not maximize the expected utility of each, or perhaps of any, person ignorant of his identity in society, since the ideal actor fails to consider the preferences persons have with respect to their possible identities.

It will be objected that our argument shows, not the failure of the average-utilitarian account of Archimedean choice, but rather our

[13] See Mill, ch. 2, para. 6.

[14] See Harsanyi, *Rational Behavior in Games and Social Situations* (Cambridge, 1977), pp. 51–5, where he defends leaving these preferences out of account by an appeal to the principle of consumer sovereignty.

own failure to grasp the full impartiality of that choice. We have supposed that the ideal actor need not maximize the expected utility of any person ignorant of his identity and role in society, because the ideal actor fails to take preferences for identities into account. But a person ignorant of his identity has no such preferences! Or rather, his preferences can only be the average of the preferences of the various persons, any one of whom he may be. A person with particular, determinate preferences for certain personal characteristics is not yet in a position of full impartiality. Full impartiality, as expressed in Archimedean choice, requires that one be ignorant, not only of the characteristics one will have and the role one will play in each of the feasible social structures among which one must choose, but also of the characteristics one now has, determining one's preferences for the characteristics of the persons in the social structures. One must assume, then, that there is an equal chance that one has the preferences of each person. If a social structure consists of persons a, b, and c respectively in situations x, y, and z, then one considers the structure as a lottery in which, if one is person a one receives the prize (a,x), if one is person b one receives the prize (b,y), and if one is person c one receives the prize (c,z). Given an equal chance of being each person, one has equal chances of receiving the utilities $U_a(x)$, $U_b(y)$, and $U_c(z)$, so that one's expected utility is, after all, $1/3[U_a(x) + U_b(y) + U_c(z)]$. The ideal actor, in maximizing expected average utility, maximizes the expected utility of each person who chooses without knowing both the identity and role he will have in the social structure chosen, and his own present identity.

But let us reflect on the choice we are ascribing to the ideal actor. In not knowing who she is, she cannot express a single set of preferences, to be represented by a single utility function. She does not have a single, unified standpoint from which she can establish a preference ordering over the social structures among which she chooses. She establishes an ordering by comparing the fulfilment of preferences belonging to different sets, reflecting different and possibly incompatible standpoints. But this ordering is not the preference ordering of any person; it is not a preference ordering at all. Its measure, average utility, is the measure of the extent of preference fulfilment, but since it is not the measure of a preference ordering, it is not a utility.

The ideal actor, in maximizing expected average utility, is not maximizing expected utility—her own or that of anyone else. Choice from the Archimedean point is therefore not a simple extension of rational choice under uncertainty. In putting uncertainty into the basis of choice, in denying the actor the unity afforded by a single set of preferences, the character of the choice is radically changed. But although this shows that Harsanyi mistakes the relationship between the average-utilitarian principle and the principle of expected utility-maximization, it does not show that he has incorrectly characterized choice from the Archimedean point. Grant that it is distinctive; why should we not suppose that its distinctiveness is captured by the average-utilitarian principle? If for a person ignorant of his identity no simple extension of expected utility-maximization is possible, since such a person lacks knowledge of his utility function, then why should maximization of average expected utility not recommend itself as the appropriate substitute, tailored to Archimedean circumstances?

In distinguishing average expected utility from the utility expectation of any individual, we have broken the link ensuring that each person would identify with the ideal actor in Archimedean choice. In recognizing that the maximization of average expected utility requires choosing a society of satisfied fools to one of dissatisfied Socrates, we may suspect that it will not be possible to find another link ensuring this identification. Indeed, we claim that the average-utilitarian account of Archimedean choice fails to understand the human individual. Although we suppose that each person seeks to maximize his utility, yet he does not consider himself merely a receptacle for preference fulfilment. To suppose that he should choose among social structures solely by maximizing the average level of preference fulfilment is to suppose, not that he should choose impartially, but that he should exhibit no concern for who he is, that he should care, not what capacities or preferences he has, but only that his capacities enable him to fulfil his preferences.

Each person, aware of his identity, must be able to identify with choice from the Archimedean point, as the choice he would have made under the conditions of ideal agency. For a choice is rational only to those able to identify with it, and impartial only if all are able to identify with it. But the choice required by average utilitarianism affords no basis for this identification. John Rawls has stated, 'Utilitarianism does not take seriously the distinction between persons.'[15] We agree, but even more, utilitarianism does not take

[15] Rawls, p. 27.

seriously the individuality of persons. Our objection is not so much that the utility of one person may be sacrificed to that of others, but that each person is treated as a means to overall preference fulfilment. Utilitarianism violates the integrity of the individual as a being with his own distinctive capacities and preferences, and so with a distinctive utility, not interchangeable with the utilities of others, that he seeks to maximize.

But the lesson to be drawn from our discussion is not directed only against utilitarianism. We should agree that if choice from the Archimedean point were to be represented in directly maximizing terms, then it would be utilitarian in character. If we treat Archimedean choice as an extension of rational choice under less unusual circumstances, we must determine a single ordering of possible outcomes in terms of which we may define a measure to be maximized. And only an ordering positively responsive to individual preference orderings, and weighting each individual ordering equally, can satisfy necessary conditions for impartiality and equal rationality. Harsanyi's demonstration, to which we referred in V.2.2, that social welfare must be an average of individual utilities, shows that an impartial maximizing choice could only be utilitarian.

Thus our primary conclusion must be that choice from the Archimedean point is not an extension of expected utility-maximization. Because it does not proceed from a well-defined and unified set of preferences, it takes on a quite distinctive character. Not only does it not involve the maximization of the expected utility of any individual, but it does not involve the maximization of any measure defined over individual utilities. What does it involve? How may we represent choice from the Archimedean point so that each person, aware of his capacities and preferences, is able to identify with it as the choice he would have made lacking this awareness? This remains our problem.

3 The ideal actor is concerned with her identity, whatever that identity may be. Her choice of principles for social interaction must reflect this concern. It must link her to every person; each must see the ideal as an ideal of himself with all particularizing and so biasing characteristics excluded from his deliberation. We may find in John Rawls's theory of justice a conscious attempt to establish this link—to characterize an ideal person behind the 'veil of ignorance' with whose choices each may identify.[16]

[16] See Ibid., pp. 12, 136–42. For a partially overlapping discussion of Rawls's

For our purposes it will be appropriate to examine Rawls's conceptions in their most general form. Although he concentrates on a special case, applicable to the circumstances of present-day developed societies, yet it is in their most general form that his conceptions must be defended if they are to link, at the deepest level, the Archimedean point with real individuals. His general conception of justice is, 'All social values . . . are to be distributed equally unless an unequal distribution of any, or all, of these values is to everyone's advantage.'[17] This conception is expressed in a fundamental principle governing interaction, the 'lexical difference principle', which underlies the more specific principles of justice on which Rawls focuses. This principle states that 'in a basic structure with n relevant representatives, first maximize the welfare of the worst-off representative man; second, for equal welfare of the worst-off representative, maximize the welfare of the second worst-off representative man, and so on.'[18] We shall not pursue the idea of representative persons beyond noting that Rawls uses it to exclude a direct concern with costs and benefits that bear an accidental and unpredictable relation to the conditions of social interaction, and which would not, then, enter into an account of persons considered as representative of social positions.

The lexical difference principle requires that social structures be designed to maximize the minimum level of utility; it prescribes *maximin* utility. Clearly it demands interpersonally comparable utilities; we may suppose that the comparison is based on the degree of preference fulfilment. But Rawls himself does not consider the problem of interpersonal comparisons; and indeed, the more specific principles he discusses are couched not in terms of utility but of 'primary goods'—goods one would want if one wanted anything.[19] Note that, by contrast with the demand for maximin utility, the principle of minimax relative concession requires that social structures be designed to maximize the minimum level of relative benefit. We have argued that, from the standpoint of persons engaged in bargaining, it is rational to agree to maximize the minimum proportion of one's possible utility gain from co-operation. Rawls argues

theory see my 'Justice and Natural Endowment: Toward a Critique of Rawls' Ideological Framework', *Social Theory and Practice* 3 (1974), pp. 3–26.

[17] Rawls, p. 62.

[18] Ibid., p. 83.

[19] See ibid., pp. 62, 92.

that, from the Archimedean point, it is just to maximize the minimum amount of utility, without distinguishing the portion of it that constitutes the co-operative surplus.

Why would the ideal actor choose the lexical difference principle? Although Rawls's arguments are complex and presented in a discursive and informal manner, we may identify at least two principal themes.[20] The first is that in choosing in ignorance of one's identity, one must take special care to prevent the worst befalling one. The second is that the terms of co-operation, in so far as they benefit some more than others, must do so in a way that will command the willing support of those less advantaged. We may suggest that present in Rawls's thought, although not explicitly stated, is the idea that if the least advantaged can identify with Archimedean choice, then everyone can, and so it satisfies the requirements of equal rationality and impartiality. It is evident that these two core considerations—avoiding the worst and eliciting the willing co-operation of the least advantaged—support a maximin principle such as lexical difference.

Rawls develops his arguments largely by contrasting his principles of justice with the utilitarian conception expressed in the maximization of the average level of utility.[21] Suppose that one is among the least advantaged. If the principles of society have been chosen on utilitarian grounds, then one will regard them very differently than if they have been chosen to maximize minimum utility. In the former case one will attribute one's own disadvantaged position to a concern with preference fulfilment that ignores the distinctness and individuality of persons. One will consider oneself sacrificed for the social whole. But in the latter case one will recognize that, even if under some alternative social structure one would have been better off oneself, yet no alternative could prevent someone from being at least as disadvantaged as one now is. While this need not console one, since one takes no interest in others' interests, yet one cannot rationally expect the principles of one's society to give one greater consideration than they afford to one's fellows. The lexical difference principle ensures that no one's interests are sacrificed in order to improve the lot of someone better off. Hence if one is among the least advantaged, one is able to identify with a choice based on

[20] The arguments are to be found primarily in *A Theory of Justice*, pp. 150–61, 175–83.

[21] See ibid., pp. 167–75.

lexical difference, although not with one based on the maximization of average utility.

As a defence of the lexical difference principle against the utilitarian alternative, Rawls's appeal to the position of the least advantaged seems very powerful. But it does not suffice for a general demonstration of the principle. For it does not show that the principle is able to command everyone's support, or that no alternative could also command the support of the least advantaged. A positive defence of Rawls's position requires an appeal to a very strong condition of mutual benefit: each person may expect his preferences to be fulfilled as far as, but only as far as, their fulfilment does not impede the equal expectation of fulfilment by any other person. Each person's title to benefit is then dependent entirely on the effect that his receipt of the benefit may have on what others receive. In particular, no person is entitled to any benefit except as a member of society, and no person is entitled to any benefit as a member of society in virtue of his contribution to the production of goods, whether in market or in co-operative interaction.

This last point may seem to be obscured by Rawls when he says, 'Those who have been favored by nature, whoever they are, may gain from their good fortune only on terms that improve the situation of those who have lost out. The naturally advantaged are not to gain merely because they are more gifted, but only to cover the costs of training and education and for using their endowments in ways that help the less fortunate as well.'[22] This may suggest that those with the capacity to be socially more productive than their fellows may expect greater benefits, because rewards would be incentives to them to realize their capacity to the fullest extent, and so to benefit everyone, and in particular the least advantaged, by maximizing social productivity. But close attention to Rawls's statement makes clear that the more productive are not entitled to a greater share of goods in virtue of their greater contribution. If giving them a greater share increases their contribution, and if this in turn raises the social minimum, then they are to receive that greater share. But their rewards are purely instrumental, means to the goal of maximizing minimum utility, and not a recognition of entitlement based on contribution.

Rawls rejects the very notion of an individual's contribution to social productivity. He insists that 'from the standpoint of society as

[22] Ibid., pp. 101–2.

a whole *vis-à-vis* any one member, there is no set of agreed ends by reference to which the potential social contributions of an individual could be assessed. ... The notion of an individual's contribution to society as itself an association falls away.'[23] But this contention seems ill-founded. For society, as Rawls himself holds, 'is a cooperative venture for mutual advantage',[24] and the idea of mutual advantage provides a standard for assessing the social contributions of individuals. We must then take Rawls to be simply asserting that an individual's contribution does not entitle him to any return from society. And this is implicit in his statement that the 'difference principle represents, in effect, an agreement to regard the distribution of natural talents as a common asset and to share in the benefits of this distribution whatever it turns out to be'.[25] If talents constitute a common asset, then no individual's talent, or his effort based on that talent, affords him any particular claim to the products of social interaction.

Rawls also rejects any attempt to divide an individual's utility into social and non-social components, or any suggestion that an individual is entitled to what he might expect apart from society plus a share of the further benefits arising from social interaction. For he insists that 'our nature apart from society is but a potential for a whole range of possibilities. ... apart from our place and history in a society, even our potential abilities cannot be known and our interests and character are still to be formed.'[26] The particular characteristics that individuate a person, and determine his preferences, are social products; they do not give rise to a basis for preference fulfilment outside of or apart from society, which is then supplemented by social interaction. In creating preferences they restrict the locus of preference fulfilment to society.

For Rawls it would seem not to be sufficient that the principles of interaction be impartial, in addressing themselves to the advancement of each person's interests without advancing those of some more than others. Rather it is necessary that these principles abstract from what he considers a morally arbitrary element in individuality, so that they consider persons apart from those charac-

[23] Rawls, 'The Basic Structure as Subject', *American Philosophical Quarterly* 14 (1977), p. 162.

[24] Rawls, *A Theory of Justice*, p. 4.

[25] Ibid., p. 101.

[26] Rawls, 'The Basic Structure as Subject', p. 162; the order of the two parts of the quotation is reversed.

teristics that are merely particularizing, and so potential sources of bias, for these are all arbitrary from a moral perspective. No one has any entitlement based on being the particular person he is, and no one has any such entitlement because the particular characteristics of persons are themselves the effects of social interaction. Each person, considered apart from his particular place and time, is a mere potentiality, and it is only as a potentiality, and so only in so far as it does not differentiate him from other persons, that his individuality may be taken into account in the principles of just interaction.

We are now in a position to construct the argument for the lexical difference principle. An individual, unaware of his identity, must choose the principles to be embodied in the basic structure of society. He recognizes that his personal characteristics, whatever they may be, are formed within these social structures, and so afford him no claim, either to extra-social benefits, or to any share of the social product. His contribution to society, in so far as it depends on these socially formed characteristics, also affords him no claim on the benefits realized in society. Hence whoever he is, he has no particular claim on the benefits of social interaction. Thus he may expect others to be willing to interact with him only on terms that afford him no benefit that deprives them of an equal benefit. Similarly they may expect his participation only on terms that afford them no benefit depriving him of an equal benefit. But since, whoever he is, he seeks his maximum benefit, this dictates the choice of the principle of maximin utility to regulate social interaction and to be embodied in the basic social structures. Whoever he may be, he may identify with this choice, since it represents the greatest demand he may make on others, in a situation in which his ignorance of his particular characteristics prevents him from tailoring his demand to the biasing capacities and talents that individuate him.

This argument does not emerge clearly in Rawls's major work, *A Theory of Justice*. There he writes, 'There is no more reason to permit the distribution of income and wealth to be settled by the distribution of natural assets than by historical and social fortune. . . . For once we are troubled by the influence of either social contingencies or natural chance on the determination of distributive shares, we are bound, on reflection, to be bothered by the influence of the other. From a moral standpoint the two seem equally arbitrary.'[27] This argument, which admits the difference between natural characteristics and social contingencies while denying its moral relevance, does not sit well with the idea of Archimedean choice. For although the ideal actor is not aware of her identity, she is aware that she has an identity. It then seems reasonable that she choose with this in mind, and consider her claim on the fruits of social interaction given that identity. She would then choose a principle to regulate interaction in such a way that the particular, natural characteristics of each person, in so far as they affect what he accomplishes, will enter into the determination of the distribution of benefits. And these particular characteristics constitute the person's natural assets. Thus we should expect, contrary to Rawls's assertion, that in Archimedean choice natural assets but not social contingencies would be taken as part of one's unknown but real identity. One brings the former to society; they enter into the formation of one's preferences, and they determine one's social contribution. They do not seem to be morally arbitrary in any sense that would or could exclude them from being taken into account in impartial choice. What the Archimedean point excludes is tailoring principles to favour one's particular assets. But why need or should it exclude tailoring principles to relate the distribution of the social product to the way in which each person's assets are exercised in production?

The answer, never given in *A Theory of Justice* but evident in the paper, 'The Basic Structure as Subject', is that natural assets prove to be social contingencies.[28] If we are troubled by the influence of the latter on the determination of distributive shares, then we must also be troubled by the influence of natural chance, because what appears as natural chance is largely social contingency. Since natural assets are social products, to let the social distribution be determined by them would be to ground one social contingency on another. Apart from society human nature is merely potential; its actualization in determinate characteristics is the result of historical and social circumstances. Although these determinate characteristics constitute individual identities, yet these identities afford no extra-social basis for claims on the benefits of society. The ideality of the actor in the Archimedean point must thus be found in her inability, through ignorance of her own identity, not only to tailor principles to fit her

[27] Rawls, *A Theory of Justice*, pp. 74–5.

[28] See Rawls, 'The Basic Structure as Subject', p. 162.

nature and circumstances, but also, and of more importance, to suppose her nature a relevant factor in considering how to distribute the fruits of interaction.[29]

Justice, we have said, is the disposition not to take advantage of one's fellows, whether as a free-rider or as a parasite. It appears that the lexical difference principle licenses those with lesser natural talents to take advantage of those naturally more fortunate, requiring the latter to use their abilities, not primarily for their own well-being, but to maximize the minimum level of well-being. But to criticize Rawls in this way we must suppose that each individual may be defined independently of social interaction, so that he brings his talents and aptitudes, attitudes and preferences, into society as part of a natural endowment. We must suppose that each person's characteristics, in enabling him to make a certain contribution to the social product, also provide him with a claim to a certain share of that product.

This is precisely what Rawls rejects, and his rejection leads him to a very different view of what justice requires The person who takes advantage of her fellows is not the less talented individual who benefits from the maximin principle, but the more talented individual who uses her talents solely for her own benefit. For she diverts to her exclusive use an undue proportion of the total assets of society. She robs her fellows of what rightfully is theirs.

We might challenge Rawls's insistence that apart from society human beings have no determinate nature. We may indeed suppose that he dramatically overstates the influence of particular historical

[29] In 'Kantian Constructivism in Moral Theory', Rawls suggests a rather different answer to why natural assets are morally arbitrary. There he represents the problem of Archimedean choice as the adoption of 'principles to serve as the effective public conception of justice for a well-ordered society' in which the citizens regard themselves as 'moral persons ... characterized by two moral powers and by two corresponding highest-order interests in realizing and exercising these powers. The first power is the capacity for an effective sense of justice.... The second moral power is the capacity to form, to revise, and rationally to pursue a conception of the good. Corresponding to the moral powers, moral persons are said to be moved by two highest-order interests ... [that] are supremely regulative as well as effective. This implies that, whenever circumstances are relevant to their fulfillment, these interests govern deliberation and conduct.' (pp. 524–5.) On this view the ideality of the actor in the Archimedean point must be found in her exclusive concern with her highest-order interests in considering how to distribute the fruits of interaction. But on this view the principles are chosen to regulate the interaction, not of rational utility-maximizers for whom morality is a matter of agreement, but of antecedently moral persons. A concern for justice is given, and Archimedean choice is then to express that concern. This is simply not our problem.

and social circumstances in shaping human beings. But we may avoid the difficult factual issues involved here—issues on which I have little competence to speak. Let us grant that human beings are social products. Do we thereby grant that society, or any group of persons however constituted, acquires any right to these products? That each individual's capacities are actualized within a social nexus does not make them collective rather than individual assets, or afford any ground for treating them as part of the common capital of the group within which the individual is formed. In putting those assets to his own use the individual does not take from others what is rightfully theirs, since those others do not own him, although it does not follow that he simply uses what is rightfully his own.

We grant, at least for the purposes of argument, that the genesis of individual identity is social. We do not grant that this genesis affects the status of the identity. To be a self one need not be self-made. And each person's concern with himself, his nature as a maximizer of individual utility, need not be affected by his awareness that social forces have shaped both that concern, and the determinate preferences that provide its content. In interacting with others each person takes his own nature simply as given, and has no reason to do otherwise.

Society is, in Rawls's words which we have quoted before, 'a cooperative venture for mutual advantage', but it is not simply an instrument or tool that we employ to increase the effectiveness of interaction, enabling each person better to achieve his individual ends. To think of society as merely instrumental is to overlook both the effects of social interaction in shaping individuals and their ends, and the fact that persons do take some interest in some interests of some of their fellows. It is to overlook both socialization and sociability. But awareness of these, although essential if we are to avoid a one-sided social instrumentalism, does not lead us to deny the role of social interaction in helping (or hindering) each individual in the pursuit of ends that involve no concern with those with whom he interacts, and need not affect the way in which we agree to regulate such interaction.

When the ideal actor chooses among feasible principles of interaction, she does so, let us not forget, as an actor. Her choice is that of a person with particular capacities, attitudes, and preferences, even though it is made in ignorance of what these are. But had she no preferences to order possible outcomes, no capacity to choose among possible actions, and no understanding of the relation between actions as objects of choice and outcomes as objects of preference, then she would not be an actor. She would not be implicated in the choice among principles of interaction.

The ideal actor needs no acquaintance with her particular characteristics to know that her rationality is expressed in seeking the most efficient link between choice and preference. To suppose that the factors that determine choice and preference are morally arbitrary is to divorce morality from the conditions of rational action. That the principles of social interaction, to be morally acceptable, must exhibit impartiality among these factors, and so must be chosen in such a way that no individual may tailor or bias the principles to favour his particular personal characteristics, does not entail that these principles discount or ignore the bases of choice and preference. Impartiality is not achieved by treating persons as if they lacked particular capacities and concerns; indeed impartiality among real individuals is violated by such treatment. In supposing that the just distribution of benefits and costs in social interaction is not to be related to the characteristics of the particular individuals who make up society, Rawls violates the integrity of human beings as they are and as they conceive themselves. In seeking to treat persons as pure beings freed from the arbitrariness of their individuating characteristics, Rawls succeeds in treating persons only as social instruments. In denying to each person a right to his individual assets, Rawls is led to collectivize those assets. In his argument morality is divorced from the standpoint of the individual actor.

We have agreed with Rawls that utilitarianism does not take seriously the distinction between persons. But we took its deepest failing to lie in not taking seriously the individuality of persons. Rawls's theory falls victim to this same charge. For the individuality of persons as actors lies in their capacities and preferences. The alternative to maximizing the production of utility is not equalizing its distribution, but rather is maximizing individual shares, where each share is proportioned to the contributions of its recipient. Only in this way do we take seriously the individuality of persons, socialized and sociable as they may be, but who nevertheless find themselves in interaction with others in whom they need take no interest, and who seek to regulate that interaction in a manner with which each can identify.

4.1 Our discussion of the utilitarian principle of maximizing average utility and the generalized Rawlsian principle of maximizing minimum utility should prepare us for a constructive analysis of the ideal actor's choice among principles of interaction and social structures. At the core of this analysis is the relationship between the ideal person, aware of herself as an actor but unaware of her particular identity, and the various real persons, one of whom she in fact is, and whose interactions are to be regulated by her choice. We have insisted, in agreement with Rawls, that each must be able to identify with the ideal actor, so that each may recognize, in the choice made from the Archimedean point, the choice he could have made, had he been subject to the constraints in knowledge that define that point. The ideal actor must therefore choose, not as if she had an equal chance of being each of the persons affected by her choice, but as if she were each of those persons. We may think of the Archimedean point as a point of convergence; beginning from individuals choosing, each from his own perspective, principles for social interaction—principles which will of course reflect the chooser's concern to maximize his own utility—we alter the perspectives until we find that the same principles would be chosen by all. Thus each person is able to place himself in the Archimedean point by considering the circumstances under which his choice among principles for social interaction would converge with the choices of his fellows. He may verify that he has determined these circumstances correctly, so that his choice does not reflect a bias related to his particular identity, by supposing himself to assume the identity of any other person selected at random, and asking whether in the circumstances envisaged that other person would make the same choice, selecting the same principles.

Because the Archimedean point requires total ignorance of identity, it might be supposed impossible to connect real persons, defined by their capacities, attitudes, and preferences, to the ideal actor. But this would be mistaken. What connects each person with the ideal choice is the idea of the choice of a rational actor. We may, as it were, trace lines of rationality from the actual perspectives from which we real persons choose to the ideal perspective afforded by the Archimedean point. These lines of rationality permit identification as the conditions for the knowledge of identity are progressively removed. In this sense the Archimedean point is the limiting point for personal identity. Choices at this limit converge because the factors that make for divergence are removed. Each person identifies with choices along the line of rationality which extends from his own perspective, and thus each identifies, in the limit, with the choice made by the ideal actor.

In choosing from the Archimedean point, the ideal person chooses as each person. This is the first key; the second key that unlocks the door screening our moral understanding is provided by a clear conception of the individual person as actor, and so as chooser. In our criticism of Rawls we endeavoured to bring out what is essential to this conception. The real individual, who must identify with the ideal choice, has his own particular and defining characteristics—capacities, talents, attitudes, preferences. He acts taking these as given, and his rationality is expressed in his endeavour to maximize the fulfilment of his preferences given his capacities and other traits of character, in the circumstances, whatever they may be, in which he finds himself. There is no other level of rationality involved. And there is no other conception of the person involved. To conceive the person in some other way, however useful this could be for other purposes, would be irrelevant to a theory of morality based on rational choice.

The principles of interaction chosen from the Archimedean point are thus principles for persons conceived as rational actors. They must address themselves to the conditions of rational agency, and so they must regulate interaction in the light of the utility-maximizing intent of rational actors. What makes these principles moral is that they regulate this interaction without reference to the particular intents, based on the particular characteristics, that each actor possesses. They address themselves to the intent that is common to all, and in a way that advances no individual expression of it over any other expression. The convergence of choice in the Archimedean point achieves this, ensuring that the intent common to all will be considered and that no individual intent can be considered. The former provides the positive condition necessary if each is to identify with the choice; the latter provides the negative condition that is equally necessary, since the inclusion of any individual intent would block identification with the choice by persons lacking that intent. The lines of rationality thus converge at the point that preserves the maximizing intent of rational actors free from all particular individuation.

But we have insisted that the individual intents, and the capacities and preferences on which they rest, are excluded from moral consideration, not because they are arbitrary, but because they are partial. The Archimedean point neutralizes their effect. Here we proceed in a manner quite different from Rawls. For in his argument the epistemic effect of ignorance of one's identity has an ontological significance quite incompatible with conceiving persons as actors. Rawls is led to the Kantian view that apart from each person's contingent self he has a real self, the moral person defined by a concern with justice and the good, and that this real self is the proper subject of all moral choice.[30] This real self, which alone escapes the nexus of social determination, is revealed by removing all knowledge of the contingent features of individual identity. But we deny that there is such a 'real self'. A person's identity is in all respects a contingent matter. But this contingency is not morally arbitrary, for morality is and can be found only in the interaction of real persons individuated by their capacities, attitudes, and preferences. In our analysis we take the individuality of persons seriously.

4.2 The ideal actor reasons from the conditions common to all individuals. She distinguishes the genetic question of how she came to be an actor from the normative question of how as an actor she should choose, and her answer to this latter question is that she rationally chooses to use her powers to fulfil her preferences to the maximum extent possible. But this determines her choice among principles for interaction in two fundamental and related ways. In so far as she is able to choose whether to interact, she chooses to interact only if she expects to benefit. And so to minimize the occasions on which she must interact whether she will or not, and to maximize the opportunities for beneficial interaction, she chooses a basic freedom of action in relation to her fellows, a freedom to advance her own interests as she sees fit in so far as others remain free to interact with her or not.

That society be 'a cooperative venture for mutual advantage' is thus dictated by the terms of choice from the Archimedean point. For the choice of the ideal actor is the choice of every person. If the ideal person chooses to benefit herself, then she must choose mutual benefit; if she chooses freedom for herself, then she must choose freedom for all. In choosing among principles of interaction and the social structures that embody them, then, the ideal actor ensures first, that each person begins with a fundamental freedom to fulfil

[30] See Rawls, *A Theory of Justice*, pp. 255–6.

his preferences or advance his interests, and second, that social institutions and practices are intended to afford mutual benefit.

These two requirements—liberty of action and mutuality of benefit—are linked. Persons who are free to advance their interests as they please so long as this does not compel interaction, will choose to interact only in so far as they benefit by doing so. On the other hand, persons lacking a fundamental freedom of action may prefer to interact with others, given the constraints limiting their choices, even if this interaction would not benefit them were they free. The ideal actor thus chooses to be free so that she may choose only genuinely beneficial interaction, and being free, she of course then chooses to interact only in beneficial ways.

In choosing freedom of action and mutual benefit through interaction, the ideal actor imposes only very weak and hardly controversial limitations on the range of acceptable social structures. Even so, we may question whether at any time in human history these limitations have been generally respected. For it is not sufficient to ensure merely that each individual benefits from all of his interactions with others taken as a whole, and contrasted with a hypothetical state of nature in which he would live a completely solitary existence. Rather it is necessary that no type of interaction be sanctioned that, taken in its full extent, permits some persons to benefit by imposing costs on others. If some type of interaction is avoidable, and if it is then freely chosen by those who engage in it, it cannot afford some the expectation of overall benefit by affording others the expectation of overall cost.

The freedom chosen from the Archimedean point is therefore not the freedom of Hobbesian or anarchistic interaction, in which each may pursue his greatest benefit without concern for the effects of this pursuit on others. If interaction is to be mutually beneficial, then it must preclude the unilateral imposition of costs by one person on another. There may—indeed in the world as we know it perhaps there must—be situations in which the mere presence of several persons occasions mutual disadvantage, and in an over-populated world these situations will become increasingly prevalent. But we shall not here confront the ideal actor with the problems posed by a choice of evils. Supposing the possibility of mutual benefit, the ideal actor must choose to prohibit the unilateral taking of advantage. No one may better himself through interaction that worsens the position of another, where the base point in relation to which we determine bettering and worsening is the absence of the other party to the interaction. And so the ideal actor must choose the proviso as one of the principles for interaction.

In choosing the proviso, the ideal actor exhibits no altruistic or even impartial concern for her fellows. She has no interest in refraining from taking advantage of them, no desire not to better her position by worsening theirs, should this prove the most effective way to maximize her own utility. But the conditions of Archimedean choice prevent the ideal actor from choosing principles of interaction that would permit her to indulge her single-minded concern with maximizing her own utility, when this could be achieved only at the expense of others. In choosing to benefit herself through interaction, the ideal actor can only choose mutual benefit. And in choosing mutual benefit, she chooses to prohibit the taking of advantage, since any interaction that, considered in its full scope, may be represented as bettering the position of one person by worsening that of another, cannot afford mutual benefit.

The proviso is both the weakest constraint on the actions of an individual that is compatible with the requirement that, in so far as possible, interaction be mutually advantageous, and the strongest constraint on the actions of an individual compatible with his freedom to advance his own interests. It defines the initial position from which market competition and co-operation, the forms of social interaction, proceed, as the intersection between individual liberty and mutual benefit.

What is the scope of the proviso, as chosen by the ideal actor? Is it a general constraint on action, or a constraint only on those particular actions that relate directly to competition and co-operation? The ideal actor chooses only beneficial interaction; it might therefore seem that she chooses the proviso only as a limited constraint, acceptance of which disposes persons not to take advantage of their fellows only in so far as they are participants in specific joint activities. But this would be mistaken. For the ideal actor recognizes that the disposition to seek out opportunities for market and co-operative interaction is itself advantageous, given the costs of the state of nature and the benefits of society. In conformity with Hobbes's first law of nature, the ideal actor chooses to endeavour peace as far as she has hope of obtaining it. She must exhibit a continuing willingness to engage in social interaction, pursuing mutual advantage whenever and wherever it may be found. And so, in choosing the principles by which interaction is to be regulated, she chooses the proviso as a general constraint, acceptance of which shows each person's readiness to forgo his own direct endeavour to maximize his utility when all may benefit from co-operation.

Society, as the framework within which market competition and co-operation occur, is itself a single co-operative enterprise. The proviso is the constraint on each individual's pursuit of maximum utility that makes this enterprise possible. The ideal actor thus chooses that each person refrain from taking advantage of his fellows even if no particular agreement or role specifically grounds such a constraint on his behaviour. From the Archimedean point the proviso appears, not only as the determinant of the initial position of particular transactions, but as the principle that, mutually accepted by any group and persons, provides the cornerstone of a structure of institutions and practices by which the group becomes a society.

The ideal actor, in disposing herself to social interaction, chooses the proviso, but how far does this disposition extend? We are not—most of us—disposed to refrain from taking advantage of insects; we enjoy the honey and do as we please with the bees. Does the ideal actor choose the proviso as a constraint on all human interaction? Or may its scope be limited—so that it constrains the interactions of members of a particular gender, or race, or class, or faith? From an Archimedean point, is it possible to establish a distinction between *us* and *them*, so that the ideal actor may choose that *we* refrain from taking advantage among ourselves, while allowing us to come down on *them* like the wolf on the fold?

Were the interests of certain persons or groups of persons necessarily opposed, as on the Dobuan view of yams or the Marxian view of classes, then the ideal actor, although ignorant of her particular identity, would recognize that her hope of obtaining peace, of benefiting from social interaction, was limited in extent. No one could identify with the choice of a principle requiring constraint where no benefit could arise. Were Marx right, the ideal actor would limit the proviso to intra-class activities, leaving each class (or its members) free to endeavour to benefit at the expense of others.[31] But we do not accept any necessary opposition of interests.

[31] See J. Elster, *Ulysses and the Sirens: Studies in rationality and irrationality* (Cambridge, 1979), p. 97, for an illuminating comparison of Hobbes and Marx relevant to this point.

The presumption of the benefits of market and co-operative interaction extends to each person, in interaction with all others. That there are particular occasions in which unequal circumstances defeat this presumption cannot affect a choice made in abstraction from all such particulars. The ideal actor agrees with Hume that 'History, experience, reason sufficiently instruct us . . . in the gradual enlargement of our regards to justice, in proportion as we become acquainted with the extensive utility of that virtue.'[32] She chooses the proviso as constraining interactions among all of humankind.

4.3 The ideal actor, having established the basic framework within which social interaction is to occur by her choice of freedom constrained by the proviso, must now proceed to consider principles for that interaction. First, she must ensure that she, and so each person, enjoys the greatest expectation of utility compatible with the comparable expectation of every other person. Not only mutual benefit, but optimality, is the object of Archimedean choice.

Given freedom constrained by the proviso, so that force and fraud are absent from interaction, a market emerges. In the circumstances of perfect competition, this market results in an optimal outcome, reached by exchanges in which each pays, and pays only, the costs for the benefits he receives. No unfairness enters in market interaction; since the proviso excludes unfairness in determining each person's market endowment, the market outcome is thus both optimal and fair. And the exchanges that bring it about are freely made by all; the market respects the liberty of each to choose whether or not to interact with his fellows.

The ideal actor therefore chooses the market in conditions of perfect competition. No other choice is compatible with her insistence on freedom constrained only by the proviso, and optimality. Since each person in the market pays the costs of the benefits he enjoys, any alternative to the market, involving a different distribution of costs and benefits, would necessarily involve a displacement of costs through which some would better their situation by worsening that of their fellows. Any alternative would therefore constrain freedom so that advantage might be taken.

The ideal actor is, therefore, not a socialist. Or rather, she is not an ideal socialist; she would not choose social ownership of the means of production under circumstances which permit the perfectly competitive market to operate. She would not choose socialism

[32] Hume, *Enquiry*, iii. i, p. 192.

because the constraint on individual freedom required by the transfer of the factors of production from individuals to society could be justified neither by the proviso nor by the demand for optimality. The remedy for violations of the proviso in the determination of individual initial factor endowments is not the collectivization of these endowments, but the fair redistribution of factors among individuals so that the market may operate. The ideal for Archimedean choice is a free market economy.

But let us remember that this argument is not sufficient as either a defence or a condemnation of any actual social arrangements. For it is perfectly compatible with what we have said that the actual imperfections in market arrangements, which affect not the endowments of individuals but the efficacy of voluntary exchange in relating costs to benefits, may justify some form of social control or even social ownership. Our argument is incompatible with socialist theory, just as it is incompatible with utilitarian theory. But it is possible, however unlikely, that different theories will lead to the same practice.

We should also note that in choosing the market, the ideal actor does not commit herself to any particular view of inheritance, or to any view of entitlement to factor rent. There are evident problems in relating inheritance to the mutual unconcern presupposed in Archimedean choice. And rent, which may be redistributed without affecting the efficiency of the market, and which arises only from the relations of those interacting, may not be claimed as part of a pre-market endowment. We shall examine both inheritance and rent in Chapter IX.

But we should not conclude this subsection with these qualifications, important as they are. For the connection between rational choice, impartiality, and market interaction that our argument reveals deserves strong emphasis. The market, as we saw in Chapter IV, creates a morally free zone, but it is itself a rational and moral creation. The conditions for market interaction are not always present, but their absence is never without loss for rational actors. From the Archimedean point the market is chosen as itself an ideal.

4.4 With the proviso and the market in place, the ideal actor must turn to interaction in which the presence of externalities leads to a sub-optimal outcome if each is free to advance his interests without constraint. How, without allowing the taking of advantage, is optimality to be attained? Since the ideal actor, in choosing benefit for herself, must choose mutual benefit, how is this mutuality to be extended to those institutions and practices that promote co-operation as the answer to market failure?

The demand for optimality is met by the choice of an appropriate joint strategy for interaction, embodied in the social structure. But to meet the demand for fairness, it is not sufficient to ensure that the chosen social structure provides that, in each type of interaction, no one may expect to benefit by imposing costs on another. For the structure itself may favour some persons differentially, in the potentialities it actualizes or represses, and in the activities it requires or prohibits. Suppose for example that two persons are of roughly comparable talents, energies, and interests, but that one is provided with an education fitting him for a stimulating and socially valuable career, well remunerated and highly esteemed, whereas the other is denied such an education, and finds that in consequence she is able to pursue only a less interesting, poorly rewarded, lowly regarded occupation. The returns to these individuals may correspond closely to the contributions they actually make to the production of goods. Each pays for benefits received. His greater benefits are not obtained by imposing costs on her. Yet their contributions to social interaction and so their returns which, to ensure mutual benefit throughout, must be equally proportional to those contributions, reflect social contingencies determined by a particular social structure, in which males are encouraged to actualize capacities repressed in females. We should of course find this structure unfair, not because it allows individuals to take advantage of their fellows, for it does not, and not because it fails to relate benefits to contributions, for it does not, but because it fails to relate benefits to the contributions each person would have made had each enjoyed similar opportunities and received similar encouragement.

To accommodate this, we must suppose that the ideal actor considers, not only the internal workings of each of the social structures among which she must choose, but also the comparative workings of the different structures. She must ensure, not only that no individual actually benefits at the expense of another, but also that no individual benefits differentially from the particular social structure selected. Again, her concern is in no way altruistic or impartial. She is concerned solely to ensure that she benefits from social interaction, not merely overall but throughout. But this requires her to choose principles of interaction that ensure full mutual benefit for each type of interaction, considered in relation to feasible alternatives.

The principles chosen from the Archimedean point must therefore provide that each person's expected share of the fruits of social interaction be related, not to what he actually contributes, since his actual contribution may reflect the contingent permissions and prohibitions found in any social structure, but to the contribution he would make in that social structure most favourable to the actualization of his capacities and character traits, and to the fulfilment of his preferences, provided that this structure is a feasible alternative meeting the other requirements of Archimedean choice. (That structure in which I am Emperor and you my humble servants, however favourable to my megalomania, is disqualified because it blatantly ignores the proviso.) To measure an individual's potential contribution in that admissible social structure most favourable to him, we relate it, following the argument of V.4.3, to the claim he would make on the surplus realized through social interaction. If we call this his maximum social benefit, then we may say that in choosing a social structure, the ideal actor must provide that in so far as possible, individuals may expect equal proportions of their maximum social benefits. In this way the ideal actor relates the choice of a social structure to the idea of society as a single co-operative enterprise.

Lest it be thought that the idea of potential contribution is completely indeterminate, since different social and historical conditions shape human beings in incomparably different ways, we should note that the comparison among social structures required to determine potential contribution and maximum social benefit must be restricted to structures that are feasible alternatives. The ideal actor does not range over societies past, present, and future, in both the actual and all possible worlds, to find that which best suits each individual person. Rather she compares the actual historical and social circumstances in which an individual finds himself with the alternatives available in that place and at that time, given the available technology and the existing conceptual horizon. These boundaries are vague, but they keep the required comparison meaningful.

The ideal actor chooses not to be taken advantage of in interaction. She chooses, therefore, principles determining a social structure in which her expectation of benefit from co-operation, relative to the maximum benefit she might receive in some feasible social structure, is no less than that received by her fellows, or if equality is sub-optimal, no less than some person must receive whatever social structure be chosen. Were she aware of her identity, and in a position to choose among principles of social interaction, she could and of course would make a more advantageous choice, reflecting her particular capacities and preferences, but from the Archimedean point she is unable to do this. Given her ignorance she can choose only to maximize minimum relative benefit from social interaction. And so she chooses, from the Archimedean point, the principle of minimax relative concession, since as we showed in V.4.3 it is equivalent to maximin relative benefit. The proviso, the market, and co-operation based on minimax relative concession, together express the fundamental concerns of the ideal actor, freedom of individual action and mutual benefit through interaction, as these concerns are extended and applied to society conceived as an overall structure for co-operation.

4.5 The principles of social interaction chosen from the Archimedean point are the same principles of rational agreement that underlie co-operation. This should not surprise us. For if each person is to identify with the choice made by the ideal actor, then her choice must be modelled, not on an individual decision under uncertainty, but on a bargain or contract acceptable to all individuals. The ideal actor may not collapse the identities of the persons, any one of whom she may be, into a single identity, or their utilities into a single utility which she would then endeavour to maximize. She must maintain their separate identities and utilities, and so must choose as if she were bargaining as each person. This is the essential feature of Archimedean choice.

The Archimedean point may seem a peculiar artifice, introduced solely to ensure impartiality in choice. And so you and I may ask what Archimedean choice is to us. Why concern ourselves with principles chosen under the limiting condition of ignorance of one's identity which it requires? But that ignorance is appropriate to the selection of those principles embodied in the institutions and practices that constitute our social womb. Reflecting on the processes of socialization that enter deeply into determining the particular individuals we are, we understand that to assess them and the principles underlying them, we must find a standpoint with which each of us can identify, and yet that is independent of our particular characteristics. This is exactly the standpoint of Archimedean choice. In identifying with the choices of the ideal actor, we justify to ourselves the social processes by which we have come to be. We enter into the choice of what literally we cannot choose in a way that gives meaning to the idea of our rational autonomy. An autonomous person is one who consciously identifies with the processes that have shaped him as a rational actor.

Far from introducing a peculiar and artificial standpoint for choice, the Archimedean point offers the familiar perspective of agreement. A decision made in complete ignorance of one's identity proves coincident with an agreement made among persons individuated in all possible ways. The lines of rationality that lead from each individual to converge in the ideal actor are the same lines that lead from each to converge on a rational bargain. Thus the Archimedean point is the position you and I occupy when we find ourselves in fully voluntary and equal agreement with our fellows. Archimedean choice yields the social contract.

However, Archimedean choice does not itself yield compliance with the social contract. Although each person identifies with the ideal actor's choice of social principles, he is not thereby rationally committed to personal compliance with those principles. The rationality of compliance, as we have argued in Chapter VI, depends on the characteristics and circumstances of the individuals involved in interaction. It is not determinable from the Archimedean point.

The ideal actor chooses, not compliance, but those processes of socialization that promote the circumstances in which narrow compliance is rational. Given the benefits each may expect from co-operation, each has reason to prefer that everyone be sufficiently translucent that the disposition to comply with the proviso and the principle of minimax relative concession is itself utility-maximizing. And each has reason to prefer that everyone be affectively engaged by compliance, so that the familiar feelings of respect and resentment, of self-respect and guilt, are linked appropriately with the fair and unfair behaviour of others and oneself. Although our primary concern is with the principles that would be chosen from the Archimedean point, we should not forget the importance of the choice of affections, in so far as these can be shaped by socialization.

Moral theory offers an Archimedean point analysis of human interaction. The theory of rational choice offers an analysis from the standpoint of each interacting individual. In exhibiting the harmony between these analyses, we have shown that the moral demand for impartiality can be accommodated within the rational demand for individual utility-maximization by attending to the conditions of agreed interaction among equally rational persons. This completes our theoretical exposition; what remain are a sketch of how morals by agreement may be applied to the evaluation of social practices, and a discussion of the viability of social life informed by contractarian morality.

IX

PERSONS, PEOPLES, GENERATIONS

1 John Locke wrote that 'an Hobbist . . . will not easily admit a great many plain duties of morality'.[1] Although our understanding of human motivation and rationality is less restrictive than Hobbes's, yet the moral theory we have developed is clearly 'Hobbist' in its emphasis on mutual constraint. Our wider perspective has enabled us to establish individual rights of a recognizably Lockean character, as well as principles of justice. Yet we may agree that the moral constraints arising from what are, in the fullest sense, conditions of mutual advantage, do not correspond in every respect to the 'plain duties' of conventional morality. Animals, the unborn, the congenitally handicapped and defective, fall beyond the pale of a morality tied to mutuality. The disposition to comply with moral constraints, without which moral relationships fall victim to the scorn of the Foole, may be rationally defended only within the scope of expected benefit.

In showing that minimax relative concession is a principle both of justice and of rational choice, we give morality the secure foundation first demanded in the challenge put to Socrates by Glaucon and Adeimantus.[2] But (to borrow an advertiser's paradox) our argument gives us all we ever wanted in a morality—and less.[3] It gives us all, in providing a rational foundation that does not play fast and loose with our conception of rationality; it gives us less, in providing that foundation only within the confines of mutual benefit.

In this chapter we shall consider exactly what our moral theory does entail for our assessment of some of the core relationships of social morality. We shall see that our theory gives rise to very different standards for evaluating the distribution of private and of public goods. We shall consider the implications of our argument for the distribution of factor rent, showing that we take a position between the simple individualism of Robert Nozick and the implicit collectivism of John Rawls. We shall examine the implications of

[1] See note 26 to ch. I, above.
[2] *Republic*, 357a–367e.
[3] The advertiser is the Miller Brewing Company.

differences in initial acquisition for the relationships between peoples or nations. We shall show how, with the aid of very simple and plausible empirical assumptions, we may partially order differing ways of life in terms of their level of advancement, and justify the supplanting of a less advanced by a more advanced way. We shall show how moral relationships among normal adult members of society may be extended to involve the young as future contributors and the aged as past contributors, giving a contractarian rationale for practices of inheritance and investment that seems to avoid the unintuitive consequences of both utilitarian and Rawlsian views.

We shall find no simple fit, or lack of fit, between our theory and the supposedly 'plain duties' of conventional morality. Trusting theory rather than intuition, we should advocate the view of social relationships sketched in this chapter without regard to the intellectual fashions of the moment.[4] If the reader is tempted to object to some part of this view, on the ground that his moral intuitions are violated, then he should ask what weight such an objection can have, if morality is to fit within the domain of rational choice. We should emphasize the radical difference between our approach, in which we ask what view of social relationships would rationally be accepted *ex ante* by individuals concerned to maximize their utilities, from that of moral coherentists and defenders of 'reflective equilibrium', who allow initial weight to our considered moral judgements.[5]

We do not claim that the only way to refute our claims in this chapter is to provide a superior moral theory. For we may have misunderstood the implications of our own position. There are formidable difficulties in applying a moral theory to circumstances far more complex than those envisaged in the idealized framework employed in its construction. And so we embark on the present chapter in a spirit of exploration, distinguishing what seem justifiable inequalities from unjustifiable ones, and human advancements from retrogressions, but ready to admit that, even if our theory of

[4] For a contrary view, see T. Nagel, *Mortal Questions* (Cambridge, 1979), p. x. 'I believe one should trust problems over solutions, intuition over arguments, and pluralistic discord over systematic harmony. Simplicity and elegance are never reasons to think that a philosophical theory is true: on the contrary, they are usually grounds for thinking it false.' But why should philosophy differ so from science? Nevertheless, there is no better account of the view contrary to that underlying *Morals by Agreement*.

[5] See J. Rawls, *A Theory of Justice* (Cambridge, Mass., 1971), p. 20. Also N. Daniels, 'Wide Reflective Equilibrium and Theory Acceptance in Ethics', *Journal of Philosophy* 76 (1979), pp. 256–82.

morals by agreement be fully acceptable, much that we say here must be tentative and controversial.

2 Equality is not a fundamental concern in our theory. In arguing that social institutions and practices are justified by appeal to a hypothetical *ex ante* agreement among fully informed and rational persons, we have appealed to the equal rationality of the bargainers to show that their agreement satisfies the moral standard of impartiality. But impartial practices respect persons as they are, the inequalities among them as well as the equalities. Since the perfectly competitive market provides a framework for interaction that leaves each individual with the full liberty enjoyed by a Robinson Crusoe, we should not be surprised that the natural inequalities that would be manifested by different Robinson Crusoes reappear as market inequalities. Since no one is in a position to take advantage of any other person, pure market inequalities no more reveal unfairness than do inequalities among isolated, non-interacting individuals. Those who are able to supply more factor services to the market may expect to enjoy a preferred share of the private goods, such as food, clothing, housing, private transportation and recreation, that the market provides.

Pure market societies are frequently criticized for the inequalities that allegedly they promote. But where market inequality is a legitimate basis for criticism, it is the failure of the market occasioned by the presence of externalities, giving rise to free-ridership or to parasitism, that is the true source of fault. Public goods are supplied by the market in a manner that is neither efficient nor fair. In its proper realm, the market is in fact an equalizing force in human affairs, eliminating the violations of the proviso that characterize slave, serf, and caste societies. The effect of subordinating the market to some form of political control is typically to reintroduce violations of the proviso and to run roughshod over fairness in the terms of co-operation, as the so-called socialist societies of the Eastern bloc bear eloquent witness. Rather than suppressing the market, what is needed is its supplementation by co-operative institutions and practices that assure the optimal supply of public goods.

Co-operation gives rise to a much more equal distribution of goods produced than does the market. For as we showed in V.4.2–3, in producing the co-operative surplus different individuals make equivalent contributions. Where this surplus constitutes a single, transferable good, co-operators contribute equally to its production and are therefore entitled to share equally in its distribution. Now it might be supposed that in the case of pure public goods, defined by their non-excludability, equal distribution is assured.[6] If national defence and unpolluted air are supplied to one person, they are supplied to all. And if all must share in the goods, then entitlements are irrelevant. But since excludability and non-excludability are ideal limits, most of the goods constituting the co-operative surplus can be differentially supplied; public educational institutions need not open their doors to all. And in any case, it is the net surplus that, on our argument, is to be distributed equally; even if the good of national defence or unpolluted air must be supplied equally to all, the cost need not be equally borne.

Are we then committed to the view that pure public goods should be supplied on the basis of equal contributions from all members of society? If national defence is supplied equally to all, should it be paid for by equal contributions from all? If this were required by the principle of minimax relative concession, then not only the existing system of progressive taxation, but the proposed flat-rate alternative, long advocated by such economists as Milton Friedman, would surely be both irrational and unjust.[7] To the extent to which co-operatively or publicly produced goods are divided equally among the members of society, taxation should also be equal, so that each receives an equivalent share of the net co-operative surplus.

This argument is specious, resting on a failure to note that minimax relative concession applies to the distribution of the co-operative surplus considered, not as a bundle of goods, but as a set of individual utilities. Consider a rational bargain over the division of costs of producing a pure public good. In the non-co-operative outcome, which serves as initial position, the good is not produced. Each person claims the maximum level of the good that can be produced without cost to himself, and that leaves every other person at least as well off as if the good were not produced at all. The actual level at which persons then agree to produce the good, and the actual division of costs among them, is determined by applying minimax relative concession, or equivalently, maximin relative benefit. For each possible level and division of costs, the net gain of each person

[6] See the discussion of pure public goods in H. van den Doel, *Democracy and Welfare Economics*, trans. B. Biggins (Cambridge, 1979), pp. 25–30.

[7] See M. Friedman, *Capitalism and Freedom* (Chicago, 1962), pp. 174–6.

is measured as a proportion of the gain he would receive from his claim, and the level and distribution maximizing the minimum proportionate net gain is selected.

In general, if two persons pay equally, in money or resources, for a pure public good, then the person with fewer resources will lose a greater proportion of the gain he would realize were he to obtain the good without cost. Thus he makes a greater relative concession than his fellow. But the principle of minimax relative concession will normally equalize relative concessions. It will not, then, require persons to pay equal taxes, but rather will demand larger payments from those better off. It may then be plausible to suppose that a flat rate tax yields equal relative benefits. The rate itself, of course, must be set to yield an optimal supply of publicly produced goods.

Private goods are provided separately at fixed prices. Public goods are provided in a single package at prices varying with the resources of the purchasers. Co-operation proves more equalizing in its effects than does the market. In a society governed by the principle of minimax relative concession, police and judicial protection, national defence, land, water, and air free from pollution, are supplied to all on the basis of proportionate taxation. The intuitively different ways in which we regard inequalities in private and in public goods prove to reflect, not the incoherence of our views, but a deep difference in the workings of social institutions that satisfy a single standard of rationality and impartiality.

3.1 In discussing market interaction we have omitted one inequality in return that is not determined by the cost of supplying factor services. As we noted in IV.3.2, persons in the market may receive factor rent. Rent is determined by factor scarcity; it is the premium certain factor services command, over and above the full cost of supply, because there is no alternative to meet the demand.

There is a demand for hockey, expressed in the purchase of tickets admitting their bearers to hockey games. This demand is met by the activities of hockey players, who therefore are able to command payment for their services matching this demand less other costs. But there is an additional demand for the unique hockey skills of Wayne Gretzky, expressed by the fact that half-empty arenas fill up when Gretzky and the Edmonton Oilers come to town. There is no substitute available to meet this demand. Gretzky is therefore in a position to extract payment for his services over and above the cost to him, including the opportunity cost, of supplying those services;

he is in a position to extract factor rent. Gretzky would, quite likely, be willing to play hockey for a lower salary than he receives; the difference between the least amount that would induce him to play as well as he does and his actual remuneration is then his rent.

Suppose that factor rent could be identified in practice and were taxed at a rate of 100 per cent. The distribution of the surplus represented by rent does not affect the optimality of the outcome. Even a confiscatory tax, resulting in a complete redistribution of rent, would be merely redistributive in its effects. It would not and could not affect the supply of factor services, and so the production of goods. Taxation on market remuneration generally affects the workings of the market in an adverse manner, by changing the terms on which factor services are provided. But a tax on rent, however large that tax may be, would not lead to any form of inefficiency.

Not only would optimality be unaffected by taxing rent, but also natural freedom, assured by the market, would be unaffected. Each person would remain able, without interference, to direct his capacities to the service of his preferences. Knowing that one would be unable to obtain factor rent would not lead any rational person to choose to alter his interactions with others. If Wayne Gretzky chooses, rationally, to play hockey, then the opportunity cost to him of doing so is determined by the net benefit he would expect from the best available alternative to playing hockey. If, as a result of anticipated taxation on remuneration from playing hockey, he were to choose an alternative career, then that taxation would necessarily affect his opportunity cost and so would not be levied only on rent. A tax on rent cannot affect the preferential ordering of alternative courses of action and so cannot affect one's freedom.

It may be supposed that the proviso, in giving each person the right to his basic endowment—his natural capacities—gives him the right to factor rent deriving from the endowment. Wayne Gretzky has the right to his unique hockey skills; he may use them as he pleases; does he not therefore have the right to the rent which they command? But his right to use his hockey skills as he pleases is not affected by the distribution of rent; we have just seen that a confiscatory tax on rent would not, and could not, affect his willingness to play hockey. Each person's right to his basic endowment is a right to the exclusive use of that endowment in market and co-operative interaction. But market interaction is not affected by the distribution of the surplus represented by rent; each person's exclusive use of his capacities in market interaction is left untouched if rent is confiscated. What about each person's right to his capacities for co-operative interaction?

Society may be considered as a single co-operative enterprise. The benefit represented by factor rent is part of the surplus afforded by that enterprise, for it arises only in social interaction. But then that benefit is to be distributed among the members of society on the terms established by minimax relative concession. Each person, as a contributor to social interaction, shares in the production of the benefit represented by factor rent. Wayne Gretzky's talents command factor rent because they are scarce, but their scarcity is not a characteristic inherent in his talents, but a function of the conditions of supply, and so of the relation between his talents and those of others, and a function also of the conditions of demand, and so of the relation between his talents and the interest of others in attending hockey games.

The right to use one's capacities as one sees fit in co-operation with others thus does not entail a right to receive factor rent, but only a right to share, with others, in the surplus represented by such rent. In so far as this surplus takes the form of a single, transferable good, each member of society is entitled to an equal portion of it. Inequalities from factor rent are excluded if we apply the principle of minimax relative concession to the overall terms of social co-operation. But we should warn against an overly egalitarian application of this result. For it is not easy to distinguish rent from payment for costs of supply. In many activities, the willingness shown by persons to strive for maximum performance may be related to the rewards received by those who prove most successful. The high level of remuneration received by a few may then not be factor rent, but rather a 'jackpot'. Just as lottery prizes must involve substantial inequality, with a few large pay-offs, to induce widespread participation, so in many human activities substantial inequality in reward may be the condition necessary to induce widespread effort. It may be that Wayne Gretzky is receiving, not only factor rent, but also the jackpot needed to encourage all hockey players to strive to perfect themselves. The co-operative surplus does not include payments that meet costs of supply, and unequal payments to induce effort cover such costs. In practice, the equal distribution of factor rent might have little effect on inequalities of wealth.

3.2 Discussion of factor rent by recent moral theorists have reached conclusions quite different from ours. Readers familiar with Robert Nozick's *Anarchy, State, and Utopia* will no doubt have recognized in our discussion of Wayne Gretzky an intended parallel to Nozick's treatment of Wilt Chamberlain (Americans introduce basketball players, Canadians hockey players).[8] He is concerned to show 'how liberty upsets patterns'.

Begin with whatever distribution of goods conforms to your favourite conception.

> Now suppose that Wilt Chamberlain is greatly in demand by basketball teams, being a great gate attraction.... He signs the following sort of contract with a team: In each home game, twenty-five cents from the price of each ticket of admission goes to him.... The season starts, and people cheerfully attend his team's games; they buy their tickets, each time dropping a separate twenty-five cents of their admission price into a special box with Chamberlain's name on it.... Let us suppose that in one season one million persons attend his home games, and Wilt Chamberlain winds up with $250,000, a much larger sum than the average income and larger even than anyone else has. [Remuneration in professional sports was, of course, much lower in the far-off days of the early 1970s when Nozick wrote.] Is he entitled to this income? Is this new distribution ... unjust? If so, why?[9]

Nozick, of course, wants to claim that the new distribution is not unjust. Each person who pays to see Chamberlain play voluntarily chooses to do so; each benefits, and Chamberlain benefits. Each is entitled to the money he has (it is part of a distribution of goods that satisfies the requirements of justice); must not Chamberlain be entitled to the outcome of the transfers each voluntarily makes with what is initially his own?

What is the nature of the payment Chamberlain receives? Is it only the prospect of $250,000 that induces him to play another season of basketball? Were the terms of the contract he proposes to be refused, would he then prefer to retire? If so, then the payment to him covers only the cost of supply (in this case, primarily the opportunity cost) for the service he provides in playing basketball. The contract represents a standard market exchange, and we must agree with Nozick that interference with it would constitute a denial of liberty.

Or would Chamberlain choose to play, even if he were to receive, say, only $100,000? If so, then that portion of the payment in excess

[8] See R. Nozick, *Anarchy, State, and Utopia* (New York, 1974), pp. 160–3.

[9] Ibid., p. 161.

of $100,000 constitutes rent, and interference with it would not affect Chamberlain's decision to play. Nozick would suppose that Chamberlain is entitled to whatever rent he can receive through voluntary exchange (constrained by a form of the Lockean proviso). But we should argue that the terms of social co-operation, set by the principle of minimax relative concession, rule out a contract that includes factor rent. Certainly the principle does interfere with a particular liberty—specifically, the freedom to collect factor rent. But this is no part of the freedom of a solitary being; the surplus represented by rent arises only through interaction. And so it is not a necessary part of market freedom conceived as an extension of the natural freedom enjoyed by a Robinson Crusoe.

In a society governed by the principle of minimax relative concession, Chamberlain need forgo no more advantageous alternative if he is to play basketball. He is free to demand a remuneration sufficient to make basketball his most preferred activity, and to refuse to play should such remuneration not be forthcoming. But he is not free to pursue the maximum possible remuneration, where this would include factor rent. He is entitled only to enough so that, over and above full payment for costs, he shares equally in the social surplus of which factor rent is a component. The claim of liberty bears very differently on Chamberlain's proposed contract, depending on whether he is demanding payment for opportunity costs, or seeking to extract rent for his unique talents.

If Nozick would treat the right to factor rent as a component of liberty, John Rawls would not only demand its confiscation, but its redistribution so that, in effect, the surplus represented by rent would be enjoyed by those lacking the factors. We have already quoted Rawls as saying, 'The naturally advantaged are .. to gain ... only to cover the costs of training and education and for using their endowments in ways that help the less fortunate as well.'[10] In other words, each is entitled to payment for the costs of the factor services he provides. But factor rent will be subject to the difference principle, and so will be redistributed to maximize the welfare of those worst off—or, to stay more closely with Rawls's particular formulation of the requirements of justice, to maximize the minimum level of social and economic primary goods.

It would seem, from Rawls's statement that persons are entitled to gain 'for using their endowments in ways that help the less fortu-

[10] Rawls, pp. 101–2.

nate', that he supposes that each person has the right to use his capacities and talents as he chooses, so that he is entitled to payment for costs arising from opportunities forgone. If persons lacked this right—if, for example, it were supposed that each individual had the obligation to use his capacities in whatever way would maximize the welfare of those worst off—then no one would be entitled to payment for so using his capacities. Alternative uses would be ruled out as contrary to the requirements of justice, and so there would be no legitimate opportunity costs to be met.

From the lexical difference principle, expressing Rawls's general conception of justice that 'All social values . . . are to be distributed equally unless an unequal distribution . . . is to everyone's advantage',[11] and the claim that 'the distribution of natural talents' is to be regarded 'as a common asset',[12] it might seem to follow that no person has a right to his basic endowment of physical and mental capacities, entitling him to payment for opportunity costs. Indeed, this right may seem incompatible with maximizing the welfare of those worst off. But Rawls's special conception of justice, which he holds to be that particularization of the general conception applicable to our social and economic circumstances, is expressed by two principles, of which the first and prior requires that 'Each person is to have an equal right to the most extensive total system of equal basic liberties compatible with a similar system of liberty for all.'[13] From this principle the right to one's basic endowment would seem to follow, and so the entitlement to payment for opportunity costs in return for the provision of factor services.

We shall not consider further whether Rawls's special conception of justice, affording each person a right to his basic endowment, is compatible with his general conception. For our purposes, what is significant is that Rawls implicitly distinguishes factor rent from payment for factor services, agreeing with our view that each person is entitled to the latter, but supposing that the former, instead of being divided equally among all co-operators, is to be used to the benefit of the least advantaged. And this is a denial of basic liberty in the context of co-operation. If each contributes equally to the production of the co-operative surplus, then each is entitled to an equal share in that surplus. Rawls fails to recognize this entitlement.

4.1 We argued in Chapter VII that an individual might rightfully appropriate land or other goods previously in common use for

[11] Ibid., p. 62. [12] Ibid., p. 101. [13] Ibid., p. 250.

her own exclusive use, provided the effect of such appropriation was to leave other persons at least as well off as before. The appropriator betters herself without worsening the situation of others. However, it might be objected that she does curtail the opportunities of others, and so worsens their situation. In making the most advantageous acquisition for herself, the appropriator precludes her fellows from making an equally advantageous acquisition. It may then be urged that we should take more seriously Locke's own words, 'enough, and as good', and insist that any opportunity that an individual may rightfully exercise must leave, if not similar, then equally advantageous opportunities for others. Although one person may in fact do better than her fellows as a result of non-co-operative appropriations, yet she would violate the proviso were it not possible for them to do equally as well.

But the role of the proviso is to prohibit the taking of advantage. In making the best appropriation open to one, one does not take advantage of others simply because they now lack the opportunity that one was the first to seize. The winner of a race does not take advantage of the other runners, at least if participation in the race is itself advantageous. The runners all prefer a situation in which benefit is unequal, so that there are winners and losers, to one in which all benefit equally, but there are no races.

Were the world such as the Dobu have been said to conceive it, so that all goods were in fixed supply, then the proviso would indeed limit appropriation by the requirement that as good an opportunity be left for others, so that one should take only an equal share of land or of other goods. For in such a world races would not be advantageous for all participants. Of course, in such a world social interaction itself would not be advantageous, so that no one would have reason to adhere to the proviso. But in our world, in which human effort increases the total supply, particularly of material goods, a restriction to equal appropriation would disadvantage everyone. Those who seize personally beneficial opportunities frequently also create new opportunities as a result of their activities. The first-comer may of course be the greatest beneficiary of her own activity. But everyone may reasonably expect to benefit more, from the opportunities that the activity creates, than if the first-comer had constrained her appropriation by leaving opportunities for others equal to the one she took for herself. One leaves others more, or rather, one creates more for them, by not leaving them literally 'as good'. The recognition of this fundamental practical truth has been one of the central ideas of modern Western society, enabling it to succeed to an extent unparalleled in human history in harnessing the seizure of personally advantageous opportunities by some individuals to the creation of enlarged opportunities for others.

But not every activity that forecloses certain opportunities is licensed by the proviso; not every such activity may be expected to create new and enlarged prospects. Clearly it is not enough to leave others as they were before, able to carry on with their present activities and to reap benefits equal to those they attained in the past, if one also deprives them of opportunities previously available for bettering themselves without affording them new alternatives. And this has very significant implications for the scope of legitimate appropriation, both among persons and among peoples. Consider, as in VII.4.1, an island inhabited by persons who originally cultivate the land non-co-operatively, but claim no private holdings. Eve appropriates some of the land for herself, taking care to leave the others with enough so that they are as well off as before her appropriation. But then oil is discovered on her land. Her right to the land need not extend to a right to the oil. It may be that the benefit all derive from individual rights related to agricultural production, which licenses Eve's original appropriation, does not extend to individual rights related to the development of mineral or other resources. Here any individual acquisition may worsen the situation of some persons. Or it may be that, even if individual rights in mineral resources are in principle mutually beneficial, yet the particular allocation of rights that would result from extending rights justifiably acquired in land to rights to resources on that land may not benefit all.

Eve is not able to claim justifiably that her situation is worsened if her alleged right to the oil on her land is rejected. If someone acquires land to farm, with no concern for and no knowledge of the oil beneath her fields, then her position cannot be worsened if she lacks an exclusive right to what is only later discovered. The rights acquired in an act of appropriation are determined by the context of the act, and by the use or uses made of what is appropriated. Here we may see the very real relevance of Locke's insistence that what is rightfully acquired be put to use, even if his own understanding of this requirement, as merely forbidding wastage, is itself defective.

The key point on which to focus is that the effect of rights to oil may be very different from the effect of rights to land. In acquiring a plot of land, even the best land on the island, Eve may initiate the possibility of more diversified activities in the community as a whole, and more specialized activities for particular individuals with ever-increasing benefits to all. But if she also gains title to the oil on her land, then she may become proprietor of the only oil well on the island. She may be a monopolist, and most persons may be made worse off by a private monopoly than by common control. Of course, were she to be a monopolist she need not make her fellows actually worse off than they were when, prior to the discovery of oil, their activities were restricted to agriculture. But she may well curtail rather than enlarge their opportunities for betterment by the control she would exercise over what might become their primary source of energy.

Because rights are temporally open-ended, consideration of their long-term implications, especially for the extent of opportunities, must not be ignored in determining whether they satisfy the proviso. Individually beneficial appropriation does not itself violate the proviso merely because the literal Lockean 'as good' is not satisfied. But appropriation must occur in a context of expanding opportunities, if literally unequal acquisitions are to enter into the initial position for market and co-operative interaction.

4.2 The example sketched in the preceding subsection has evident application to the contemporary world. Arabs and Albertans (to mention but two) have affirmed their right to the oil beneath their lands. And under the rules of the present international order the claims of the Arabs, but not those of the Albertans, are firmly based—the former have the good fortune to constitute nations, while the latter make up a mere province. But the present international order may not afford a rational and fair basis for co-operative interaction among the world's peoples. Arabs and Albertans may be expanding opportunities for themselves while curtailing others' prospects for development. Both may of course have certain historic claims to compensation for past injustices. But that is another matter—not a possible foundation for the simple right to whatever may be found in the territory one happens to occupy.

The rights assigned to the personae of the international order—to nations—open the door to prospects of oligopolic and monopolistic control which may well be in violation of the proviso, when the effect on opportunities for development is taken into account. But we may find what seem to be more serious violations arising, not from the recognition of rights legitimating the direct access of peoples to the resources of the lands they occupy, but from the use of resources to which others have recognized rights, even if this use is not always achieved by direct or overt coercion.

If one nation industrializes and enjoys affluence, while others do not, remaining at the level of subsistence agriculture, there need be no injustice. The industrialized country may fully respect the proviso, enriching itself in ways that create new prospects for its neighbours, whether or not they take advantage of them. But if it seeks, whether through coercion or agreement, to appropriate the presently unused resources of its undeveloped neighbours, so that they are no longer able to choose their own paths of development, but rather must decide between continuing their original way of life, and supplying the needs of their industrialized partner—growing its coffee, or bananas, or meat, or rubber, or newsprint—then even if the immediate effect of partnership is to enhance the standard of living and to broaden the opportunities for individual advancement in the undeveloped nations, yet the long-term effect may rather be to diminish those opportunities, condemning the undeveloped to permanent dependence and impoverishment. If a nation may take advantage of others by acquiring an effective monopoly over certain widely needed resources, yet it may equally be taken advantage of if others exploit the resources that are in the long run the key to its own development.

Of course the undeveloped agrarian neighbours may be in no position to challenge their industrialized partner; it may simply dictate the terms of interaction. In the short run at least, predation may succeed. But we should not conclude that this legitimates the *de facto* rights that form the base point of this interaction. Differential access to resources, and differing levels of development, are factors that militate against adherence to the proviso in the present state of nations. To point this out, and to show that the existing basis for international co-operation is in part unjust, so that those disadvantaged by it will accept it rationally only in so far as it is coercively maintained, is not to accuse those who benefit from superior access or greater development of deliberate wrongdoing. Indeed, in so far as the state of nations remains a state of nature, those who profit at the expense of their neighbours are behaving in a straightforwardly maximizing manner in circumstances in which constrained maximization would not be reciprocated. The proviso is a rational constraint on the interactions of nations only if there is the prospect of an international order of co-operation. But we must remember that the *de facto* natural distribution resulting from the interaction of nations in a state approaching that of nature will not yield an allocation of rights acceptable as a basis for more co-operative relationships. If we measure these rights against the proviso, then we must look to the mutual enhancement and enlargement of opportunities as a fundamental criterion for judging what may reasonably be claimed by each partner as its initial endowment in a fair world order.

4.3 The encounter of two peoples at different levels of development raises issues about the rightful basis and character of their interaction that extend beyond the particular question of opportunities. Let us imagine a planet whose surface is covered by stormy seas, broken by two large, widely separated islands. Each island is inhabited by creatures sufficiently human-like that we shall consider them our own kind; the one island is inhabited by purple people, the other by green people. Before the time at which our story begins the two peoples have lived in complete isolation from each other; neither the green nor the purple people have been aware that other humans inhabited their planet.

The purple people have developed an ideally just society. The rights of each purple person are rooted firmly in the proviso. A free market extends its sway wherever it affords optimality; elsewhere, externalities are countered by policies and practices that satisfy minimax relative concession. To ensure long-run equity (a problem we shall examine in more detail in the last section of this chapter), policies concerning population, conservation, and development have been designed to provide benefits to each person, whenever he may live, that are equivalent, relative to his rights, personal characteristics, and the possible modes of social interaction, to those of each other person. The green people, on the other hand, live in totally chaotic squalor. Heedless of both their fellows and their future, they have exhausted themselves in strife, squandered their resources, propagated themselves without constraint, so that they are on the brink of catastrophic collapse. At this point in their respective histories, an exploration party from the land of purple people discovers the greens, and reports back on their condition.

Consensus is reached among the purple people on several matters.

Any contact between the two groups must be at their instigation, since the greens lack means both of transport and of communication across the sea. The combined resources of the two islands could not support their combined populations at the level of well-being enjoyed by the members of purple society. Maximization of either the average or the minimum level of well-being would require a massive transfer of resources from purple people to green.

The purple people have no reason to embrace a utilitarian response to the situation we have just outlined—a response that would deem it obligatory for the purples to undertake a massive transfer of resources to the greens. The purples may of course respond sympathetically to the greens' plight. They may even consider themselves obliged not to worsen the greens' unfortunate situation, although whether our theory can countenance such an obligation is a matter we must consider. But the purples neither would nor could have reason to consider themselves obliged to worsen their own situation in order to maximize overall average utility.

Clearly the purple people have not violated the proviso with respect to the greens. They cannot have done, since there has been no past interaction. Thus there is no present injustice in the situation of the two peoples, despite the marked inequality in their conditions. Injustice can arise only in so far as the actions of one person or group affect another. Thus the existing situation constitutes an acceptable initial position for the application of the principles of rational bargaining. The inequalities that it contains will be preserved in any rational co-operative arrangement among purples and greens. They are not part of the co-operative surplus to be distributed between the two peoples according to the terms of co-operation.

How may we expect the surplus to be divided? Given the very different levels of development of the two peoples, and their very different positions, co-operation between them will not, in all likelihood, yield a single, transferable good to be shared equally between them. In so far as the benefits of co-operation are comparable, it would seem evident that the greens have far more to gain than do the purples from interaction between the two. Hence equivalent shares of the co-operative surplus, as required by minimax relative concession, will provide the green people with greater absolute benefits.

It might therefore be supposed that, starting from a position of great inequality, the two peoples would gradually move closer in their levels of development and well-being. But this need not be the case; absolute inequality between the two may even increase, although co-operation benefits the greens more than it does the purples. For as we shall show in the final section of this chapter, rational co-operation with a society must in general result in a positive rate of growth, and so in increasing material well-being over time. It may be that this internal rate of growth is so much greater among the purple people than among the green people that its effects more than offset the greater benefits received by the greens from co-operation. An increase in the inequalities between two co-operating peoples is not a sign that the terms of co-operation between them are unfair, or contrary to the requirements of minimax relative concession.

The application of our moral theory to interaction between purples and greens may seem quite straightforward. Co-operation begins from the situation as it is when the two peoples first come into contact; co-operation itself tends to benefit the less advanced group more because it has more to gain; despite this, co-operation need not lead, over time, to any reduction in the inequalities between the groups. But there are complications that we have not considered. Need the purples embark on co-operation with the greens?

Some of the purple people might well oppose any form of interaction with their newly discovered fellow humans. They might do this, even though they could expect to benefit, if only marginally, from exchanges with the green people. For they might suppose that this gain would be accompanied by the serious cost of maintaining a relationship that, however just, would come in time to be resented by the greens in virtue of its inequality. Ideally rational persons would no doubt not exhibit such resentment, but the greens are not ideally rational. Furthermore, the purples might suppose that a highly unequal relationship would strain their own feelings—that their sympathy would motivate them not only to share the benefits of co-operation, but to transfer goods from themselves to the less fortunate greens. And they might prefer not to find themselves in a position in which their own sympathetic feelings, combined with the greens' feelings of resentment, might leave them worse off than if no interaction were to occur, so that neither sympathetic nor resentful feelings would develop. In effect it may be urged that in this highly unequal situation other-directed feelings would not be a source of enrichment to human life.

If some of the purple people prefer to ignore the greens, others may suggest that the purples simply make what use they can of the island inhabited by the greens, without seeking to cause its present occupants direct harm or disadvantage, but without concern for the indirect effects of their use. Or, more radically, they may suggest that the purples actively engage in predation, taking what they can from the greens and from the island they inhabit. The second of these proposals quite intentionally violates the proviso. The first does not, in so far as the purples envisage no benefits from interaction with the greens, since it affords them only the expectation of the utility they might obtain were the other island uninhabited. Which of these proposals might be preferred would depend on particular circumstances; either could be the straightforwardly utility-maximizing policy. In effect their advocates claim that the purple people have no good reason to extend their disposition to constrained maximization so that interaction with the green people falls within its scope.

We might characterize these non-co-operative policies as treating the greens not as fellow human beings, not as 'us', but as animals, as 'them'. Behaviour towards animals is quite straightforwardly utility-maximizing, although it may be affected by particular feelings for certain animals. In grounding morals in rational choice, we exclude relations with non-human creatures from the sphere of moral constraint. Why should the purple people not consider the greens merely as animals?

There are several grounds on which purple people might defend constrained maximization, adherence to the proviso, and acceptance of minimax relative concession, in their relationship with the greens. First, they might insist that, whatever the short-term advantages, in the long run the purples may expect to benefit from constraint. As interaction between the purples and greens continues, the greens may become better able to defend their interests. Co-operation, on fair terms, may then be advantageous for both. But if the purple people have acted as predators, or even if they have simply disregarded the greens, then they may face implacable hostility, or at best a demand for compensation as a precondition to co-operation, and this compensation may involve greater costs than would be required by a continuing adherence to the proviso. Restoring a fair initial position for co-operation may be less beneficial than never departing from it. Thus it may be argued that expected advantage requires the purples to dispose themselves to co-operate with the greens.

But second, the purples may already be disposed to such co-operation. In developing their own ideally just society, they may have introduced patterns of socialization disposing them to constrained maximization with all whom they consider fellow human beings, and they may have no alternative but so to consider the greens. They are disposed to treat all beings with certain capacities and attitudes as potential partners in co-operative arrangements, and the green people may have these capacities and attitudes. Perhaps, had they known that they would in time encounter the green people, they would have disposed themselves differently. But even were this so, they need have no reason to seek changes in their patterns of socialization. The benefits and costs anticipated in establishing certain patterns may be quite different from those required to alter those patterns. Thus the purple people, without any irrationality, may simply never consider approaching the greens from a non-co-operative stance. They will, of course, not engage in active co-operation except in the context of explicit or implicit agreement, but they may from the outset show their disposition to such agreement by strict adherence to the proviso.

And third, the purple people may possess a certain measure of sympathy for all whom they consider human. They may take a positive interest in the interests of others, and this may suffice to ground a disposition not to worsen the situation of other persons except where the alternative would be to accept a significant worsening in their own situation. They may then not want to seize the resources of the newly discovered island without thought for the plight of the greens. Without recognizing any positive obligation towards the green people, and without accepting any duty that would require them to divest themselves of benefits they presently enjoy in order to better the greens' unfortunate situation, the purples may consider themselves obliged, in virtue of their sympathetic feelings, to do nothing that would worsen that situation. Although the purples have not the least reason to reproach themselves for the present plight of the greens, yet they would reproach themselves were they to affect the greens adversely.

Such a reaction is not, and cannot be, required by reason alone. The demands of sympathy are quite distinct from those of rational choice, and only confusion results from treating them together. A morality of feeling must be examined quite apart from morals by agreement. But we may suppose that for some persons, a willingness to approach interaction co-operatively, rather than to behave as a predator, and so to constrain the maximization of one's own utility in accordance with the proviso and the principle of minimax relative concession, may be grounded in sympathetic feelings.

As we take leave of the purple and green people, we should relate their fiction to fact. The relations among the more and less developed nations of our world are in important respects not parallel to the relations between purples and greens. But at least some contemporary moral thinkers argue in such a way that, even were they parallel, one would suppose the situation unjust, and hold that the developed countries were obliged to make sacrifices for the benefit of the less developed. For it is sometimes supposed that the mere fact of inequality—and mere fact that some peoples are so much better off than others, and that their well-being increases so much more rapidly—is indicative of injustice. Our story should reveal the fallaciousness of this view. It may be that Laos or Mali, Bourkina Fasso or Ethiopia, would be even poorer, and America or Switzerland even richer, were they to inhabit different islands with no contact between them. It may be that inequalities are increasing, not because the well-to-do are profiting at the expense of the poor, but because the internal rate of growth that the wealthy nations can fairly sustain exceeds what is possible for the poor, and more than balances the benefits that co-operation brings to less developed countries.

We do not suggest that the present international order is a model of just and rational co-operation. We are quite willing to suppose that at least some existing disparities and inequalities may be traced to exploitation, to interaction in violation of the proviso and minimax relative concession. But we may not assume this simply because the disparities exist. We must ask how they came about. If nations are to interact in a rational, fair, non-exploitative way, then it is necessary to determine whether their past relationships involve violations of the proviso which require both compensation and an adjustment in existing *de facto* rights. It is necessary also to determine whether the present modes of interaction benefit each nation in ways equivalent to the benefits afforded others. Until we are able to answer these questions, not of course with precision but with some reasonably assured approximation, then we are in no position to evaluate the present international order, however much certain facts or alleged facts may arouse our feelings. In the world of purple and green people the inequalities are justified. In our world they may or may not be; we do not know.

5.1 Interaction between peoples who practise different ways of life raises issues of great practical complexity which our moral theory may help to illuminate. Throughout human history, contact between different ways of life has tended to result in conflict and, not infrequently, conquest, rather than peaceable coexistence. The idea that ways of life have a right to survive—an idea expressed in that extraordinary conception, cultural genocide—is a recent arrival on the moral scene. It is also a thoroughly misguided idea. Individuals matter; ways of life matter only as expressing and nurturing human individuality. On the basis of our theory, and some few factual but hardly controversial assumptions about what human beings prefer, we shall come to a clearer understanding of the circumstances in which one way of life justifiably supplants another.

We begin by formulating four criteria for classifying one way of life as more advanced than another, as exhibiting a higher stage of human development. The first, and perhaps the least important, is *density of population*: other things being equal, *A* is a more advanced way of life than *B* if it enables a larger number of persons to inhabit a given territory. The second is *duration of life*: other things being equal, *A* is a more advanced way of life than *B* if it enables those who practise it to enjoy, on average, a longer life span. The third is *material well-being*: other things being equal, *A* is a more advanced way of life than *B* if it enables those who practise it to enjoy, on average, a greater abundance, and more varied kinds, of material goods. And the fourth, and most important, is *breadth of opportunity*: other things being equal, *A* is a more advanced way of life than *B* if those who practise it enjoy, on average, a choice among more diverse and varied vocational and avocational roles. These four criteria induce a partial ordering on ways of life, in terms of advancement or human development. We shall not attempt to weight the criteria in such a way as to provide more than a partial ordering.

How may we defend these criteria? We appeal to what seem plain facts about human preferences. Although not all human beings wish to reproduce, yet most do, and certainly most wish the opportunity to do so, should they choose. A society that supports a larger population, with longer life spans, gives persons more effective opportunities for successful reproduction. Again, although not all human beings wish long lives, yet most do, and wish them also for friends and kin. A society that offers greater average duration of life answers this wish.

The desire for material well-being is manifested primarily among those who believe it possible—who see the world as a place of increasing wealth. Among those who do see the world in this way, the desire is widespread and even more widespread is the wish to have the opportunity to seek greater material well-being should one so choose. A society that affords a higher average level of material well-being answers this wish; it gives its members an option lacking in a materially impoverished society.

Again, the desire for a broad range of vocational and avocational opportunities, among which one may choose, is manifested primarily by persons who are socialized to conceive themselves as free, autonomous individuals, and not as born to play some predetermined social role. The members of a primitive group of hunter-gatherers do not think in terms of choosing among diverse opportunities. But preference development here is unidirectional; as persons come to be aware of a broadening range of opportunities, they want to be free to choose among them, as persons find themselves faced with a narrowing range, they regret the loss of freedom that it brings. A society that broadens the range of opportunities effectively available to its members provides ever more fully for the varied capacities and talents, the varied preferences and attitudes, that individuate human beings. In VIII.4.2, we saw that the fundamental choice of the ideal actor is to use her powers to fulfil her preferences to the maximum extent possible. But then the ideal actor must also choose a society that affords its members the widest choice among vocational and avocational roles, the broadest range of opportunities, as the most effective means to realize that fundamental choice.

The four criteria give us a normative perspective from which we may assess many of the interactions among peoples practising different ways of life. It will not have escaped the reader's attention, or—at this stage of our argument—surprised him, to realize that among human societies the criteria are satisifed preeminently by our own, modern Western civilization. We note but one illustration. At the beginning of the present century, average duration of life, worldwide, was between thirty and forty years.[14] Eighty years later, it is over sixty years. Since the hypothetical minimum for human beings is about twenty years (the species could not effectively reproduce itself, and so survive, were average duration of life lower), in the present century the life span of men and women has increased at least as much, and perhaps significantly more, than it had throughout all previous human history. That increase may be attributed primarily to specifically Western ideas of sanitation, and a technology to implement those ideas, supplemented by specifically Western advances in nutrition, agricultural productivity, and transportation. Whatever the motivation of the merchants, soldiers, and missionaries who set out from Europe and America, their contact with the other peoples of the world has finally led to the doubling of those peoples' life expectancies. As an imperial legacy, there have been worse.

5.2 We return for a final visit to our imaginary island. Suppose that Eve, appropriating land for her exclusive use, takes so much that the others are unable to live as well as before if they continue to treat the remaining land as a commons. However, Eve provides effective opportunities for them to increase their well-being by changing their way of life. On the land that she acquires, she introduces new techniques of food production, increasing yield to such an extent that some of the others may cease to be self-sufficient, becoming instead specialized artisans and craftspersons, exchanging their products for her surplus food and living better in consequence. The others, who remain food-growers, may learn the new techniques which Eve freely shares with them, and, dividing up the remaining land into individual holdings, implement these new techniques to benefit from both increased harvests and exchanges with the artisans and craftspersons. Thus although the other inhabitants of the island are no longer free to continue in their old ways without loss, yet everyone is able to benefit by changing her ways, and so is compensated for the loss of benefits from her original activities by the expanded opportunities which offer new and greater benefits.

Is this compensation sufficient to satisfy the proviso? Eve betters her situation in relation to, and indeed through interaction with, her fellows. In so doing she provides them with the opportunities to better their own situations, but only if they seize these opportunities

[14] See N. Eberstadt, 'The Health Crisis in the U.S.S.R.', *New York Review of Books* 28, no. 2 (1981), p. 23. For average duration of life at the turn of the century, he accepts an estimate closer to thirty than to forty years. But elsewhere I have read estimates closer to the latter.

can they avoid finding themselves worse off than before her appropriation. We may suppose that initially they prefer not to change their ways and exercise the new opportunities. Their preferences are related to their old circumstances. But we may also suppose that, consistently with our discussion in the preceding subsection, if they change, they will then not want to return to their former way of life, not merely because they have acquired new aims and desires which that way could not satisfy, but because they prefer their new lifestyle, with its wider opportunities and greater material well-being, to what they suppose they would have experienced had they not changed. They will find themselves, not in the position of the habitual smoker who cannot do without a cigarette but wishes she had never started smoking, but in the position of the successful weight-loser, who underwent the agony of dieting but finds his slimmer self enjoying a happier life.

Eve offers what we have seen to be two of the criteria of human advancement. She offers her fellows the opportunity to choose among different vocational roles—farmer, artisan, craftsperson, and the increased affluence created by exchanges among persons fulfilling these roles. Of course, expansion and diversification do not occur without some contraction. Opportunities for automobile manufacturers and mechanics displace opportunities for horsebreeders and blacksmiths, to mention the classic example. Such contraction represents the unavoidable cost of human development. However, if individuals are neither excluded from nor coerced into the overall expansion of opportunity, with its accompanying enhancement of material well-being, then their situation is not worsened in order to better that of others, and they have no complaint in justice against the change. Eve's appropriation is vindicated.

The proviso does not require that one leave others as well off as before in their existing activities, if new and effective opportunities for betterment are provided. We have so far supposed that these opportunities are optional; those faced with them may choose between changing and staying as they are. Is this choice itself necessary to avoid violating the proviso? Or may we argue that so long as others may benefit by changing their ways, it is not unjust if they are compelled to change? May Eve force some of her fellows to become craftspersons, and others independent landowners, rather than allow them to decide whether they will give up life on their commons?

To this question our answer must be firmly negative. For Eve to compel others to change would be for her to violate the right each person has to use her body and capacities as she sees fit, provided only that in her use she does not violate the proviso. Eve may provide opportunities for change, and indeed must provide them to justify her appropriation, but she may not force others to accept these opportunities without violating their basic rights. Since the right to one's own person affords the initial step in transforming the Hobbesian state of nature, it may not later be revoked. Thus appropriation would be unjust were it not to allow others to live as before, even if less well. The right to acquire land or other goods for one's exclusive use is not a right to compel others to interact with one against their will even if such interaction is to their benefit.

Before continuing we should note that the opportunities for others to improve their situation, must be effectively available. Eve must afford every assistance necessary to ensure that the new ways are known and accessible to those who must choose between adopting them and suffering loss. The practical importance of this in applying the proviso will be evident.

Let us now change our story in one significant respect. Suppose that an outsider, whom we shall call Columbus, appears on our island where land is treated as a commons. May he join the original inhabitants, using the land with them? We may suppose that his arrival worsens their situation; it creates greater population pressure on the land. However, if Columbus is entirely self-sufficient and does not profit in any way from the presence of the original inhabitants, then he does not better his situation in relation to what he would expect were they absent. He does not violate the proviso by his use of the island, although equally, the original inhabitants do not violate the proviso in seeking to exclude him. For in excluding him they do not better their situation in relation to his absence.

However, if Columbus seeks to interact with the original inhabitants, benefiting from their presence and activities, then the situation is quite different. In merely using land, unless he profits from their prior cultivation of it, he does not benefit in any way from what they do. But if he proposes to trade with them, then the cost to them of his presence falls within the framework of interaction as a displaced cost, an externality. The proviso comes into play. Unless he proposes to act simply as a predator, he must accept the initial position determined by the proviso. Since this requires the internalization of all costs, he must provide benefits for the original inhabitants sufficient to compensate them for his presence. Only when he has done this is there a fair basis for exchange.

Let us suppose that the principal benefit Columbus brings is a more advanced agricultural technology. And let us suppose further that he seeks, not to share the land in common with the original inhabitants, but to appropriate some portion for his exclusive use, so that he may implement an agrarian revolution. He must worsen the lot of the original inhabitants if they continue as before, since they are to be confined to a smaller area. But the increased yield on the land that he farms enables him to play the role of Eve in our previous story. He produces surplus food, which he willingly exchanges with the others for other goods that some may now specialize in producing, leading to wider opportunities and enhanced well-being for all. The original inhabitants must choose between their old way of life with diminished well-being, and the new way offered by Columbus with broader horizons and greater material benefits.

Columbus is an outsider, taking from what had been used exclusively by others. The original inhabitants may claim that the island is theirs, that they are making full use of it to maintain themselves, and that his attempt to appropriate a portion of it for his exclusive use is theft. He may plead in return that the original inhabitants have indeed a right in the island, fully recognized in the circumstances of his own appropriation, but not a right to the island. From his standpoint a part of the resources and capacities of the island is going to waste. It is possible for a larger number of persons to inhabit it, each at a higher material standard, by implementing his more advanced technology. Again the criteria of 5.1 are brought into the argument. And just as the rights acquired in an act of appropriation are determined by the context of the act and the uses made of what is appropriated, so the limitations set on appropriation by previous use are determined by the nature of that use in relation to the criteria for advancement. If an act of appropriation occurs in the context of new uses that make possible a larger population living in greater material comfort, then it need involve no violation of the proviso, even if the appropriator is an outsider.

In the state of nature, if not always in society, efficient use is a condition of rightful possession. Although rights are temporally open-ended, they are subject to alteration in the light of changed possibilities. The relevance of efficient use to rightful possession within an established social framework depends of course on the implicit or explicit terms of agreement underlying that framework. Hence in a court of law the plea of the outsider, that he may appropriate on the basis of new uses making advancement possible, may prove invalid. But in the court of nature, where what each must show is only that he does not worsen the situation of others by seeking to better his own situation through interaction with them, then the outsider may justify his appropriation if he provides those whose present activities he affects adversely with new and broader prospects enhancing their well-being. Columbus' appropriation, like that of Eve, is vindicated.

5.3 In calling the outsider Columbus, we suggest the relevance of our story to the assessment of relationships between the native inhabitants of North America and the first Europeans to arrive among them.[15] We shall argue that much of the European appropriation of North America might have taken place without violating the proviso, and so without treating the native inhabitants unjustly. We shall not argue that what actually occurred was free from injustice. But a hypothetical just appropriation is nevertheless important for present practice. If it is possible to show how, without injustice, Europeans might have come to live in North America with rights to the lands they occupy, valid even against claims by the native inhabitants, then redress for the actual injustices committed should be feasible without requiring Europeans to abandon their existing rights. If on the other hand there is no way in which Europeans might have occupied North America, except by a predatory seizure which would give rise to no rights, and which would violate the proviso if offered as determining the initial position for co-operative interaction with the native inhabitants, then effective redress is not possible, and fair co-operation would require a basis very different from the actual present situation.

We imagine, then, the continent of North America inhabited by Indians and Inuit, using it as a vast commons. Suppose that the level of population is as great as is compatible with the level of material well-being, given the technology available to the natives. Then the

[15] For a discussion of this problem, see M. McDonald, 'Aboriginal Rights', in W. R. Shea and J. King-Farlow (eds.), *Contemporary Issues in Political Philosophy* (New York, 1976), pp. 27–48. McDonald argues that 'this country [Canada] ought to recognise aboriginal rights *on the basis of original acquisition*' (p. 47).

incursion of outsiders must in itself lower the existing level of well-being or reduce the native population, and lower the future expectations of at least some of the inhabitants, so that such an incursion, if taken to include a claim even to share in the commons without justifiable opposition from the natives, must be itself unjustifiable, a claim to rights beyond what the proviso licenses.

But the European arrives with a superior technology, enabling more people to live longer and more abundantly, with wider, albeit somewhat different, opportunities than previously was possible. If Indians and Inuit are given the effective prospect of adapting their life-styles in order to share in this enhancement of life, while being left free to continue their old ways, with reduced expectations, should they so choose, then their situation is not worsened and they can have no complaint in justice against the incursion of Europeans and the appropriation by them of much, although of course not of all, of the continent.

The most cursory reading of the history of the European appropriation of North America shows that the native inhabitants were not offered an effective choice between adapting to European ways and preserving their old life-styles. Reservations were provided to permit the old ways to continue, but entry into the white man's society was effectively denied. Thus the condition of the natives was worsened and the proviso violated. But this violation was an unnecessary, if unsurprising, effect of an incursion based on a technology that offered a potentially justifiable mode of acquisition. Hence it should now be possible for the non-native inhabitants of North America to offer the natives a bargain or agreement based on a fair initial position, without abandoning the bulk of their appropriation.

The European appropriation—as any state of nature acquisition—did not rest on consent. A fair bargain must itself involve consent, or at least hypothetical consent rationally grounded, but initial appropriation is not a bargain. It occurs under conditions in which each actor is free to advance his own interests except where he would take advantage of some other actor in so doing. To require consent in the acts of appropriation that establish initial rights would invite free-ridership. It would impose a barrier, quite probably insuperable, to human advancement, where such advancement can be accomplished only through major changes in ways of life. The native peoples of North America can have no complaint, in reason or justice, against the failure of the Europeans to gain their prior consent before establishing themselves in the new world. Such consent would no doubt have been impossible to obtain; the Indian and Inuit peoples could have had no prior understanding of the new technology which enlarged opportunities but supplanted their old ways.

These old ways were effectively doomed by the arrival of the Europeans. They were highly effective adaptations to an environment that the native inhabitants were unable to transform. But European technology rendered these adaptations obsolete. The problems with which the natives grappled were dissolved by that technology—to be replaced, to be sure, by new and different problems, but related to a more advanced level of human development. The modes of production and structures of belief that had served the natives well lost all meaning in the light of a superior technology and a more comprehensive science. The effect of the European incursion was to turn cultural practices that had been necessary to survival into a form of play. For the European offered a way of life that could sustain more people, with longer life expectancies, at a higher level of material well-being, and with an extended horizon of opportunity.

To say that European technology rendered the culture of Indians and Inuit obsolete is neither to denigrate that culture nor to diminish the achievements of those individuals who developed it. The obsolescence of cultures shows only that human advancement, as measured by the criteria of 5.1, continues. Those who would condemn the supplanting of one culture by another as 'cultural genocide' would seem to prefer that human beings serve as live museum pieces in an unending re-enactment of past roles, rather than that they be freed to participate in the course of human development. The proviso, by licensing those appropriations that make evident the obsolescence of ways of life, stimulates their adherents to seize the new opportunities enabling them to become once more participants in that development. Unfortunately, and unjustifiably, the European chose all too frequently to show the Indian or Inuit the obsolescence of her way of life, without extending to her the opportunity to participate in the way that supplanted it.

There is a further dimension to the European appropriation of North America that we have so far ignored. Not only the effect on the native inhabitants, but also that on the other peoples of the world, must be taken into account. In the short run these effects were minimal, but as we have seen, short-run considerations do not suffice to ground permanent acquisition. If the European presence in North America is supposed to exclude African and Asian peoples from the continent, except as immigrants on terms acceptable to the proprietors, then does it not involve a contraction in the opportunities of these other peoples?

Africans or Asians would have done better, had they developed the technology that would have enabled them to reach America first, and to appropriate it for themselves. But the inability to act first does not in itself worsen one's situation. We must ask whether Africans or Asians would have benefited if America had simply remained in Indian and Inuit possession. The facts may be unclear. But it is surely plausible to hold that the European incursion into North America was an integral part of a tremendous expansion of global productive capacity that has effectively broadened horizons, bettered living conditions, added to life expectancies, and expanded populations of peoples throughout the world. That these benefits have been distributed unequally is in itself no proof of injustice. More seriously, some peoples have shared but slightly in the improvements. Even this need not show injustice, since it is possible that these peoples have chosen to persist in their old ways of life despite the costs involved. But surely few believe that all peoples have in fact been afforded an effective chance to participate fairly in the increase in global well-being and the overall human advancement made possible by European technology. Yet the very real and extensive injustices that have occurred would seem to be incidental in relation to our particular concern; they could have been avoided without invalidating the European appropriation of North America, or indeed without hindering the other events that have multiplied human productive capacity.

In considering the appropriation, by members of a more advanced society, of lands previously inhabited only by members of societies less advanced, we have ventured on matters of great complexity. We intend our discussion not to be conclusive, but to show the relevance of the proviso to problems of appropriation among peoples, and to indicate the type of conclusions to which its application may lead. And in particular, we wish to rescue from the indiscriminate obloquy that has fallen upon the imperial idea, that very real and significant strand in which the more advanced power seeks to better its own situation in a manner that makes effectively available to others the prospect of increasing their numbers, prolonging their lives, adding to their material goods, and enlarging their opportunities.

6.1 Relations among persons of different generations may seem to fall ouside the scope allowed to rational morality by our theory. While supposing mutual unconcern, we have nevertheless generated impartial constraints on the maximization of individual utility by appealing to the benefits of co-operation. But co-operation is possible only among contemporaries who actually interact. Although an individual can do much to benefit or harm his descendants, only those whose lives overlap with his can benefit or harm him in return. He has then no reason to concern himself with others. In maximizing his utility without regard for future persons whose lives will not overlap with his own, he runs no risk of attaining a sub-optimal outcome. Any constraint he might accept would result in a simple transfer of utilities from himself to future persons; it could not lead to mutual benefits. Any costs that his actions impose on future persons are strictly incidental to the benefits he receives. They cannot, then, involve violations of the proviso. So an individual does his descendants no injustice in not concerning himself with them. If the world is not left a fit place for their habitation, much less their well-being, this merely characterizes the circumstances in which they find themselves; their rights are not affected.

If this is indeed the position to which reason leads us, then we must accept it, admitting another, and very deep, difference between our intuitive morality and what conforms to rational choice. We might then be led to suppose that moral relationships among persons of different generations require an affective basis. Rejecting the assumption of mutual unconcern, we might explore the morality of feeling. Characteristically persons do take an interest at least in their immediate descendants. And this interest expresses in a desire to leave the world a better place, or at least no worse a place, than they themselves found it. Human communities endure in time; persons regard their descendants as members of the same society as themselves. Thinking in this way, they consider the adverse effects of their activities on future members of their society as indeed displaced costs, violating the proviso-based requirement that they be internalized. Thus we might introduce the idea that human beings are engaged in a partnership over time in creating and maintaining a society—a way of life in which all share. We might come to Burke's conception of society as based on a contract among past, present, and future generations.[16] We should then be able to apply our moral theory to determine a framework of rights and obligations among the members of different generations, based on the fiction of agreement despite the fact of no interaction.

But need we depart from the assumption of mutual unconcern? Does not the argument for ignoring those descendants whose lives do not overlap with our own in effect ignore the real significance of generational overlap? The generations of humankind do not march on and off the stage of life in a body, with but one generation on stage at any time. Each person interacts with others both older and younger than himself, and enters thereby into a continuous thread of interaction extending from the most remote human past to the farthest future of our kind. Mutually beneficial co-operation directly involves persons of different but overlapping generations, but this creates indirect co-operative links extending throughout history. Each person, in considering the terms on which he is to co-operate with those in an earlier generation than himself, must keep in mind his need to establish similar terms with those of a later generation, who in turn must keep in mind their need to co-operate with members of a yet later generation, and so on. Thus, although each individual might be prepared to agree with his contemporaries that they should exhaust the world's resources without thought for those yet to be born, the need to continue any agreement as time passes, to extend it to those who are born as it ceases for those who die, ensures that, among rational persons, the terms must remain constant, so that exhaustion of the world's resources does not present itself as an option. No matter when one lives, one should expect the same relative benefits from interaction with one's fellows as were enjoyed by one's predecessors and as will be enjoyed in turn by one's successors.

Let us begin, then, from our assumption of mutual unconcern, and ask what conditions govern the transfer of rights of jurisdiction and ownership from persons to their temporal successors, and what conditions govern the terms of co-operative arrangements in which it is expected that participants will be replaced by their descendants.

[16] See Edmund Burke, *Reflections on the Revolution in France* (London, 1790); intro. A. J. Grieve (London, 1910), p. 93.

Specifically, let us consider the conditions governing inheritance and investment.

6.2 Problems of inheritance may seem to be dissolved by the assumption of mutual unconcern.[17] A person who takes literally no interest in her fellows and their interests must be entirely indifferent as to what befalls her possessions and privileges when she is no longer able to derive benefit from them. During her lifetime she will arrange for their disposition in whatever way maximizes her present utility. She will contract with others for rights that she may use and enjoy while alive in return for rights that will pass to them at her death. Should she fail to dispose of all of her possessions and privileges in this way, then at her death they will return to an unowned condition. They will be available for appropriation by others. Since the existence of such unowned goods is likely to cause inconvenience within society, we may suppose that some procedure for their disposition will be established that, if it satisfies minimax relative concession, will afford each member of society an equivalent share in the expected benefit from these goods. Inheritance as such will not exist; it is not a practice that fully mutually unconcerned persons would have reason to institute or to accept.

Let us approach inheritance from a more realistic perspective. We suppose, as is clearly the case, that most persons are concerned with the disposition of their privileges and possessions, that most, indeed, wish to share with spouses and provide for offspring. Mutual unconcern obtains, not between the parties to the relationship constituted by bequest and inheritance, but between the members of society for whom an acceptable practice of inheritance is to be defined, so that each may recognize the transfer of rights that it involves. What rights must persons, who take no interest in either the individual making a bequest or the individual receiving an inheritance, rationally recognize?

Have we not answered this question in our account of legitimate appropriation? If an individual acquires a right to the exclusive use of a certain piece of land, or some other good, or a right to the exclusive exercise of some privilege, then surely she is entitled to dispose of that right as she pleases, and so to bequeath it to another person at death. But matters are not so simple. We have asserted

[17] For an earlier discussion of inheritance, relevant to but partially superseded by the present treatment, see my 'Economic Rationality and Moral Constraints', *Midwest Studies in Philosophy* 3 (1978), pp. 84–8.

that rights are temporally open-ended, but we have not defended this assertion. We have supposed that rights are transferable, but may there not be limits on the admissible modes of transfer? An individual's rights constitute her endowment for market and co-operative interaction. She is then entitled to exchange her rights in the market, or in co-operative practices. It does not follow that she is entitled to dispose of her rights in other ways, such as gift or bequest. Perhaps no one is entitled to acquire a right, except by initial appropriation where there is no previous right-holder, or by a market transaction in which the previous holder receives payment or compensation. We might then envisage a society in which rights expire with their holder, and may be disposed of only by market exchange—or by abandonment, in which case the possession or privilege is reallocated by some social procedure satisfying minimax relative concession. Once more, inheritance does not exist.

However, we do not suppose that rational persons would reject temporally open-ended rights that may be disposed of, not only by market exchange, but also by gift or bequest as the holder wishes. For it is evident that the desire to acquire land and other goods that may be passed on to one's offspring has been a powerful motivating factor in the productive activities that have increased material well-being and expanded the range of individual opportunities. The individual who claims a permanent and bequeathable right in some good may then be benefiting herself by invoking a practice which redounds to the expected advantage of everyone. The argument we offered to support the individual appropriation of land and other goods in VII.4.1 may be extended to ground a right of bequest.

The right to dispose of one's possessions by gift or bequest is not an integral part of the right to the exclusive use of those possessions that is required for market and co-operative interaction. Its rationale depends on a concern with the disposition of one's goods that presupposes taking an interest in particular other persons. And this presupposition is foreign to the market and unnecessary for co-operation. But its rationale is addressed to persons who are mutually unconcerned. I recognize your right to bequeath your possessions as you please, even though I may take no interest in you, because the practice of bequest satisfies the proviso, in enabling those who engage in it to benefit without in any way taking advantage of their fellows.

But if bequest is not to run foul of the proviso, it must observe certain limits. For each person's inheritance constitutes a significant component of her initial factor endowment, and the extent of an individual's endowment affects, not only the opportunities she enjoys, but also the opportunities available to others. Consider a community of small landowners, all of whom benefit from the stimulus to production that arises from private holdings, and from the limited specialization and resulting exchanges that their holdings make possible. Suppose, for whatever reason, that all of the landowners choose to leave their property to one man, whose charismatic personality (and promise to them of reward in heaven) has charmed them all. His inheritance would make him a monopolist in land, leaving others in the position of landless labourers. A right to such an extensive holding—to all of the arable land of the community—would seem clearly to violate the proviso. The right of bequest must not be so extensive as to afford any individual an inheritance that she could not acquire in some other way without restricting the opportunities or reducing the well-being of her fellows.

The acceptable limits of inheritance are not subject to a priori determination. If the right of bequest does not serve as a stimulus to production, adding to the expected benefits of all members of the community, we may suppose that inheritances will be more narrowly circumscribed than if the desire to provide for one's offspring is a strong motive to the individual investment of time and effort. We must be content here with such general conclusions, which indicate how, on our theory, problems about the rights of bequest and inheritance are resolved.

6.3 The problem of the rational rate of investment—of savings from present production to increase future production—receives a very clear solution from our theory, based on the representation of society as an ongoing bargain or agreement among mutually unconcerned persons.[18] One of the core components in social progress, as we noted in 5.1, is the per capita increase in the supply of material goods. Assuming that investment is productive, so that there is a positive rate of accumulation rather than a negative rate, or positive rate of depletion, then this progress is achieved by investing a portion of present production as capital for future production rather

[18] For previous discussions, see my 'The Social Contract: Individual Decision or Collective Bargain?', *Philosophy and Public Affairs* 6 (1977), pp. 63–5, and 'Social Choice and Distributive Justice', *Philosophia* 7 (1978), pp. 249–50.

than using it for present consumption. But if this increases the future supply of consumable goods, it does so by diminishing the present supply. Those who save to provide capital for future production would then do better, in terms of their own utilities, were they to consume instead. Since saving makes more goods available in the future than could be provided at present, it constitutes a transfer from those with fewer goods to those with more. On the face of it such a transfer would seem to violate the principle of minimax relative concession. Hence our theory would seem to require a zero rate of investment, and thereby would deny the rationality of choosing social progress.

But this is not so. Let us consider the terms of a rational bargain among persons in different generations. The initial bargaining position may be supposed to be the same, to whatever generation one belongs. For this position is determined by state-of-nature interaction constrained by the proviso. And we may assume that the state of nature affords roughly constant expectations to individuals over time, given that the members of each generation are protected by the proviso from activities of their predecessors that would deplete the resources available to them and curtail their opportunities. Thus we take individual differences in the pay-offs of the initial bargaining position to reflect factors that are not temporally dependent. The initial position of the average individual is the same, to whichever generation she may belong.

But the maximum claim that each may rationally advance is time dependent. Each person's maximum claim is her greatest possible return from co-operation, given that others receive at least what they would expect from state-of-nature interaction constrained by the proviso. Thus if one is a member of the initial generation, one's claim is based on the fruits of social interaction among the members of that generation, and on nothing else. If one is a member of the second generation, then one's claim is based on the fruits of social interaction among the members of one's own generation, and also on the fruits of the investment, by the initial generation, of their entire co-operative surplus—of what they could produce over and above what they would have expected in the absence of co-operation. If one is a member of the third generation, then one's claim is based on the fruits of interaction among the members of one's own generation, and also on the fruits of the investment, by the first two generations, of their entire co-operative surplus. And so on, so that as long as investment is productive, the members of each generation may advance greater maximum claims than the members of preceding generations.

Applying the principle of minimax relative concession to the maximum claims, and assuming the invariance of the initial bargaining position, we find of course that the members of each generation receive more, in absolute terms, than did their predecessors. In a bargain among generations, there is no single, transferable good to be shared among all, but instead there is a steadily increasing good to be shared in proportionately equal amounts. Members of each generation receive the same proportion of their claim as did their predecessors and as will their successors, but the productivity of investment guarantees continuing enrichment.

The rational rate of investment is thus determined by applying minimax relative concession to claims based on the rate of possible accumulation. We may compare this solution to those offered by the principle of maximin absolute well-being, and the utilitarian principle of maximum average well-being. Although in many circumstances these alternative principles lead to identical prescriptions, yet here their applications differ markedly, and our own position falls between them.

To maximize the minimum level of absolute well-being one would prohibit any transfer from those with fewer goods to those with more. Hence one would prohibit any saving by the initial generation; they must consume all of the goods which they produce. But then each generation is in the position of the initial generation; each must consume all that it produces, since otherwise it would have less so that others might have more. Or rather, each must save only to the extent necessary to counteract any depletion of resources, since each generation must leave its successors as favourably placed as itself. In maximizing the minimum level of absolute well-being we should invoke the proviso, but there would be no inter-generational co-operation, and the rational rate of investment would normally be zero.[19]

On the other hand, given plausible assumptions about the productive effects of investment, to maximize average well-being over time would require a very high rate of investment. For even given the

[19] To avoid this conclusion, Rawls adjusts his account of motivation, treating persons 'as representing family lines, say, with ties of sentiment between successive generations', *A Theory of Justice*, p. 292.

usual assumption that the utility derived from each unit of a good decreases as one's total wealth increases, a sufficiently high rate of return on investment in terms of goods affords a lower but still positive rate of return in terms of utilities. Since individuals have no entitlements in themselves, the utilitarian may find herself as the advocate of restricting current consumption to whatever is needed to ensure maximum productivity, and eschewing all present luxury, the costs to present persons being outweighed in her calculations by the much greater eventual benefits to future persons.

Between these extremes, our theory, equalizing relative rather than absolute benefits, requires progress without ignoring the claims of present persons. Viewing society as a bargain in which the terms remain constant over time, so that each generation offers its successor the same agreement that it accepted from its predecessor, we are able to give a clear account of justice between generations.

X

THE RING OF GYGES

1.1 The story is familiar.[1] It is said that Gyges, king of Lydia, possessed a ring which, should its collet be turned, made its wearer invisible. Gyges' ancestor had been a shepherd, servant to the then king. One day, while he was tending his flock, a great storm occurred; the earth opened and the shepherd descended to a cavern where he saw a bronze horse, hollow with an opening in its body containing a giant corpse wearing a gold ring. The shepherd took the ring for himself. Later, meeting with his fellow shepherds, he happened by chance to turn the collet of the ring, and became invisible to them; turning the collet again, he was once more visible. Realizing the power this gave him, the shepherd contrived to be one of the messengers reporting to the king on the flocks. With the power to make himself unseen at will, he found his way to the queen's bed; her satisfaction with this encounter induced her to join him in a rather different errand to the king's chamber. And so the shepherd established himself and his descendants on the throne of Lydia.

The moral of this story is pointed for us by Glaucon, in expounding the thesis that injustice is superior to justice, which he wants Socrates to refute.

> Now if there were two such rings, and the just man would put one on, and the unjust man the other, no one, as it would seem, would be so adamant as to stick by justice and bring himself to keep away from what belongs to others and not lay hold of it, although he had license to take what he wanted from the market without fear, and to go into houses and have intercourse with whomever he wanted, and to slay or release from bonds whomever he wanted, and to do other things as an equal to a god among humans. And in so doing, one would act no differently from the other, but both would go the same way.[2]

The ring puts its wearer outside the circumstances of justice. And these are the circumstances of weakness. As Glaucon argues before telling the story,

[1] *Republic*, 359c–360b.

[2] Ibid., 360b-c; trans. A. Bloom, p. 38.

They say that doing injustice is naturally good, and suffering injustice bad, but that the bad in suffering injustice far exceeds the good in doing it; so that, when they do injustice to one another and suffer it and taste of both, it seems profitable—to those who are not able to escape the one and choose the other—to set down a compact among themselves neither to do injustice nor to suffer it. . . . And this . . . is the genesis and being of justice; it is a mean between what is best—doing injustice without paying the penalty—and what is worst—suffering injustice without being able to avenge oneself. The just is in the middle between these two, cared for not because it is good but because it is honored due to a want of vigor in doing injustice. The man who is able to do it and is truly a man would never set down a compact with anyone not to do injustice and not to suffer it. He'd be mad.[3]

Glaucon's problem is not our familiar Prisoner's Dilemma. Indeed, he supposes that persons agree to justice as a response to Prisoner's Dilemma-type situations in which each would lose more at the hands of others than she could gain at their expense. But Glaucon insists that a person has reason to agree to the constraints of justice only because of her weakness, manifested in her inability to take net advantage of others. The truly strong person would reject not only compliance but co-operation itself, ignoring both Hobbes's third law of nature, that men perform their covenants, and his second law, that each lay down some portion of her initially unlimited right of nature provided others do so as well. Possessed of the ring, the shepherd finds no benefit in agreement with his fellows.

It may seem that what Glaucon says about justice, we must say about morality. It is a mean between what is best—bettering one's situation at whatever cost to others, and what is worst—having one's situation worsened at others' pleasure. We care for morality, not for its own sake, but because we lack the strength to dominate our fellows or the self-sufficiency to avoid interaction with them. The person who could secure her ends either independently of others or by subordinating them would never agree to the constraints of morality. She would be irrational—mad.

That a rational morality is a necessary evil would seem to be confirmed by the arguments of both Hobbes and Hume. For Hobbes, the laws of nature, the 'true and onely Moral Philosophy' as he calls them, are the basis of all constraint;[4] it is the second law that tells us to give up some portion of our initial, unlimited natural

[3] Ibid., 358e–359b, pp. 36–7.
[4] Hobbes, *Leviathan*, ch. 15, p. 79.

right. But as Hobbes notes, 'Seeing all men by Nature had Right to All things, they had Right every one to reigne over all the rest. But ... it concerned the safety of every one, laying by that Right, to set up men ... by common consent, to rule and defend them: whereas if there had been any man of Power Irresistible; there had been no reason, why he should not by that Power have ruled, and defended both himselfe, and them, according to his own discretion.'[5] This, Hobbes insists, is the basis of God's sovereignty over men—a point worth keeping in mind to relate to the idea that the ring of Gyges conveys the power 'to do other things as an equal to a god among humans'. But our immediate concern is with the implications of Hobbes's argument for morality. As a type of constraint, it is clear that it has no rational claim on those with power sufficient to dominate their fellows; such persons have no reason to give up any portion of their unlimited permissive right, or their adherence to straightforward maximization.

Although Hume bases morality on the sympathetic and so tuistic feelings of persons, yet his account of justice falls into the contractarian tradition.[6] Each person's primary obligation to justice is founded on interest; where this interest is lacking, justice has no place. Hume notes that

> Were there a species of creatures intermingled with men, which, though rational, were possessed of such inferior strength, both of body and mind, that they were incapable of all resistance, and could never, upon the highest provocation, make us feel the effects of their resentment; the necessary consequences ... is that we ... should not, properly speaking, lie under any restraint of justice with regard to them.... Our intercourse with them could not be called society, which supposes a degree of equality; but absolute command on the one side, and servile obedience on the other.... as no inconvenience ever results from the exercise of a power, so firmly established in nature, the restraints of justice and property, being totally *useless*, would never have place in so unequal a confederacy.[7]

Hume further notes that justice depends on individual insufficiency, on the need that persons have for each other.

> Were the human species so framed by nature as that each individual possessed within himself every faculty, requisite both for his own preservation and for the propagation of his kind ... It seems evident, that so solitary

[5] Ibid., ch. 31, p. 187.

[6] See my 'David Hume, Contractarian', *Philosophial Review* 88 (1979), pp. 3–38.

[7] Hume, *Enquiry*, iii. i, pp. 190–1.

a being would be as much incapable of justice, as of social discourse and conversation. Where mutual regards and forbearance serve to no manner of purpose, they would never direct the conduct of any reasonable man. . . . And as each man is here supposed to love himself alone, and to depend only on himself and his own activity for safety and happiness, he would, on every occasion . . . challenge the preference above every other being, to none of which he is bound by any ties, either of nature or of interest.[8]

Hume rejects any conception of practical rationality. But where he speaks of interest, we may speak of reason. We may then reinterpret Hume as spelling out Glaucon's thesis in more detail, insisting that a rational morality requires the relative equality and individual insufficiency of those constrained by it. We are dependent on others whom we cannot master; we should then accommodate ourselves to them. But in realizing this, we realize also that we are less than the beings we should wish to be. As a remedy for and reminder of human weakness, morality can have no deep hold on human beings. If this harsh conclusion does not emerge in Hume, it is only because he accepts an affective morality, based on the sympathetic transmission of feelings from one person to another. But such a morality has no basis in utility-maximizing rationality.

Morality as a necessary evil will not invite the reverence thought fitting by Kant, but will it not do its job none the less?[9] In seeking to be persuaded that justice should be prized for its own sake, was not Glaucon asking to be deceived? Perhaps he was. But we shall find that the idea that morality reflects only human weakness and insufficiency subverts its role in making possible society as 'a cooperative venture for mutual advantage'. Fortunately, we shall also find that morality is misrepresented in Glaucon's tale and its seeming confirmation in the arguments of Hobbes and Hume. In the final chapter of our enquiry we shall link morals by agreement positively to our conception of ideal human beings as liberal individuals.

1.2 Glaucon portrays justice as a conventional, social imposition on nature. He speaks of persons as doing and suffering injustice prior to accepting the constraints that constitute justice, but more correctly he should say that, although persons naturally do what will come to be counted unjust, originally they stand outside all moral constraint where, as Hobbes says, 'The notions of . . . Justice

[8] Ibid., iii. i, pp. 191–2.

[9] See Kant's paean to duty in *Critique of Practical Reason*, pp. 86–9.

and Injustice have ... no place.'[10] If morality is a matter of agreement, then prior to agreement nothing is either just or unjust. For Glaucon, natural man is pre-social and pre-moral. And it is from the standpoint of this pre-social, pre-moral being that morality appears a necessary evil.

Alasdair MacIntyre insists that the conception of natural man 'suffers from a fatal internal incoherence'.[11] The terms used to characterize this allegedly pre-social creature, such as 'selfish' and 'aggressive', 'are defined in terms of established norms of behavior', and so constitute 'a vocabulary drawn from social life'. MacIntyre supposes that Glaucon, and the Sophistic tradition for which Glaucon speaks, confuse Homeric society with nature, and the Homeric hero, the *agathos*, with natural man. Glaucon does not evaluate morality from the standpoint of nature, but rather he evaluates one morality, that of the fifth-century *polis*, from the standpoint of another, that of the *agathos*.

Our concern is not with the historical accuracy of MacIntyre's charge. For him, as for us, Glaucon plays an illustrative and representative role. MacIntyre claims that Western moral philosophy has repeatedly committed the Sophistic error of supposing that there is an extra-moral standpoint, natural or rational, from which morality can be grasped and either defended or attacked.[12] We shall deny this. But our denial will invite MacIntyre to press a second charge—that the attempt to use natural man as an Archimedean point in moral theory endangers the point of the moral enterprise.

To show that the idea of natural man is, at least in principle, a coherent one, we should begin by noting that in characterizing a being as asocial, we are concerned, not with her origins, but with her motivations and values. Human beings are language-using animals, and it has been claimed that language is necessarily a social product, at least to the extent that its use requires the internalization of a set of conventions. Without entering into the complex issues raised by this claim, let us simply grant that human beings are necessarily 'conventionalized'. Our question is then whether the conventions that enter into the make-up of a person must introduce any element of sociality into either her valuation or her motivations. And it seems clear that they need not.

[10] Hobbes, *Leviathan*, ch. 13, p. 63.

[11] A. MacIntyre, *A Short History of Ethics* (New York, 1966), p. 18.

[12] See ibid.

The condition for asocial valuation is simply non-tuism; the non-tuist takes no interest in the interests of those with whom he interacts. His utility function, measuring his preferences, is strictly independent of the utility functions of those whom he affects. But non-tuism does not ensure asocial motivation. Even if one takes no interest in others' interests, one may take an interest in states of affairs that cannot be specified except with reference to others. The condition for asocial motivation is nicely defined by Michael Laver; we allow 'only those assumptions about the motivations of individuals which can be precisely defined with reference to a single individual'.[13] Thus in accounting for the motivation of person *x*, we may refer only to those features of states of affairs that involve *x* and no one else.

Asociality does not require that all motivation meet this strict condition. We may allow socially defined secondary motives. In a world in which resources are scarce, so that the aggregate demand for many goods exceeds their total supply, the asocial person may be led to an instrumentally selfish and aggressive stance in relation to others. She may seek to dominate others as the best way to assure herself the supply of asocially-characterized goods that meet her needs. But her aggressiveness is to be understood, in the same way as any other social disposition, as purely instrumental to her more basic, non-tuistic and asocial concerns.

MacIntyre may then be right to insist that natural man must be characterized in a vocabulary drawn from social life. In so far as natural man interacts with her fellows, she will exhibit certain social dispositions. But if these dispositions are based strictly on her secondary motives, then they are compatible with her underlying asociality. She does not suffer from a fatal internal incoherence.

The challenge to moral convention that is posed by natural man does not assume a conflict between different moral or social standards, as MacIntyre supposes when he insists that the Sophists appeal to the standpoint of the *agathos* to undermine the morality of the *polis*. Rather, the challenge is implicit in the idea that sociality is a matter of convention, so that what is revealed when all social practices and institutions are removed is a being asocial in motivation and non-tuistic in values. MacIntyre claims that 'the sophists . . . failed to distinguish . . . the difference between the concept of a

[13] M. Laver, *The Politics of Private Desires* (Harmondsworth, Middx., 1981), p. 13.

man who stands outside and is able to question the conventions of some one given social order and the concept of a man who stands outside social life as such.'[14] But in fact the Sophists grasped, for the first time in human thought, the standpoint of a person who does stand outside social life, not in her capacities, not in being able to live without society, but in her motivations, in being able to view society as purely instrumental to goals that do not require social life for their formulation. If MacIntyre is correct to see the Sophistic natural man as the Homeric hero, then the Sophists found, by abstracting from the social circumstances of the *agathos*, the basis for their radical challenge to the very idea of a moral order.

But although MacIntyre rejects the conceptual coherence of the Sophists' core insight, he seems to understand it and to grasp its implications with great acuity. For he realizes that the Sophistic argument does more than represent morality as a necessary evil reluctantly accepted by those unable either to dominate their fellows or to live without them. Rather, MacIntyre argues, the Sophist portrays morality as a smoke-screen, a device by which the clever are able to free themselves from the very constraints that it seems to impose.

MacIntyre notes,

> Natural man portrayed in Thrasymachean guise [and it will be remembered that Glaucon takes up Thrasymachus' argument] has two main characteristics. His psychological make-up is simple: he is out to get what he wants, and what he wants is narrowly circumscribed. Power and pleasure are his exclusive interests. But to get what he wants this wolf has to wear the sheep's clothing of the conventional moral values. His masquerade can only be carried through by putting the conventional moral vocabulary to the service of his private purposes. He must say . . . what people want to hear, so that they will put power into his hands. Thus . . . [he must] learn the craft . . . of molding people by rhetoric. He must take them by the ear before he takes them by the throat.[15]

Treating morality as the product of agreement among asocial persons may seem to represent it as a necessary evil. MacIntyre paints a darker picture. Not only may the clever cast off morality's chains, but they may use them to fetter their fellows. Morality may seem to make reluctant co-operators of us all. In fact it divides us into foxes and gulls.

1.3 There are circumstances in which it is rational for one person

[14] MacIntyre, p. 18. [15] Ibid.

to take advantage of another. Reason and justice there part company, leaving justice with no hold on the non-tuistic individual. This much we conceded to Hobbes's Foole in VII.5.2, but we limited our concession by insisting that the separation of justice and reason results from a lack of equal rationality among persons. And we claimed that this lack is accidental. But perhaps this is too easy an escape from the Foole's hold. Perhaps the lack of equal rationality is contrived by those who see the prospect of preserving their unjust advantages beneath a moral façade.

The idea that a contractarian morality invites use as an instrument of domination is introduced by Jean-Jacques Rousseau in his *Discours sur l'inégalité*. Beginning from an essentially Hobbesian state of nature, he argues that

> The rich especially soon came to feel the disadvantages of a perpetual war in which they bore all the costs, for although everyone risked his life, they risked also their goods. . . . Lacking reasons adequate to justify himself and forces sufficient to defend himself . . . the rich man, spurred by necessity, finally conceived the most profound project ever to enter the human mind: to employ in his favour the very forces that attacked him, to make defenders of his adversaries. . . . 'Let us unite', he said to them, 'to protect the weak from oppression, to restrain the ambitious, and to give each secure possession of what belongs to him: let us institute rules of justice and peace to which all shall be obliged to conform, excepting no one, and which will compensate to some degree for the caprices of fortune, in placing powerful and weak alike under mutual duties.' . . . Such was, or might well have been, the origin of society and of laws, putting new fetters on the weak and conferring new powers on the rich . . . establishing forever the law of property and inequality, converting a clever usurpation into an irrevocable right, and, for the benefit of the ambitious few, subjecting from that time forth all humankind to work, to slavery, and to misery.[16]

Agreement institutes a society of unequals in which wealth confers power and ultimately mastery. In accepting constraints, the rich acquire an instrument of domination and the poor are subjected to an instrument of suppression. One may question the rationality of the poor in disposing themselves to comply with such constraints. But rationality itself becomes a privilege of the dominant, who then rationally encourage the irrationality of their fellows.

We claimed in Chapter VII that when justice and reason part

[16] Jean-Jacques Rousseau, *Discours sur l'inégalité*, 1755, in *The Political Writings*, ed. C. E. Vaughan, 2 vols. (Cambridge, 1915), vol. i, pp. 180–1; my translation.

company, the cause is to be found either in false views of the world and the practices and institutions to which such views give rise, or in the accidental technological differences between societies. Either cause leads to the unequal rationality that prevents justice. Following Rousseau's account, which echoes many of the Sophists' ideas, we must ask whether these causes are not rationally maintained by those who are then able to dominate their fellows. Not only is contractarian morality available for use as an instrument of domination, but reason endorses this use.

In an important critique of instrumental rationality, Mary Gibson argues that those who can undermine the rationality of others rationally should do so. She claims that 'in a competitive society, it is, in general, in the interests of each person to be as rational as possible but to have his or her competitors be as irrational as possible (within certain limits, of course). It is in the interests of capitalists ... to keep workers from recognizing and acting effectively upon their interests.... Hence we have a system in which persons have an interest in seeing that the optimum conditions for rationality are *not* met.'[17]

Were optimum conditions for rationality met, then, following our earlier argument, coercion would be needed were one individual or group to maintain an unfair advantage over others. The long-term costs of coercion, both those directly incurred in maintaining an apparatus of repression, and those opportunity costs arising from the loss of occasions for co-operation, are likely to outweigh its benefits. But if some persons or groups can be encouraged to behave irrationally, failing either to recognize their interests or effectively to pursue them, then a less overtly coercive order can be maintained in which advantage is readily taken.

Gibson claims that a competitive society is 'a system in which various kinds of deception are in the interests of persons who are in a position to carry out such deceptions on a rather large scale'.[18] Not only are persons deceived about their interests and the products that may meet their interests, but the deceivers deceive themselves 'concerning the fact that [they are] doing these things'. This self-deception we may identify with the maintenance of an ideology in which the unfairness of practices is concealed from both victims and beneficiaries. The result is that 'the availability of accurate infor-

[17] Mary Gibson, 'Rationality', *Philosophy and Public Affairs* 6 (1977), p. 218.
[18] Ibid.

mation reported in an intelligible and non-misleading way, which is essential to the effective carrying out of a rational life-plan, is also undermined'.

To the extent to which this ideological concealment is effective, we may suppose that the idea of morals by agreement, the idea of society as a co-operative venture for fair mutual advantage, masks the reality of a society based on the false agreement sketched by Rousseau. Those who are not deceived by the façade, and who are in favoured positions, may see themselves as able to avoid the constraints of morality. To them morality will appear, not as the price to be paid for effective co-operation, but only as a constraint to be accepted by those insufficiently strong or clever to do better for themselves. And this brings us back to the thesis stated by Glaucon. Among equals, morality would be a necessary evil. But in the real world morality is an instrument of domination, representing as equal what is not, and as mutual constraint what is one-sided oppression. Justice is conventionally acknowledged to be superior to injustice, and indeed, a society of unjust persons must do worse than a society of just persons. But the strong and clever person, recognizing the natural superiority of successful and unrequited injustice, is able to use the moral beliefs of her fellows as a means for freeing herself from the constraints they impose.

Rousseau and Gibson seem to confirm the insight of the Sophists. If morality is represented as a conventional constraint on the natural mode of human behaviour, as a necessary evil rather than as integral to human good, then any genuine adherence to morality is undermined. At first one may suppose that there is no kicking against the pricks—that to get what one wants, given one's weakness and insufficiency, requires interaction with others, and advantageous interaction requires constraint. But then one may come to believe that one is not so weak as may seem. One can manipulate others, encouraging them to act in ways favourable to one's own interests, although unfavourable to theirs did they but understand them. And more important, one can use the very language of constraint as one's instrument for freeing oneself. Where naked self-interest would condemn one, the veneer of morality enables one to take advantage of others in the guise of co-operating with them. Taking them by the ear before one takes them by the throat may be too crude; one takes them by the ear merely to turn their heads.

2.1 Morals by agreement, it has been said (for I have said it), are the morals of economic man.[19] And economic man is the natural man of our time. His motivation is most succinctly expressed in the word of Samuel Gompers, whose reply to what labour demanded was 'More!'[20] Economic man, whether capitalist or worker, is an indefinite appropriator, seeking to subdue more and more of the world to his power exercised in the service of his preferences.

Economic man is properly a theoretical entity, entering into our best theories for conceptualizing and explaining human interaction. But it is not his explanatory role that is of concern here. For economic man has entered into the ground of our self-consciousness, of the way in which we, heirs to a tradition of social thought that has matured in western Europe and America since the seventeenth century, understand ourselves. I have argued elsewhere that our belief in economic man, or in human beings as radically contractarian, runs deeper than our conscious disavowals; economic man is a caricature, or distortion, who has come more and more to shape our reality.[21]

But as the heir of the Homeric *agathos*, economic man sees the moral and political orders as conventional constraints, curbing the natural expression of his desires. The rational defence of these constraints reveals them to be necessary evils, and, as we have argued in the preceding section of this chapter, the natural response to what is claimed to be a necessary evil is to make it unnecessary. As the morality of economic man, morals by agreement are a sham.

Were the conception of economic man our last word about ourselves, morality would have a precarious future. For moral constraints can have no hold on those who see in them only instruments of domination. Their honeyed words proving of no avail, economic men and women would have no choice but to take their fellows by the throat. Suppose it granted that our argument in earlier chapters is sound, so that relative to certain conditions, relating to both our circumstances and our dispositions, the rationality of moral constraints is fully demonstrated. Yet it may be that the very characteristics of human nature that enter into the grounding of these constraints, serve also to undermine the conditions under which compliance with them would be rational. It may seem that we

[19] 'Reason and Maximization', *Canadian Journal of Philosophy* 4 (1975), p. 433.

[20] See G. Seldes, *The Great Quotations* (New York, 1966), p. 285.

[21] See 'The Social Contract as Ideology', *Philosophy and Public Affairs* 6 (1977), esp. pp. 135–8.

need moral constraints because of our asociality and non-tuism, but that, being asocial and non-tuistic, we act to bring about circumstances in which the alleged impartiality of these constraints is an imposture. And if the imposture is recognized, the constraints cease to be effective. This, we might suppose, is very close to the deep message of both Plato and Rousseau. Socrates charms Glaucon; he does not answer him.[22]

Have we, then, developed an account of morality that rests on a conception of human nature that in turn makes the morality chimerical? We shall deny this. Our theory of morality, although it makes use of the idea of economic man, is not committed to that idea as a full and adequate account of human nature. Economic man remains a caricature, albeit a useful one for both explanatory and normative purposes. Morals by agreement would afford economic man a beneficial constraint, if only he could be constrained. Because we real human beings share some of his characteristics, morals by agreement afford us a beneficial constraint, and because we are nevertheless not economic men and women, we can be constrained. Morality does not undermine itself.

So we shall argue. But it will be well to keep in mind that here argument is not enough. In so far as the idea of economic man is part of our way of understanding ourselves, part of our idea of what it is to be human, and in so far as this idea persists even in the face of conscious disavowal, then the rational bonds of morals by agreement may be too weak to hold us. We need exorcism in addition to argument. But that I have no power to provide. We shall sketch the distinctive features of economic man, showing what moral and social capacities he lacks. Then, in the concluding chapter, we shall incorporate what he lacks into the idea of the *liberal individual*. We shall argue that the liberal individual is capable of essential justice, so that for him morality is not a necessary evil, far less an instrument of domination. We shall sketch briefly the idea of an essentially just society, which encourages free affectivity and individualistic community. That both the liberal individual and the essentially just society are problematic and threatened ideas will, however, provide a more sombre note in our conclusion.

2.2 Economic man seeks more. But 'more' is ambiguous; we may suppose that economic man seeks either more than what he himself initially has, or more than what his fellows have. The person

[22] An interpretation of the *Republic* lurks here, but this is not the occasion for it.

who seeks more than her fellows, who would outdo them, is not asocial in her motivation. If outdoing others is among her primary or intrinsic goals, then she is motivated by Rousseauean *amour propre*.[23] And as Rousseau argues, such a person must not be identified with natural, asocial man, for she exists only in her relation to others, taking indeed her very sense of self from that relation.[24] If economic man is the true heir of the Sophists' natural man, then his concern to outdo others can only be derivative. In seeking more, he seeks more than what he himself now has.

Economic man is an appropriator. His fundamental relation to things is that expressed in Genesis, to subdue and have dominion over them.[25] Although individual appropriation excludes others, it is not essentially a social relationship; one appropriates most literally and completely what one makes into part of one's body, what one takes as food and drink. Beyond this, one appropriates what one makes one's instrument, available at will to serve one's preference. Persons enter only incidentally; in the presence of others one's appropriation is secure only if their use of what is appropriated is subject to one's will.

Appropriation has no natural upper bound. Economic man seeks more. But appropriation, as other activities, exhibits the principle of diminishing marginal utility; the more one appropriates, the less the benefit and the greater the cost of an additional appropriative act—if not in every case, yet in general. A cost/benefit analysis determines the effective extent of economic man's appropriations.

We must not suppose that economic man has either metaphysical or moral scruples against appropriating other persons. But he may find them not only recalcitrant to his appropriative activity, but eager to appropriate him in turn. Appropriation expresses one-sided instrumentality; where this is infeasible the favoured habitat of economic man is the perfectly competitive market. For the market is the locus of interactions undertaken voluntarily by persons lacking all tuistic motivation. Market interactions are a network of contractual arrangements, and this network is itself founded on an overall social contract, expressive of the two-sided instrumentality that constitutes society from the standpoint of economic man. Market 'competitors', we must remember, are neither enemies nor friends;

[23] See Rousseau, *Discours sur l'inégalité*, note o, p. 217.
[24] See ibid., p. 195.
[25] See Genesis 1: 28.

they have no natural concern with each other, but only the artificial, instrumental concern expressed in contract.

The characterization of the market as competitive is perhaps unfortunate. For 'competition' suggests a zero-sum situation in which a gain for one person entails a loss for another. But as we noted in Chapter IV, in the perfectly competitive market each person must expect to improve his condition. The underlying idea of the market is not that of a game. The market is the framework of asocial rather than of opposed interaction; it is an optimal environment for those who must engage in mutually instrumental interaction. And awareness of this environment distinguishes economic man from his predecessors; as we shall see, society offers him more than protection against his fellows.

In relating to other persons within the context of the market, economic man exhibits a *radically contractarian* view of human relationships. With respect to the things that he can dominate, that he can treat instrumentally without being treated instrumentally in return, economic man is an appropriator; with respect to the persons whom he cannot dominate, whom he can treat instrumentally only if he lets himself be treated instrumentally in turn, he is a contractarian.

Economic man is a radical contractarian in that all of his free or non-coercive interpersonal relationships are contractual. For him, voluntary social relationships require a rationale; contract provides it. The idea underlying contract, that persons who take no interest in one another's interests may nevertheless be able to interact in a mutually advantageous and therefore voluntarily acceptable manner, is, as we have noted, one of the great liberating ideas in human history, freeing persons from the requirement that they be affectively dependent on their fellows. But economic man carries this liberation to its full extreme; his exclusively asocial motivation precludes voluntary non-contractual interpersonal relationships. He is not only freed from compulsory affective dependence; he is incapable of voluntary affection.

Hobbes offers the most unified and compelling psychological portrayal of economic man.[26] But the society that with matchless consistency he generates from purely asocial motivations, is primarily an instrument for cutting the costs of human interaction, for

[26] See C. B. Macpherson's introduction to *Leviathan* (Harmondsworth, Middx., 1968), pp. 30–9.

eliminating the hostility found in the natural condition of humankind. It is true that when Hobbes catalogues the ills of this natural condition, he refers to the lack of arts, letters and society (that is social intercourse), of commodious building, navigation, and mechanical contrivances, but the emphasis is on the shortness and nastiness of life. Hobbes had little sense of the positive benefits of interaction, and no sense at all, or so it would seem, of the progressive benefits—of the prospect of, not merely an improved lot, but a continually improving lot, for human beings in a condition of society.

The psychological grasp of asociality implicit in Hobbes's argument is thus not matched by a comparable degree of social or economic insight. And those later thinkers, following in the wake of Adam Smith, who grasped the idea of social progress, failed to equal Hobbes in the consistency with which they portrayed economic man. The result has been to obscure the implications of asocial motivation for the stability of social institutions and practices.

When Rousseau writes of the agreement that institutes a society of unequals, he, like Hobbes, ignores the positive and progressive benefits that even an unequal society can effect. Thus he represents the situation of the poor as being actually worsened as a consequence of the new power relationships that society institutes. But it may plausibly be objected that, although the stability brought about by the new rules of 'justice and peace' limits some of the opportunities for individual aggrandizement previously available, yet the net effect on expectations is a positive one. Each person may reasonably expect to do better as a consequence of the benefits of market and co-operative interaction, even if these benefits are not fairly or equitably distributed. If among economic men moral and political constraints come to serve as instruments of domination, perpetuating and strengthening inequalities, yet they may also serve as instruments of improvement.

Thus there is an important difference between economic man and his predecessors. The natural man of Sophistic thought lived in an environment perceived as essentially incapable of improvement. Society itself could bring order into human affairs, and order was itself a great good. But once this good was realized, then as long as the stability of society was not undermined, social interaction constituted a zero-sum game. Gains were at the expense of losses. But in the world of economic man, order is only the first good brought about by society. Although goods are scarce, yet given the appropriate social institutions and practices, human interaction is capable of increasing the supply of goods indefinitely. Every person can then be better off; gains occur without losses.

In so far as moral constraints contribute to the order that underlies progress, morality must appear in a more favourable light than Glaucon's account would imply. Glaucon suggests that moral constraints are accepted as a result of comparing the benefits of inflicting injustice with the costs of suffering injustice. But it is not so much the direct benefits and costs of our actions that are at issue here. Rather, moral constraints are accepted because of the indirect benefits—not the relief from suffering injustice but the gains of interaction within an orderly, stable framework. Constraints on force and fraud make the market possible, but no one suffers injustice simply because it is absent.

Yet, even if morality is more than a necessary evil, it would seem that it is not freed from being an instrument of domination. All that our argument shows is that what lies behind the façade is more than simple, one-sided exploitation—that morality proves to be more than a device to enable one group to benefit at the expense of another. Those who are able to use the language of constraint as their instrument for casting off constraint do not thereby deny their fellows the benefits of order and improvement; they simply ensure that the largest share of those benefits goes to themselves.

2.3 Seeking to dominate and exploit his fellows, economic man may be supposed to try to undermine their rationality. This is, indeed, the burden of Mary Gibson's claim that 'in a competitive society, it is . . . in the interests of each person . . . to have his or her competitors be as irrational as possible'.[27] But this claim is too strong, conceding too much to the zero-sum view of human competition which may have seemed self-evident to Homeric heroes, but which an appreciation of the market has taught economic men to reject. The market, which flourishes only in the absence of force and fraud, makes possible movement through time in a desirable direction, encouraging not merely a static accommodation to given preferences, but also a dynamic and flexible accommodation as both new preferences and new technologies of satisfaction appear. But a high degree of instrumental rationality is needed to grasp the discipline over immediate gratification that is a precondition of this

[27] Gibson, p. 218.

improvement. To be sure, we could imagine beings who cared little or nothing for their future selves, and who would lack use for this discipline, but if we suppose that economic man is motivated by at least a moderate degree of prudence, or long-term self-concern, then he will find it in his interest to interact with persons whose rationality enables them to understand the means to satisfy that prudence. The irrationality of others threatens to set one's plans and endeavours at nought.

Gibson's critique is therefore misstated. But she is right to insist that economic man has a merely instrumental concern with the rationality of others. And this does lead him to seek to undermine in others the full reflective and critical rationality characterized in Chapter II. Where overt coercion is too crude and inefficient an instrument, and honeyed words fail, economic man works others to his will through the manipulation of their preferences, and in so doing, he comes to a view of justice that makes morality an instrument of domination in a deeper sense than we have yet considered.

In extending to economic man the asociality of his predecessors, we must again be careful not to deny the place of society in shaping his asocial and non-tuistic values and motivations. And we must not suppose economic man ignorant of the effects of socialization. He is concerned with society as an instrument or tool for the attainment of personal ends—a tool that he must, like it or not, share with others. But he is aware that, in enabling persons better to attain their asocial ends, social institutions and practices also react on and reshape those ends. Thinking of persons as sets of preferences, represented by utility functions, and sets of capacities and possessions, represented by production functions, economic man is aware that neither utility functions nor production functions are fully fixed, but that both are alterable by the use of the very instrument that serves them.

A just society maximizes minimum relative benefit among its members. If we take the preferences and endowments of individuals as given, then we may use the principles of justice to determine and assess social institutions and practices. But we may proceed in the other direction. We cannot simply take social institutions and practices as given and use the principles of justice to determine individual preferences and endowments, since the social institutions and practices must be supposed to determine preferences and endowments directly, and this determination may or may not satisfy the requirements of justice. Rather, we may ask what social institutions and practices do satisfy the requirements of justice, not by directly maximizing minimum relative benefit for given individuals, but rather by determining individual preferences and endowments in such a way that maximin relative benefit is achieved.

In Aldous Huxley's *Brave New World* we have the exemplar of a society designed to shape individuals so that they fit its institutions and practices, and fulfil the functions required for its survival.[28] Huxley, like most anti-Utopian novelists, arbitrarily introduces a flaw into the socialization procedures, but we may for the moment suppose success. Society proves to be the perfect instrument of its members because it so designs them that they find it their perfect instrument. In the *Republic*, Socrates argues that in the just city, each does that for which she is naturally most fit.[29] The 'brave new world' turns this conception around; it is just because each is made most fit for what she does. We need not suppose that there is a unique society meeting this standard. What any 'brave new world' requires to be just, is the satisfaction of a coherence condition: the preferences and capacities created by the social institutions and practices must be identical with the preferences and capacities best satisfied by those institutions and practices. Let us say that a society that designs its socialization procedures to meet this coherence condition is *artificially just*.

The idea of an artificially just society may seem far removed from the purely instrumental view of society embraced by economic man. Artificial justice may seem to be the perfection of collectivism, of shaping the individual to fit the social whole, whereas economic man is the pure individualist, concerned with society only in so far as it is shaped to satisfy him. Yet in fact the two are closely related. The ideal of social instrumentalism is simply that of perfect fit between individual preferences and social practices. Nothing in the ideal specifies how this fit is to be brought about. Economic man places no value on preferences, except as material for satisfaction. And so he has no intrinsic concern with the manipulation of preferences, or of persons, to fit social practices. Indeed, manipulation is relevant to economic man only from the standpoint of the manipulator. And here we see the evident appeal of artificial justice.

We think of the market as producing goods to satisfy persons. But

[28] See A. Huxley, *Brave New World* (London, 1932).

[29] See *Republic*, 433a–434c.

the advertiser may think of producing persons to be satisfied by goods. Economic man is manifested in the activities of such a manipulative advertiser quite as much as in the activities of the commodity producer. What difference is there between creating a demand for a given supply, and creating a supply for a given demand?

For us, the difference is that the individuals in an artificially just society must lack the capacity to change in certain humanly possible ways. Their preferences must be fixed in two respects—as outputs of social causation and as inputs for social fulfilment. Any variation that would destroy the fit between the two must be eliminated. But we may then question whether these inhabitants of 'brave new world' are fully rational. They act rationally, to maximize their utilities. But are the preferences whose measure they act to maximize fully reflective? Do these persons possess a full self-critical capacity, so that they may subject their preferences to reflective assessment, and alter them, and so their preferentially based behaviour, in the light of that assessment?

If each person may subject her preferences to self-critical reflection without affecting the fair and optimal fulfilment she receives from a given social structure, then 'brave new world' must so shape its members that each reflectively endorses its *status quo*. We need not consider whether this is possible in principle. For we are considering the human design of society and the social design of human beings within the limits of technologically and imaginatively possible experience. And here we may conclude that only by suppressing full reflective rationality can the fit between the preferences socially produced and those socially fulfilled be assured. The flaw in Huxley's *Brave New World*, which we may now non-arbitrarily introduce, is that this capacity to reflect is not sufficiently eliminated.

In so far as society shapes the individual, viewing society as a mere tool leads to considering it as a tool for shaping individuals. As a tool its efficacy is judged from the standpoint of the user. Economic man, judging in terms of his asocial interests, seeks to use the tool, not to produce human beings with reflective rationality, but rather to produce instrumentally rational creatures with preferences satisfied by the tool. The justice he pursues is artificial, the fit of persons to society, and in his pursuit he is rightly seen to threaten the full rationality of his fellows.

2.4 Although economic man finds in society a source of continuing and increasing benefit that was not recognized by his pre-market predecessors, yet his asocial motivation severely restricts the scope of such benefit. For an asocial actor seeks only goals that can be specified in terms of a single person—herself. Thus she can take no direct pleasure in or satisfaction from essentially social activities. Note that taking pleasure in an activity does not require tuistic motivation. I may take pleasure from conversing with you. This is an essentially social activity. I may take pleasure in it whether or not you do. But even if I am indifferent to your pleasure, my motivation is not asocial. The source of my pleasure cannot be specified independently of reference to you—to a person other than myself.

There are a great many activities that are social in scope even if the satisfaction they provide is purely individual and independent. In many and diverse cases, from athletic activities to musical, from political activities to military, human beings find satisfaction in participation. To be sure, the participation must be related to some end, but it would be wrong to think of the participation as valued purely instrumentally. Indeed, someone may value ends in part because they afford occasions for participation, for joint or co-operative effort. And the person who thus esteems participation does not see her lack of self-sufficiency as a weakness. Indeed, such a person does not see a self-sufficient life as fully human.

Reasoning from an evolutionary perspective, we may suppose that the value we find in participation is itself instrumentally related to our insufficiency. We may agree with Hume that did each individual possess 'every faculty, requisite both for his own preservation and for the propagation of his kind', we should be incapable of any form of social activity.[30] But this does not make the value of participation itself instrumental. There is nothing contradictory, or paradoxical, or even surprising, in an instrumental explanation of certain of our intrinsic values. Not being sufficient, then, we value participation with our fellows, but we value it for its own sake and not merely as a means to overcoming that insufficiency.

In understanding this, we should realize how alien economic man is from our real selves. For his asocial motivation makes him incapable of finding more than instrumental value in participation, or more generally, in any activity requiring interaction with his fellows. Thus his lack of sufficiency is simply an evil, making him

[30] Hume, *Enquiry*, iii. 1, p. 191.

dependent on other persons, with interests separate from his own, for his own satisfaction. Participation, far from being a good, is simply a reminder of his dependence. Economic man endorses Rousseau's view that the division of labour diminishes his freedom in making him dependent on the wills of others.[31] The idea that the division of labour may be a source of enrichment as well as efficiency, that it may open new sources of satisfaction, clearly presupposes the possibility of social motivation. This is a theme to which we shall return in our sketch of individualistic community with an intrinsically just society.

In finding no value in participation, economic man also finds a lessened instrumental value in morality. For morality as we understand it affords a set of constraints peculiarly conducive to valued participatory activity. Morals by agreement ensure a rationally acceptable distribution of the goods realized in such activity. And so the participant does not find himself victimized. He need not sacrifice his fair share of other goods in order to gain the satisfactions of participation. And he gains no more than a fair share, so that he does not have to fear the justifiable resentment of his fellows.

We shall expand on these ideas in the next chapter. Here our concern is to note what economic man lacks, and to relate what he lacks to what morality provides. Morals by agreement may indeed be the only morality that economic man can understand, but their value to him is lessened by his indifference to many of the activities that they help to make possible.

2.5 Morality does not engage the affections of economic man. Taking no interest in others' interests, he equally takes no interest in constraints derived from their interests, except in so far as adherence to them is instrumental to his own asocial concerns. Now it may seem that this affective disregard for morality is a presupposition of our own, or of any, contractarian theory, which treats the rationale for moral principles as strictly non-tuistic. But this would be a mistake. Just as human beings may find participation with their fellows intrinsically valuable, even though their participatory activities have a non-tuistic rationale and explanation in their weakness and non-self-sufficiency, so human beings may find morality affec-

[31] See Rousseau, *Discours sur l'inégalité*, pp. 169–79. See also my discussion in 'The Politics of Redemption', *Trent Rousseau Papers*, ed. J. McAdam, M. Neumann, and G. Lafrance (Ottawa, 1980), especially pp. 73–80.

tively engaging for its own sake, even though their moral principles have a non-tuistic rationale.

We must distinguish two ways in which moral considerations may be thought to engage our affections. First, we might suppose that human beings have the capacity for an affective morality. Such a morality may be conceived as a set of constraints, not on the maximization of the actor's utility, but rather on the maximization of her asocial concerns, motivated by interests that she takes in her fellows. The constraints are not rationally binding whatever one's interests or preferences, but binding in virtue of, and solely in virtue of, certain directly tuistic interests. Economic man has no such interests, and we have eschewed any appeal to such interests in developing a rationale for morality. We do not deny that real persons, unlike economic men, are constrained by tuistic interests in the pursuit of their asocial concerns, and of course we do not deny that such moral thinkers as David Hume have developed accounts of affective morality based on such interests. But an affective morality, a morality of feeling, of benevolence, binds in a way quite different from a rational morality—so different that there is no perspicuous connection between the two. We could wish that the vocabulary linking the two in our conceptual scheme might be reformed.

But we should not thereby want to reject all connection between morality and the affections. For we should not confuse the capacity for a so-called affective morality with a second way in which moral considerations engage us, through an affective capacity for (rational) morality. Economic man lacks this capacity, just as he lacks the capacity for valuing participation. He lacks any affective concern with or acceptance of the constraints that he may nevertheless recognize as rationally binding. Morals by agreement can speak only to his intellect, but not to his feelings.

Persons with an affective capacity for morality have their emotions and feelings engaged by what they recognize as moral considerations. The capacity may itself be neutral with respect to the nature or binding force of these considerations; although our concern is with rationally based constraints, we may suppose that those who believe in objective authority may have their emotions engaged by its demands upon them. A person who possesses a sense of duty displays an affective capacity for morality; he is moved to do his duty just because it is his duty. A person who possesses a sense of justice also displays an affective capacity for morality; she is moved to do what is just because she so considers it. Note that an affective capacity for morality presupposes a prior conception of morality; one cannot be moved by a sense of duty unless one antecedently believes some action to be one's duty.

In distinguishing an affective capacity for morality from the capacity for a so-called affective morality, this last point deserves emphasis. The capacity for an affective morality does not presuppose any prior conception of morality. It is simply the capacity to be constrained in one's asocial pursuits by concern for others; it is identified as moral in that it introduces constraints, not in that it motivates one to adhere to constraints that one already recognizes. An affective capacity for morality, on the other hand, introduces no constraints, but disposes one emotionally and motivationally to adhere to constraints previously and independently accepted.

Glaucon claims that were the just man to put on the ring of Gyges, he would behave no differently from the unjust man.[32] In so claiming Glaucon thinks of the just man merely as someone who recognizes the need to accept certain constraints, but whose emotions are in no way engaged by them. The 'just man' thus lacks any sense of justice, any capacity to be moved by considerations of justice as such. It is then not surprising that, given the ring of Gyges, he would behave as did the Lydian shepherd. But this shows only that he is not truly the just man. Properly understood, the just man is the person who, recognizing a certain course of action to be just, finds her feelings engaged by that recognition and so finds herself moved to adhere to that course of action because of its justice. To be sure, she may be moved in other ways as well, but for the just person, this motivation is essential.

Economic man lacks the capacity to be truly the just man. He understand the arguments for moral constraint, but he regards such constraint as an evil from which he would be free. Given the opportunity to use morality as an instrument of domination, he unhesitatingly does so, because his concern with morality is purely an instrumental one, and his goals to which morality is instrumental are asocial.

Morals by agreement have a non-tuistic rationale. Their constraints bind rationally, and independently of all particular prefer-

[32] See *Republic*, 360b–c.

ences. But it does not follow that morals by agreement bind only non-tuists. We may distinguish the pure non-tuist, whose affections cannot be engaged except by his own concerns, from the person who demands a non-tuistic rationale for constraint, but whose affections may then be engaged by constraints so justified. She does not allow herself to be disadvantaged or worsened by tuistic concerns, but she does not seek to take advantage of or better herself in relation to others by seeking to circumvent constraints non-tuistically justified.

Throughout our argument, non-tuism has served as an assumption required to ensure that morality is not affectively dependent, so that it speaks directly to reason and not to particular, contingent emotions or feelings. Non-tuism has not been treated as literally characterizing human beings. And so we may now suppose that persons have, in particular, an affective capacity for morality, not so that we may show certain moral constraints to be justified, but rather so that we may show that, for persons with such a capacity, moral constraints do not constitute a necessary evil, and are not willingly circumvented in making morality an instrument of domination. We are now ready to address the charge that morals by agreement are no more than a façade by which a non-tuistic and asocial being most effectively pursues his private ends. We are ready to show that morals by agreement are more than the morals of economic man.

XI

THE LIBERAL INDIVIDUAL

1.1 In a passage curiously reminiscent of Hobbes's description of the state of nature, Skepticus, one of the disciples of Bernard Suits's Grasshopper, says, 'In Utopia man cannot labour, he cannot administer or govern, there is no art, no morality, no science, no love, no friendship.'[1] Skepticus suggests that 'Perhaps the moral ideal of man is just a supreme orgasm', but the Grasshopper shows his proposal to be quite untenable. Utopia, the condition in which 'all of the instrumental activities of human beings have been eliminated',[2] would seem as bleak as the state of nature, in which those instrumental activities are doomed to fail.

The Grasshopper at first thinks not. For what remains when all instrumental activities are eliminated, are games, where 'playing a game is the voluntary attempt to overcome unnecessary obstacles.'[3] And if games are possible then so is striving, and with striving 'both admiration and sharing are again possible, and so love and friendship . . . emotional content is provided for art. And perhaps morality will also be present . . . in the form of what we now call sportsmanship.'[4] What the Grasshopper envisages is a culture based, not as our own and all past cultures, on scarcity, whether 'economic, moral, scientific, erotic', but on plenitude. And so it will be a culture whose 'institutions . . . foster sport and . . . games that will require for their exploitation . . . as much energy as is expended today in serving the institutions of scarcity.'

But then the Grasshopper has a vision 'of the downfall of Utopia, a vision of paradise lost. I saw [he says] time passing . . . and I saw the Strivers and the Seekers coming to the conclusion that if their lives were merely games, then those lives were scarcely worth living.'[5] And so they delude themselves into believing that their games are 'vitally necessary tasks which had to be performed in order for mankind to survive. Thus, although all of the apparently productive

[1] B. Suits, *The Grasshopper: Games, Life and Utopia* (Toronto, 1978), p. 170.

[2] Ibid., p. 167.

[3] Ibid., p. 41.

[4] Ibid., p. 176.

[5] Ibid., p. 177.

activities of man were games, they were not believed to be games. . . . And if it had been possible to convince these people that they were in fact playing games, they would have felt that their whole lives had been as nothing—a mere stage play or empty dream.'

Before the Grasshopper can reflect on the fear expressed in his vision, that paradise could be gained only to be lost, he dies, and Suits's book ends. But this fear seems soundly based. In considering why, we shall reach a deeper understanding of the good of justice, an understanding that will reveal the constraints of morality to be something quite other than an imposture.

In considering the Grasshopper's message, two points deserve special attention. The first is that Utopia assumes the complete absence of scarcity. More than material factors are included; the Grasshopper sees our present world as one of emotional deprivation. The person who seeks emotional fulfilment is as much a seeker engaged in instrumental activity, as the person who seeks to assuage hunger or thirst. More controversially perhaps, the Grasshopper insists that lack of knowledge is also a form of scarcity; the search for knowledge, as opposed to the enjoyment taken in contemplation, is also an activity unfit for Utopia.

Now in ruling out all forms of instrumental activity from Utopia, the Grasshopper is following in a distinguished tradition of which Aristotle is an early representative.[6] All of those activities that Aristotle took to be unworthy of perfection are instrumental concerns unsuited to Utopia. But the Grasshopper and Aristotle part company when they consider what would remain, after mere instrumentality is removed. For Aristotle the only form of perfect activity is contemplation. But the life of contemplation, however appropriate it may be for the Unmoved Mover, is, he admits, too high for man. And the Grasshopper never supposes that human beings in Utopia might engage in an activity whose fundamental character differs from those we know—an activity related entirely to possessing, rather than to seeking or to striving. Rather, the Grasshopper insists that the Utopian condition of human beings must lie in performing the same kind of activities as before, but with their objective instrumentality removed; the striving and the seeking must be related to unnecessary obstacles voluntarily imposed. Utopian activities may appear similar to those in which persons now engage, but in Utopia these activities will be games. Thus scientific

[6] See Aristotle, *Nicomachean Ethics*, bk. x, chs. 6–7; *Metaphyics*, bk. xii, chs. 7, 9.

researchers will be in the position of students who work through problems even though the solutions are in the back of the book.

We may express the Grasshopper's underlying thesis about value by saying that what proves of intrinsic value in human life is engagement in instrumental activities—seeking and striving. In a non-Utopian condition these activities also have instrumental value, so that we do not pursue them purely for their own sake. But in Utopia their instrumental value is annulled; they have the pure intrinsic value of games.

The second point demanding our attention emerges from the Grasshopper's vision. For here, the thesis about value is extended in a way fatal to the possibility of a true Utopia. What has intrinsic value in human life is not just engagement in instrumental activities, but engagement in activities that have instrumental value. To strive or to seek, where there is no further point to the striving or seeking, is 'a mere stage play or empty dream'. In our non-Utopian world, games have point because they are part of a life that is not mere game-playing. They offer us respite from activities that relate to necessary obstacles. And so games have instrumental value for us; we enjoy the freedom to create our own obstacles. But in Utopia we should have nothing but that freedom. In our world the point of games is to have no point beyond themselves; in Utopia they would lack that point.

But is there not a paradox here? How can intrinsic value depend on instrumental value? How can the only thing worth doing for its own sake be the doing of something for the sake of something further? Surely the Grasshopper's view of intrinsic value—or at any rate, our interpretation of it—is completely incoherent. To avoid this charge, we must complicate our account slightly. Certainly the activities that have instrumental value must have a point beyond themselves, and this point cannot be merely engagement in such activities. We must then allow certain intrinsically valuable states of affairs, desired for their own sake. But we need not suppose that these states of affairs, however valuable, are sufficient for a life that humans find worth living. We can agree that a life of seeking and striving, if it is to be judged worth living, may require arriving and possessing; we may equally agree that a life of arriving and possessing, if it too is to be judged worth living, may require seeking and striving. We may then say that seeking and striving are intrinsically valuable only in so far as they have real goals, so that their intrinsic value is not independent of their having instrumental value, which in turn requires that other things have intrinsic value.

The claims we are making here are clearly psychological. They concern human good, and questions about human good demand empirical investigation. Our concern is not to establish these claims but only to suggest their plausibility. For they enable us to show how, for those beings of whom they are true, a morality that is neither a necessary evil nor a means of domination is possible. Perhaps we are not such beings. But perhaps, as I think, we are.

1.2 If a fulfilling human life must include activities with instrumental value, then paradise can be gained only to be lost. Paradise is gained when all obstacles to fulfilment are overcome, but when all obstacles are overcome, instrumental activities lose their point and cease to afford fulfilment. And with the loss of paradise, we come to a new understanding of the place of scarcity in human affairs. In the broadest sense, it is scarcity that gives rise to activities with instrumental value. If they are necessary to human fulfilment, then scarcity is necessary too. The idea of a human society based not on scarcity but on plenitude is chimerical; to overcome scarcity would be to overcome the conditions that give human life its point.

Karl Marx paid capitalist society its highest compliment in supposing it to have overcome scarcity through the creation of productive forces. For Marx, communism had become possible only because humankind could pass from a condition of scarcity to one of plenitude. Marx was mistaken. But in a much-criticized passage in the *German Ideology*, in which Marx for once speculates on the character of a society of plenitude, he reveals a profound insight into what would be necessary for such a condition.

The effect of scarcity in human affairs is to bring about the division of labour, in which

> each man has a particular, exclusive sphere of activity, which is forced upon him and from which he cannot escape. He is a hunter, a fisherman, a shepherd, or a critical critic, and must remain so if he does not want to lose his means of livelihood; while in communist society, where nobody has one exclusive sphere of activity but each can become accomplished in any branch he wishes, society regulates the general production and thus makes it possible for me to do one thing today and another tomorrow, to hunt in the morning, fish in the afternoon, rear cattle in the evening, criticise after

dinner, just as I have a mind, without ever becoming hunter, fisherman, shepherd or critic.[7]

It has been correctly noted that technological advances in the productive sphere make nonsense of Marx's vision. But the nonsense shows that Marx failed to separate his vision sufficiently from the conditions of production, and did not realize that he was describing Utopia, in which society would not need to regulate the general production because scarcity would be fully overcome; there would be no genuinely necessary productive activity for human beings. In such circumstances a person may hunt, fish, rear cattle, criticize, just as she has a mind. And indeed, a person must be able to do these things; in Utopia there can be no scarcity even in the modes of self-realization. Every form of life must be equally and fully accessible to everyone.

It should be evident that this is quite impossible. Even if we suppose material scarcity entirely overcome, there would remain scarcity in the forms of human fulfilment. No human being is capable of realizing in herself, all of the possible modes of human activity. She cannot be a concert pianist in the morning, a nuclear physicist in the afternoon, a neuro-surgeon in the evening, and a novelist after dinner, because the talents and efforts needed for each of these activities make up the core of a whole life, leaving no room for the others. She can be all men and women at most dilettantishly (and what counts as being a dilettantish neuro-surgeon?), but acting dilettantishly precludes the real, full commitment that self-realization requires.

Scarcity in the forms of human fulfilment seems a fixed feature of human life. Each of us can realize in herself only one of the many possible lives that together make up human flourishing. Even if we detach each of these lives from its instrumental point, supposing that we could be fulfilled in activities engaged in only as games, we find scarcity recurring in the varieties of games that an individual could master.

Marx saw, more clearly than has often been realized, what Utopia would entail. He saw that in Utopia no person would have to make real choices among activities or forms of life. 'Choosing' would be merely a device for temporal ordering; choosing to hunt in the

[7] Karl Marx and Frederick Engels, *The German Ideology*, pt. 1, ed. C. J. Arthur (New York, 1970), p. 53.

morning would not entail choosing not to fish, since that would remain available in the afternoon. But Utopia is then impossible, for we cannot escape the need to make real choices. Let all problems of production be solved. If the Grasshopper's fears are sound, then human activities would lose their point. But let this fear be momentarily waived. Let us suppose that productive scarcity is not a necessary condition of humanly fulfilling activities. Yet scarcity in consumption would remain. Each of us has but one life to lead, and there are many possible and incompatible lives to be led.

Scarcity is the humanly necessary evil. Faced with scarcity, choice as a device that, in selecting some activities, rejects others, is necessary, and the rule of rational choice is maximally to fulfil one's preferences. The supposition that to conceive a human being as a maximizer of expected utility is to conceive him in a limited way, determined by the particular conditions of our own Western society, but neither generally applicable nor ideally appropriate, is mistaken. Utopia, in which maximization would not be expressive of human rationality, is illusory; only a god, of whom we can have no conception, could inhabit such a realm.

But economic man is not therefore the human ideal. For his non-tuism is as inapplicable to the human condition as the Utopian idea of plenitude. Faced with scarcity, but aware of others like himself, a rational being can be no more unaware of the need for participating than the need for seeking and striving. And the same intrinsic value that human beings find in seeking and striving, is found also, and perhaps even more fully, in participating. For participation addresses not only productive scarcity, but also the scarcity of consumption.

Here we appeal to the conception of the social nature of human beings held by Rawls, who acknowledges his indebtedness to Wilhelm von Humboldt.[8] Noting that an individual could avoid one-sidedness in her own development by a harmonious combination of her activities through time, von Humboldt went on to say, 'What is achieved, in the case of the individual, by the union of past and future with the present, is produced in society by the mutual co-operation of its different members; for, in all stages of his life, each individual can achieve only one of those perfections, which represent the possible features of human character. It is through a social union, therefore, based on the internal wants and capacities of its

[8] J. Rawls, *A Theory of Justice* (Cambridge, Mass., 1971), pp. 522–7.

members, that each is enabled to participate in the rich collective resources of all the others.'[9] Rawls offers an illuminating instance of pure social union: 'consider a group of musicians everyone of whom could have trained himself to play equally well as the others any instrument in the orchestra, but who each have by a kind of tacit agreement set out to perfect their skills on the one they have chosen so as to realize the powers of all in their joint performances.'[10]

There are two important strands of thought to be noted here. The first is that each person, unable to realize all human excellences in her own person, profits directly from the realization by others, of excellences differing from, although not opposed to, her own. Each is enriched by the complementarity of realizations quite apart from the specific activities made possible. The second is that in realizing complementary excellences, persons make possible activities that no individual could engage in on her own—the activities of an orchestra as opposed to the activities of separate players. Here participation is most fully exercised, and we may suppose, even without qualifying the supposition of non-tuism, that each values both the shared activities and the sharing or participating. But beyond this, we may suppose that in valuing participation, a person comes to value her fellow participants, so that shared activities give rise to bonds among persons which lead to each taking an interest in others' interests—though to be sure, in the interests not of all other persons, but of those identified and experienced as co-participants.

Now it should be noted that the value of participating is related to what we have identified as scarcity of consumption, the inability of each individual to attain all forms of human realization. But in so far as some of these forms require shared activities—even if an individual could master all instruments, yet she could not turn herself into an orchestra (we leave aside the technological marvel that by successive recording could enable such an individual to simulate an orchestral performance)—the value of participating reveals an insufficiency in the human individual that does not itself reduce to scarcity. Not only can no individual realize all forms of human life in herself, but some forms are not individually realizable.

In X.1.1, we suggested that individual insufficiency was a defect; the person aware of her insufficiency is aware that she is less than she

[9] W. von Humboldt, *The Limits of State Action*, ed. J. W. Burrow (Cambridge, 1969), pp. 16–17.

[10] Rawls, p. 524 n.

would be. We must now reconsider that suggestion. Taking scarcity for granted, as giving instrumental point to our activities, have we reason to regret that some of those activities are necessarily shared? Have we reason to regret that some music requires an orchestra, or that some games (since we have no reason to deny the value of games in a world that is not all game-playing) are for teams? Indeed, have we reason to consider the individual defective, because the activity of child-raising seems best carried on through the co-operation of mother and father? May we not rather suppose that our social capacity to find value in participating is one of the main sources of enrichment in human life, making possible as it does the complementary realization of our varied human powers and capacities?

In valuing participation, we appreciate the importance of public life. Our conception of society embraces the forum as well as the market-place. But just as the value of seeking and striving requires these activities to have goals beyond themselves, so the value of participating requires that public life take its rationale from the varied realizations of individuality that it makes possible. Public life considered apart from its instrumental roles would become yet another game.

1.3 Morality takes on different colouration when viewed in relation to participation. For asocial seekers and strivers morality could be no more than a needed but unwelcome constraint. But for those who value participation, a morality of agreement, although still a source of constraint, makes their shared activity mutually welcome and so stable, ensuring the absence of coercion or deception. As our analysis of co-operation has shown, agreed constraint is a condition of the rational acceptability to the actors of the division of benefits realized by their shared activity. And so it is a condition of their finding participation in such activity intrinsically valuable.

A person values striving, but only, we have supposed, in so far as he considers its costs necessary to attain some valued end. If he believes that it does not satisfy the standard of efficiency implicit in maximization, then he will consider the striving misguided. Similarly, a person values participating, again only in so far as he considers its costs necessary to attain some valued end. Here it is not enough that it satisfy the standard of efficiency implicit in optimization. For if he believes that its costs to him are relatively greater than any participant need bear, then he will consider them excessive and the satisfaction he takes from participation will be reduced. He might, of course, find value in participation if the costs to others were excessive, but if each participant is to find shared activity intrinsically valuable, then it must satisfy the standard of fairness found in minimax relative concession. And this is to say that it must be voluntarily acceptable; the actors must be willing to participate without being coerced or deceived.

If persons develop tuistic values primarily in the context of shared activities, then the acceptance of moral constraints underlies these values. In the absence of a morally acceptable division of benefits, persons will come to view their shared activities as exploitative rather than co-operative, and their fellows as having interests opposed to their own. And this must be inimical to the development or continuation of tuistic bonds. It might seem that, in admitting that persons do come to take an interest in the interests of their co-participants, we undercut the rationale for requiring that moral constraints have a non-tuistic basis. But if moral constraints underlie tuistic values, then they must have a basis independent of those values. Persons come to take an interest in their fellows because they recognize their mutual willingness not to take advantage of each other, and to share jointly produced benefits on a fair basis. In accepting moral constraints they do not express their concern for each other, but rather they bring about the conditions that foster such concern.

But in valuing both participation and their fellow participators, persons come to place a new value on the moral framework within which participation flourishes. Having first engaged their reason, morality now engages their affections. They exhibit the affective capacity for morality that we found lacking in economic man. We noted in X.2.5 that an affective capacity for morality does not give rise to moral constraints but presupposes their prior recognition; the desire to do one's duty cannot determine the content of duty. And this fits our present argument. Persons rationally recognize the constraints of morality as conditions of mutually beneficial co-operation. They then come to value participation in co-operative and shared activities that meet these constraints, and to take an interest in their fellow participants. And finally they come to value the morality that first appeared to them only as a rational constraint.

Our concern here is not with empirical moral psychology. We do not seek to describe the process by which actual individuals come to manifest an affective capacity for morality. Children are not made moral beings by appealing first to their intellects and only thereafter to their feelings. Rather we are engaged in the philosopher's task of rational reconstruction. We have not supposed that actual moral constraints represent the outcome of real agreement, but we have argued that, if they are to be justified, we must be able to consider them as objects of a hypothetical *ex ante* agreement, the rationality of which we now recognize *ex post*. Similarly, we do not suppose that actual moral feelings represent the outcome of a prior valuing of participation and an awareness that voluntary participation requires the acceptance of moral constraints. Rather our argument is that, if we are to consider our moral affections to be more than dysfunctional feelings of which we should be well rid, we must be able to show how they would arise from such a valuing and awareness. We must show that a person, reflecting on his moral feelings, would consider them an appropriate extension of his concern for others in the context of valued participatory activities, and would then consider those activities appropriately valued in so far as they were morally constrained. Such a person would find his moral outlook congruent with his reflection. If morality played in his life only the role of necessary evil or of convenient deception that it plays for economic man, then we should expect that awareness of its role would undermine his moral affections.

A rational morality is contractarian. But this does not imply that it is of purely instrumental value to us. In relating morality to the provision of benefits that themselves involve no affective concern with others, we do not thereby impoverish the moral feelings of persons who have such concern. It is because we can give morality a rational basis that we can secure its affective hold.

2.1 A just society is neither a Utopia, nor a society of economic men. It provides a framework for community but is not communal. The socialization that it affords its members promotes the realization of their autonomy. The division of labour that it embraces broadens individual opportunity, and encourages the realization of a wide range of complementary human potentialities. It is a society of liberal individuals, free to establish their own goals and to choose their own affective ties with their fellows.

We may think of the relation between liberal individual and just society as expressed in Archimedean choice. From the Archimedean point the rational person chooses social practices and institutions instrumentally, but in a way that achieves full generality because she must identify, not with some particular individual, or the members of some limited set of individuals, but with any person, who might find himself in the society chosen. Her choice reflects, not the preferences of any particular individual or individuals, but the possible preferences of human beings, given only the general relations between social practices and human concerns that may reasonably be assumed, and the general constraints on circumstances set by the horizon of institutional and technological feasibility.

A society so chosen is *essentially* just. Its institutions and practices are intended to enable the maximization of minimum relative benefit, not only for a particular set of actual persons whose preferences and capacities are taken as given, or for persons whose preferences and capacities are socially conditioned to fit what the institutions offer, but for all persons interacting for mutual advantage. We may say that a particular bargain or agreement is instrumentally just in so far as it affords maximin relative benefit to the actual bargainers. And we said in X.2.3 that an arrangement is artificially just in so far as the preferences of those affected by it are shaped so that they are afforded maximin relative benefit. But neither instrumental nor artificial justice is sufficient for society conceived as the object of Archimedean choice; both limit the range of persons who receive justice. The idea of essential justice is that this range not be limited, so that institutions and practices accommodate themselves to all persons, whatever their preferences and capacities, provided only that they may be participants in a co-operative endeavour.

We may think of the perfectly competitive market, under the impact of changing utility and production functions, as continually adjusting in the direction of an equilibrium which would be actually attained only under static conditions, but which serves in practice as a regulative ideal determining the direction of market movement. In the same way we may think of the essentially just society, also under the impact of changing utility and production functions, as continually adjusting to make possible maximin relative benefit. Again, this ideal position would be reached only under static conditions; in practice it serves as a regulative ideal determining the direction of social adjustment. The neutrality of the market, with respect to the aims of market competitors, is shown in the direction of its adjustment; it adapts to whatever their aims may be, bringing their fulfilment into optimal equilibrium. Similarly the neutrality of the essentially just society, with respect to the aims of its members, is shown in its adaptation to whatever their aims may be, bringing their fulfilment into optimal relative equality.

An essentially just society is fully compatible with the critical and reflective rationality of its members. It does not need to shape individuals in order to afford them justice. We shall consider presently how the essentially just society acts as a socializing agent; here our concern is only to note that the neutrality of justice, with respect to individual aims and preferences, enables the defender of essential justice to escape the charge that society provides a strait-jacket which individuals must be tailored to fit.

In saying that an essentially just society is neutral with respect to the aims of its members, we deny that justice is linked to any substantive conception of what is good, either for the individual or for society. A just society has no aim beyond those given in the preferences of its members. As a co-operative venture for mutual advantage, it enables each to promote what she holds good. An essentially just society does not introduce a social good as a function of individual goods. This distinguishes it most clearly from a utilitarian society, which also rejects any substantive conception of the good, or any aim beyond those based on the preferences of its members, but which supposes a social good as the sum of individual goods. A utilitarian society lacks any substantive aim but is concerned to realize the greatest sum of individual goods. A just society is concerned only to enable each person to realize the greatest amount of her own good, on terms acceptable to all.

An essentially just society affords its members the opportunity to enjoy the intrinsic value of participation. But it does this, not by imposing any participatory structures, but by freeing persons from the barriers to fully voluntary co-operative interaction. We have indeed claimed that rational persons would accept the perfectly competitive market where conditions make perfect competition, or a near approximation thereto, feasible. But an essentially just society does not impose the market on its members; it does, however, remove what might be barriers to it, both in enforcing the proviso and punishing force and fraud, and in rejecting compulsory social practices and institutions that embody any substantive goal. An essentially just society can neither ban nor require capitalist acts among consenting adults.

Essential justice is an idealization; to devise institutions and practices that would adjust perfectly under changing preferences, capacities, and circumstances, that would accommodate change in persons, change of persons, and technological advances, no doubt exceeds human capability. This should not be taken as a counsel of despair. The achievements of liberal politics and market economics in moving humankind towards essential justice are not inconsiderable. But if the underpinnings of the essentially just society are provided by a theory of morals by agreement, and the provision of private goods in such a society is treated by a theory of economics by agreement, which is of course the theory of the market, then the selection and provision of public goods in such a society require a theory of politics by agreement, and this theory is conspicuously underdeveloped. Significant contributions are offered by theorists of public choice.[11] But problems of political procedure and institutional design cannot be considered here.

2.2 From the Archimedean point, a rational individual would choose essential justice. In X.2.3 we argued that artificial justice, in adapting persons to institutions, fails adequately to accommodate the rational capacity of persons to reflect self-critically on their preferences. Archimedean choice does accommodate this capacity. Even though a person, aware of his utilities and capacities, does not find himself at the Archimedean point, yet he can recognize its relevance to those choices that would determine the overall social context of his activity, because it ensures that not only his actual preferences, but those possible preferences that he might come to have, will be taken fairly into account.

The rational individual faces a fundamental uncertainty, both in understanding himself and in treating his interactions with others. This uncertainty is fundamental because it arises from the reflective dimension of rationality. The utility function that partially defines a particular individual is revisable, in part through the individual's own reflective activity. Now there are deep and difficult issues about personal identity which are connected with this revisability. Derek Parfit has examined many of these issues in considering the relationship between temporally distant 'selves'.[12] Briefly and dogmatically we advance the following position. Personal identity has an essen-

[11] In particular J. M. Buchanan, whose book *The Limits of Liberty* we have referred to in Chapter VII.

[12] See D. Parfit, 'Later Selves and Moral Principles'; also 'Personal Identity', *Philosophical Review* 80 (1971), pp. 3–27.

tially practical dimension. The self at time t_1 is identical with the later self at time t_2 to the extent that it identifies with that later self, and this identification is measured by the weight given to the expected preferences of the self at t_2 in the preferences of the self at t_1. Utility is, as we have insisted throughout, the measure of present preference, the preferences of the self at a particular time; practical rationality is the maximization of utility and so the maximization of the satisfaction of present preferences. Present preferences may or may not accommodate anticipated future preferences; this is not in principle a matter of rationality. The rational person may, but need not, be the prudent person. However, the self-critical nature of rationality adds a further dimension of great importance in determining the relation of temporally distant selves. For the fully rational person must view his future selves as linked to his present self by a process of critical reflection; future preferences emerge from present preferences by a rational, although of course experientially informed, exercise. The connection between the self at t_1 and the self at t_2 is thus neither arbitrary nor entirely accidental. And this, we suggest, disposes the rational person to identify with his later selves, in giving weight in his present preferences to those future preferences that he expects to derive from them by a rational process.

But this identification with one's future selves involves uncertainty. The rational person is partially ignorant of the preferences of the temporally extended self for whom he is concerned to provide. Now in many of his choices this ignorance has no practical effect. But in agreeing to the institutions and practices of society—his overall social environment—it must be accommodated. And this induces a movement towards the Archimedean point in choosing among social structures. For one's concern with one's possible future selves becomes, in effect, a concern to be fair to whomever one may become, and the Archimedean point ensures this fairness over the widest possible range of future selves. Although no individual need or could suppose all possible persons to be among his possible future selves, yet the difficulty of bounding one's future makes Archimedean choice a salient device for expressing one's identification with whatever preferences one may come to have.

The capacity for rational, self-critical reflection on one's grounds of action may be identified with the traditional idea of autonomy. The person who is a law unto himself is not bound by his present preferences, except in so far as they constitute his starting point for self-assessment. In the absence of any preferences and capacities he would have no basis on which to consider what person he might be. In taking over the Kantian idea of autonomy, we continue to reject the Kantian claim that reason affords substantive grounds for choice or action.[13] But we recognize that reason offers a formal ground for Archimedean choice, as congruent to the autonomy that rationality confers. And so the essentially just society is the proper habitat of the fully autonomous agent. The person who is concerned with the full exercise of his rational freedom cannot agree to social institutions and practices that are merely instrumentally just, however well adapted they may be to his present concerns and powers, because he has no guarantee that such a social structure will continue to provide fairly for his satisfaction.

The second uncertainty faced by rational individuals concerns the willingness of others voluntarily to accept social institutions and practices. Given that, as we have argued, this willingness is predicated on the fairness of society, then one can be assured of the voluntary compliance of others only in an essentially just society. For otherwise, changes in the preferences, powers, or circumstances of other persons may render social arrangements unjust, and undermine their continuing acceptability. Thus a concern with stability also induces a movement towards the Archimedean point in choosing among social structures. Again, no individual need or could suppose that he might find himself in interaction with all possible persons or in all possible circumstances. Yet the difficulty of determining plausible limits on the range either of persons or circumstances, especially in a populous and technologically advanced society, makes Archimedean choice a salient device for ensuring the stability of the institutions and practices making co-operation possible and fruitful.

Although rational persons who value participatory activities with their fellows will develop an affective concern for essential justice, yet the object of their concern is initially an instrumental value. The components of a rationally agreed morality are judged by their contribution to the satisfaction of preferences directed at quite other objects. But the instrumental character of essential justice is parallel to the instrumental character of rationality. Neither merely happens to be the best means to some particular end or ends. Rather, each

[13] One might deny that Kant makes such a claim. But we find it implicit in the idea of a categorical imperative.

proves of value given certain general features characteristic of human activity. Practical reason is of use only to a being who has the capacity and need to choose among possible actions, but given that capacity and need, reason is necessarily of value to such a being. Justice is of use only to a being who has the capacity and need to choose among possible interactions in which the value of the outcome to each person depends on the actions of all, but given that capacity and need, justice is necessarily of value to such a being. Humans value justice ultimately because it affords the basis for interactions, free of all external constraints, that enable them best to fulfil whatever preferences they have, given whatever capacities they have.

Glaucon represents justice as a necessary evil because he supposes that it affords us only a second-best means to our ends. But he is mistaken. The co-operation that justice makes possible, considered both in terms of what it brings about, and in terms of the participatory activity that it involves, is not a second-best way of realizing what could, but for some particular obstacles, better be realized in some other way. In co-operating we make the most effective use of our powers to attain ends that would otherwise lie beyond our individual capacities. And we find value in ways that no solitary being could experience. It is of course true that an all-powerful and all-sufficient being would have no use for co-operation, and so for its virtue, justice. But we are neither all-powerful nor all-sufficient. We may not then sensibly suppose that co-operation, which enhances our limited powers and overcomes our individual insufficiency, is a necessary evil. Indeed, to represent co-operation, and so justice, as necessary evils is to view being human as itself evil.

Although Glaucon misrepresents justice, there is an important political lesson to be drawn from his parable. Justice is a virtue suited to human powers and desires. The tale of the Lydian shepherd shows the consequences of conferring the power to act 'as an equal to a god' on someone who retains human desires. Bonds of justice lose their hold on those who may enjoy benefits without paying their costs. We do well, then, to curb that mortal god, Leviathan, lest it find justice an unnecessary evil.

2.3 Morals by agreement capture the understanding of economic man; they capture the affections of the liberal individual. The characteristics that constitute liberal individuality are to be found, explicitly or implicitly, in our preceding discussion, and we need only recapitulate and re-emphasize them here. First of all, the liberal individual is an active being, who finds satisfaction in the seeking and striving that constitute activity as we humans conceive it. Of course, to reiterate what we noted in 1.1, if one finds intrinsic value in instrumentally valuable activity, then one must also find it in the end of that activity; the good life must combine attainment with striving. But in so far as the latter is essential, the habitat of the liberal individual must be one of scarcity, whether material, mental, or emotional.

Second, the liberal individual has her own independent conception of the good. That conception need not rest on purely asocial motivation, for the liberal individual is not an asocial being. But the goods of different individuals characteristically reflect both harmonies and conflicts of interest. The good of each person expresses his preferences, but, we have insisted, his considered preferences. Thus the liberal individual must have the capacity to reflect on her preferences, and to alter them in the light of this reflection; this capacity makes her autonomous.

Thus third, the liberal individual is fully rational, where rationality embraces both autonomy and the capacity to choose among possible actions on the basis of one's conception of the good as determined by one's reflective preferences. Defining utility as the measure of considered preference, the liberal individual is rational in being a maximizer of expected utility. Here we emphasize the self-critical dimension of practical rationality, since this seems lacking from the crude conception of merely economic rationality.

As an autonomous being, the liberal individual is aware of the reflective process by which her later selves emerge from her present self, so that her preferences are modified, not in a random or uncontrolled way, but in the light of her own experience and understanding. This gives her the sense of a temporally extended being, whose life is a single development, capable of being integrated and unified. Thus although the liberal individual need not be strictly prudent and take an atemporal view of her preferences and their satisfaction, she views the present not in isolation, but in relation to both her past and her possible futures. And so she is able to constrain her maximizing behaviour in terms of policies and principles, given that such constraint seems to her rational. She has then the practical capacity for what we have identified as moral behaviour.

But beyond this practical capacity, she also has the emotional or affective capacity. For the liberal individual realizes that she must choose among many possible ways of life, and that the breadth and richness of her choices depend on the existence of other persons choosing in other ways. She therefore sees her life in a social context, as made possible through interaction with others—interaction which of course also makes possible their lives. Valuing this breadth of opportunity and richness of fulfilment, the liberal individual comes to value participation as well as individual seeking and striving, and, although not a natural tuist, comes to value those whom she encounters as fellow participators. Her habitat is then characterized both by scarcity and society, and the intrinsic satisfaction she takes from society is not dissociated from its instrumental role in meeting scarcity. Valuing participation and her fellow participators, she values also the constraints that make it possible; both intellect and emotion make her a moral being.

But there is another characteristic of the liberal individual that demands emphasis here—free affectivity. The liberal individual does not lack emotional ties to other persons, but those she has are of her own volition, or more properly, represent the joint volition of the persons tied. Just as each individual has her own conception of the good, and makes her own choice among possible ways of life, so each individual makes her own choice of others as objects of affection. She is not bound by fixed social roles, either in her activities or in her feelings. Although social affective relationships are essential to the liberal individual, there are no essential social relationships.

Now the idea of free affectivity should not be confused with traditional notions of 'free love'. In particular, there is no reason for persons whose affections are free, subject to their autonomous control, not to enter into enduring and binding relationships with others. What is essential to free affectivity is that the bonds be of the person's own making. Imposition, not commitment, is incompatible with individual autonomy in the sphere of the emotions.

Free affectivity is linked to essential justice. Only in a society that can be viewed by its members as a genuine co-operative venture for mutual advantage, could we expect the purely voluntary relationships formed among persons to be sufficient social cement. There are two related reasons for this. On the one hand, a society recognized as promoting mutual advantage in a fair way needs fewer personal bonds to maintain it; persons interact co-operatively because of the impersonal benefits involved. Recognizing other persons as partners in a mutually beneficial enterprise enables those who take no interest in others' interests nevertheless to interact constructively with them. And on the other hand, in a society viewed as a fair co-operative venture, we may expect a genuine civic friendship to blossom. Interpersonal bonds that would not exist among persons who viewed one another in a traditionally competitive way (a way which we distinguished from market competition) or as enemies, are naturally generated in a framework of mutual benefit. An essentially just society thus fosters interpersonal bonds while being less dependent on them for its continuance. And so an essentially just society can afford to let interpersonal bonds be freely chosen by its members.

In the absence of an affective capacity for morality among its members, free affectivity would prove rapidly destabilizing for any society. An affective capacity for morality is needed if the constraints required by essential justice are to be willingly honoured. Without an emotional commitment by its members to maintain the framework of mutual benefit, a society could ensure its stability only by imposing on them, through processes of socialization, loyalty to a more substantive goal, which would define roles that individuals would not be free to accept or reject. Free love may have arisen as a reaction against emotional responsibility—an understandable reaction in so far as that responsibility was thrust upon persons, independently of their preferences and volitions. But free affectivity is precisely the assumption of personal responsibility for one's emotions.

The idea of free affectivity will no doubt seem threatening to the defenders of substantive community, whether radical or reactionary. Where their concern may seem most justified is, no doubt, in the sphere of purely private or domestic society. Although there is nothing in free affectivity to preclude the assumption of the emotional commitment requisite to the successful raising of children, yet it may be supposed, with some evidence, that too few adults may be prepared to assume this commitment in a freely chosen way. The fair bargain among generations that we discussed in IX.6 was, it will be remembered, essentially a public bargain, concerning social rates of investment. It involved no direct emotional demands. The raising of children, in a society whose technology affords other ways of providing for old age, is a quite different matter.

Free affectivity is not an unproblematic ideal. We may not assume that a society of liberal individuals would generate the intergenerational concerns that would ensure its viability over time. But equally, we may not assume that it would not. We must suspend judgement.

2.4 In defending the normative priority of individual to community, we imply nothing about the causal basis of individuality. The self-consciousness necessary for a being to have a genuine self-conception may well be possible only as a result of socialization. And self-consciousness is at the root of our strong sense of individuality; from the perspective of the self-conscious being, grounds for acting must be self-based. In producing a self-conscious being, human society thus finds itself called into question. From the standpoint of the self-conscious being, social practices and institutions appear as the embodiment of norms, standing in need of justification to him if he is voluntarily to acquiesce in them.

But if we admit that individuality may be socially caused, so that persons are social products, then must we not reject the contention that persons are autonomous? And if we sacrifice autonomy, then are we not undermining the conception of the liberal individual, which is at the core of our answer to those who would reject morals by agreement as the pseudo-morality of economic man? The idea that socialization is a threat to autonomy is not a new one, and if we were to suppose that an autonomous being must constitute himself *ex nihilo*, we should be unable to meet it. But autonomy has no such implication. It would be absurd to identify an individual with the formal process of reflection and choice in which autonomy is manifest. This process requires material—preferences and capacities—to serve as inputs, and there is no threat to autonomy in the recognition that these inputs are not, at least initially, autonomously determined. What makes a being autonomous is his capacity to alter given preferences by a rational, self-critical, reflective procedure, not a capacity to produce preferences with no prior basis.

We may assume that an individual begins with preferences and capacities that are, at least in part, socially determined. And we assume that the capacity by which an individual reflects self-critically on his preferences and capacities is also in part socially determined. In effect, we assume that human beings are socialized into autonomy. What matters is that their preferences and, within limits, their capacities are not fixed by their socialization, which is not a process by which persons are hard-wired, but rather, at least in part, a process for the development of soft-wired beings, who have the capacity to change the manner in which they are constituted.

In 2.1 we characterized an essentially just society as neutral with respect to the aims of its members, adapting itself to enable them to bring about a fair and optimal outcome whatever their particular preferences. We may now add to that characterization, and say that an essentially just society is also neutral with respect to the socialization of its members, in so far as it ensures them the autonomy to alter their preferences through rational reflection. Both neutrality in the production of preferences and neutrality in their satisfaction are required from the Archimedean point.

Neutrality in the production of preferences must, however, be limited. We suppose that persons are soft-wired so that they may change their desires and aims. We cannot suppose that the process of socialization is neutral with respect to what we may, continuing the metaphor, term the initial wiring. The essentially just society may be neutral with respect to the alteration of preferences, but it cannot be neutral with respect to their initial production. The process of socialization brings about determinate persons, not mere possibilities to be constituted by some unimagined, and perhaps unimaginable, act of self-creation. There must then be a non-neutral moment in the socializing activity of even the essentially just society. And this non-neutral moment, even if no threat to autonomy, seems an arbitrary factor that stands in need of justification to the rational autonomous individual.

But does not the assured neutrality of the essentially just society afford this justification? Grant that each person is constituted in part by an initial set of preferences that cannot be subject to his control and that from his standpoint is an arbitrary result of the social process by which he, as an individual with determinate preferences and capacities, was brought into being. Yet if he is a member of an essentially just society, he is assured that this arbitrariness cannot affect his equitable fulfilment; whatever preferences he may have, or come to have as a result of reflection on those initially given, an essentially just society enables him to realize a fair and optimal outcome.

As must be evident, an essentially just society may not socialize its members arbitrarily. In 2.1 we noted that an essentially just society is related to a choice reflecting the possible preferences of human beings, given only the general relations between social practices and human concerns that may reasonably be assumed, and the general constraints on circumstances set by the horizon of feasibility. An essentially just society will not encourage yearnings for the impossible; it will not encourage strongly opposed aims that threaten the prospect of mutual advantage. No one has reason to complain of this, for no one has reason to see himself disadvantaged by such restrictions on possible socialization.

Indeed, we must suppose that in an essentially just society, socialization will strengthen the institutions and practices that its members rationally endorse. While leaving each person free to choose the particular objects of his affections, society must encourage the general sociability of its members, since this facilitates interaction. The assurance that interaction is subject to the constraints of justice meets the concern emphasized in feminist thought, that sociability not be a basis for exploitation. In an essentially just society no individual will be expected to sacrifice her interests to those of others in order to gain the satisfaction of social intercourse.

Furthermore, an essentially just society must be strengthened through the development of the affections and interests of the young in such a way that their mature concerns afford motivational reinforcement to the rational requirements of co-operation. Co-operative activity should be experienced as itself fulfilling. So indeed should market activity, but in so far as it does not require the constraints on utility-maximizing behaviour that are essential to fair co-operation, non-social satisfactions may be expected to play a more extensive and effective motivational role within the market than beyond it. Socialization, then, should encourage persons to want to co-operate in those situations in which co-operation is otherwise mutually advantageous to them. The desire to co-operate in such circumstances will receive the reflective endorsement of reason; the justification of the essentially just society extends to the justification of the sociability that sustains and strengthens it, and so to the justification of the socialization that instils and encourages this sociability.

Because an essentially just society makes possible the greatest possible breadth of fulfilment, encouraging persons to realize the many and varied potentialities of human beings, we must expect that a division of labour will be built in to both the institutions and the socializing procedures of the society. Such a division of labour will not, of course, be expressed in requirements overriding individual autonomy. It will not be coercive. Rather, we might expect an essentially just society to promote a broadly pluralistic conception of human realization that, given the differentiating accidents of circumstance and capacity, leads individuals to choose differing but complementary roles. Neither the objection of Marx, that the division of labour prevents the many-sided development of individual human beings, nor the objection of Rousseau, that the division of labour renders individuals dependent on the alien wills of others and so unfree, can be sustained in the circumstances of essential justice.[14] For as we have already seen, no human being is capable of realizing all of the possible modes of human activity; the fullest realization possible for each of us is the realization of some mode complementary to the realization of other modes by other persons. And in the essentially just society, no one is disadvantaged or exploited by dependence on others; the insufficiency of the individual, both in terms of producing the material goods of human life, and in terms of realizing the varied modes of human life, is most fully overcome by the shared, fair, optimal activities that such a society makes possible.

But there are more problematic aspects to socialization that may seem to threaten the very possibility of an essentially just society. All known human societies embrace both gender differentiation and status differentiation, and the two are linked; males are consistently status-superior to females.[15] Now the content of both gender and status differentiation is highly (although not totally) variable; what is constant is the form of differentiation. But given this constancy, it would be a bold person who would suppose that either gender differentiation, or its linkage with status, is eliminable. Even if we were to suppose that genderization, the conceptual differentiation and identification of human beings corresponding to physiological sexual differences, is itself entirely a social product, yet it may result

[14] Marx's view has been cited in I.2. For Rousseau, see note 31 to Chapter X. Rousseau's underlying idea is clearly formulated in *Projet de constitution pour la corse*, in *Political Writings*, vol. 2, p. 308; 'Whoever depends on another, and lacks resources in himself, can not be free' (my translation).

[15] See, for example, Ernestine Friedl, *Women and Men: An Anthropologist's View* (New York, 1975); 'We begin with the evidence that a degree of male dominance exists in all known societies' (p. 7).

from a hard-wired difference in the behavioural responses of adult human beings to sexual differences in infants and children. To treat children as male or as female, and to socialize them so that they regard themselves as essentially male or female, may be fixed.

Genderization itself threatens essential justice. Its effect is to relativize the expectations of females and males to separate ideals or standards. Social institutions and practices encourage, if they do not actually require, role differences between women and men. And these are related to affective differences; socialization promotes different forms of sociability for women and men. Even if none of these differences were related to status, yet the imposition of gendering in determining the fulfilment appropriate to women and men may be seen as inconsistent with the requirements of Archimedean choice that determine essential justice.

Differential status leaves the issue in no doubt. A society that assigns it on the basis of imposed standards cannot be supposed to satisfy the neutrality of satisfaction required for essential justice. But if the assignment of differential status is one of the fixed points of human society, essential justice is impossible. The non-neutral moment in socialization may then seem to undermine the idea of a society of autonomous, affectively free, liberal individuals.

3 We may read the first sustained enquiry into justice, Plato's *Republic*, as an attempt to defend the Greek *polis* by representing its ideal nature and showing the congruence of that nature with reason. A similar concern may be seen to inform our enquiry, as an attempt to defend Western market society by representing its ideal nature in relation to reason. But as the actual *polis* fell irredeemably short of the city that comes into being in speech, so market society falls short of the society that would manifest essential justice.[16] Plato no doubt hoped to recall the *polis* to its ideal, but his articulation came too late. Is there a further parallel here?

In concluding *The Order of Things*, Michel Foucault writes, 'As the archaeology of our thought easily shows, man is an invention of recent date. And one perhaps nearing its end.'[17] Whether invention or discovery, the liberal individual is indeed of recent date; is she the mere creature of an historical moment, her maximizing rationality and free affectivity variants on some larger theme? We have found

[16] For the idea of the 'city that comes into being in speech', see *Republic* 369a.

[17] M. Foucault, *The Order of Things: An Archaeology of the Human Sciences* (New York, 1971), p. 387.

her ecological niche in the essentially just society, which is in the fullest sense 'a cooperative venture for mutual advantage'. Her morality and her sociability are elicited and sustained by, and only by, her sense of herself as interacting with others in ways that afford fair mutual benefit. In other habitats, lacking essential justice, persons would be constrained, not autonomously by reason, but heteronomously by socially conditioned beliefs and affections. So we may ask for the prospects of the liberal individual; can her ecological niche be realized and sustained?

Historically, the individual has emerged, both practically and conceptually, in an environment in which there has been a strong positive correlation between the pursuit of individualized interest and a continuing increase in the provision of goods and services to all. However fair or unfair the distribution of benefits may be, Western society has maintained the appearance of affording its members mutual advantage. And we may attribute significant roles in the creation of this environment to the perfection of social instruments for exchange and investment, and to the development of a technology oriented to increasing production and diversification. But we lack the expertise to form a sensible expectation about the prospects for the continuation, much less the improvement, of these circumstances favourable to liberal individuality.

Equally we lack the expertise to form any reasonable expectation about the conceptual future of the individual. If our present self-understanding emerges from the disappearance of the belief that man is a creature, taking his goals and values from a divinely established order, yet it may be no more than an uneasy transitional stage to the emergence of the sense that man is an artifact, constructed through an increasingly known and alterable process of genetic engineering. And man as engineered may be no more compatible with the ideas of individuality and autonomy which underlie our enquiry than man as created.

Perhaps then we have constructed, not a theory linking morality to rational choice, but a portrayal of moral constraints and maximizing choice in an ephemeral market society. Yet we have hope of a better conclusion. Nietzsche begins the second essay of *On the Genealogy of Morals* with the question, 'To breed an animal *with the right to make promises*—is not this the paradoxical task that nature has set itself in the case of man? is it not the real problem regarding man?'[18] Nature sets itself no tasks, but in Nietzsche's metaphor we may find the core of a self-understanding that, once attained, is not lightly to be sacrificed. An animal with the right to make promises must be able to commit itself, giving itself a reason for choice and action that overrides its usual concern with fulfilling its preferences. Such an animal is able to interact with its world in a new and distinctive way, which we have sought to capture in the conception of constrained maximization. Economic man would be no more than 'a globally maximizing machine'.[19] But the liberal individual is surely 'aware of his superiority over all those who lack the right to make promises and stand as their own guarantors ... and of how this mastery over himself also necessarily gives him mastery over circumstances, over nature, and over all more short-willed and unreliable creatures'.[20] And this mastery over self is expressed when, recognizing the need for community, the individual human being, woman or man among women and men, embraces morals by agreement.

[18] Friedrich Nietzsche, *On the Genealogy of Morals*, 1887, second essay, sect. 1; trans. W Kaufmann and R. J. Hollingdale and ed. W. Kaufmann (New York, 1967), p. 57

[19] The phrase, italicized in the original, is from J. Elster, *Ulysses and the Sirens: Studies in rationality and irrationality* (Cambridge, 1979), p. 10.

[20] Nietzsche, second essay, sect. 2; pp. 59–60.

INDEX

CPSIA information can be obtained at www.ICGtesting.com
Printed in the USA
BVOW020132130712

295070BV00001B/1/A